FiSHE X415498

THE POEMS OF JOHN CLARE

JOHN CLARE

From W. Hilton's Portrait in the National Portrait Gallery

The Poems of
JOHN CLARE

Edited with an Introduction
by
J. W. Tibble

VOLUME ONE

LONDON
J. M. DENT & SONS LIMITED
NEW YORK: E. P. DUTTON & CO. INC.

INTRODUCTION

THIS edition of Clare's poems is intended to complete the work begun by Mr. Edmund Blunden and Mr. Alan Porter fifteen years ago. It is significant that the 1920 edition, a representative selection of the best of Clare's work, bore the sub-title, 'Poems chiefly from Manuscript,' and that it was followed in 1924 by *Madrigals and Chronicles*, a selection of poems entirely from manuscript. Those familiar with the story of Clare's life will know why so much of his best work remained for so long in obscurity. His first book, *Poems Descriptive of Rural Life and Scenery*, was published in 1820; *The Village Minstrel* followed in 1821, *The Shepherd's Calendar* in 1827; *The Rural Muse*, the last volume to appear during his lifetime, was published one hundred years ago, in 1835. But the poems in these four books by no means represented his work up to 1835; the poems in *The Shepherd's Calendar* were all written before 1824, and most of those in *The Rural Muse* before 1830; and even so, they included only a fraction of what he committed to manuscript between 1821 and 1830. The first posthumous edition appeared in J. L. Cherry's *Life and Remains of John Clare*, 1873; this included a selection from the poems written in Northampton Asylum between 1841 and 1864, a series of Old Songs and Ballads, and a section of Miscellaneous Poems, chiefly collected from periodicals. So Cherry, through no fault of his, for the material was withheld from him, drew little upon the store of manuscript poems mentioned above. Thus, much of Clare's best work remained unpublished until 1920; for Mr. Norman Gale's selection in 1901 contained no new poems, and Mr. Arthur Symons's selection of 1908 only sixteen, gleaned from a stray manuscript.

The immediate need in 1920 was, obviously, to bring to light the best of what lay hidden in the archives at Peterborough and Northampton. The editors' difficulty was not one of finding enough poems equal in quality to the best previously published, but of reducing their selection to the number required at the moment. And in addition to this store of new material, the hundred or more note-books at Peterborough and Northampton contained the manuscript originals of nearly all the previously published poems. Thus the need for a more comprehensive edition as soon as circumstances should permit became apparent: many of the earlier published poems which had not been included in later selections were hardly more accessible than the unpublished poems; all the earlier texts needed bringing into line with their manuscript originals; and the selections of 1920 and 1924 had by no means exhausted the store of unpublished poems.

In the present edition are gathered together for the first time the bulk of the poems published during Clare's lifetime and after his death. To these 560 poems, 300 previously unpublished have been added; even so the poems still left in manuscript considerably outnumber all those included in this edition. The number of these excluded poems calls for some comment.

In every phase of Clare's life there were circumstances which encouraged a natural tendency to prolific composition. In his early apprenticeship period he wrote with sheer delight in his new-found gift of rhyming, as most young poets do; but all the more because it was his only hope of escape from 'the dull and obstinate class from whence I struggled into light like one struggling from the nightmare in his sleep.' The spectacular success of his first book merely added a new stimulus; it was his spontaneous untutored writing that had brought him fame, and naturally he wanted to repeat that success as often as possible. Moreover it was not until he was nearly thirty that he had any opportunity for that free access to literature and contact with men of kindred and mature tastes which a poet needs for the development of his critical powers. And even in his mature period Clare was often driven to write below his best level to earn a little money as a contributor to the Annuals. By 1835 he had amassed such a quantity of manuscript that he felt the need for sorting out his work, selecting the best and destroying juvenilia and occasional verses. He had by that time acquired the critical judgment needed for the task; but it was too late. He was on the verge of a nervous breakdown and had only strength to tie up his manuscripts in bundles and leave the task of sorting them out to posterity. Finally in the asylum period he often wrote merely to escape from prison for a while, or to please some visitor who expected the mad poet to perform. And in all these periods he wrote because he was lonely, because, except for brief periods between 1820 and 1830, there was no one with whom he could share his enthusiasms and discuss his work. We can but speculate upon the difference it might have made if Clare and Keats had met and talked frequently, as they hoped to do in 1820, or if his friendship with Lamb, Cary, Darley, Reynolds, and other 'Londoners,' had not been limited to occasional visits and letters. It was this companionship with kindred and mature minds that Clare needed most.

But apart from these special circumstances, Clare's temperament made him a prolific writer; when the mood was favourable, poems left his pen as leaves whirl from a tree before an autumn gale. He commented on this in a letter to John Taylor in May 1820: 'When I am in the fit, I write as much in one week as would knock ye up a fair-sized volume; and when I lay down the pen I lay it down for a good long while. . . . I am like the boy that gets his horn-book alphabet by heart and then can say his lesson with his eyes as well shut as open. . . .' In January of this same year Edward Drury had written to Taylor: 'It is to be greatly feared that the man will be afflicted with insanity if his talent continues to be forced as it has been these four months past; he has no other mode of easing the fever that oppresses him after a tremendous fit of rhyming except by getting tipsy. A single pint of ale very often does this. . . . He has rhymed and written for three days and three nights, without hardly eating or sleeping. . . .' Twenty years later, when Drury's prophetic fear had been realized, we find Dr. Allen of High Beech asylum commenting on the ease with which verses came the moment Clare got pen or pencil in hand. The period of which Drury wrote was exceptional in that Clare was keyed up by the impending publication of his first book, and later by news of its great success; he did in fact compose enough to complete, in the first half of 1820, the two volumes of *The Village Minstrel* and still leave many poems for his third book. But if his composition did not normally proceed at this feverish pace, it was always a business which gave him intense pleasure, a pleasure accentuated by the periods of melancholy and illness which too often filled the intervals between fits of rhyming. He quoted Spenser's 'I play to please myself,' on the title-page of his *Village Minstrel*; and we find him expressing the same attitude again and again in later years; thus in 1832: 'But I wrote because it pleased me in sorrow, and when happy it makes me happier; and so I go on. . . . I pursued pleasure in many paths and never found her so happily as when I sang imaginary songs to the woodland solitudes and winds of autumn.'

'The poetry of Keats,' writes Mr. Sutherland in *The Medium of Poetry*, 'is rarely the result of emotion recollected in tranquillity, and rarely the record of an experience already completely realized. Where Wordsworth is thinking mainly of the idea to be expressed, Keats is delighting in his powers of expression. The poem with Keats is not the objective shadow cast by an experience already present in the poet's consciousness, but a thing created almost wholly out of the immediate excitement of composition.' Clare's method seems to lie midway between the two. Like Wordsworth's his poems are usually the record of an experience already completely realized, but unlike Wordsworth he seldom allowed an interval to elapse between the experience and its recording. 'I found the poems in the fields,' he said, and often enough he wrote them in the fields too, on any scrap of paper that came to hand. Like Keats, he experienced the immediate excitement of composition; but the poem did not arise primarily out of that excitement. It was not the words that excited him, the actual making of the poem, so much as the power of the words to prolong and renew that rapture which he felt in the presence of nature.

Clare was not, we feel, interested in words as words; nor did he pay much attention to their formal grouping into sentences. The unit for him was the short phrase or clause—the verbal expression of the image upon which his attention was focused. As image succeeded image, phrase followed phrase; the image expressed in a subordinate clause would distract his attention and the subject of the main sentence be forgotten and left in the air. He used few punctuation marks, an occasional dash serving many purposes. We must, of course, remember the meagre nature of Clare's formal training in the art of writing at school; thereafter until 1820 his writing was all in verse; and while he composed in that medium with astonishing fluency, the orderly exposition of a theme in prose always gave him great difficulty. In descriptive and personal passages the gifts of exact observation and vivid imagery notable in his poetry were ample compensation; he had also a fine ear for verse rhythms; but in prose and verse he often left grammar and syntax to take care of themselves.

If the resulting blemishes are obvious enough, the finer qualities of Clare's poetry are in large measure due to this pre-occupation with the immediate experience, the image seen or recollected and the emotion it evoked in him. As Mr. Murry noted in *The Problem of Style*, quoting a verse of Clare's 'Summer Images' as an example of that 'pure and limpid lyricism' which is the basic stuff of all poetry: 'An object or an incident in life arouses an overwhelming emotion in him, and a desire to express the emotion. The crystallization is, as it were, automatically accomplished; for the only way he can communicate his emotion is by describing the objects which aroused it. If his emotion was a true one, the vividness and particularity of his description will carry it over to us. . . . Thus, quite simply, the cause of the emotion becomes the symbol. The miracle is accomplished. There we have, in simplest lyricism, the achievement of perfect style.'

This spontaneity, directness, simplicity, and vividness are present in all Clare's best work; it is only when he is generalizing, dealing in ideas at second hand, recording emotions not completely realized in an image, that his expression becomes commonplace or vague. Uncertainty creeps in when he is forced to seek deliberately and consciously for the word or phrase to convey what he feels. The manuscripts show clearly enough that he seldom worked over a poem; most of the poems appear in more than one manuscript, not a few in four or five, but the later versions are either simple copies of the earlier with minor alterations only, or else they are practically new poems, rewritten with a fresh inspiration. 'Summer Images,' for example, was first written (see 1. 380) in the unrhymed stanza of Collins's 'Ode to Evening'; there are four drafts of this version; it was then entirely rewritten in a longer rhyming stanza and two fair copies made of this version (see II. 6). It is illuminating to compare the two versions and note where the re-reading has evoked in Clare a new and richer emotional experience, and where, occasionally, he is simply padding to make up the longer verse.

The earlier 'Summer Images' belongs to the *Shepherd's Calendar* period, 1821–4, when Clare first clearly emerged from his apprenticeship to the eighteenth-century poets, and his own native mode was firmly established. We no longer find the 'woolly charge,' the 'feathered race,' the 'tasteful illumination of the night,' the echoes of Thomson, Goldsmith, and John Cunningham which mingle with the authentic Clare in the earlier poems. His technique at this period is well revealed in the first version of the verse quoted by Mr. Murry:

> Jet-black and shining, from the dripping hedge
> Slow peeps the fearful snail,
> And from each tiny bent
> Withdraws his timid horn.

The image could not be conveyed with more economy, directness, and clarity, and the poems of this period abound with such description. But it is true that something is not actually present which we are accustomed to look for in poetry—the particular emotion aroused in Clare by the image. It is implied; such sharp definition and clarity can be achieved only by a man of 'more than ordinary sensibilities'; and the above verse alone would put another man of similar sensibilities in full possession of the emotion felt by Clare but not explicitly expressed. Now when he rewrote the verse some years later, he made this emotion explicit, fusing it with the image:

> And note on hedgerow baulks, in moisture sprent,
> The jetty snail creep from the mossy thorn,
> With earnest heed and tremulous intent,
> Frail brother of the morn,
> That from the tiny bents and misted leaves
> Withdraws his timid horn,
> And fearful vision weaves.

The initial clarity is retained, but the verse is greatly enriched by the projection into the image of Clare's own emotions, in lines three, four, and seven. We cannot doubt that the emotions existed when Clare wrote the original verse. In fact, it was simply because they were so obviously there, because this kind of insight was so normal to him in the presence of nature, that he often took it for granted and left it unexpressed; if he could only fix the image in its immediate clarity, he knew that the simple description alone would re-evoke in him the accompanying emotion; and he seems to have assumed that all men were so constituted. Keats made this point when, in criticizing one of Clare's early poems, he observed that 'the Description too much prevailed over the Sentiment.' Beside which, as revealing Clare's attitude to his own work in 1820, we may set his criticism of Keats: 'He often described Nature as she appeared to his fancies, and not as he would have described her had he witnessed the things he described.'

However, we have here the main clue to the further development of Clare's technique. We find the fusion of emotion and image described above more and more common in the poems written in the ten years following 1824. What was it that compelled Clare to do something which was, in a sense, unnatural to him? His own role, as he saw it, was to hold the mirror up to nature, to set down the immediate impression in its first clarity. Yet from the first there were circumstances which often prevented him from resting content with the immediate impression, which made him contrast what was with what had been, and thrust to the front the emotional and personal elements in the experience. The turning back to the Golden Age of childhood was not, with Clare, simply a consequence of growing old, enclosure by the shades of the prison house; it was due to enclosure of another kind which changed the face of his beloved countryside and degraded the village society and tradition into which he was born. The change was not in him but in nature itself; wherever he went about the fields and woods he saw change—heaths enclosed, pastures ploughed up, trees destroyed. The first poem printed in this edition is a regret for a Helpstone that was no more; but the full force of the change was not felt until later, when change in nature became linked with the loss of his first love, Mary Joyce, and the decline of his own fortunes which had seemed so bright in 1820. There was, indeed, always enough left to give him abundant delight; but the sense of loss and decay increased with the years; in the earlier poems it either appeared as an excuse for that mood of gentle melancholy which young poets often affect, or else issued in impersonal description or satire, as in 'The Parish.' After 1824 we meet it more and more frequently in the form of a poignant emotion suffusing the imagery. After 1824 he wrote no more narrative and few long descriptive poems; his work became essentially lyrical. Mr. Blunden has charted this process in his *Nature in English Literature*, with special reference to the poem 'Autumn' (ii. 3), which also appears in several manuscripts and is closely connected with 'Summer Images.' 'A great part of his verse is the history of the transference of love in him from woman to Nature.' His early inspiration, his rural muse, Nature, conventionally personified, becomes the 'Sweet Vision, with the wild dishevelled hair,' the 'wild sorceress' of 'Autumn,' upon whose glances, gestures, and adornments he feasts with the eye of a lover; she assumes more and more clearly the lineaments of his lost love, Mary Joyce, whom he sometimes saw so vividly in dreams that he could no longer doubt her existence as his 'guardian genius' (i. 404). She was at once Mary Joyce, the spirit of love, the spirit of nature, his muse, and the guardian of his fame. And certainly Clare needed her guardianship in 1832 when the removal from Helpstone led him to take stock of his fortunes and review all the hopes that had fallen by the wayside. The result is seen when poems like 'The Flitting' (ii. 251) and 'Remembrances' (ii. 257) are compared with earlier auto-biographical poems such as 'The Village Minstrel.' He has now found a direct and poignant expression for those sorrows and joys which in the earlier poems 'no words can utter and no tongue can tell.' Moreover, in 'Song's Eternity' and other lyrics (ii. 264–76), we have the first appearance of the mood and tone of the asylum lyrics; emotion, image, and idea, are purged of their personal reference without losing directness and intensity.

But Clare had not yet been forced to accept that sacrifice of the man to the poet which made this kind of vision normal to him; earth was not yet 'but a name.' And as the strain intensified in the years succeeding 1832, it resulted in a cleavage between the two elements which had been forced together against Clare's natural inclination. In 1835–6 we find him trying to escape from the emotional turmoil, deliberately and defiantly excluding it from his verse and turning to stark, objective description of natural scenes. Of the series of sonnets written at this time (II. 333–75) Mr. Blunden has noted: 'The vividity of the observation and ancient hardness and directness of the expression give them an unmistakable individuality.' We feel in them what almost amounts to a contempt for artistic polish, and for all personal and emotional intrusions, and for man, except as part of the natural scene. When he does write personally it is in this mood:

> I hate the very noise of troublous man
> Who did and does me all the harm he can.
> Free from the world I would a prisoner be
> And my own shadow all my company.

But below the surface the emotional turmoil intensified, and after the breakdown of 1837 and when Clare was indeed a prisoner, it found its own expression in the verses taken from the High Beech note-books (II. 379–98). Here the personal takes charge; and under the half-delusion, half-pretence that he was Byron, he describes without restraint his mental Odyssey. The verses are overcharged with emotion; they are the raw material of poetry rather than poetry itself; but even in this troubled underworld of lost hopes, Clare's 'guardian' accompanied him, appearing in her different guises—Mary Joyce, now his 'first wife' as well as 'nature's self,' the spirit of love, which 'lives on in every kind of weather,' nature, freedom.

The addition of freedom to the list of Clare's 'esteems' is the clue to an understanding of the asylum poetry. The significance lies not in his longing for freedom—the asylum was always 'prison' to him—but in his achievement of that freedom in his verses. The price of freedom was a dissociation of the man and the poet; the man struggled on, unreconciled to prison, wrestling with delusions and melancholy; the poet escaped from 'earth and its delusions,' 'wrote till earth was but a name,' and kept his 'spirit with the free.' He had at last reached a plane of vision upon which emotion was no longer a disturbing factor but could be 'recollected in tranquillity,' its cause becoming its symbol. As Mr. Symons wrote in the discerning Introduction to his selection, 'Here, for the first time, Clare's lyrical faculty gets free. Strangely enough, a new joy comes into his verse, as if at last he is at rest. It is only rarely, in this new contentment, this solitude even from himself, that recollection returns. . . . He seems to accept nature now more easily, because his mind is in a kind of oblivion of everything else; madness being, as it were, his security. He writes love songs that have an airy fancy, a liquid and thrilling note of song.'

Clare's achievement both in the best of these asylum lyrics and in the best of his earlier nature poems has been generously acknowledged since 1920. It is the purpose of this edition to give these poems their proper setting in the general body of his works, and to give full representation to every aspect and period. There are 'certain ardours and purposes of men' which are beyond Clare's range, but within the limits he set himself there is variety enough. This variety, like that of the country round Helpstone, the 'Clare country,' may not be obvious to the tourist in search of beauty spots. But it lies quietly in wait to delight the eye which has learned to look for the infinite richness of detail in Nature's underworld, and the ear which can discover the ceaseless variation of mood and tone within the repeated theme of days and seasons. Nor should his preoccupation with the 'diminutives of Nature,' and the delicacy of his etching, lead us to overlook the native vigour and robustness of his expression, a vigour fed by the tradition which gave him his store of dialect words and old ballads. We may be grateful too for Clare's chronicling of village life, customs, and occupations, as they existed in his childhood, and for his vivid picture in 'The Parish' of the effect of enclosure on village life. The satirical mode was not natural to him, and his debt to the eighteenth-century satirists was openly acknowledged; yet his adaptation of his models to fit his local and particular theme is skilful and trenchant enough. Very different is the approach and mood of the Village Tales; again, Clare's natural gifts did not lie in the direction of narrative or dramatic verse; yet these bucolics have a quiet charm of their own if the reader can surrender himself to it. Clare's interest here is not so much in the story itself as in the undertones and undercurrents of emotion evoked in the characters, especially

xiv

the effects of success and disappointment in love. Clare's imaginative projection is often as successful here as in his faithful delineation and interpretation of the world of nature.

The poems are arranged in chronological sections. The chronological arrangement does not usually extend to the poems within each section, for most of them can only be dated approximately on evidence of style, handwriting, and the manuscripts in which they occur. The texts of all previously published poems have been collated with the manuscript originals, and many emendations and additions have been made. The particular problems which confront an editor of Clare's poems call for brief comment. To reprint the texts exactly as they appear in manuscript would make too many demands on the reader's patience, nor would it be in accordance with Clare's wishes. He bequeathed the task of supplying punctuation and regularizing spelling to his editors. In this edition the punctuation of the early editions has been lightened and the number of capitals reduced to agree more both with Clare's own usage and modern custom. The poems published in Clare's lifetime were well edited, but somewhat over-edited, by John Taylor; Clare passed the proofs of these poems and some of the emendations are undoubtedly his. Hence some readings not found in manuscript have been retained, together with Taylor's minor corrections of grammatical and other blemishes. But Taylor frequently standardized dialect forms and toned down vigorous expressions, and these have been restored, for Clare accepted such changes reluctantly. In the poems published after Clare's death and in all new poems, the manuscript versions have been faithfully followed save in the matter of punctuation and spelling. It should be remembered that the originals of the asylum poems are still untraced and we have to rely on transcripts made by a scribe who often had obvious difficulty in reading the original. Cherry used the original poems, and his version often differs from that of the transcripts; but his editing does not inspire great faith; he was sometimes driven to use asterisks where he could not read the text, and his note in the Introduction is ominous: 'Of those which are printed, scarcely one was found in a state in which it could be submitted to the public without more or less of revision and correction.'

As so many of the poems in this edition are either previously unpublished or reprinted from scarce early editions, it has been thought inadvisable to burden the pages with references to textual matters. The insertion of new lines and stanzas in previously published poems is indicated in footnotes; a list of corrections of earlier readings, with some variant readings from manuscript, will be found at the end of Volume II. The glossary provides a complete list of the dialect words used in these poems. For a number of these words Clare is the sole or chief authority, and the list includes some additions to and corrections of the entries in Wright's *Dialect Dictionary*.

The pioneer work of Mr. Edmund Blunden on the Clare manuscripts prepared the way for this edition, and I am indebted to him, to Messrs. Cobden-Sanderson, and to the Beaumont Press, for permission to reproduce the text of poems published in 1920 and 1924; moreover, access to Mr. Blunden's store of transcripts of unpublished poems has materially lightened my task, and I am most grateful to him for his generosity in this and in other respects. My thanks are also due to Professor Lascelles Abercrombie for his continued interest and advice; and to Mr. Charles Lee for his vigilant reading of the proofs and for many helpful suggestions arising therefrom.

For permission to transcribe and publish from the Clare manuscripts at Peterborough and Northampton, I am indebted to Mr. J. W. Bodger, secretary of the Peterborough Archaeological Society and curator of the Peterborough Museum, and to Mr. Reginald W. Brown, Librarian of the Northampton Public Library.

J. W. T.

University College,
    Exeter,
        January 1935.

ERRATA

Volume I, page	206,	line	13	*For* grount *read* grunt.
,,	,, 357	,,	25	*For* nuddling *read* huddling.
Volume II	,, 58	,,	22	*For* greave *read* gleave.
,,	,, 108	,,	22	*For* It is *read* 'Tis.
,,	,, 198	,,	31	*For* polygot *read* polyglot.
,,	,, 223	,,	9	*For* eddying *read* edding.
,,	,, 422	Title		*For* I. Inskip *read* T. Inskip.
,,	,, 485	,,		*For* Loved *read* Love.

CONTENTS

Poems now first published, or in some few cases first collected from periodicals, are left undated.

The volume in which previously published poems first appeared is indicated by the date after the title:

1820 Poems Descriptive of Rural Life and Scenery.

1821 The Village Minstrel.

1827 The Shepherd's Calendar.

1835 The Rural Muse.

1865 The Life of John Clare: F. Martin.

1873 Life and Remains of John Clare: J. L. Cherry.

1908 Poems by John Clare: Arthur Symons.

1920 John Clare: Poems: Edmund Blunden and Alan Porter.

1924 Madrigals and Chronicles: Edmund Blunden.

VOLUME ONE

POEMS WRITTEN AT HELPSTONE, 1809–19

xix

POEMS WRITTEN AT HELPSTONE, 1819–21

POEMS WRITTEN AT HELPSTONE, 1821–4

VOLUME TWO

POEMS WRITTEN AT HELPSTONE, 1824–32

POEMS WRITTEN AT NORTHBOROUGH, 1832–5

xxviii

POEMS WRITTEN AT HIGH BEECH, EPPING, 1837–41, AND AT NORTHBOROUGH, 1841

POEMS WRITTEN IN NORTHAMPTON ASYLUM, 1842–64

xxx

xxxi

POEMS WRITTEN AT HELPSTONE
1808–19

HELPSTONE

(The dates given at the end of poems in this section were supplied by Clare in 1819)

HAIL, humble Helpstone! where thy valleys spread,
And thy mean village lifts its lowly head,
Unknown to grandeur, and unknown to fame,
No minstrel boasting to advance thy name:
Unletter'd spot! unheard in poets' song,
Where bustling labour drives the hours along,
Where dawning genius never met the day,
Where useless ignorance slumbers life away,
Unknown nor heeded, where low genius tries
Above the vulgar and the vain to rise.

Mysterious Fate! who can on thee depend?
Thou opes the hour, but hides its doubtful end:
In Fancy's view the joys have long appear'd,
Where the glad heart by laughing plenty's cheer'd,
And Fancy's eyes as oft, as vainly, fill,
At first but doubtful, and as doubtful still.
So little birds, in winter's frost and snow,
Doom'd, like to me, want's keener frost to know,
Searching for food and 'better life,' in vain
(Each hopeful track the yielding snows retain),
First on the ground each fairy dream pursue,
Though sought in vain; yet bent on higher view,
Still chirp, and hope, and wipe each glossy bill;
And undiscourag'd, undishearten'd still,
Hop on the snow-cloth'd bough, and chirp again,
Heedless of naked shade and frozen plain:
Till, like to me, these victims of the blast,
Each foolish, fruitless wish resign'd at last,
Are glad to seek the place from whence they went
And put up with distress, and be content.

Hail, scenes obscure! so near and dear to me,

3

The church, the brook, the cottage, and the tree:
Still shall obscurity rehearse the song,
And hum your beauties as I stroll along.
Dear, native spot! which length of time endears,
The sweet retreat of twenty lingering years;
And, oh! those years of infancy the scene,
Those dear delights, where once they all have been,
Those golden days, long vanish'd from the plain,
Those sports, those pastimes, now belov'd in vain;
When happy youth in pleasure's circle ran,
Nor thought what pains awaited future man,
No other thought employing, or employ'd,
But how to add to happiness enjoy'd:
Each morning wak'd with hopes before unknown,
And eve, possessing, made each wish their own;
The day gone by left no pursuit undone,
Nor one vain wish, save that it went too soon;
Each sport, each pastime, ready at their call,
As soon as wanted they possess'd them all:
These joys, all known in happy infancy,
And all I ever knew, were spent in thee.
And who but loves to view where these were past?
And who, that views, but loves them to the last?
Feels his heart warm to view his native place,
A fondness still those past delights to trace?
The vanish'd green to mourn, the spot to see
Where flourish'd many a bush and many a tree?
Where once the brook, for now the brook is gone,
O'er pebbles dimpling sweet went whimpering on;
Oft on whose oaken plank I've wondering stood
(That led a pathway o'er its gentle flood),
To see the beetles their wild mazes run,
With jetty jackets glittering in the sun:
So apt and ready at their reels they seem,
So true the dance is figur'd on the stream,
Such justness, such correctness they impart,
They seem as ready as if taught by art.
In those past days, for then I lov'd the shade,
How oft I've sigh'd at alterations made,

4

To see the woodman's cruel axe employ'd,
A tree beheaded, or a bush destroy'd:
Nay e'en a post, old standard, or a stone
Moss'd o'er by age, and branded as her own,
Would in my mind a strong attachment gain,
A fond desire that there they might remain;
And all old favourites, fond taste approves,
Griev'd me at heart to witness their removes.

Thou far fled pasture, long evanish'd scene!
Where nature's freedom spread the flow'ry green,
Where golden kingcups open'd into view,
Where silver daisies in profusion grew;
And, tottering, hid amidst those brighter gems,
Where silken grasses bent their tiny stems:
Where the pale lilac, mean and lowly, grew,
Courting in vain each gazer's heedless view;
While cowslips, sweetest flowers upon the plain,
Seemingly bow'd to shun the hand, in vain:
Where lowing oxen roam'd to feed at large,
And bleating there the shepherd's woolly charge,
Whose constant calls thy echoing valleys cheer'd,
Thy scenes adorn'd, and rural life endear'd;
No calls of hunger pity's feelings wound,
'Twas wanton plenty rais'd the joyful sound:
Thy grass in plenty gave the wish'd supply,
Ere sultry suns had wak'd the troubling fly;
Then blest retiring, by thy bounty fed,
They sought thy shades, and found an easy bed.

But now, alas! those scenes exist no more;
The pride of life with thee, like mine, is o'er,
Thy pleasing spots to which fond memory clings,
Sweet cooling shades, and soft refreshing springs.
And though Fate's pleas'd to lay their beauties by
In a dark corner of obscurity,
As fair and sweet they bloom'd thy plains among,
As bloom those Edens by the poets sung;
Now all's laid waste by desolation's hand,

5

Whose cursed weapons level half the land.
Oh! who could see my dear green willows fall,
What feeling heart, but dropt a tear for all?
Accursed Wealth! o'er-bounding human laws,
Of every evil thou remain'st the cause:
Victims of want, those wretches such as me,
Too truly lay their wretchedness to thee:
Thou art the bar that keeps from being fed,
And thine our loss of labour and of bread;
Thou art the cause that levels every tree,
And woods bow down to clear a way for thee.[1]

Sweet rest and peace! ye dear, departed charms,
Which industry once cherish'd in her arms;
When ease and plenty, known but now to few,
Were known to all, and labour had its due;
When mirth and toil, companions through the day,
Made labour light, and pass'd the hours away;
When nature made the fields so dear to me,
Thin scattering many a bush and many a tree;
Where the wood-minstrel sweetly join'd among,
And cheer'd my needy toilings with a song;
Ye perish'd spots, adieu! ye ruin'd scenes,
Ye well-known pastures, oft frequented greens!
Though now no more, fond Memory's pleasing pains,
Within her breast your every scene retains.
Scarce did a bush spread its romantic bower,
To shield the lazy shepherd from the shower;
Scarce did a tree befriend the chattering pie,
By lifting up its head so proud and high;
No, not a secret spot did then remain,
Throughout each spreading wood and winding plain,
But, in those days, my presence once possess'd,
The snail-horn searching, or the mossy nest.

Oh, happy Eden of those golden years
Which memory cherishes, and use endears,
Thou dear, beloved spot! may it be thine

[1] The preceding ten lines were omitted in the fourth edition of *Poems Descriptive*; Lord Radstock objected to them because they smacked of 'radical slang.'

To add a comfort to my life's decline,
When this vain world and I have nearly done,
And Time's drain'd glass has little left to run;
When all the hopes, that charm'd me once, are o'er,
To warm my soul in ecstasy no more,
By disappointments prov'd a foolish cheat,
Each ending bitter, and beginning sweet;
When weary age the grave, a rescue, seeks,
And prints its image on my wrinkled cheeks—
Those charms of youth, that I again may see,
May it be mine to meet my end in thee;
And, as reward for all my troubles past,
Find one hope true—to die at home at last!

1809.

THE FATE OF AMY

A TALE

BENEATH a sheltering wood's warm side,
   Where many a tree expands
Its branches o'er the neighbouring brook,
   A ruin'd cottage stands:

Though now left desolate, and lost
   Its origin, and all,
Owls hooting from the roofless walls,
   Rejoicing in its fall,

A time was once, remembrance knows,
   Though now the time's gone by,
When that was seen to flourish gay,
   And pleasing to the eye.

On that same ground the brambles hide
   And stinking weeds o'er-run,
An orchard bent its golden boughs,
   And redden'd in the sun.

7

Yon nettles where they're left to spread,
  There once a garden smil'd;
And lovely was the spot to view,
  Though now so lost and wild;

And where the sickly elder loves
  To top the mouldering wall,
And ivy's kind encroaching care
  Delays the tottering fall,

There once a mother's only joy,
  A daughter lovely, fair
As ever bloom'd beneath the sun,
  Was nurs'd and cherish'd there.

The cottage then was known around;
  The neighbouring village swains
Would often wander by to view
  That charmer of the plains.

Where softest blush of roses wild
  And hawthorn's fairest blow
But meanly serve to paint her cheek
  And bosom's rival snow,

The loveliest blossom of the plains
  The artless Amy prov'd,
In nature's sweetest charms adorn'd,
  Those charms by all belov'd.

Sweet Innocence! the beauty's thine
  That every bosom warms:
Fair as she was, she liv'd alone
  A stranger to her charms.

Unmov'd the praise of swains she heard,
  Nor proud at their despair,
But thought they scoff'd her when they prais'd,
  And knew not she was fair.

Nor did she for the joys of youth
    Forsake her mother's side,
Who then by age and pain infirm'd
    On her for help relied.

No tenderer mother to a child
    Throughout the world could be;
And, in return, no daughter prov'd
    More dutiful than she.

The pains of age she sympathiz'd
    And sooth'd and wish'd to share:
In short, the aged, helpless dame
    Was Amy's only care.

But age had pains, and they were all:
    Life's cares they little knew;
Its billows ne'er encompass'd them,
    They waded smoothly through.

The tender father, now no more,
    Did for them both provide;
The wealth his industry had gain'd,
    All wants to come supplied.

Kind heaven upon their labours smil'd;
    Industry gave increase;
The cottage was contentment's own
    Abode of health and peace.

Alas! the tongue of Fate is seal'd,
    And kept for ever dumb:
To-morrow's met with blinded eyes;
    We know not what's to come.

Blithe as the lark, as crickets gay
    That chirrup'd on the hearth,
This sun of beauty's time was spent
    In inoffensive mirth.

Meek as the lambs that throng'd her door,
  As innocent as they,
Her hours pass'd on, and charms improv'd
  With each succeeding day.

So, smiling on the sunny plain,
  The lovely daisies blow,
Unconscious of the careless foot
  That lays their beauty low.

So blows the lily of the vale
  (Ye beauties, oh, be wise!);
Untimely blasts o'ertake its bloom,
  It withers, and it dies.

The humble cottage lonely stood
  Far from the neighbouring vill;
Its church, that topp'd the willow groves,
  Lay far upon the hill;

Which made all company desir'd
  And welcome to the dame,
And oft to tell the village news
  The neighbouring gossips came.

Young Edward mingled with the rest:
  An artful swain was he,
Who laugh'd, and told his merry jests,
  For custom made him free:

And oft with Amy toy'd and play'd
  While, harmless as the dove,
Her artless, unsuspecting heart
  But little thought of love.

But frequent visits gain'd esteem,
  Each time of longer stay;
And custom did his name endear:
  He stole her heart away.

So fairest flowers adorn the wild,
  And, most endanger'd, stand
The soonest seen—a certain prey
  To some destroying hand.

Her choice was fix'd on him alone;
  The rest but vainly strove;
And worse than all the rest is he,
  But blind the eyes of love.

Of him full many a maid complain'd,
  The lover of an hour,
That, like the ever changing bee,
  Sipp'd sweets from every flower.

Alas! those slighted pains are small,
  If all such maidens know;
But she was fair, and he design'd
  To work her further woe.

Her innocence his bosom fir'd,
  So long'd to be enjoy'd;
And he, to gain his cruel ends,
  Each subtle art employ'd.

Ah! he employ'd his subtle arts,
  Alas, too sad to tell;
The winning ways which he employ'd
  Succeeded but too well.

So artless, innocent, and young,
  So ready to believe,
A stranger to the world was she,
  And easy to deceive.

Ah! now farewell to beauty's boast,
  Charms so admir'd before;
Now innocence has lost its sweets,
  Her beauties bloom no more.

The flowers, the sultry summer kills,
    Spring's milder suns restore;
But innocence, that fickle charm,
    Blooms once, and blooms no more.

The swains who lov'd, no more admire,
    Their hearts no beauty warms;
And maidens triumph in her fall,
    That envied once her charms.

Lost was that sweet simplicity;
    Her eye's bright lustre fled;
And o'er her cheeks, where roses bloom'd,
    A sickly paleness spread.

So fades the flower before its time,
    Where canker-worms assail;
So droops the bud upon its stem,
    Beneath the sickly gale.

The mother saw the sudden change,
    Where health so lately smil'd;
Too much—and, oh! suspecting more—
    Grew anxious for her child.

And all the kindness in her power
    The tender mother shows,
In hopes such kindly means would make
    Her fearless to disclose.

And oft she hinted, if a crime,
    Through ignorance beguil'd—
Not to conceal the crime in fear,
    For none should wrong her child.

Or, if the rose that left her cheek
    Was banish'd by disease,
'Fear God, my child!' she oft would say,
    'And you may hope for ease.'

And still she pray'd, and still had hopes
  There was no injury done;
And still advis'd the ruin'd girl
  The world's deceit to shun.

And many a cautionary tale
  Of hapless maiden's fate,
From trusting man, to warn her, told;
  But told, alas! too late.

A tender mother's painful cares
  In vain the loss supply;
The wide-mouth'd world, its sport and scorn
  Than meet, she'd sooner die.

Advice but aggravated woe;
  And ease, an empty sound;
No one could ease the pains she felt,
  But he who gave the wound.

And he, wild youth, had left her now,
  Unfeeling as the stone:
Fair maids, beware, lest careless ways
  Make Amy's fate your own.

Ill-fated girl! too late she found,
  As but too many find,
False Edward's love as light as down,
  And vows as fleet as wind.

But one hope's left, and that she sought,
  To hide approaching shame;
And Pity, while she drops a tear,
  Forbears the rest to name.

The widow'd mother, though so old,
  And ready to depart,
Was not ordain'd to live her time;
  The sad news broke her heart.

Borne down beneath a weight of years,
  And all the pains they gave,
But little added weight requir'd
  To crush her in the grave.

The strong oak braves the rudest wind;
  While, to the breeze, as well
The sickly, aged willow falls—
  And so the mother fell.

Beside the pool the willow bends,
  The dew-bent daisy weeps;
And where the turfy hillock swells,
  The luckless Amy sleeps.

1808.

NOON

ALL how silent and how still,
Nothing heard but yonder mill;
While the dazzled eye surveys
All around a liquid blaze;
And amid the scorching gleams,
If we earnest look, it seems
As if crooked bits of glass
Seem'd repeatedly to pass.
Oh, for a puffing breeze to blow!
But breezes are all strangers now;
Not a twig is seen to shake
Nor the smallest bent to quake;
From the river's muddy side
Not a curve is seen to glide;
And no longer on the stream
Watching lies the silver bream,
Forcing, from repeated springs,
'Verges in successive rings.'
Bees are faint, and cease to hum;
Birds are overpower'd and dumb.
Rural voices all are mute,
Tuneless lie the pipe and flute;

Shepherds, with their panting sheep,
In the swaliest corner creep;
And from the tormenting heat
All are wishing to retreat.
Huddled up in grass and flowers,
Mowers wait for cooler hours;
And the cow-boy seeks the sedge,
Ramping in the woodland hedge,
While his cattle o'er the vales
Scamper, with uplifted tails;
Others not so wild and mad,
That can better bear the gad,
Underneath the hedgerow lunge,
Or, if nigh, in waters plunge.
Oh! to see how flowers are took,
How it grieves me when I look:
Ragged-robins, once so pink,
Now are turn'd as black as ink,
And the leaves, being scorch'd so much,
Even crumble at the touch;
Drowking lies the meadow-sweet,
Flopping down beneath one's feet;
While to all the flowers that blow,
If in open air they grow,
Th'injurious deed alike is done
By the hot relentless sun.
E'en the dew is parched up
From the teasel's jointed cup:
O poor birds! where must ye fly,
Now your water-pots are dry?
If ye stay upon the heath,
Ye'll be chok'd and clamm'd to death:
Therefore leave the shadeless goss,
Seek the spring-head lin'd with moss;
There your little feet may stand,
Safely printing on the sand;
While, in full possession, where
Purling eddies ripple clear,
You with ease and plenty blest,

Sip the coolest and the best.
Then away! and wet your throats;
Cheer me with your warbling notes;
'Twill hot noon the more revive;
While I wander to contrive
For myself a place as good,
In the middle of a wood:
There aside some mossy bank,
Where the grass in bunches rank
Lifts its down on spindles high,
Shall be where I'll choose to lie;
Fearless of the things that creep,
There I'll think, and there I'll sleep,
Caring not to stir at all,
Till the dew begins to fall.

1809.

EVENING

Now grey-ey'd hazy Eve's begun
  To shed her balmy dew,
Insects no longer fear the sun,
  But come in open view.

Now buzzing, with unwelcome din,
  The heedless beetle bangs
Against the cow-boy's dinner-tin,
  That o'er his shoulder hangs.

And on he keeps in heedless pat,
  Till, quite enrag'd, the boy
Pulls off his weather-beaten hat,
  Resolving to destroy.

Yet thoughtless that he wrongs the clown,
  By blows he'll not be driven,
But buzzes on, till batter'd down
  For unmeant injury given.

Now from each hedgerow fearless peep
  The slowly-pacing snails,
Betraying their meand'ring creep
  In silver-slimy trails.

The dew-worms too in couples start,
  But leave their holes in fear;
For in a moment they will part,
  If aught approaches near.

The owls mope out, and scouting bats
  Begin their giddy round;
While countless swarms of dancing gnats
  Each water pudge surround.

And 'side yon pool, as smooth as glass,
  Reflecting every cloud,
Securely hid among the grass,
  The crickets chirrup loud.

That rural call, '*Come mulls! come mulls!*'
  From distant pasture-grounds,
All noises now to silence lulls
  In soft and ushering sounds;

While echoes weak, from hill to hill,
  Their dying sounds deplore,
That whimper faint and fainter still,
  Till they are heard no more.

The breezes, once so cool and brief,
  At eve's approach all died;
None's left to make the aspen leaf
  Twirl up its hoary side.

But breezes all are useless now;
  The hazy dun, that spreads
Her moist'ning dew on every bough,
  Sufficient coolness sheds.

The flowers, reviving from the ground,
  Perk up again and peep,
While many different tribes around
  Are shutting up to sleep.

Now let me, hid in cultur'd plain,
  Pursue my evening walk,
Where each way beats the nodding grain,
  Aside the narrow balk;

While fairy visions intervene,
  Creating dread surprise,
From distant objects dimly seen,
  That catch the doubtful eyes.

And fairies now, no doubt, unseen,
  In silent revels sup,
With dew-drop bumpers toast their queen,
  From crow-flower's golden cup.

Although about these tiny things
  Folks make so much ado,
I never heed the darksome rings
  Where they are said to go:

But superstition still deceives,
  And fairies still prevail;
While stooping genius e'en believes
  The customary tale.

Oh, loveliest time! oh, sweetest hours
  The musing soul can find!
Now, Evening, let thy soothing powers
  At freedom fill the mind.

1809.

IMPROMPTU ON WINTER

O WINTER, what a deadly foe
Art thou unto the mean and low!
What thousands now half pin'd and bare
Are forced to stand thy piercing air
All day, near numbed to death wi' cold
Some petty gentry to uphold,
Paltry proudlings hard as thee,
Dead to all humanity.
Oh, the weather's cold and snow,
Cutting winds that round me blow,
But much more the killing scorn!
Oh, the day that I was born
Friendless—poor as I can be,
Struck wi' death o' poverty!
But why need I the winter blame?
To me all seasons come the same:
Now winter bares each field and tree
She finds that trouble sav'd in me
Stript already, penniless,
Nothing boasting but distress;
And when spring chill'd nature cheers,
Still my old complaint she hears;
Summer too, in plenty blest,
Finds me poor and still distrest;
Kind autumn too, so liberal and so free,
Brings my old well-known present, Poverty.

1809–10.

RUINS OF DESPAIR

YON mouldering wall composed of naught but mud
(Which has for ages in that manner stood)
Is rightly styled the 'Ruins of Despair,'
For naught but wretchedness assembles there,
All sons of grief and daughters of despair,

Within that hut:—but how can life live there?
That's strange indeed!—while these old walls of mud
(Which have for ages in that manner stood)
Keep daily mouldering in a lost decay,
Leaning on props that want themselves a stay.
Well may those rankling nettles thrive and grow,
So duly watered with the tears of woe.
Lo on the floor, with gulling holes o'erspread,
Their wretched feet betray a shoeless tread;
The Ruins' covering naught but loose-laid straw
Which winds blow off and leave a frequent flaw;
These snows drive in upon the wretch's head;
These hasty rains a threaten'd deluge shed.
Thrice wretched, wretched 'Ruins of Despair,'
What griefs are thine!—Oh, how can life live there?
A rag-stuft hole, where bits of lead remain,
Proof of what was—but now without—a pane;
A roof unceiled displays the rafters bare,
Here dangling straws and cobwebs dropping there;
No white-washed walls to pictured taste incline;
Instead of pictures threatened carvings shine.
The dismal hearth is nothing but a hole,
To wood a stranger and the same to coal;
Light straw and rubbish make their sorry fires,
Kindled no quicker than the flame expires.
Instead of chairs great stones bedeck the ground
(Rough seats indeed), and closely ranged around
On these the wretched tribe spend half their days,
Dithering and weeping o'er the dying blaze,
A blaze that does more paint than heat supply,
Tinging their faces with a smoky dye.
No shelves, no cupboards, no conveniences there;
'Twas planned in grief and finished with despair;
They make their shelves and cupboards on the floor
In a dark hole behind the broken door;
There an old pitcher broke beyond excuse
(For want concealed by them is little use)
Stands with the filthy shadow of a pan
Filthy and nauseous—oh, what being can

Endure! Grief-searching muse, give o'er,
On such a dismal scene essay no more;
Stay thy too-curious search, forbear! forbear!
No more describe the 'Ruins of Despair'!

ON A LOST GREYHOUND

LYING ON THE SNOW

AH, thou poor, neglected hound!
  Now thou'st done with catching hares,
Thou mayst lie upon the ground,
  Lost, for what thy master cares.
To see thee lie, it makes me sigh:
  A proud, hard-hearted man!
But men, we know, like dogs may go,
  When they've done all they can.

And thus, from witnessing thy fate,
  Thoughtful reflection wakes;
Though thou'rt a dog, with grief I say't,
  Poor man thy fare partakes:
Like thee, lost whelp, the poor man's help,
  Erewhile so much desir'd,
Now harvest's got, is wanted not,
  Or little is requir'd.

So now, the overplus will be
  As useless negroes, all
Turn'd in the bitter blast, like thee
  Mere cumber-grounds, to fall:
But this reward, for toil so hard,
  Is sure to meet return
From Him, whose ear is always near,
  When the oppressed mourn.

For dogs, as men, are equally
  A link of nature's chain,
Form'd by that hand that formed me,
  Which formeth naught in vain.

21

All life contains, as 'twere by chains,
    From Him still perfect are;
Nor does He think the meanest link
    Unworthy of His care.

So let us both on Him rely,
    And He'll for us provide;
Find us a shelter warm and dry,
    And everything beside.
And while fools, void of sense, deride
    My tenderness to thee;
I'll take thee home, from whence I've come:
    So rise, and gang with me.

Poor, patient thing! he seems to hear
    And know what I have said;
He wags his tail, and ventures near,
    And bows his mournful head.
Thou'rt welcome: come! and though thou'rt dumb,
    Thy silence speaks thy pains;
So with me start, to share a part,
    While I have aught remains.

A REFLECTION IN AUTUMN

Now autumn's come, adieu the pleasing greens,
    The charming landscape, and the flow'ry plain!
All have deserted from these motley scenes,
    With blighted yellow ting'd, and russet stain.

Though desolation seems to triumph here,
    Yet this is spring to what we still shall find:
The trees must all in nakedness appear,
    Reft of their foliage by the blust'ry wind.

Just so 'twill fare with me in autumn's life;
    Just so I 'd wish: but may the trunk and all
Die with the leaves; nor taste that wintry strife,
    When sorrows urge and fear impedes the fall.

1809.

THE ROBIN

Now the snow hides the ground, little birds leave the wood,
And fly to the cottage to beg for their food;
While the robin, domestic, more tame than the rest,
With its wings drooping down, and rough feathers undrest,
Comes close to our windows, as much as to say,
'I would venture in, if I could find a way:
I'm starv'd, and I want to get out of the cold;
Oh! make me a passage, and think me not bold.'
Ah, poor little creature! thy visits reveal
Complaints such as these to the heart that can feel;
Nor shall such complainings be urged in vain;
I'll make thee a hole, if I take out a pane.
Come in, and a welcome reception thou'lt find;
I keep no grimalkin to murder inclin'd.
But oh, little robin! be careful to shun
That house, where the peasant makes use of a gun;
For if thou but taste of the seed he has strew'd,
Thy life as a ransom must pay for the food:
His aim is unerring, his heart is as hard,
And thy race, though so harmless, he'll never regard.
Distinction with him, boy, is nothing at all;
Both the wren, and the robin, with sparrows must fall.
For his soul (though he outwardly looks like a man)
Is in nature a wolf of the Apennine clan;
Like them his whole study is bent on his prey:
Then be careful, and shun what is meant to betray.
Come, come to my cottage, and thou shalt be free
To perch on my finger and sit on my knee:
Thou shalt eat of the crumbles of bread to thy fill,
And have leisure to clean both thy feathers and bill.
Then come, little robin! and never believe
Such warm invitations are meant to deceive:
In duty I'm bound to show mercy on thee,
Since God don't deny it to sinners like me.

1809.

THE UNIVERSAL EPITAPH

No flattering praises daub my stone,
  My frailties and my faults to hide;
My faults and failings all are known—
  I liv'd in sin—in sin I died.

And oh! condemn me not, I pray,
  You who my sad confession view;
But ask your soul if it can say
  That I'm a viler man than you.

1809.

HER I LOVE

Rose, in full-blown blushes dyed,
  Pink, maturely spread,
Carnations, boasting all their pride
  Of melting white and red,
Are charms confess'd by every eye;
  But, ah! how faint they prove
To paint superior charms, when nigh
  The cheek of her I love.

Ripe cherry on its parent tree,
  With full perfection grac'd,
Red coral in its native sea,
  To all advantage plac'd;
What charms they boast, the eye to please
  And beauty to improve:
But, ah! all's lost, when match'd with these
  The lips of her I love.

The pulpy plum, when ripeness swells
  Its down-surrounding blue—
The dews besprent on heather-bells,
  Reflecting brighter hue—

24

The azure sky, when stars appear
    Its blueness to improve,
Fade into dullest shades, when near
    The eyes of her I love.

Sweet is the blossom'd bean's perfume,
    By morning breezes shed;
And sweeter still the jonquil's bloom,
    When eve bedews its head;
The perfume sweet of pink and rose,
    And violet of the grove:
But ah! how sweeter far than those,
    The kiss of her I love.

ADDRESS TO A LARK

SINGING IN WINTER

Ay, little larky! what's the reason,
Singing thus in winter season?
Nothing, surely, can be pleasing
    To make thee sing;
For I see naught but cold and freezing,
    And feel its sting.

Perhaps, all done with silent mourning,
Thou think'st that summer is returning,
And this the last, cold, frosty morning,
    To chill thy breast;
If so, I pity thy discerning:
    And so I've guess'd.

Poor little songster! vainly cheated,
Stay, leave thy singing uncompleted,
Drop where thou wast beforehand seated,
    In thy warm nest;
Nor let vain wishes be repeated,
    But sit at rest.

25

'Tis winter; let the cold content thee:
Wish after nothing till it's sent thee,
For disappointments will torment thee,
　　Which will be thine:
I know it well, for I've had plenty
　　Misfortunes mine.

Advice, sweet warbler! don't despise it:
None knows what's what but he that tries it;
And then he well knows how to prize it,
　　And so do I:
Thy case, with mine I sympathize it,
　　With many a sigh.

Vain Hope! of thee I've had my portion;
Mere flimsy cobweb! changing ocean!
That flits the scene at every motion,
　　And still eggs on,
With sweeter view, and stronger notion
　　To dwell upon:—

Yes, I've dwelt long on idle fancies,
Strange and uncommon as romances,
On future luck my noddle dances,
　　What I would be;
But, ah! when future time advances,
　　All's blank to me.

Now twenty years I've pack'd behind me,
Since hope's deluding tongue inclin'd me
To fuss myself.　But, warbler, mind me,
　　It's all a sham;
And twenty more's as like to find me
　　Just as I am.

I'm poor enough, there's plenty knows it,
Obscure, how dull, my scribbling shows it:
Then sure 'twas madness to suppose it,
　　What I was at,
To gain preferment!—there I'll close it:
　　So mum for that.

Let mine, sweet bird, then be a warning:
Advice, in season, don't be scorning;
But wait till spring's first days are dawning
    To glad and cheer thee;
And then, sweet minstrel of the morning,
    I'd wish to hear thee.

1815.

THE VILLAGE FUNERAL

To yon low church, with solemn-sounding knell,
    Which t'other day, as rigid fate decreed,
Mournfully knoll'd a widow's passing-bell,
    The village funeral's warned to proceed.

Mournful indeed! the orphans' friends are fled:
    Their father's tender care has long been past;
The widow's toil was all their hope of bread,
    And now the grave awaits to seize the last.

But that providing Power, for ever nigh,
    The universal friend of all distress,
Is sure to hear their supplicating cry,
    And prove a father to the fatherless.

Now from the low mud cottage on the moor,
    By two and two sad bend the weeping train;
The coffin, ready near the propt-up door,
    Now slow proceeds along the wayward lane:

While, as they nearer draw in solemn state,
    The village neighbours are assembled round,
And seem with fond anxiety to wait
    The sad procession in the burial ground.

Yet every face the face of sorrow wears;
    And, now the solemn scene approaches nigh,
Each to make way for the slow march prepares,
    And on the coffin casts a serious eye.

27

Now walks the curate through the silent crowd,
  In snowy surplice loosely banded round;
Now meets the corse; and now he reads aloud,
  In mournful tone, along the burial ground.

The church they enter, and adown the aisle,
  Which more than usual wears a solemn hue,
They rest the coffin on set forms awhile,
  Till the good priest performs the office due.

And though by duty aw'd to silence here,
  The orphans' griefs so piercing force a way;
And, oh! so moving do their griefs appear,
  The worthy pastor kneels, in tears, to pray.

The funeral rites perform'd, by custom thought
  A tribute sacred and essential here,
Now to the last, last place the body's brought,
  Where all, dread fate! are summon'd to appear.

The churchyard round a mournful view displays,
  View where mortality is plainly penn'd;
Drear seem the objects which the eye surveys,
  As objects pointing to our latter end.

There the lank nettles sicken ere they seed,
  Where from old trees eve's cordial vainly falls
To raise or comfort each dejected weed,
  While pattering drops decay the crumbling walls.

Here stand, far distant from the pomp of pride,
  Mean little stones, thin scatter'd here and there,
By the scant means of poverty applied,
  The fond memorial of her friends to bear.

O Memory! thou sweet, enliv'ning power,
  Thou shadow of that fame all hope to find;
The meanest soul exerts her utmost power
  To leave some fragment of a name behind.

Now crowd the sad spectators round to see
   The deep sunk grave, whose heap of swelling mould,
Full of the fragments of mortality,
   Makes the heart shudder while the eyes behold.

Aw'd is the mind, by dreaded truths imprest,
   To think that dust, which they before them see,
Once liv'd like them; chill Conscience tells the rest:
   That like that dust themselves must shortly be.

The gaping grave now claims its destin'd prey,
   'Ashes to ashes—dust to dust,' is given;
The parent earth receives her kindred clay,
   And the soul starts to meet its home in heaven.

Ah, helpless babes! now grief in horror shrieks,
   Now sorrow pauses dumb: each looker-on
Knows not the urging language which it speaks—
   A friend—provider—this world's all—is gone!

Envy and malice now have lost their aim,
   Slander's reproachful tongue can rail no more;
Her foes now pity, where they us'd to blame;
   The faults and foibles of this life are o'er.

The orphans' grief and sorrow, so severe,
   To every heart in pity's language speak;
E'en the rough sexton can't withhold the tear,
   That steals unnotic'd down his furrow'd cheek.

Who but is griev'd to see the fatherless
   Stroll in their rags unnotic'd through the street?
What eye but moistens at their sad distress
   And sheds compassion's tear whene'er they meet?

Yon workhouse stands as their asylum now,
   The place where poverty demands to live,
Where parish bounty scowls his scornful brow,
   And grudges the scant fare he's forc'd to give.

Oh, may I die before I'm doom'd to seek
  That last resource of hope, but ill supplied,
To claim the humble pittance once a week,
  Which justice forces from disdainful pride!—

Where the lost orphan, lowly bending, weeps,
  Unnotic'd by the heedless as they pass,
There the grave closes where a mother sleeps,
  With brambles platted on the tufted grass.

1815.

TO HEALTH

HAIL, soothing balm! Ye breezes blow,
  Ransack the flower and blossom'd tree;
All, all your stolen gifts bestow,
  For health has granted all to me.

And may this blessing long be mine,
  May I this favour still enjoy;
Then never shall my heart repine,
  Nor yet its long continuance cloy.

And though I cannot boast, O health!
  Of aught beside, but only thee,
I would not change this bliss for wealth,
  No, not for all the eye can see.

Wealth without thee is useless made,
  Void of the smallest happy spark;
Yes, just as useless to give aid
  As mirrors set to light the dark.

Thy voice I hear, thy form I see,
  In silence, echo, stream, or cloud;
Now, that strong voice belongs to thee
  Which woods and hills repeat so loud.

30

The leaf, the flower, the spiry blade,
  The hanging drops of pearly dew,
The russet heath, the woodland shade,
  All, all can bring thee in my view.

With thee I seek the woodland shade
  Beset in briery wilds among;
With thee I tread the tufted glade,
  Transported by the woodlark's song.

With thee I wander where the sheep
  In groups display a chequer'd train,
Where weedy waters winding creep;
  Nor wilt thou fallow-clods disdain.

Then hail, sweet balm! Ye breezes blow,
  Ransack the flower and blossom'd tree;
All, all your stolen gifts bestow,
  For health has granted all to me.

NARRATIVE VERSES

WRITTEN AFTER AN EXCURSION FROM HELPSTONE TO BURGHLEY PARK

THE faint sun tipt the rising ground,
  No blustering wind, the air was still;
The blue mist, thinly scatter'd round,
  Verg'd along the distant hill:
Delightful morn! from labour free
  I jocund met the south-west gale,
While here and there a humming bee
  Skimm'd lightly o'er the flow'ry vale.

O joyful morn! on pleasure bent,
  Down the green slopes and fields I flew;
And through the thickest covert went,
  Which hid me from the public view:

Nor was it shame, nor was it fear,
　　No, no, it was my own dear choice;
I love the briery thicket, where
　　Echo keeps her mocking voice.

The sun's increasing heat was kind,
　　His warm beams cheer'd the vales around;
I left my own fields far behind,
　　And, pilgrim-like, trod foreign ground;
The glowing landscape's charms I caught,
　　Where'er I look'd or wander'd o'er,
And every wood and field methought
　　A greener, brighter clothing wore.

Delicious morn! thou'lt always find,
　　When an hour's pastime intervenes,
A vacant opening in my mind
　　To think and cherish thy fond scenes;
Though no huge rock approach'd my sight,
　　Nor lofty mountain rear'd its head,
Enough for wonder and delight
　　All around my path was spread.

Sometimes musing on the sky,
　　Then list'ning to the waterfall,
Now marking sunbeams mounted high
　　Glistering shine on Walkherd Hall—
Thus I often made a stand,
　　Thus I mark'd each curious spot,
And, seemingly to court my hand,
　　I now and then a cowslip got.

But, Barnack Sinnoms, thine's the place,
　　Where antique forms are dimly shown;
There, o'er thy moss-grown hills, I trace
　　Scenes which never will be known:
The deep-sunk moat, the stony mound,
　　Brought o'er my mind a pensive fit;
But 'ah,' thought I, while looking round,
　　'Their heads don't ache that made yon pit.'

Oh, thou long-remember'd morn,
  How blest was I in these dear vales,
When snugly hid beneath the thorn
  I mus'd o'er Bloomfield's 'Rural Tales':
And there, sweet bard! thy 'forest-song,'
  Describ'd with energy sublime,
Fraught with such music, charm'd my tongue,
  And turn'd my simple thoughts to rhyme.

Thus ever varying my mind,
  Ever running like the rill,
Soon I left these scenes behind
  In quest of others brighter still;
Yet not for ever! no, ye vales,
  I love your pleasant shades too well,
And often since to view your dales
  I've brush'd along the upland swell.

Now nothing, save a running stream,
  For a while my eye engag'd,
Whose plaintive murmurs sooth'd my dream,
  And all aspiring thoughts assuag'd;
Now, when near its mossy bank,
  I well remember how I lay,
Stretching o'er the oaken plank
  To see the dancing beetles play.

Though the stranger passing by
  Scarcely gave a single look,
Yet for a whole day could I lie
  And pore upon this little brook;
Well pleas'd to view its winding rounds,
  And see the eddying purls it made,
But still its daisy-skirted bounds,
  Like 'Barnham Water,' want a shade.

The passing hours jogg'd on apace,
  And in their progress seem'd to say,
'Haste, and gain that destin'd place,
  Or soon thou'lt lose the flitting day':

I instantly obey'd their call,
  Nor went to where the footpath lay,
But clamber'd o'er an old rough wall,
  And stole across the nearest way.

No spire I caught, nor woody swell,
  My eye confin'd to lower bounds,
Yet not to mark the flow'ret's bell,
  But watch the owners of the grounds;
Their presence was my only fear,
  No boughs to shield me if they came,
And soon amid my rash career
  I deem'd such trespassing to blame.

For troubled thoughts began to rise,
  Of ills almost beyond relief
Which might from this one cause arise,
  And leave me then to want reprief;
So arguing with myself how vain
  An afterthought, 'still to keep free,'
Made me to seek the road again,
  And own the force of liberty.

For oh, its unabated power
  Did then my breast with raptures fill,
And sure it was a happy hour
  That led me up to Barnack Hill;
There uncontroll'd I knew no bounds,
  But look'd o'er villages a crowd,
And cots and spires to farthest rounds,
  While far trees seem'd a misty cloud.

When tir'd with such far-stretching views,
  I left the green hill's sideling slope,
But oh, so tempting was the muse,
  She made me wish, she made me hope;
I wish'd and hop'd that future days
  (For scenes prophetic fill'd my breast)
Would grant to me a crown of bays
  By singing maids and shepherds drest.

These for a while gave such delight,
  And occupied my mind so strong,
That not one view could tempt my sight
  But all unheeded pass'd along;
Save only when that destin'd place,
  As yet unknown, though long endear'd,
Enrich'd with many a nameless grace,
  Through fancy's flitting eye appear'd.

HELPSTONE GREEN

Ye injur'd fields, ye once were gay,
  When nature's hand display'd
Long waving rows of willows grey,
  And clumps of hawthorn shade;
But now, alas! your hawthorn bowers
  All desolate we see,
The spoilers' axe their shade devours,
  And cuts down every tree.

Not trees alone have own'd their force,
  Whole woods beneath them bow'd;
They turn'd the winding rivulet's course,
  And flowery pastures plough'd;
To shrub or tree throughout thy fields
  They no compassion show;
The uplifted axe no mercy yields,
  But strikes a fatal blow.

Whene'er I muse along the plain
  And mark where once they grew,
Remembrance wakes her busy train
  And brings past scenes to view:
The well-known brook, the favourite tree,
  In fancy's eye appear,
And next, that pleasant green I see,
  That green for ever dear.

O'er its green hills I've often stray'd
  In childhood's happy hour,
Oft sought the nest along the shade
  And gather'd many a flower,
And there, with playmates often join'd
  In fresher sports to plan;
But now increasing years have coin'd
  Those children into man.

The green's gone too—ah, lovely scene!
  No more the kingcup gay
Shall shine in yellow o'er the green,
  And shed its golden ray;
No more the herdsman's early call
  Shall bring the cows to feed,
No more the milkmaid's evening bawl
  In 'Come mull' tones succeed.

Both milkmaid's shouts and herdsman's call
  Have vanish'd with the green,
The kingcups yellow, shades and all,
  Shall never more be seen;
But the thick-cultur'd tribes that grow
  Will so efface the scene,
That after-times will hardly know
  It ever was a green.

Farewell, thou favourite spot, farewell!
  Since every effort's vain,
All I can do is still to tell
  Of thy delightful plain;
But that joy's short—increasing years,
  That did my youth presage,
Will now, as each new day appears,
  Bring on declining age.

Reflection pierces deadly keen,
  While I the moral scan—
As are the changes of the green
  So is the life of man:

Youth brings age with faltering tongue,
    That does the exit crave;
There's one short scene presents the throng,
    Another shows the grave.

TO THE VIOLET

SWEET tiny flower of darkly hue,
    Lone dweller in the pathless shade;
How much I love thy pensive blue
    Of innocence so well display'd!

What time the watery skies are full
    Of streaming dappled clouds so pale,
And sideling rocks, more white than wool,
    Portending snowy sleet, or hail;

I 'gin to seek thy charming flower
    Along each hedgerow's mossy seat,
Where, dithering many a cold blea hour,
    I've hugg'd myself in thy retreat.

What makes me cherish such fond taste,
    What makes such raptures spring for thee,
Is that thou lov'st the dreary waste
    Which is so well belov'd by me.

For solitude should be my choice
    Could I this labouring life resign,
To see the little birds rejoice,
    And thy sweet flowers in clusters shine.

I'd choose a cave beside some rock,
    Clos'd in all round with ash and thorn,
That near my door thy tribe might flock
    To shed their sweets in early morn.

But, ah! that way would never prove
    Means to sustain impending life;
I must forgo those scenes I love,
    And still beat on with needy strife.

Sweet flower! we must reverse the plan,
    Nor cherish such romantic views;
I'll strive to seek thee when I can,
    Through noontide heat or evening dews.

To spring return, with all thy train
    Of flow'rets cloth'd in varied hue,
I long to see that morn again
    Which brings to light the violet blue.

SONG OF PRAISE

IMITATION OF THE 148TH PSALM

WARM into praises, kindling muse,
With grateful transport raise thy views
    To Him, who moves this ball,
Who whirls, in silent harmony,
The earth, the ocean, air, and sky—
    Oh, praise the Lord of all!

Ye angels—hymning round your King,
Praise Him who gives you power to sing,
    Ye hosts—with raptures burn;
Who station'd you in bliss, proclaim!
Oh, bless your Benefactor's name,
    Betokening kind return.

Ye spreading heavens, arching high,
Ye scenes unknown beyond the sky,
    Creation's Maker own:
'Let there be light'—your Ruler said;
And instant your blue curtain spread
    In triumph round His throne.

Thou moon, meek guardian of the night,
Ye planets of inferior light,
　　Ye lamps of rays divine,
Ye suns—dart forth your splendid rays
To Him who metes your nights and days,
　　And suffers you to shine.

Oh, praise His name, His mercy bless,
Ye poor, like me, in 'whelmed distress;
　　Oh, hail protection given:
When sin and sorrow die away,
Our hopes His promise still shall stay
　　Of recompensing heaven.

Thunders that fright the trembling ground,
Ye forked lightnings, flashing round,
　　Or quench'd in 'whelming shower;
While skies in vollied rolls are rent—
While nature pauses, silent bent—
　　Adore Almighty Power.

Ye minstrel birds, wild woodland's charms,
Whose song each child of nature warms
　　With your lov'd haunts in view;
From Him you borrow'd every note,
Then open wide your chanting throat
　　To give the tribute due.

Mis-shapen germs of parent earth,
Waiting, dependent for your birth,
　　The sun's enlivening rays;
Emerging from your silent tomb,
To join the hailing myriads, come,
　　And kindle into praise.

Bowing adorers of the gale,
Ye cowslips, delicately pale,
　　Upraise your loaded stems;
Unfold your cups in splendour, speak!
Who deck'd you with that ruddy streak,
　　And gilt your golden gems?

Violets, sweet tenants of the shade,
In purple's richest pride array'd,
  Your errand here fulfil;
Go bid the artist's simple stain
Your lustre imitate, in vain,
  And match your Maker's skill.

Daisies, ye flowers of lowly birth,
Embroiderers of the carpet earth,
  That stud the velvet sod;
Open to spring's refreshing air,
In sweetest smiling bloom declare
  Your Maker, and my God!

Thou humble clothing of the trees,
Moss, in whose meanness genius sees
  A world of wonders shine;
Put on your satin-smoothening green,
And let your Maker's power be seen,
  And workmanship divine.

Creation's universal round,
That beat the air, or press the ground,
  Or plough the seas, the same,
All join in chorusing accord,
Exalt your Maker and your Lord,
  And praise His holy name:

Till o'er this sin-consuming world
Destruction's fated doom is hurl'd,
  And ruin's self decays;
Then, freed from sin and Adam's fall,
All join, and hail Him Lord of all,
  In everlasting praise.

THE WOOD-CUTTER'S NIGHT SONG

G. M. H.
"roundy wells"

Welcome, red and roundy sun,
  Dropping lowly in the west;
Now my hard day's work is done,
  I'm as happy as the best.

Joyful are the thoughts of home,
  Now I'm ready for my chair,
So, till morrow-morning's come,
  Bill and mittens, lie ye there!

Though to leave your pretty song,
  Little birds, it gives me pain,
Yet to-morrow is not long,
  Then I'm with you all again.

If I stop, and stand about,
  Well I know how things will be,
Judy will be looking out
  Every now-and-then for me.

So fare-ye-well! and hold your tongues,
  Sing no more until I come;
They're not worthy of your songs
  That never care to drop a crumb.

All day long I love the oaks,
  But, at nights, yon little cot,
Where I see the chimney smokes,
  Is by far the prettiest spot.

Wife and children all are there,
  To revive with pleasant looks,
Table ready set, and chair,
  Supper hanging on the hooks.

Soon as ever I get in,
  When my faggot down I fling,
Little prattlers they begin
  Teasing me to talk and sing.

Welcome, red and roundy sun,
    Dropping lowly in the west;
Now my hard day's work is done,
    I'm as happy as the best.

Joyful are the thoughts of home,
    Now I'm ready for my chair,
So, till morrow-morning's come,
    Bill and mittens, lie ye there!

TO THE BUTTERFLY

LOVELY insect, haste away,
Greet once more the sunny day;
Leave, oh, leave the murky barn,
Ere trapping spiders thee discern;
Soon as seen, they will beset
Thy golden wings with filmy net,
Then all in vain to set thee free,
Hopes all lost for liberty.
Never think that I belie,
Never fear a winter sky;
Budding oaks may now be seen,
Starry daisies deck the green,
Primrose groups the woods adorn,
Cloudless skies, and blossom'd thorn
These all prove that spring is here,
Haste away then, never fear.
Skim o'er hill and valley free,
Perch upon the blossom'd tree;
Though my garden would be best,
Couldst thou but contented rest:
There the school-boy has no power
Thee to chase from flower to flower,
Harbour none for cruel sport,
Far away thy foes resort;
Naught is there but liberty,

42

Pleasant place for thee and me.
Then hither bend thy roving flight,
In my garden take delight.
Though the dew-bent level dale
Rears the lily of the vale,
Though the thicket's bushy dell
Tempts thee to the foxglove's bell,
Come but once within my bounds,
View my garden's airy rounds,
Soon thou'lt find the scene complete,
And every flow'ret twice as sweet:
Then, lovely insect, come away,
Greet once more the sunny day.
Oft I've seen, when warm and dry,
'Mong the bean-fields bosom-high,
How thy starry gems and gold
To admiration would unfold:
Lo! the arching heavenly bow
Doth all his dyes on thee bestow,
Crimson, blue, and watery green,
Mix'd with azure shade between;
These are thine—thou first in place,
Queen of all the insect race!
And I've often thought, alone,
This to thee was not unknown;
For amid the sunny hour,
When I've found thee on a flower
(Searching with minutest gleg),
Oft I've seen thy little leg
Soft as glass o'er velvet glides
Smoothen down thy silken sides;
Then thy wings would ope and shut;
Then thou seemingly wouldst strut:
Was it nature, was it pride?
Let the learned world decide.
Enough for me (though some may deem
This a trifling, silly theme)
Wouldst thou in my garden come,
To join the bee's delightful hum;

These silly themes then, day and night,
Should be thy trifler's whole delight.
Then, lovely insect, haste away,
Greet once more the sunny day.

MAY-DAY

Now happy swains review the plains,
    And hail the first of May;
Now linnets sing to welcome spring,
    And every soul is gay.

Hob, joyful soul, high rears the pole,
    With wild-flower wreaths entwin'd;
Then tiptoe round the maidens bound,
    All sorrow lags behind.

Branches of thorn their doors adorn,
    With every flow'ret lin'd
That earliest spring essays to bring,
    Or searching maids can find.

All swains resort to join the sport,
    E'en age will not disdain,
But oft will throng to hear the song,
    And view the jocund train.

I often too had us'd to go,
    The rural mirth to share,
But what, alas! time brought to pass,
    Soon made me absent there.

My Colin died, the village pride,
    O hapless misery!
Then sports adieu, with him they flew,
    For he was all to me.

And May no more shall e'er restore
    To me those joys again,
There's no relief but urging grief,
    For memory wakens pain.

To think how he, so dear to me,
 Had us'd to join the play;
And oh, so dear such pleasures were,
 He gloried in the day.

But now, sad scene, he's left the green
 And Lubin here to mourn:
Then flowers may spring, and birds may sing,
 And May-day may return;

But never more can they restore
 Their rural sports to me—
No, no, adieu! with him they flew,
 For he was all to me.

ADDRESS TO PLENTY

IN WINTER

OH, thou Bliss! to riches known,
Stranger to the poor alone,
Giving most where none's requir'd,
Leaving none where most's desir'd;
Who, sworn friend to miser, keeps
Adding to his useless heaps
Gifts on gifts, profusely stor'd,
Till thousands swell the mouldy hoard:
While poor, shatter'd Poverty,
To advantage seen in me,
With his rags, his wants, and pain,
Waking pity but in vain,
Bowing, cringing at thy side,
Begs his mite, and is denied,
Oh, thou Blessing! let not me
Tell, as vain, my wants to thee;
Thou, by name of Plenty styl'd,
Fortune's heir, her favourite child.

'Tis a maxim—hunger feed,
Give the needy when they need;
He whom all profess to serve
The same maxim did observe:
Their obedience here, how well,
Modern times will plainly tell.
Hear my wants, nor deem me bold,
Not without occasion told:
Hear one wish, nor fail to give;
Use me well, and bid me live.

'Tis not great, what I solicit;
Was it more, thou couldst not miss it:
Now the cutting winter's come,
'Tis but just to find a home,
In some shelter, dry and warm,
That will shield me from the storm.
Toiling in the naked fields,
Where no bush a shelter yields,
Needy Labour dithering stands,
Beats and blows his numbing hands;
And upon the crumping snows
Stamps, in vain, to warm his toes.
Leaves are fled, that once had power
To resist a summer shower;
And the wind so piercing blows,
Winnowing small the drifting snows,
The summer shade of loaded bough
Would vainly boast a shelter now;
Piercing snows so searching fall,
They sift a passage through them all.
Though all's vain to keep him warm,
Poverty must brave the storm.
Friendship none, its aid to lend;
Health alone his only friend,
Granting leave to live in pain,
Giving strength to toil in vain,
To be, while winter's horrors last,
The sport of every pelting blast.

Oh, sad sons of Poverty!
Victims doom'd to misery;
Who can paint what pain prevails
O'er that heart which want assails?
Modest shame the pain conceals;
No one knows, but he who feels.
Oh, thou charm which Plenty crowns,
Fortune! smile, now winter frowns:
Cast around a pitying eye;
Feed the hungry, ere they die.
Think, oh! think upon the poor,
Nor against them shut thy door;
Freely let thy bounty flow
On the sons of want and woe.

Hills and dales no more are seen
In their dress of pleasing green;
Summer's robes are all thrown by,
For the clothing of the sky;
Snows on snows in heaps combine,
Hillocks, rais'd as mountains, shine,
And at distance rising proud,
Each appears a fleecy cloud.
Plenty! now thy gifts bestow;
Exit bid to every woe;
Take me in, shut out the blast,
Make the doors and windows fast;
Place me in some corner, where,
Lolling in an elbow chair,
Happy, blest to my desire,
I may find a rousing fire;
While in chimney-corner nigh,
Coal, or wood, a fresh supply,
Ready stands for laying on,
Soon as t'other's burnt and gone.
Now and then, as taste decreed,
In a book a page I'd read;
And, inquiry to amuse,
Peep at something in the news;

See who's married, and who's dead,
And who, though bankrupt, beg their bread:
While on hob, or table nigh,
Just to drink before I'm dry,
A pitcher at my side should stand,
With the barrel nigh at hand,
Always ready as I will'd,
When 'twas empty, to be fill'd;
And, to be possess'd of all,
A corner cupboard in the wall,
With store of victuals lin'd complete,
That when hungry I might eat.
Then would I, in Plenty's lap,
For the first time take a nap;
Falling back in easy lair,
Sweetly slumb'ring in my chair,
With no reflective thoughts to wake
Pains that cause my heart to ache,
Of contracted debts, long made,
In no prospect to be paid,
And, to want, sad news severe,
Of provisions getting dear:
While the winter, shocking sight,
Constant freezes day and night,
Deep and deeper falls the snow,
Labour's slack, and wages low.
These, and more, the poor can tell,
Known, alas, by them too well,
Plenty! oh, if blest by thee,
Never more should trouble me.
Hours and weeks will sweetly glide,
Soft and smooth as flows the tide,
Where no stones or choking grass
Force a curve ere it can pass:
And as happy, and as blest,
As beasts drop them down to rest,
When in pastures, at their will,
They have roam'd and eat their fill,
Soft as nights in summer creep,

So should I then fall asleep;
While sweet visions of delight,
So enchanting to the sight,
Sweetly swimming o'er my eyes,
Would sink me into ecstasies,
Nor would pleasure's dreams once more,
As they oft have done before,
Cause be to create a pain,
When I woke, to find them vain:
Bitter past, the present sweet,
Would my happiness complete.
Oh! how easy should I lie,
With the fire up-blazing high
(Summer's artificial bloom),
That like an oven keeps the room,
Or lovely May, as mild and warm:
While, without, the raging storm
Is roaring in the chimney-top,
In no likelihood to drop;
And the witchen-branches nigh,
O'er my snug box towering high,
That sweet shelter'd stands beneath,
In convulsive eddies wreathe.
Then while, tyrant-like, the storm
Takes delight in doing harm,
Down before him crushing all,
Till his weapons useless fall;
And as in oppression proud
Peal his howlings long and loud,
While the clouds, with horrid sweep,
Give (as suits a tyrant's trade)
The sun a minute's leave to peep,
To smile upon the ruins made;
And to make complete the blast,
While the hail comes hard and fast,
Rattling loud against the glass;
And the snowy sleets, that pass,
Driving up in heaps remain
Close adhering to the pane,

Stop the light, and spread a gloom,
Suiting sleep, around the room:
Oh, how blest 'mid these alarms,
I should bask in Fortune's arms,
Who, defying every frown,
Hugs me on her downy breast,
Bids my head lie easy down,
And on winter's ruins rest.
So upon the troubled sea,
Emblematic simile,
Birds are known to sit secure,
While the billows roar and rave,
Slumbering in their safety sure,
Rock'd to sleep upon the wave,
So would I still slumber on,
Till hour-telling clocks had gone,
And, from the contracted day,
One or more had click'd away.
Then with sitting wearied out,
I for change's sake, no doubt,
Just might wish to leave my seat,
And, to exercise my feet,
Make a journey to the door,
Put my nose out, but no more;
There to village taste agree,
Mark how times are like to be,
How the weather's getting on,
Peep in ruts where carts have gone.
Or, by stones, a sturdy stroke,
View the hole the boys have broke,
Crizzling, still inclin'd to freeze;
And the rime upon the trees.
Then, to pause on ills to come,
Just look upward on the gloom;
See fresh storms approaching fast,
View them busy in the air,
Boiling up the brewing blast,
Still fresh horrors scheming there.
Black and dismal, rising high

From the north, they fright the eye:
Pregnant with a thousand storms
Huddled in their icy arms,
Heavy hovering as they come,
Some as mountains seem—and some
Jagg'd as craggy rocks appear
Dismally advancing near;
Earth unable seems to bear
The huge mass that's moving there.
Fancy, at the cumbrous sight,
Chills and shudders with affright,
Fearing lest the air in vain
Strives her station to maintain,
And wearied, yielding to the skies,
The world beneath in ruin lies.
So may Fancy think and feign;
Fancy oft imagines vain;
Nature's laws, by wisdom penn'd,
Mortals cannot comprehend;
Power Almighty Being gave,
Endless Mercy stoops to save;
Causes, hid from mortals' sight,
Prove 'whatever is, is right.'

Then to look again below,
Labour's former life I'd view,
Who, still beating through the snow,
Spite of storms their toils pursue,
Forc'd out by sad necessity,
That sad fiend that forces me.
Troubles, then no more my own,
Which I but too long had known,
Might create a care, a pain;
Then I'd seek my joys again,
Pile the fire up, fetch a drink,
Then sit down again and think;
Pause on all my sorrows past,
Think how many a bitter blast,
When it snow'd, and hail'd, and blew,

I have toil'd and batter'd through,
And how many a lengthen'd day,
Half the night as one may say,
Weary lowking in a barn,
Humble twenty pence to earn.
Then to ease reflective pain, ⎫
To my sports I'd fall again, ⎬
Till the clock had counted ten, ⎭
When I'd seek my downy bed,
Easy, happy, and well fed.

Then might peep the morn, in vain,
Through the rimy misted pane;
Then might bawl the restless cock,
And the loud-tongued village clock;
And the flail might lump away,
Waking soon the dreary day:
They should never waken me,
Independent, blest, and free;
Nor, as usual, make me start,
Yawning sigh with heavy heart,
Loath to ope my sleepy eyes,
Weary still, in pain to rise,
With aching bones and heavy head,
Worse than when I went to bed.
With nothing then to raise a sigh,
Oh, how happy should I lie
Till the clock was eight, or more,
Then proceed as heretofore.
Best of blessings! sweetest charm!
Boon these wishes while they're warm;
My fairy visions ne'er despise;
As reason thinks, thou realize:
Depress'd with want and poverty,
I sink, I fall, denied by thee.

1817.

ELEGY ON THE RUINS OF PICKWORTH

(RUTLANDSHIRE)

THESE buried ruins, now in dust forgot,
   These heaps of stone the only remnants seen,—
'The Old Foundations' still they call the spot,
   Which plainly tells inquiry what has been—

A time was once, though now the nettle grows
   In triumph o'er each heap that swells the ground,
When they, in buildings pil'd, a village rose,
   With here a cot, and there a garden crown'd.

And here while grandeur, with unequal share,
   Perhaps maintain'd its idleness and pride,
Industry's cottage rose contented there,
   With scarce so much as wants of life supplied.

Mysterious cause! still more mysterious plann'd
   (Although undoubtedly the will of heaven):
To think what careless and unequal hand
   Metes out each portion that to man is given.

While vain extravagance, for one alone,
   Claims half the land his grandeur to maintain,
What thousands, not a rood to call their own,
   Like me but labour for support in vain!

Here we see luxury surfeit with excess;
   There want, bewailing, beg from door to door,
Still meeting sorrow where he meets success,
   By lengthening life that liv'd in vain before.

Almighty Power!—but why do I repine,
   Or vainly live thy goodness to distrust?
Since reason rules each provident design,
   Whatever is must certainly be just.

Ye scenes of desolation spread around,
   Prosperity to you did once belong;
And, doubtless, where these brambles claim the ground,
   The glass once flow'd to hail the ranting song.

The ale-house here might stand, each hamlet's boast;
   And here, where elder rich from ruin grows,
The tempting sign—but what was once is lost;
   Who would be proud of what this world bestows?

How contemplation mourns their lost decay,
   To view their pride laid level with the ground;
To see, where labour clears the soil away,
   What fragments of mortality abound.

There's not a rood of land demands our toil,
   There's not a foot of ground we daily tread,
But gains increase from time's devouring spoil,
   But holds some fragment of the human dead.

The very food, which for support we crave,
   Claims for its share an equal portion too;
The dust of many a long-forgotten grave
   Serves to manure the soil from whence it grew.

Since first these ruins fell, how chang'd the scene!
   What busy, bustling mortals, now unknown,
Have come and gone, as tho' there naught had been,
   Since first oblivion call'd the spot her own.

Ye busy, bustling mortals, known before,
   Of what you've done, where went, or what you see,
Of what your hopes attain'd to (now no more)
   For everlasting lies a mystery.

Like yours, awaits for me that common lot;
   'Tis mine to be of every hope bereft:
A few more years and I shall be forgot,
   And not a vestige of my memory left.

1818.

WHAT IS LIFE?

AND what is Life?—An hour-glass on the run,
A mist retreating from the morning sun,
   A busy, bustling, still repeated dream;
Its length?—A minute's pause, a moment's thought;
   And happiness?—A bubble on the stream,
That in the act of seizing shrinks to naught.

What are vain Hopes?—The puffing gale of morn,
That of its charms divests the dewy lawn,
   And robs each flow'ret of its gem—and dies;
A cobweb hiding disappointment's thorn,
   Which stings more keenly through the thin disguise.

And thou, O Trouble?—nothing can suppose
(And sure the power of wisdom only knows)
   What need requireth thee:
So free and liberal as thy bounty flows,
   Some necessary cause must surely be.
But disappointments, pains, and every woe
   Devoted wretches feel,
The universal plagues of life below,
   Are mysteries still 'neath Fate's unbroken seal.

And what is Death? is still the cause unfound?
That dark, mysterious name of horrid sound?—
   A long and lingering sleep, the weary crave.
And Peace? where can its happiness abound?—
   Nowhere at all, save heaven, and the grave.

Then what is Life?—When stripp'd of its disguise,
   A thing to be desir'd it cannot be;
Since everything that meets our foolish eyes
   Gives proof sufficient of its vanity.
'Tis but a trial all must undergo;
   To teach unthankful mortals how to prize
That happiness vain man's denied to know,
   Until he's call'd to claim it in the skies.

1818.

55

THE HARVEST MORNING

Cocks wake the early morn with many a crow;
Loud striking village clock has counted four;
The labouring rustic hears his restless foe,
And weary, of his pains complaining sore,
Hobbles to fetch his horses from the moor:
Some busy 'gin to teem the loaded corn,
Which night throng'd round the barn's becrowded door;
Such plenteous scenes the farmer's yard adorn,
Such busy bustling toils now mark the harvest morn.

The bird-boy's pealing horn is loudly blow'd;
The wagons jostle on with rattling sound;
And hogs and geese now throng the dusty road,
Grunting and gabbling, in contention, round
The barley ears that litter on the ground.
What printing traces mark the wagon's way;
What busy bustling wakens echo round;
How drive the sun's warm beams the mist away;
How labour sweats and toils, and dreads the sultry day!

His scythe the mower o'er his shoulder leans,
And whetting, jars with sharp and tinkling sound,
Then sweeps again 'mong corn and crackling beans,
And swath by swath flops lengthening o'er the ground;
While 'neath some friendly heap, snug shelter'd round
From spoiling sun, lies hid the heart's delight;
And hearty soaks oft hand the bottle round,
Their toils pursuing with redoubled might—
Great praise to him be due that brought its birth to light.

Upon the wagon now, with eager bound,
The lusty picker whirls the rustling sheaves,
Or, ponderous resting creaking fork aground,
Boastful at once whole shocks of barley heaves:
The loading boy revengeful inly grieves
To find his unmatch'd strength and power decay;
The barley horn his garments interweaves;
Smarting and sweating 'neath the sultry day,
With muttering curses stung, he mauls the heaps away.

A motley group the clearing field surround:
Sons of humanity, oh, ne'er deny
The humble gleaner entrance in your ground;
Winter's sad cold and poverty are nigh.
Grudge not from Providence the scant supply:
You'll never miss it from your ample store.
Who gives denial—harden'd, hungry hound—
May never blessings crowd his hated door!
But he shall never lack, that giveth to the poor.

Ah, lovely Emma! mingling with the rest,
Thy beauties blooming in low life unseen,
Thy rosy cheeks, thy sweetly swelling breast,
But ill it suits thee in the stubs to glean.
O Poverty! how basely you demean
The imprison'd worth your rigid fates confine;
Not fancied charms of an Arcadian queen,
So sweet as Emma's real beauties shine:
Had fortune blest, sweet girl, this lot had ne'er been thine.

The sun's increasing heat now mounted high,
Refreshment must recruit exhausted power;
The wagon stops, the busy tool's thrown by,
And 'neath a shock's enjoy'd the bevering hour.
The bashful maid, sweet health's engaging flower,
Lingering behind, o'er rake still blushing bends,
And when to take the horn fond swains implore,
With feign'd excuses its dislike pretends.
So pass the bevering hours, so harvest morning ends.

O rural life! what charms thy meanness hide;
What sweet descriptions bards disdain to sing;
What loves, what graces on thy plains abide:
Oh, could I soar me on the muse's wing,
What rifled charms should my researches bring!
Pleas'd would I wander where these charms reside;
Of rural sports and beauties would I sing,
Those beauties, Wealth, which you in vain deride,
Beauties of richest bloom, superior to your pride.

1818.

THE POET'S WISH

A WISH will rise in every breast
For something more than what's possess'd,
Some trifle still, or more or less,
To make complete one's happiness.
And, faith! a wish will oft incline
To harbour in this breast of mine;
And oft old Fortune hears my case,
Told plain as nose upon her face;
But vainly do we beggars plead,
Although not ask'd before we need:
Old Fortune, like sly Farmer Dapple,
Where there's an orchard flings her apple;
But where there's no return to make ye,
She turns her nose up, 'Deuce may take ye.'
So rich men get their wealth at will,
And beggars—why, they're beggars still.

But 'tis not thought of being rich
That makes my wishing spirit itch;
'Tis just an independent fate,
Betwixt the little and the great;
No out-o'-the-way nor random wish,
No ladle carv'd for silver dish,
'Tis but a comfortable seat,
While without work both ends would meet.
'Tis just get hand to mouth with ease,
And read and study as I please:
A little garret, warm and high,
As loves the muse sublime to fly,
With all my friends encircled round
In golden letters, richly bound;
Dear English poets! luckless fellows,
As born to such, so fate will tell us;
Might I their flow'ry themes peruse,
And be as happy in my muse,
Like them sublimely high to soar,
Without their fate—so cursed poor!

While one snug room, not over small,
Contain'd my necessary all,
And night and day left me secure
'Mong books, my chiefest furniture,
With littering papers, many a bit
Scrawl'd by the muse in fancied fit.
And curse upon that routing jade,
My territories to invade,
Who finds me out in evil hour,
To brush and clean and scrub and scour,
And with a dreaded brush or broom
Disturbs my learned lumber-room.
Such busy things I hate to see,
Such troublers ne'er shall trouble me:
Let dust keep gathering on the ground,
And roping cobwebs dangle round,
Let spiders weave their webs at will,
Would cash, when wanted, pockets fill,
To *pint* it just at my desire,
My drooping muse with ale inspire,
And fetch at least a roll of bread,
Without a debt to run or dread.
Such comforts, would they were but mine,
To something more I'd ne'er incline:
But happiest then of happy clowns,
   I'd sing all cares away;
And pitying monarchs capp'd with crowns,
   I'd see more joys than they.

   Thus wish'd a bard, whom fortune scorns,
To find a rose among the thorns;
And musing o'er each heavy care,
His pen stuck useless in his hair,
His muse was dampt, nor fir'd his soul,
And still unearn'd his penny roll;
Th'unfinish'd labours of his head
Were listless on the table spread;
When lo! to bid him hope no more,
A rap—an earthquake! jars the door;

His heart drops in his shoes with doubt:
'What fiend has found my lodging out?'
Poor trembling tenants of the quill!—
'Here, sir, I bring my master's bill.'—
He heav'd a sigh, and scratch'd his head,
And credit's mouth with promise fed:
Then sat in terror down again,
Invok'd the muse, and scrigg'd a strain,
A trifling something glad to get,
To earn a dinner, and discharge the debt.

SUMMER EVENING

THE sinking sun is taking leave,
And sweetly gilds the edge of eve,
While huddling clouds of purple dye,
Gloomy hang the western sky.
Crows crowd croaking overhead,
Hastening to the woods to bed.
Cooing sits the lonely dove,
Calling home her absent love.
With 'Kirchup! kirchup!' 'mong the wheats,
Partridge distant partridge greets,
Beckoning hints to those that roam,
That guide the squander'd covey home.
Swallows check their winding flight,
And twittering on the chimney light.
Round the pond the martins flirt,
Their snowy breasts bedaub'd with dirt,
While the mason, 'neath the slates,
Each mortar-bearing bird awaits:
By art untaught, each labouring spouse
Curious daubs his hanging house.
Bats flit by in hood and cowl;
Through the barn-hole pops the owl;
From the hedge, in drowsy hum,
Heedless buzzing beetles bum,

Haunting every bushy place,
Flopping in the labourer's face.
Now the snail hath made his ring,
And the moth with snowy wing
Circles round in winding whirls,
Through sweet evening's sprinkled pearls
On each nodding rush besprent,
Dancing on from bent to bent:
Now to downy grasses clung,
Resting for a while he's hung;
Strong, to ferry o'er the stream,
Vanishing as flies a dream,
Playful still his hours to keep,
Till his time has come to sleep;
In tall grass, by fountain-head,
Weary then he drops to bed.
From the hay-cock's moisten'd heaps,
Startled frogs take vaunting leaps,
And along the shaven mead,
Jumping travellers, they proceed:
Quick the dewy grass divides,
Moistening sweet their speckled sides;
From the grass or flow'ret's cup,
Quick the dew-drop bounces up.
Now the blue fog creeps along,
And the bird's forgot his song.
Flowers now sleep within their hoods,
Daisies button into buds;
From soiling dew the buttercup
Shuts his golden jewels up;
And the rose and woodbine they
Wait again the smiles of day.
'Neath the willow's wavy boughs,
Dolly, singing, milks her cows;
While the brook, as bubbling by,
Joins in murmuring melody.
Dick and Dob, with jostling joll,
Homeward drag the rumbling roll;
Whilom Ralph, for Doll to wait,

Lolls him o'er the pasture gate.
Swains to fold their sheep begin;
Dogs loud barking drive them in.
Hedgers now along the road
Homeward bend beneath their load;
And from the long furrow'd seams,
Ploughmen loose their weary teams:
Ball, with urging lashes weal'd,
Still so slow to drive a-field,
Eager blundering from the plough,
Wants no whip to drive him now;
At the stable-door he stands,
Looking round for friendly hands
To loose the door its fast'ning pin,
And let him with his corn begin.
Round the yard, a thousand ways,
Beasts in expectation gaze,
Catching at the loads of hay
Passing fodd'rers tug away.
Hogs with grumbling, deaf'ning noise,
Bother round the server boys;
And, far and near, the motley group
Anxious claim their suppering-up.
From the rest, a blest release,
Gabbling home, the quarrelling geese
Seek their warm straw-litter'd shed,
And, waddling, prate away to bed.
'Nighted by unseen delay,
Poking hens, that lose their way,
On the hovel's rafters rise,
Slumbering there, the fox's prize.
Now the cat has ta'en her seat,
With her tail curl'd round her feet;
Patiently she sits to watch
Sparrows fighting on the thatch.
Now Doll brings th'expected pails,
And dogs begin to wag their tails;
With strokes and pats they're welcom'd in,
And they with looking wants begin:

Slove in the milk-pail brimming o'er,
She pops their dish behind the door.
Prone to mischief boys are met,
'Neath the eaves the ladder's set,
Sly they climb in softest tread,
To catch the sparrow on his bed;
Massacred, O cruel pride!
Dash'd against the ladder's side.
Curst barbarians! pass me by;
Come not, Turks, my cottage nigh;
Sure my sparrows are my own,
Let ye then my birds alone.
Come, poor birds! from foes severe
Fearless come, you're welcome here;
My heart yearns at fate like yours,
A sparrow's life's as sweet as ours.
Hardy clowns! grudge not the wheat
Which hunger forces birds to eat:
Your blinded eyes, worst foes to you,
Can't see the good which sparrows do.
Did not poor birds with watching rounds
Pick up the insects from your grounds,
Did they not tend your rising grain,
You then might sow to reap in vain.
Thus Providence, right understood,
Whose end and aim is doing good,
Sends nothing here without its use;
Though ignorance loads it with abuse,
And fools despise the blessing sent
And mock the Giver's good intent.—
O God! let me what's good pursue,
Let me the same to others do
As I'd have others do to me,
And learn at least humanity.

Dark and darker glooms the sky;
Sleep 'gins close the labourer's eye;
Dobson leaves his greensward seat,
Neighbours where they neighbours meet

Crops to praise, and work in hand,
And battles tell from foreign land.
While his pipe is puffing out,
Sue he's putting to the rout,
Gossiping, who takes delight
To shool her knitting out at night,
And back-bite neighbours 'bout the town—
Who's got new caps, and who a gown,
And many a thing her evil eye
Can see they don't come honest by.
Chattering at a neighbour's house,
She hears call out her frowning spouse;
Prepar'd to start, she soodles home,
Her knitting twirling o'er her thumb,
As, loath to leave, afraid to stay,
She bawls her story all the way:
The tale so fraught with 'ticing charms,
Her apron folded o'er her arms,
She leaves the unfinished tale, in pain,
To end as evening comes again,
And in the cottage gangs with dread,
　　To meet old Dobson's timely frown,
Who grumbling sits, prepar'd for bed,
　　While she stands chelping 'bout the town.

　　The night-wind now, with sooty wings,
In the cotter's chimney sings:
Now, as stretching o'er the bed,
Soft I raise my drowsy head,
Listening to the ushering charms
That shake the elm tree's mossy arms;
Till sweet slumbers stronger creep,
　　Deeper darkness stealing round,
Then, as rock'd, I sink to sleep,
　　Mid the wild wind's lulling sound.

SUMMER MORNING

THE cocks have now the morn foretold,
  The sun again begins to peep;
The shepherd, whistling to his fold,
  Unpens and frees the captive sheep.

O'er pathless plains, at early hours,
  The sleepy rustic sloomy goes;
The dews, brush'd off from grass and flowers,
  Bemoistening sop his harden'd shoes;

For every leaf that forms a shade,
  And every flow'ret's silken top,
And every shivering bent and blade,
  Stoops, bowing with a diamond drop.

But soon shall fly those pearly drops;
  The red, round sun advances higher,
And stretching o'er the mountain tops,
  Is gilding sweet the village spire.

Again the bustling maiden seeks
  Her cleanly pail, and eager now,
Rivals the morn with rosy cheeks
  And hastens off to milk her cow;

While echo tells of Colin near,
  Blithe, whistling o'er the misty hills:
The powerful magic fills her ear,
  And through her beating bosom thrills.

'Tis sweet to meet the morning breeze,
  Or list the giggling of the brook,
Or, stretch'd beneath the shade of trees,
  Peruse and pause on nature's book;

When nature every sweet prepares
  To entertain our wish'd delay—
The images which morning wears,
  The wakening charms of early day!

Now let me tread the meadow paths,
    While glittering dew the ground illumes,
As, sprinkled o'er the withering swaths,
    Their moisture shrinks in sweet perfumes;

And hear the beetle sound his horn;
    And hear the skylark whistling nigh,
Spring from his bed of tufted corn,
    A hailing minstrel in the sky.

First sunbeam, calling night away,
    To see how sweet thy summons seems,
Split by the willow's wavy grey,
    And sweetly dancing on the streams:

How fine the spider's web is spun,
    Unnoticed to vulgar eyes;
Its silk thread glittering in the sun
    Art's bungling vanity defies.

Roaming while the dewy fields
    'Neath their morning burthen lean,
While its crop my searches shields,
    Sweet I scent the blossom'd bean:

Making oft remarking stops,
    Watching tiny nameless things
Climb the grass's spiry tops,
    Ere they try their gauzy wings.

So emerging into light
    From the ignorant and vain,
Fearful genius takes her flight,
    Skimming o'er the lowly plain.

Now in gay, green, glossy coat,
    On the shivering, benty balk,
The free grasshopper chirps his note,
    Bounding on from stalk to stalk.

And the bee at early hours
　　Sips the tawny bean's perfumes;
While butterflies infest the flowers,
　　Just to show their glossy plumes.

So industry oft seeks the sweets,
　　Which weary labour ought to gain;
And oft the bliss the idle meets,
　　And heaven bestows the bliss in vain.

Pleas'd I list the rural themes
　　Heartening up the ploughman's toil;
Urging on the jingling teams,
　　As they turn the mellow soil.

Industry's care abounds again,
　　As now the peace of night is gone;
Many a murmur wakes the plain,
　　Many a wagon rumbles on.

The swallow wheels his circling flight,
　　And o'er the water's surface skims;
Then on the cottage chimney lights,
　　And twittering chants his morning hymns.

Station'd high, a towering height,
　　On the sun-gilt weathercock,
Now a jackdaw takes his flight,
　　Frighted by the striking clock.

Snug the wary watching thrush
　　Sits to prune her speckled breast,
Where the woodbine, round the bush
　　Weaving, hides her mortar'd nest,—

Till the cows, with hungry low,
　　Pick the rank grass from her bower;
Startled then—dead leaves below
　　Quick receive the pattering shower.

67

Now the scythe the morn salutes,
  In the meadow tinkling soon;
While on mellow-tootling flutes
  Sweetly breathes the shepherd's tune.

Where the bank the stream o'erlooks,
  And the wreathing worms are found,
Anglers sit to bait their hooks,
  On the hill with wild thyme crown'd.

While the treach'rous watching stork
  With the heedless gudgeon flies,
Bobbing sinks the varnish'd cork,
  And the roach becomes a prize.

'Neath the blackthorn's stunted bush,
  Cropp'd by wanton oxen down,
Whistling o'er each culling rush,
  Cow-boys plat a rural crown.

As slow the hazy mists retire,
  Crampt circle's more distinctly seen;
Thin scatter'd huts, and neighbouring spire,
  Drop in to stretch the bounded scene.

Brisk winds the lighten'd branches shake,
  By pattering, plashing drops confess'd;
And, where oaks dripping shade the lake,
  Print crimpling dimples on its breast.

The misted brook, its edges reek;
  Sultry noon is drawing on;
The east has lost its ruddy streak,
  And morning sweets are almost gone.

In tortur'd haste, retreating cows
  Plunge headlong in the spangled flood,
Or sweeping by the oaken boughs
  Brushing trace the tangled wood.

In all directions buzzing by,
    Waken'd by the sultry heat,
Once again the tiresome fly
    Bold, intruding plagues repeat.[1]

Now as morning takes her leave,
    And while swelter'd nature mourns,
Let me, waiting soothing eve,
    Seek my cot till she returns.

DAWNINGS OF GENIUS

GENIUS! a pleasing rapture of the mind,
A kindling warmth to learning unconfin'd,
Glows in each breast, flutters in every vein,
From art's refinement to th'uncultur'd swain.
Hence is that warmth the lowly shepherd proves,
Pacing his native fields and willow groves;
Hence is that joy, when every scene unfolds,
Which taste endears and latest memory holds;
Hence is that sympathy his heart attends,
When bush and tree companions seem and friends;
Hence is that fondness from his soul sincere,
That makes his native place so doubly dear.
In those low paths which poverty surrounds,
The rough rude ploughman, off his fallow-grounds
(That necessary tool of wealth and pride),
While moil'd and sweating by some pasture's side,
Will often stoop inquisitive to trace
The opening beauties of a daisy's face;
Oft will he witness, with admiring eyes,
The brook's sweet dimples o'er the pebbles rise;
And often, bent as o'er some magic spell,
He'll pause, and pick his shaped stone and shell:
Raptures the while his inward powers inflame,
And joys delight him which he cannot name;

[1] Two preceding stanzas added from MS.

Ideas picture pleasing views to mind,
For which his language can no utterance find;
Increasing beauties, fresh'ning on his sight,
Unfold new charms, and witness more delight;
So while the present please, the past decay,
And in each other, losing, melt away.
Thus pausing wild on all he saunters by,
He feels enraptur'd though he knows not why,
And hums and mutters o'er his joys in vain,
And dwells on something which he can't explain.
The bursts of thought with which his soul's perplex'd,
Are bred one moment, and are gone the next;
Yet still the heart will kindling sparks retain,
And thoughts will rise, and fancy strive again.
So have I mark'd the dying ember's light,
When on the hearth it fainted from my sight,
With glimmering glow oft redden up again,
And sparks crack brightening into life, in vain;
Still lingering out its kindling hope to rise,
Till faint, and fainting, the last twinkle dies.
    Dim burns the soul, and throbs the fluttering heart,
Its painful pleasing feelings to impart;
Till by successless sallies wearied quite,
The memory fails, and fancy takes her flight.
The wick confin'd within its socket dies,
Borne down and smother'd in a thousand sighs.

THE LAMENTATIONS OF ROUND OAK WATERS

OPPRESS'D with grief a double share,
    Where Round Oak Waters flow
I one day took a sitting there,
    Recounting many a woe.
The grass, all dropping wet with dew,
    Low bent their tiny spears;
The lowly daisy bended too
    More lowly with my tears.

And there I fancied uncontrolled;
   My sorrows as they flew,
Unnoticed as the waters rolled,
   Were all unnoticed too.
But soon I found I was deceived:
   For wakened by my woes,
The naked stream, of shade bereaved,
   In grievous murmurs rose:
'Ah, luckless youth! to sorrow born,
   Shunned son of Poverty,
The world's made gamely sport and scorn
   And grinning infamy;
Unequalled tho' thy sorrows seem—
   And great indeed they are—
Oh, hear my sorrows for my stream,
   You'll find an equal there.
I am the genius of the brook;
   And like to thee I moan,
By Naiads and by all forsook,
   Unheeded and alone.
Distress and sorrow quickly proves
   The friend sincere and true;
Soon as our happiness removes
   Pretenders bid adieu.
Here I have been for many a year,
   And here my brook has been;
How pleasures lately flourished here,
   Thyself hast often seen.
The willows waving with the wind
   And here and there a thorn
Did please thy melancholy mind
   And did my banks adorn;
And here the shepherd with his sheep
   And with his lovely maid
Together where these waters creep
   In loit'ring dalliance played;
And here the cow-boy loved to sit
   And plait his rushy thongs
And dabble in the fancied pit

And chase the minnow throngs;
And when thou didst the horses tend
  Or drive the ploughman's team,
Thy mind did naturally bend
  Towards my pleasing stream,
And different pleasures filled thy breast,
  And different thy employ,
And different feelings thou possess'd
  From any other boy.
The sports which they so dearly lov'd
  Thou couldst not bear to see,
And joys which they as joys approv'd
  Ne'er seem'd as joys to thee;
The joy was thine could thou but steal
  From all their gambols rude,
In some lone thicket to conceal
  Thyself in solitude.
There didst thou joy and love to sit
  The briers and brakes among,
To exercise thy infant wit
  In fancied tale or song;
And there the insect and the flower
  Would court thy curious eye,
To muse in wonder on that power
  Which dwells above the sky,
But now, alas! my charms are done
  For shepherds and for thee:
The cow-boy with his green is gone
  And every bush and tree;
Dire nakedness o'er all prevails;
  Yon fallows bare and brown
Are all beset with posts and rails
  And turnèd upside down;
The gently curving, darksome balks,
  That stript the cornfields o'er
And prov'd the shepherd's daily walks,
  Now prove his walks no more;
The plough has had them under hand
  And overturned them all,

And now along the elting-land
    Poor swains are forced to maul;
And where yon furlong meets the lawn,
    To ploughmen ah! how sweet,
When they had their long furrow drawn,
    Its eddings to their feet,
To rest 'em while they cleaned their plough
    And light the loaded shoe—
But ah! there's ne'er an edding now
    For either them or you.
The balks and eddings are no more,
    The pastures too are gone,
The greens, the meadows and the moors
    Are all cut up and done;
There's scarce a greensward spot remains
    And scarce a single tree;
All naked are thy native plains,
    And yet they're dear to thee.
But oh, my brook, my injured brook,
    'Tis that I most deplore,
To think how once it used to look,
    How it must look no more.
Oh, then what trees my banks did crown!
    What willows flourished here!
Hard as the axe that cut them down
    The senseless wretches were.
But sweating slaves I do not blame,
    Those slaves by wealth decreed;
No, I should hurt their harmless name
    To brand them with the deed;
Although their aching hands did wield
    The axe that gave the blow,
Yet 'twas not them that owned the field
    Nor plann'd its overthrow.
No, no, the foes that hurt my field
    Hurt these poor moilers too,
And thy own bosom knows and feels
    Enough to prove it true.
Their foes and mine are lawless foes,

And laws themselves they hold
  Which clipt-wing'd justice can't oppose
    But forcèd yields to gold.
  These are the foes of mine and me;
    These all our ruin plann'd,
  Altho' they never fell'd a tree
    Or took a tool in hand.
  Ah, cruel foes, with plenty blest,
    So hankering after more,
  To lay the greens and pastures waste
    Which profited before!
  Poor greedy souls! What would they have
    Beyond their plenty given?
  Will riches keep them from the grave
    Or buy them rest in heaven?'

1818.

A SUNSET

Ah, just as well as if but yesternight
  I do remember on that self-same hill
I dropt me down with exquisite delight;
  The very hawthorn bush is standing still
From whence I sought a twig of blooming may
  And stuck it to my bosom when at rest.
Oh, 'twas a lovely eve; the lambs at play
  Scampt round and round the hill, and in the west
The clouds of purple and of crimson dye
  Were huddled up together in a heap,
And o'er the scented wide world's edge did lie
  Resting as quiet as if lulled to sleep.
I gazed upon them with a wishing eye,
  And longed but vainly for the painter's power
To give existence to the mingling dye
  And snatch a beauty from an evening hour.
But soft and soft it lost itself in night,
  And changed and changed in many a lumined track;
I felt concerned to see it leave the sight
  And hide its lovely face in blanking black.

RECOLLECTIONS AFTER AN EVENING WALK

Just as the even-bell rang, we set out
To wander the fields and the meadows about;
And the first thing we mark'd that was lovely to view
Was the sun hung on nothing, just bidding adieu:
He seem'd like a ball of pure gold in the west,
In a cloud like a mountain blue, dropping to rest;
The skies all around him were ting'd with his rays,
And the trees at a distance seem'd all on a blaze,
Till, lower and lower, he sank from our sight,
And the blue mist came creeping with silence and night.
The woodman then ceas'd with his hatchet to hack,
And bent away home with his kid on his back;
The mower, too, lapt up his scythe from our sight,
And put on his jacket, and bid us good night;
The thresher once lumping, we heard him no more,
He left his barn-dust, and had shut up his door;
The shepherd had told all his sheep in his pen,
And humming his song, sought his cottage agen:
But the sweetest of all seeming music to me
Were the songs of the clumsy brown-beetle and bee;
The one was seen hast'ning away to his hive,
The other was just from his sleeping alive—
'Gainst our hats he kept knocking as if he'd no eyes,
And when batter'd down he was puzzled to rise.
The little gay moth, too, was lovely to view,
A-dancing with lily-white wings in the dew;
He whisk'd o'er the water-pudge flirting and airy,
And perch'd on the down-headed grass like a fairy.
And there came the snail from his shell peeping out,
As fearful and cautious as thieves on the rout;
The sly jumping frog, too, had ventur'd to tramp,
And the glow-worm had just 'gun to light up his lamp;
To sip of the dew the worm peep'd from his den,
But dreading our footsteps soon vanish'd agen:
And numbers of creatures appear'd in our sight,
That live in the silence and sweetness of night,
Climbing up the tall grasses or scaling the bough,

But these were all nameless, unnotic'd till now.
And then we wound round 'neath the brook's willow row,
And look'd at the clouds that kept passing below;
The moon's image too, in the brook we could see't,
As if 'twas the other world under our feet;
And we listen'd well pleas'd at the guggles and groans
The water made passing the pebbles and stones.
And then we turn'd up by the rut-rifted lane,
And sought for our cot and the village again;
For night gather'd round, and shut all from the eye,
And a black sultry cloud crept all over the sky;
The dew on the bush, soon as touch'd it would drop,
And the grass 'neath our feet was as wet as a mop:
And, as to the town we approach'd very fast,
The bat even popp'd in our face as he past;
And the crickets sang loud as we went by the house,
And by the barn-side we saw many a mouse
Quirking round for the kernels that, litter'd about,
Were shook from the straw which the thresher hurl'd out.
And then we came up to our cottage once more,
And shut out the night-dew, and lock'd up the door;
The dog bark'd a welcome, well-pleas'd at our sight,
And the owl o'er our cot flew, and whoop'd a 'good night.'

A SIGH IN A PLAYGROUND

O HAPPY spot! how much the sight of thee
Wakes the endearments of my infancy:
The very trees, through which the wild winds sigh,
Seem whispering now some joys of youth gone by;
And each spot round, so sacred to my sight,
Hints at some former moment of delight.
Each object there still warmly seems to claim
Tender remembrance of some childish game;
Still on the slabs, before yon door that lie,
The top seems spinning, in fond memory's eye;
And fancy's echo still yon field resounds

With noise of blind-man's-buff, and fox-and-hounds.
Ah, as left rotting 'neath its mossy crown
The pile stands sacred o'er some past renown,
So thou, dear spot, though doubtless but to me,
Art sacred from the joys possess'd in thee,
That rose, and shone, and set—a sun's sojourn;
As quick in speed—alas, without return!

ADDRESS TO THE SLUGGARD

AWAKE, thou sluggard! could thy drowsy soul
Lay sloth aside, be resolute enough
To trace the fields and silver-studded woods
While each grass-point and velvet-knobbèd flower
Bends arching with a gem: Oh, couldst thou but
Meet the first breath which morning zephyr breathes,
Pilfering and culling, skimming woods and fields,
Who like a robber lingers for the chance
When wakening nature opens all her stores,
Molests her entrance and unbid intrudes
With forcing rape to sip her sweetest charms,
Then in a heedless and make-gamely fit
Scatters their beauties o'er a thankless world:
    Oh, wouldst thou but
List to the hymn of daybreak when the woods
Echo in harmony, with lark and thrush
And blackbird music thrilling, low, and sweet:
    Oh, couldst thou feel
The thrilling, burning ecstasy of soul,
The throbbing beat that heaves the bosom's charm
While musing on the work of power divine,
When in each meanest mite on earth or sea
Its Maker's image wonderfully shines,
When genius, left in wonder's void to pause,
Thrills into adoration's silent praise
And bent enraptured hails the Lord of all:
   Didst thou know this, thy stocky bed,
Which seems to thee so comfortable now

Lost in its drowsy apathy and ease,
Would like a dungeon seem and please no more;
But when night's curtain lapt thee up to sleep
And shut in darkness nature's weary eye,
As sickness' bed is to the fated wretch
To thee its necessary rest would seem,
A forced relief as loath to be enjoyed.

EPIGRAM

For fools that would wish to seem learned and wise,
    This receipt a wise man did bequeath:
'Let 'em have the free use of their ears and their eyes;
    'But their tongue,' says he, 'tie to their teeth.'

ON BEAUTY

Beauty, how changing and how frail!
    As skies in April showers,
Or as the summer's minute-gales,
    Or as the morning flowers.

As April skies, so beauty shades;
    As summer gales, so beauty flies;
As morning flower at evening fades,
    So beauty's tender blossom dies.

ON AN INFANT'S GRAVE

Beneath the sod where smiling creep
    The daisies into view,
The ashes of an infant sleep,
    Whose soul's as smiling too;
Ah! doubly happy, doubly blest
    (Had I so happy been!),
Recall'd to heaven's eternal rest,
    Ere it knew how to sin.

Thrice happy infant! great the bliss
    Alone reserv'd for thee;
Such joy 'twas my sad fate to miss,
    And thy good luck to see;
For oh! when all must rise again,
    And sentence then shall have,
What crowds will wish with me, in vain,
    They'd fill'd an infant's grave.

ON CRUELTY

COMPASSION sighs, and feels, and weeps,
    Retracing every pain
Inhuman man, in vengeance, heaps
    On all the lower train.

Ah, Pity! oft thy heart has bled,
    As galling now it bleeds;
And tender tears thy eyes have shed
    To witness cruel deeds.

The lash that weal'd poor Dobbin's hide,
    The strokes that cracking fall
On dogs, dumb cringing by thy side—
    Ah! thou hast felt them all.

The burthen'd asses, 'mid the laugh
    To see them whipp'd, would move
Thy soul to breathe in their behalf
    Humanity and love.

E'en 'plaining flies to thee have spoke,
    Poor trifles as they be;
And oft the spider's web thou'st broke,
    To set the captive free.

The pilfering mouse, entrapp'd and cag'd
    Within the wiry grate,
Thy pleading powers has oft engag'd
    To mourn its rigid fate.

How beat thy breast with conscious woes,
    To see the sparrows die:
Poor little thieves of many foes,
    Their food they dearly buy.

Where nature groans, where nature cries
    Beneath the butcher's knife,
How vain, how many were thy sighs,
    To savé such guiltless life.

And ah! that most inhuman plan,
    Where reason's name's ador'd,
Unfriendly treatment man to man
    Thy tears have oft deplor'd.

Nor wise nor good shall e'er deride
    The tear in Pity's eye;
Though laugh'd to scorn by senseless pride,
    From them it meets a sigh.

FALLING LEAVES

HAIL, falling leaves! that patter round,
    Admonishers and friends;
Reflection wakens at the sound—
    So, Life, thy pleasure ends.

How frail the bloom, how short the stay,
    That terminates us all!
To-day we flourish green and gay,
    Like leaves to-morrow fall.

Alas! how short is fourscore years,
    Life's utmost stretch—a span;
And shorter still, when past, appears
    The vain, vain life of man.

These falling leaves once flaunted high,
    O pride! how vain to trust:
Now wither'd on the ground they lie,
    And mingled with the dust.

So Death serves all—and wealth and pride
    Must all their pomp resign;
E'en kings shall lay their crowns aside,
    To mix their dust with mine.

The leaves, how once they cloth'd the trees,
    None's left behind to tell;
The branch is naked to the breeze;
    We know not whence they fell.

A few more years, and I the same
    As they are now, shall be,
With nothing left to tell my name,
    Or answer, 'Who was he?'

Green turf's allow'd forgotten heap
    Is all that I shall have,
Save that the little daisies creep
    To deck my humble grave.

TO AN APRIL DAISY

WELCOME, old matey! peeping once again;
    Our meeting 'minds me of a pleasant hour:
Spring's pencil pinks thy cheek that blushy stain,
    And summer glistens in thy tinty flower.

Hail, beauty's gem! disdaining time nor place,
    Carelessly creeping on the dunghill's side;
Demeanour's softness in thy crimpled face
    Decks thee in beauties unattain'd by pride.

Hail, venturer! once again that fearless here
    Encampeth on the hoar hill's sunny side;
Spring's early messenger! thou'rt doubly dear;
    And winter's frost by thee is well supplied.

Now winter's storms shall cease their pelting rage,
    But winter's woes I need not tell to thee;
Far better luck thy visits well presage,
    And be it thine and mine that luck to see.

Ah, may thy smiles confirm the hopes they tell;
    To see thee frost-bit I'd be griev'd at heart;
I meet thee happy, and I wish thee well,
    Till ripening summer summons us to part.

Then like old mates, or two who've neighbours been,
    We'll part, in hopes to meet another year;
And o'er thy exit from this changing scene,
    We'll mix our wishes in a tokening tear.

AN EFFUSION TO POESY

ON RECEIVING A DAMP FROM A GENTEEL OPINIONIST IN POETRY,
OF SOME SWAY, AS I AM TOLD, IN THE LITERARY WORLD

Despis'd, unskill'd, or how I will,
Sweet Poesy! I'll love thee still;
Vain (cheering comfort!) though I be,
I still must love thee, Poesy.
A poor, rude clown, and what of that?
I cannot help the will of fate,
A lowly clown although I be;
Nor can I help it loving thee.
Still must I love thee, sweetest charm!
Still must my soul in raptures warm;
Still must my rudeness pluck the flower,
That's plucked in an evil hour,
While Learning scowls her scornful brow,
And damps my soul—I know not how.
Labour! 'cause thou'rt mean and poor,
Learning spurns thee from her door;
But despise me as she will,
Poesy! I love thee still.
When on pillow'd thorns I weep,
And vainly stretch me down to sleep,
Then, thou charm from heav'n above,
Comfort's cordial dost thou prove:
Then, engaging Poesy!

Then how sweet to talk with thee.
And be despis'd, or how I will,
I cannot help but love thee still.
Endearing charm! vain though I be,
I still must love thee, Poesy.
Still must I! ay, I can't refrain:
Damp'd, despis'd, or scorn'd again,
With vain, unhallow'd liberty
Still must I sing thee, Poesy.
And poor, and vain, and press'd beneath
Oppression's scorn although I be,
Still will I bind my simple wreath,
Still will I love thee, Poesy.

ON YOUTH

Aʜ, youth's sweet joys! why are ye gone astray?
    Fain would I follow could I find a plan:
To my great loss are ye exchang'd away
    For that sad sorrow-ripening name—a Man.
Far distant joys! the prospect gives me pain:
    Ah, happiness! and hast thou no return?
No kind concern to call thee back again,
    And bid this aching bosom cease to mourn?
    The daisies' hopes have met another spring,
Poor standard tenants on a stormy plain;
    The lark confirms it on his russet wing;
And why alone am I denied?—In vain:
            Ah, youth is fled!
    A second blossom I but vainly crave:
    The flower, that opes with peace to come,
        Is budding in the grave.

TO AN INSIGNIFICANT FLOWER

OBSCURELY BLOOMING IN A LONELY WILD

AND though thou seem'st a weedling wild,
   Wild and neglected like to me,
Thou still art dear to nature's child,
   And I will stoop to notice thee.

For oft, like thee, in wild retreat,
   Array'd in humble garb like thee,
There's many a seeming weed proves sweet,
   As sweet as garden-flowers can be.

And, like to thee, each seeming weed
   Flowers unregarded, like to thee,
Without improvement, runs to seed,
   Wild and neglected like to me.

And, like to thee, when beauty's cloth'd
   In lowly raiment like to thee,
Disdainful pride, by beauty loath'd,
   No beauties there can ever see.

For, like to thee, my Emma blows,
   A flower like thee I dearly prize;
And, like to thee, her humble clothes
   Hide every charm from prouder eyes.

But though, like thee, a lowly flower,
   If fancied by a polish'd eye,
She soon would bloom beyond my power,
   The finest flower beneath the sky.

And, like to thee, lives many a swain
   With genius blest; but, like to thee,
So humble, lowly, mean, and plain,
   No one will notice them—or me.

So, like to thee, they live unknown,
   Wild weeds obscure; and, like to thee,
Their sweets are sweet to them alone:
   The only pleasure known to me.

Yet when I'm dead, let's hope I have
   Some friend in store, as I'm to thee,
That will find out my lowly grave,
   And heave a sigh to notice me.

1818.

PATTY OF THE VALE

WHERE lonesome woodlands close surrounding
   Mark the spot a solitude,
And nature's uncheck'd scenes abounding
   Form a prospect wild and rude,
A cottage cheers the spot so glooming,
   Hid in the hollow of the dale,
Where, in youth and beauty blooming,
   Lives sweet Patty of the Vale.

Gay as the lambs her cot surrounding,
   Sporting wild the shades among,
O'er the hills and bushes bounding,
   Artless, innocent, and young,
Fresh, as blush of morning roses
   Ere the midday suns prevail,
Fair, as lily-bud uncloses,
   Blooms sweet Patty of the Vale.

Low and humble though her station,
   Dress though mean she's doom'd to wear,
Few superiors in the nation
   With her beauty can compare.
What are riches ?—not worth naming,
   Though with some they may prevail;
Theirs be choice of wealth proclaiming,
   Mine is Patty of the Vale.

Fools may fancy wealth and fortune
   Join to make a happy pair,
And for such the god importune,
   With full many a fruitless prayer;

I, their pride and wealth disdaining
   Should my humble hopes prevail,
Happy then, would cease complaining,
   Blest with Patty of the Vale.

MY LOVE'S LIKE A LILY

My love's like a lily, my love's like a rose,
My love's like a smile the spring mornings disclose;
And sweet as the rose, on her cheek her love glows,
   When sweetly she smileth on me:
But as cold as the snow of the lily, my rose
   Behaves to pretenders, whoever they be;
In vain higher stations their passions disclose,
   To win her affections from me.

My love's like a lily, my love's like a rose,
My love's like the smile the spring mornings disclose;
And fair as the lily, and sweet as the rose,
   My love's beauty bloometh to me:
And smiles of more pleasure my heart only knows,
   To think that pretenders, whoever they be,
But vainly their love and their passions disclose;
   My love remains constant to me.

THE FIRST OF MAY

A BALLAD

Fair blooms the rose upon the green,
   Pretending to excel;
But who another rose has seen,
   A different tale can tell.
The morning smiles, the lark's begun
   To welcome in the May:
Be cloudless, skies! look out, bright sun!
   And haste my love away.

Though graceful round the maidens move,
    That join the rural ball,
Soon shall they own my absent love
    The rival of them all.
Go, wake your shepherdess, ye lambs!
    And murmur her delay:
Chide her neglect, ye hoarser dams!
    And call my love away.

Ye happy swains, with each a bride,
    Were but the angel there,
While slighted maids despair'd and sigh'd,
    You'd court th'unequall'd fair.
Dry up, ye dews! nor threat'ning hing,
    To soil her best array:
Ye birds! with double vigour sing,
    And urge my love away.

Welcome, sun! the dews are fled,
    The lark has rais'd his song;
The daisy nauntles up its head—
    Why waits my love so long?
As flow'rets fade, the pleasures bloom,
    All hastening to decay:
The day steals on, and showers may come:
    This instant haste away.

What now, ye fearful cringing sheep!
    Who meets your wondering eyes?
What makes you 'neath the maples creep,
    In homaging surprise?
No ladies tread our humble green:
    Ah! welcome wonders, hail!
I witness your mistaken queen
    Is Patty of the Vale.

THE FOUNTAIN

Her dusky mantle eve had spread;
The west sky glower'd with copper red;
Sun bid 'good night,' and slove to bed,
  'Hind black cloud's mimick'd mountain;
When weary from my toil I sped,
  To seek the purling fountain.

Labour had gi'en it up for good,
Save swains their folds that beetling stood,
While Echo, list'ning in the wood,
  Each knock kept 'stinctly counting;
The moon just peep'd her horned hood,
  Faint glimmering in the fountain.

Ye gently dimpling, curling streams,
Rilling as smooth as summer-dreams,
Ill pair'd to yours life's current seems,
  When hope, rude cataracts mounting,
Bursts cheated into vain extremes,
  Far from the peaceful fountain.

I'd just streak'd down, and with a swish
Whang'd off my hat, soak'd like a fish,
When 'bove what heart could think or wish—
  For chance there's no accounting—
A sweet lass came with wooden dish,
  And dipt it in the fountain.

I've often found a rural charm
In pastoral song my heart to warm,
But, faith, her beauties gave alarm,
  'Bove all I'd seen surmounting;
And when to the spring she stretch'd her arm,
  My heart chill'd in the fountain.

Simple, witching, artless maid,
So modestly she offer'd aid,

'And will you please to drink?' she said;
    My pulse beat past the counting;
Oh! Innocence such charms display'd,
    I can't forget the fountain.

Ere, lonely, home she 'gan proceed,
I said—what's secrecy indeed,
And offer'd company as need,
    The moon was highly mounting;
And still her charms—I'd scorn the deed—
    Were pure as was the fountain.

Ye leaning palms, that seem to look
Pleas'd o'er your image in the brook,
Ye ashes, harbouring pie and rook,
    Your shady boughs be mounting;
Ye Muses, leave Castalia's nook,
    And sacred make the fountain.

1818.

FAMILIAR EPISTLE,

TO A FRIEND

THIS morning, just as I awoken,
A black cloud hung the south unbroken;
Thinks I, just now we'll have it soakin';
        I rightly guess'd.
'Faith! glad were I to see the token;
        I wanted rest.

And, 'fex! a pepsing day there's been on't;
But caution'd right with what I'd seen on't,
Keeping at home has kept me clean on't;
        Ye know my creed:
Fool-hardy work, I ne'er was keen on't—
        But let's proceed.

I write to keep from mischief merely,
Fire-side comforts 'joying cheerly;
And, brother chip, I love ye dearly,
      Poor as ye be!
With honest heart and soul, sincerely;
      They're all to me.

This scrawl, mark thou the application,
Though hardly worth thy observation,
Meaneth an humble invitation
      On some day's end:
Of all ragg'd-muffins in the nation,
      Thou art the friend.

I've long been aggravated shocking,
To see our gentry folks so cocking:
But sorrow's often catch'd by mocking,
      The truth I've seen;
Their pride may want a shoe or stocking,
      For like has been.

Pride's power's not worth a roasted onion:
I'd's lief be prison mouse wi' Bunyan,
As I'd be king of our dominion,
      Or any other;
When shuffled through—it's my opinion
      One's good as t'other.

Nor would I gi'e, from off my cuff,
A single pin for all such stuff:
Riches—besh-t! a pinch of snuff
      Would dearly buy ye;
Who's got ye, keeps ye, that's enough:
      I don't envy ye.

If fate's so kind to let's be doing,
That's—just keep cart on wheels a-going;
O'er my half-pint I can be crowing
      As well's another:
But when there's this and that stands owing,
      Oh, curse the bother!

For had I money, like a many,
I'd balance, even to a penny.
Want! thy confinement makes me scranny:
     That spirit's mine,
I'd sooner gi'e than take from any;
     But worth can't shine.

O Independence! oft I bait ye;
How blest I'd be to call ye matey!
Ye fawning, flattering slaves, I hate ye:
     Mad, harum-scarum!
If rags and tatters underrate me,
     Free still I'll wear 'em.

Pox take all sorrows, now I'll bilk 'em;
What's past may go so: time that shall come,
As bad, or worse, or how it will come,
     I'll ne'er despair;
Poor as I am, friends shall be welcome
     As rich men's are.

So from my heart, old friend, I'll greet ye:
No outside brags shall ever cheat ye;
Wi' what I have, wi' such I'll treat ye,
     Ye may believe me;
I'll shake your rags whene'er I meet ye,
     If ye deceive me.

So mind ye, friend, what's what, I send it:
My letter's plain, and plain I'll end it:
Bad's bad enough, but worse won't mend it;
     So I'll be happy,
And while I've sixpence left I'll spend it
     In cheering nappy.

A hearty health shall crown my story:
Dear, native England! I adore ye;
Britons, may ye with friends before ye
     Ne'er want a quart,
To drink your king and country's glory
     Wi' upright heart!

I've oft meant tramping o'er to see ye;
But, d—d old Fortune (God forgi'e me!),
She's so cross-grain'd and forked wi' me,
      Be e'er so willing,
Spite o' my jingling powers 'tin't i' me
      To scheme a shilling.

And Poverty, with cursed rigour,
Spite of industry's utmost vigour,
Dizens me out in such a figure
      I'm sham'd being seen;
'Sides my old shoon (poor Muse, ye twig her)
      Wait roads being clean.

Then here wind-bound till Fate's conferr'd on't,
I wait ye, friend; and take my word on't,
I'll, spite of fate, scheme such a hurd on't,
      As we won't lack:
So no excuses shall be heard on't.
      Yours, random Jack.

                1819.

A SIGH

AGAIN freckled cowslips are gilding the plain,
   And crow-flowers yellow again o'er the lea,
Again the speck'd throstle comes in with her strain,
   And welcomes the spring—but no spring can I see.

I once hail'd the throstle, her singing begun,
   And bath'd in spring's dew when her flower met my eyes;
I sought for the kingcup all cloth'd in the sun,
   And gather'd my cowslips, and joy'd in the prize.

They brought nature's spring, and they comforted me,
   They wip'd winter off, and did pleasure restore;
But, alas! in their tidings a change can I see,
   Fate's added a postscript, 'Thy spring is no more.'

BALLAD

WINTER's gone, the summer breezes
  Breathe the shepherd's joys again,
Village scene no longer pleases,
  Pleasures meet upon the plain;
Snows are fled that hung the bowers,
  Buds to blossoms softly steal,
Winter's rudeness melts in flowers:
    Charmer, leave thy spinning wheel,
        And tend the sheep with me.

Careless here shall pleasures lull thee,
  From domestic troubles free;
Rushes for thy couch I'll pull thee,
  In the shade thy seat shall be;
All the flower-buds will I get
  Spring's first sunbeams do unseal,
Primrose, cowslip, violet:
    Charmer, leave thy spinning wheel,
        And tend the sheep with me.

Cast away thy 'twilly willy,'
  Winter's warm protecting gown,
Storms no longer blow to chill thee;
  Come with mantle loosely thrown,
Garments, light as gale's embraces,
  That thy lovely shape reveal;
Put thou on thy airy dresses:
    Charmer, leave thy spinning wheel,
        And tend the sheep with me.

Sweet to sit where brooks are flowing,
  Pleasant spreads the gentle heat,
On the green's lap thyme is growing,
  Every molehill forms a seat:
Fear not suns 'cause thou'rt so fair,
  In the thorn-bower we'll conceal;
Ne'er a sunbeam pierces there:
    Charmer, leave thy spinning wheel,
        And tend the sheep with me.

SONG

Of all the days in memory's list,
　　Those motley banish'd days;
Some overhung with sorrow's mist,
　　Some gilt with hopeful rays;
There is a day 'bove all the rest
　　That has a lovely sound,
There is a day I love the best—
　　When Patty first was found.

When first I look'd upon her eye,
　　And all her charms I met,
There's many a day gone heedless by,
　　But that I'll ne'er forget;
I met my love beneath the tree,
　　I help'd her o'er the stile,
The very shade is dear to me
　　That blest me with her smile.

Strange to the world my artless fair,
　　But artless as she be,
She found the witching art when there
　　To win my heart from me:
And all the days the year can bring,
　　As sweet as they may prove,
There'll ne'er come one like that I sing,
　　Which found the maid I love.

MY MARY [1]

Who lives where beggars rarely speed,
And leads a hum-drum life indeed,
As none beside herself would lead?
　　　　　　　　　My Mary.

[1] This poem and the next were omitted from the third and fourth editions of *Poems Descriptive*.　They offended the taste of some of Clare's patrons.

Who lives where noises never cease,
And what with hogs and ducks and geese
Can never have a minute's peace?
                              My Mary.

Who, nearly battled to her chin,
Bangs down the yard through thick and thin,
Nor picks her road, nor cares a pin?
                              My Mary.

Who, save in Sunday's bib and tuck,
Goes daily waddling like a duck,
O'er head and ears in grease and muck?
                              My Mary.

Unus'd to pattens or to clogs,
Who takes the swill to serve the hogs,
And steals the milk for cats and dogs?
                              My Mary.

Who, frost and snow, as hard as nails,
Stands out o' doors, and never fails
To wash up things and scour the pails?
                              My Mary.

Who bustles night and day, in short,
At all catch jobs of every sort,
And gains her mistress' favour for't?
                              My Mary.

And who is oft repaid with praise,
In doing what her mistress says,
And yielding to her whimmy ways?
                              My Mary.

For there's none apter, I believe,
At 'creeping up a mistress' sleeve,'
Than this low kindred stump of Eve,
                              My Mary.

Who, when the baby's all unfit,
To please its mamma kisses it,
And vows no rose on earth's so sweet?
                              My Mary.

But when her mistress is not nigh,
Who swears, and wishes it would die,
And pinches it and makes it cry?
                              My Mary.

Oh, rank deceit! what soul could think—
But gently there, revealing ink:
At faults of thine thy friend must wink,
                              My Mary.

Who, not without a 'spark o' pride,'
Though strong as grunter's bristly hide,
Doth keep her hair in papers tied?
                              My Mary.

And, mimicking the gentry's way,
Who strives to speak as fine as they,
And minds but every word they say?
                              My Mary.

And who, though's well bid blind to see
As her to tell ye A from B,
Thinks herself none o' low degree?
                              My Mary.

Who prates and runs o'er silly stuff,
And 'mong the boys makes sport enough,
So ugly, silly, droll and rough?
                              My Mary.

Ugly! Muse, for shame of thee,
What faults art thou a-going to see
In one, that's 'lotted out to be
                              My Mary?

Who, low in stature, thick and fat,
Turns brown from going without a hat,
Though not a pin the worse for that?
                    My Mary.

Who's laugh'd at too by every whelp,
For failings which she cannot help?
But silly fools will laugh and chelp,
                    My Mary.

For though in stature mighty small,
And near as thick as thou art tall,
The hand made thee that made us all,
                    My Mary.

And though thy nose hooks down too much,
And prophesies thy chin to touch,
I'm not so nice to look at such,
                    My Mary.

No, no; about thy nose and chin,
Its hooking out, or bending in,
I never heed or care a pin,
                    My Mary.

And though thy skin is brown and rough,
And form'd by nature hard and tough,
All suiteth me! so that's enough,
                    My Mary.

DOLLY'S MISTAKE

OR, THE WAYS OF THE WAKE

ERE the sun o'er the hills, round and red, 'gan a-peeping,
    To beckon the chaps to their ploughs,
Too thinking and restless all night to be sleeping,
    I brush'd off to milking my cows;

To get my jobs forward, and eager preparing
  To be off in time to the wake,
Where yielding so freely a kiss for a fairing,
  I made a most shocking mistake.

Young Ralph met me early, and off we were steering,
  I cuddled me close to his side;
The neighbours, while passing, my fondness kept jeering,
  'Young Ralph's timely suited!' they cried.
But he bid me mind not their evil pretensions,
  'Fools mun,' says he, 'talk for talk's sake';
And, kissing me, 'Doll, if you've any 'prehensions,
  'Let me tell you, my wench, you mistake.'

My cows when we pass'd them kept booing and mooing,
  In truth, but they made me to stare;
As much as to say, 'Well, now, Dolly, you're going,
  Mind how you get on at the fair.'
While bidden 'good speed' from each gazing beholder,
  'Good journey away to the wake,'
The mowers stopp'd whetting, to look o'er their shoulder,
  Saying 'Dolly, don't make a mistake.'

I couldn't but mind the fine morning so charming,
  The dew-drops they glitter'd like glass;
And all o'er the meads were the buttercups swarming,
  Like so many suns in the grass;
I thought as we pass'd them, if such a thing could be,
  What a fine string of beads they would make;
But when I could think of such nonsense, it would be
  Because I had made no mistake.

So on his arm hanging, with stories beguiling,
  Of what he would buy me when there,
The road cutting short with his kissing and smiling,
  He 'veigl'd me off to the fair:
Such presents he proffer'd before I could claim 'em,
  To keep while I liv'd for his sake,
And what I lik'd best, o'er and o'er begg'd me name 'em,
  That he mightn't go make a mistake.

And, lud, what a crushing and crowding were wi''em,
  What noises are heard at a fair!
Here some sell so cheap, as they'd even go gi''em,
  If conscience would take, they declare:
Some so good, 'tis e'en worth more than money to buy 'em,
  Fine gingerbread nuts and plum-cake;
For truth they bid Ralph, ere he treated me, try 'em,
  And then there could be no mistake.

A sly Merry Andrew was making his speeches,
  With chaps and girls round him a swarm,
And, 'Mind,' said he, fleering, 'ye chubby-fac'd witches,
  Your fairings don't do you some harm.'
The hay-cocks he nam'd, in the meads passing by 'em,
  When weary we came from the wake,
So soft, so inviting, for rest we mun try 'em;
  What a fool should I be to mistake.

But promis'd so faithful, behaviour so clever,
  Such gifts as Ralph cramm'd in my hand,
How could I distrust of his goodness? Oh, never!
  And who could his goodness withstand?
His ribbons, his fairings, past counting, or nearly,
  Some return when he press'd me to make,
Good manners mun give, while he lov'd me so dearly:
  Ah! where could I see the mistake?

Till dark night he kept me, with fussing and lying,
  How he'd see me safe home to my cot;
Poor maiden, so easy, so free in complying,
  I the showman's good caution forgot:
All by-ways he led me, 'twas vain to dispute it,
  The moon blush'd for shame, naughty rake!
Behind a cloud sneaking—but darkness well suited
  His baseness, who caus'd the mistake.

In vain do I beg him to wed and have done wi't,
  So fair as he promis'd we should;
We cou'dn't do worse than as how we've begun wi't,
  Let matters turn out as they would:

But he's always a-talking 'bout wedding expenses,
    And the wages he's gotten to take;
Too plain can I see through his evil pretences,
    Too late I find out the mistake.

Oh, what mun I do with my mother reprovin',
    Since she will do nothing but chide?
For when old transgressors have been in the oven,
    They know where the young ones may hide.
In vain I seek pity with plaints and despairings,
    Always ding'd on the nose with the wake:
Young maidens! be cautious who give you your fairings;
    You see what attends a mistake.

CRAZY NELL

A TRUE STORY

THE sun was low sinking behind the far trees,
And, crossing the path, humming home were the bees;
And darker and darker it grew by degrees,
    And crows they flock'd quawking to rest:
When, unknown to her parents, Nell slove on her hat,
And o'er the fields hurried—scarce knew she for what;
But her sweetheart, in taking advantage and that,
    Had kiss'd, and had promis'd the best.

Poor maidens! of husbands so much they conceit,
The daisy scarce touch'd rose unhurt from her feet,
So eager she hasten'd her lover to meet,
    As to make him to wait was unjust;
On the wood, dim discover'd, she fixed her eyes—
Such a queer spot to meet in—suspicions might rise;
But the fond word 'a sweetheart' such goodness implies,
    Ah, who would a lover distrust!

More gloomy and darker—black clouds hung the wind,
Far objects diminish'd before and behind,
More narrow and narrow the circle declin'd,
    And silence reign'd awfully round,

When Nelly within the wood-riding sat down;
She listen'd, and lapp'd up her arms in her gown;
Far, far from her cottage, and far from the town,
    And her sweetheart not yet to be found.

The minutes seem'd hours—with impatience she heard
The flap of a leaf, and the twit of a bird;
The least little trifle that whisper'd or stirr'd,
    Hope pictur'd her lover as nigh:
When wearied with sitting, she wander'd about,
And open'd the wood-gate, and gave a look out;
And fain would have halloo'd, but fear had a doubt
    That thieves might be lurking hard by.

Far clocks count eleven—'He won't be long now,'
Her anxious hopes whisper'd—hoarse wav'd the wood bough;
—'He heeds not my fears, or he's false to his vow!'
    Poor Nelly sat doubtful, and sigh'd:
The man who had promis'd her husband to be,
And to wed on the morrow—her friends all could see
That a good-for-naught sort of a fellow was he,
    And they hoped nothing worse might betide.

At length, as in fear, slowly tapp'd the wood-gate;
'Twas Ben!—she complain'd so long painful to wait:
Deep design hung his looks, he but mumbled, ''Tis late,'
    And pass'd her, and bid her come on.
The mind plainly pictures that *night-hour* of dread,
In the midst of a wood! where the trees overhead
The darkness increased—a dungeon they spread,
    And the clock at the moment toll'd one!

Nell fain would have forc'd, as she follow'd, some chat,
And trifled, on purpose, with this thing and that,
And complain'd of the dew-droppings spoiling her hat;
    But nothing Ben's silence would break.
Extensive the forest, the roads to and fro,
And this way and that way, above and below,
As crossing the ridings, as winding they go—
    'Ah! what road or way can he seek?'

Her eye, ever watchful, now caught an alarm;
Lights gleam, and tools tinkle, as if nigh a farm:
'Oh, don't walk so fast, Ben—I'm fearful of harm!
    She said, and shrugg'd closer behind.
'That light's from my house!' 'twas the first word she caught
From his lips, since he through the dark wood had her brought.
A house in a wood!   Oh, good God! what a thought;
    What sensations then rush'd on her mind!

The things which her friends and her neighbours had said
Afresh at that moment all jump'd in her head;
And mistrust, for the first time, now fill'd her with dread:
    And as she approach'd, she could see
How better, for her, their advice to have ta'en;
And she wish'd to herself then she had—but in vain:
—A heap of fresh mould, and a spade, she saw plain,
    And a lantern tied up to a tree.

'Here they come!' a voice whispers;—'Haste! put out the
        light.'
'No: dig the grave deeper!'—'Very dark is the night.'
Slow mutterings mingled.—Oh, dismal the sight!
    —The fate of poor Nelly was plain.
Fear chill'd through her heart—but Hope whisper'd her—Fly!
Chance seiz'd on the moment, a wind-gust blew high,
She slipt in the thicket—he turn'd not his eye,
    And the grave-diggers waited in vain.

At that fearful moment, so dreadfully dark,
How welcome the song of the shepherd, or lark;
How cheery to listen, and hear the dog bark,
    As through the dark wood she fled fast:
But, horror of horrors, all nature was hush!
Not a sound was there heard—save a blackbird, or thrush,
That, started from sleep, flusker'd out of the bush,
    Which her brushing clothes shook as they past.

Fear now truly pictur'd: she ne'er turn'd her head
Either this way or that way—straight forward she fled;

And Fancy, still hearing the horrors with dread,
    On faster and fearfuller stole.
The matted leaves rustle—the boughs swiftly part,
Her hands and her face with the brambles did smart;
But, oh! the worst anguish was felt at her heart—
    Ben's unkindness struck death to her soul.

Now glimmering lighter the forest appears,
And Hope, the sweet comforter, soften'd her fears;
Light and liberty, Darkness! thy horror endears;
    Great bliss did the omen impart:
The forest, its end, and its terrors gone by,
She breath'd the free air, and she saw the blue sky;
Her own fields she knew—to her home did she fly,
    And great was the joy of her heart.

Oh, prospect endearing! the village to view,
The morn sweet appearing,—and gay the cock crew,
When, mangled by brambles and dabbled in dew,
    She gave a loud rap at the door:
The parents in raptures wept over their child;
She mutter'd her terrors—her eyes rolled wild—
'They dig the grave deeper!—Your Nelly's beguil'd!'
    She said, and she siled on the floor.

Poor Nell soon recover'd; but, ah! to her cost,
Her sense and her reason for ever were lost:
And scorch'd by the summer, and chill'd by the frost,
    A maniac, restless and wild,
Now crazy Nell rambles; and still she will weep,
And, fearless, at night into hovels will creep.
Fond parents! alas, their affliction is deep,
    And vainly they comfort their child.

THE DISAPPOINTMENT

'Ah, where can he linger?' said Doll, with a sigh,
    As bearing her milk-burthen home:
'Since he's broken his vow, near an hour has gone by,
    So fair as he promis'd to come.'
—She'd fain had him notice the loudly-clapt gate,
    And fain call'd him up to her song;
But while her stretch'd shade prov'd the omen too late,
    Heavy-hearted she mutter'd along.

She look'd and she listen'd, and sigh follow'd sigh,
    And jealous thoughts troubled her head;
The skirts of the pasture were losing the eye,
    As eve her last finishing spread;
And hope, so endearing, was topmost to see,
    As 'tween-light was cheating the view,
Everything at a distance—a bush, or a tree,
    Her love's pleasing picture it drew.

The pasture-gate creak'd, pit-a-pat her heart went,
    Fond thrilling with hope's pleasing pain,
She certainly thought that a signal it meant,
    So she turn'd, to be cheated again;
Expectations and wishes throbb'd warm to her side,
    Too soon the sweet feeling was lost,
Chill damps quick ensuing, when nigh she descried
    Her nasty cows rubbing the post.

By fancy soon tickled, by hopes led astray,
    Again did she hope, but in vain;—
A twitch at her sleeve!—'twas the shepherd's fond way,
    And she look'd o'er her shoulder again;
But a bramble had caught at her gown passing by;
    Disappointment, how great is thy smart!
How deep was the sorrow explain'd in that sigh,
    Like a bramble-thorn twang'd through her heart!

Quite wearied she soodled along through the dew,
    And oft look'd and listen'd around,

And loudly she clapt every gate she came through,
    To call her lost love to the sound;
And whenever to rest she her buckets set down,
    She jingled her yokes to and fro,
And her yokes she might jingle till morn—a rude clown,
    Ere he it seem'd offered to go.

Passing maids wonder'd much as she came to the town,
    To see her so still on her way;
She ne'er stopped to name a young man or new gown,
    So much as she used to say:
Some ask'd if her tongue she had lost on the plain,
    Some inquir'd if she ow'd any spite;
But short were the answers she made them again,
    'Yes,' or 'no,' and a mutter'd 'good night.'

She'd cause to be silent, and knew it too well,
    And said to herself passing by,
'Disappointments like mine if to you they befell,
    Ye would then be as sulky as I.'
Now nigh home and Roger, her bosom glow'd hot,
    And jealousies rose on her cheek;
She'd be bound his delay a new sweetheart had got
    And if he came now she'd not speak.

She sat herself down soon as got in the house,
    No dossity in her to stir;
The cat at her presence left watching the mouse,
    And the milk she might lap it for her,
Eat it all an she would, for she car'd not a pin,
    She'd other fish frying as then;
And soon as chance offer'd that she could begin,
    She 'gan weigh her doubts to hersen.

'Ah, the gipsy, she told me my fortune last night,
    Too true have I prov'd what she said:
'' You love him too warmly that loves you too light,''
    And grievous she shaked her head;

"He scorns you—the lines of your hands," she said, "meet,"
　　I was fit to drop under my cow;
"It's as plain as the nose on your face for to see't,"
　　I could not believe it till now.

'How could I, when now but a day or two's gone,
　　Since he fuss'd me so up in the grove,
And preach'd like a parson as leading me on,
　　And seem'd like a saint fall'n in love?
He smilingly bid me behold the stiff bean,
　　How it held up the weak winding pea—
"And so on my arm," said he, "Dolly may lean,
　　For I'll be a prop unto thee."

'And oft did he show me, as proofs of his love,
　　The gate, and the stile, where we came,
And many a favourite tree in the grove,
　　Where he had been marking my name:
And these made him staunch in my foolish esteem;
　　But deuce take such provings, forsooth,
They're like flimsy nick-nacks, that cheat in a dream,
　　When the morning sun wakes with the truth.

'Last week I the first time 'gan doubt his respect,
　　When at market he left me behind;
He made no excuses to hide his neglect,
　　Plain proof that he'd changed his mind:
When I said how I loiter'd in hopes he would come,
　　And when all my troubles he learn'd,
How late and how wet I was ere I got home,
　　He ne'er seem'd a morsel concern'd.

'And magpies that chatter'd, no omen so bad,
　　The dreams of my being a bride,
Odd crows that are constantly fix'd in my pad,
　　Plain prov'd that bad luck would betide:
The coffin-spark burning my holiday gown,
　　As nothing's so certain a sign;
The knives I keep crossing whenever laid down,
　　Were proofs of these sorrows of mine.

'A good-for-naught looby, he nettled me sore,
    I minded him oft when at church,
How under the wenches' fine bonnets he'd glower,
    As smiling they came in the porch:
Lord knows, scores of times he has made me to sin,
    For, being so bother'd and vex'd,
'Bout the parson's good preaching I car'd not a pin,
    And never once thought of the text.

'Like a fool, with full many a lying excuse,
    To see him I've stole in the street,
And drest to entice him; but all's of no use,
    'Tis folly such things to repeat:
No, no, his behaviour, a good-for-naught chap,
    I'll see no uneasiness in it;
The wreath he last bought me, to dress my new cap.
    I'll burn it to ashes this minute.'

Thus she vented her griefs, and gave ease to her sighs.
    Till the tinkled latch startled her dumb,
And ended her tale in a pause of surprise,
    While hope whisper'd comfort, 'He's come!'
He enter'd, and begg'd she'd excuse the late hour,
    She doubts his assertions awhile,
Then as the glad sun breaks the clouds in a shower,
    Tears melt in a welcoming smile.

Ah, sad disappointment! your damp chilly pain
    And all jealous doubts you impart,
Description but mixes her colours in vain
    To picture your horrors at heart.
Gall'd jealousy, like as the tide, ebbs to rest,
    Subsiding as gradually o'er;
Contented she smother'd her sighs on his breast,
    And the kiss seem'd as sweet as before.

WILLIAM AND ROBIN

WILLIAM

WHEN I meet Peggy in my morning walk,
She first salutes the morn, then stays to talk:
The biggest secret she will not refuse,
But freely tells me all the village-news;
And pleas'd am I, can I but haply force
Some new-made tale to lengthen the discourse,
For—oh, so pleasing is her company,
That hours, like minutes, in her presence fly!
I'm happy then, nor can her absence e'er
Raise in my heart the least distrust or fear.

ROBIN

When Mary meets me I find naught to say,
She hangs her head, I turn another way;
Sometimes (but never till the maid's gone by)
'Good morning!' falters, weaken'd by a sigh;
Confounded I remain, but yet delight
To look back on her till she's out of sight.
Then, then's the time that absence does torment:
I jeer my weakness, painfully repent,
To think how well I might have then confest
That secret love which makes me so distrest:
But, when the maiden's vanish'd for a while,
Recruited hopes my future hours beguile:
I fuss myself another time I'll tell,
Which, if not better, will be quite as well;
Thus days, and weeks, and months I've dallied o'er,
And am no nearer than I was before.

WILLIAM

Such ways as these I ever strove to shun,
Nor was I bashful when I first begun:
Freely I offered posies to the maid,
Which she as freely with her smiles repaid;
Yet had I been, like you, afraid to own

My love, her kindness had been still unknown.
And, now the maiden's kindness to requite,
I strive to please her morning, noon, and night:
The garland and the wreath for her I bind,
Compos'd of all the fairest I can find;
For her I stop the straggler going astray,
And watch her sheep when she's not in the way;
I fetch them up at night, and shift the pen,
And in the morning let them out agen;
For her in harvest when the nuts are brown,
I take my crook to pull the branches down;
And up the trees that dismally hang o'er
The deep black pond, where none durst go before,
I heedless climb, as free from fear as now,
And snatch the clusters from the topmost bough;
Well pleas'd to risk such dangers that can prove
How much her William does his Peggy love.

ROBIN

I search the meadows, and as well as you
I bind up posies, and sweet garlands too;
And if I unawares can hear exprest
What flower she fancies finer than the rest,
Grow where it will, I search the fields about,
And search for't daily till I find it out;
And when I've found it, oh ! what tongue can tell
The fears and doubts which in my bosom swell;
The schemes contriving, and the plans I lay,
How I to her the garland may convey,
Are various indeed;—sometimes I start,
Resolv'd to tell the secret of my heart,
Vowing to make the gather'd garland prove
How much I languish, and how much I love:
But soon resolves and vows allay their heat,
And timid weakness reassumes her seat.
The garland then, which I so painful sought,
Instantly seems as if 'twere good for naught:
'Ah, gaudy thing!' I sigh, 'will Mary wear
Such foolish lumber in her auburn hair ?'

109

Thus doubts and fears each other thought confound,
And, thus perplex'd, I throw it on the ground—
Walk from't, distrest—in pensive silence mourn,
Then plan a scheme, and back again return:
Once more the garland in my hand I take,
And of the best a smaller posy make,
Resting assur'd that such a nosegay will
To gain her favour prove a better still,
And then my hopeful heart's from grief reviv'd
By this new plan, so seeming well-contriv'd;
So off I go, and gain the spot—ah, then
I sneak along—my heart misgives again,
And as I nearer draw, 'Well now,' thinks I,
'I'll not speak to her, but pass silent by':
Then from my coat that precious gift I take,
Which I beforehand treasur'd for her sake;
And after all my various scheming so,
The flowers, as worthless, to the ground I throw.
And then, if getting through the hedge-bound plain,
Having no sense to find the same again,
Her little lambkins raise a piteous cry,
Calling for help—whether far off or nigh
It matters not, can I but hear their moan
(Of hers more tender am I than my own)
The journey's naught at all, no steps I grudge,
But with great pleasure to their aid I trudge;
Yet this is never to the maiden known,
Nor ever done save only when alone,
Fearing from it that other swains should prove,
Or she herself, the favour to be love.
Though in her absence I so fond appear,
Yet when she's there I'm careless, as it were;
Nor can I have the face, although my mind
At the same time's most willingly inclin'd,
To do the least kind act at all for her,
Nor join the tale where she does interfere.
If from her looks a smile I e'er obtain,
I feel o'erjoy'd but never smile again;
And when I hear the swains her beauty praise,

And try with artful, fond, alluring ways
To snatch the posy from her swelling breast,
And loose the ribbon round her slender waist,
Then more familiar touch her curling hair,
And praise her beauty as beyond compare;
At this sad pains around my heart will sting,
But I ne'er look, nor tell a single thing.

ROSY JANE

THE eve put on her sweetest shroud,
   The summer-dress she's often in,
Freck'd with white and purple cloud,
   Dappled like a leopard's skin;
The martin, by the cotter's shed,
   Had welcom'd eve with twittering song;
The blackbird sang the sun to bed,
   Old Oxey's briery dells among:

When o'er the field tripped rosy Jane,
   Fair as the flowers she treaded on;
But she was gloomy for her swain,
   Who long to fight the French had gone;
She milk'd, and sang her mournful song,
   As how an absent maid did moan,
Who for a soldier sorrowed long,
   That went and left her, like her own.

Though dreadful drums have ceas'd their noise,
   And peace proclaim'd returning Joe,
Delays so lingering dampt her joys,
   And expectation nettled woe:
Hope, mix'd with fear and doubts the while,
   Look'd for his coming every hour;
As one, when spring begins to smile,
   Awaits the early opening flower.

With doubtful eyes we view the bud;
 Though sweet the sun smiles on it then,
A blighting storm may tear the wood,
 And blast our promises agen:
With soldiers, danger's always near;
 Poor Jane had deepest cause to sigh—
To-day, peace smiles with little fear,
 The next, war bursts, and Joe may die.

Each morn, from window of her cot,
 Adown the road she strain'd her eye;
Each eve she wander'd to the spot
 Where Joe had bid his last 'Good-bye';
Where love had breath'd its last, last vow,
 Where each their keep-sake trifles gave;
His prov'd love warm'd her bosom now—
 'This will I carry to my grave.'

So said he, looking on the box
 With poesy on the lid bespread;
So said he, while the curling locks
 Her own hand sever'd from her head;
While she wip'd off the tear-drops free
 With 'kerchief marked with his name,
And vow'd his ribbon then should be
 Her Sunday head-dress till he came.

Thus Jenny's heart was drooping sad;
 Her hopes and fears were then at strife,
Lest false should prove her soldier-lad,
 And home return with foreign wife:
Yet the last oath her love had ta'en
 Would hearten up her soul awhile—
'Should war return me safe to Jane,
 No maid on earth shall me beguile.'

Thus Jane sat milking, full of thought,
 As doubtful how the case might prove—
'Luck comes unlook'd for and unsought,'
 So gossips say of wealth and love:

How true their wisdom turneth out,
    How oft fulfill'd we little know;
But Jane proves once, without a doubt,
    What dames oft told to soothe her woe.

Old Joe the woodman, with his kid,
    Went home as warn'd the setting sun;
And stand and rest he often did,
    To talk with Jane about his son:
True to his sunset-clock he kep',
    His Goody and his cot to find,
When strange to say, with strutting step,
    To-night a soldier skipt behind.

His jacket shone so red, so gay
    His feather o'er his cap did hing,
And in the fine genteelly way
    He'd learn'd his ribbon'd cane to swing:
Unus'd to see the flashing sight,
    The startled thrush broke off her strain;
The sheep forgot their grass to bite,
    And stared up at the passing swain.

Jane's skewing cow was struck with fear,
    And kick'd the bucket i' the muck,
Which made her shed another tear,
    To think she'd naught but sorrow's luck;
But woodman Joe revers'd the plan,
    And bawl'd, 'My wench, ne'er mind your fall:
Dry up your tears; I bring the man
    Shall hide your loss, and pay for all.'

Ah, sure enough, 'twas him she wist;
    She 'member'd well the face of Joe,
And almost swooned while he kiss'd,
    So sudden pleasure banish'd woe:
'My Jane,' he cried, thy tears dry up ';
    His heart with love was beating warm,
He took the empty milkpail up,
    And led her homeward on his arm.

Old Joe stumpt 'hind them on the road,
 Heart-lighten'd from war-breeding woes,
And when the son begg'd take his load,
 He said the sticks would spoil his clothes:
Since he so happy went from toil,
 'Twas many a long and weary day;
And, stumping on, would often smile,
 To think what dame at home would say.

The swain was busied all the way
 To tell his Jane of all he'd seen,
And talk about the parting day,
 When last they met upon the green;
And show the 'bacco box the while,
 And to the parting vow refer,
And hint, when absent many a mile,
 How such things made him think of her.

And still her lock of hair he'd got,
 And near his heart the prize possess'd;
But Jenny's wonder knew it not,
 Weav'd in a brooch upon his breast:
His wisdom fill'd her with surprise,
 Since he had left his ploughs and carts;
She thought, than home-bred louts, how wise
 The people were in foreign parts.

Ere half-way home Joe had her led,
 With eager speed each passing swain
The news around the village spread,
 'Jane's sweetheart Joe's return'd again!'
Old Goody stopped her wheel, and smil'd,
 And sought her cloak 'tween joy and pain,
And took her stick, to meet her child
 She little hoped to see again.

Ah, come and gone were many years
 Since Joe with soldiers took his quart,
And laugh'd to scorn his mother's tears—
 That thorny thought still prick'd his heart:

Poor tottering soul, her head was grey,
    And grief and age had wrink'd her brow,
So alter'd since his parting day,
    He hardly knew his mother now.

But tear-drops ready stood to start
    At whispering nature's warm command,
'Oh, here's my mother!' leapt his heart—
    He instant grasp'd her trembling hand:
O'ercome with joy, 'My boy!' she said,
    And on his propping arm reclin'd,
'Death now may come without a dread,
    I've found the all I wish'd to find.'

That night around the cottage hearth
    Did meet the friends of maid and swain,
And every heart was fill'd with mirth,
    And blest I ween were Joe and Jane:
Though Joe's old folks did lowly prove,
    And Jane's could boast cows, ploughs, and carts,
They said they'd ne'er control her love,
    But wish'd them joy with all their hearts.

Joe told the wonders that he knew,
    And all the dangers of the wars;
And then, to prove his story true,
    Unbrac'd his coat to show his scars:
The old folks saw, and blest their child;
    Each drank to the intended bride,
And brought her milk-loss up, and smil'd,
    And wish'd no worse luck might betide.

Next day being Sunday, folks believ'd
    They would be ask'd at church that day;
But Joe the gossips' thoughts deceiv'd,
    And brought it in a nearer way:
He long ago did ring provide,
    And wealth in dangerous wars had ta'en,
So he with licence bought his bride,
    And crown'd the bliss of rosy Jane.

SONNETS

THE GIPSIES' EVENING BLAZE

To me how wildly pleasing is that scene
   Which doth present, in evening's dusky hour,
A group of gipsies, centred on the green,
   In some warm nook where Boreas has no pow'r;
Where sudden starts the quivering blaze behind
   Short, shrubby bushes, nibbled by the sheep,
   That mostly on these short sward pastures keep;
Now lost, now seen, now bending with the wind:
And now the swarthy sibyl kneels reclin'd;
   With proggling stick she still renews the blaze,
   Forcing bright sparks to twinkle from the flaze.
When this I view, the all-attentive mind
   Will oft exclaim (so strong the scene pervades),
   'Grant me this life, thou spirit of the shades!'

1809.

A SCENE

THE landskip's stretching view, that opens wide,
   With dribbling brooks, and river's wider floods,
   And hills, and vales, and darksome lowering woods,
With grains of varied hues and grasses pied;
   The low brown cottage in the shelter'd nook;
The steeple, perking just above the trees
Whose dangling leaves keep rustling in the breeze;
   And thoughtful shepherd bending o'er his hook;
And maidens stript, haymaking too, appear;
   And Hodge a-whistling at his fallow plough;
   And herdsman hallooing to intruding cow:
All these, with hundreds more, far off and near,
   Approach my sight; and please to such excess,
   That language fails the pleasure to express.

1810.

THE ANT

Thou little insect, infinitely small,
   What curious texture marks thy minute frame!
How seeming large thy foresight, and withal,
   Thy labouring talents not unworthy fame,
To raise such monstrous hills along the plain,
   Larger than mountains, when compar'd with thee:
To drag the crumb dropt by the village swain,
   Huge size to thine, is strange, indeed, to me.
But that great instinct which foretells the cold,
   And bids to guard 'gainst winter's wasteful power,
Endues this mite with cheerfulness to hold
   Its toiling labours through the sultry hour:
So that same soothing power, in misery,
Cheers the poor pilgrim to eternity.

1810.

THE SETTING SUN

This scene, how beauteous to a musing mind,
   That now swift slides from my enchanted view;
The sun sweet setting yon far hills behind,
   In other worlds his visits to renew:
What spangled glories all around him shine;
   What nameless colours, cloudless and serene
(A heav'nly prospect, brightest in decline),
   Attend his exit from this lovely scene.
So sets the Christian's sun, in glories clear;
So shines his soul at his departure here:
   No clouding doubts, nor misty fears arise,
To dim hope's golden rays of being forgiven;
   His sun, sweet setting in the clearest skies,
In faith's assurance wings the soul to heaven.

1814.

THE PRIMROSE

WELCOME, pale Primrose! starting up between
   Dead matted leaves of ash and oak, that strew
   The every lawn, the wood, and spinney through,
Mid creeping moss and ivy's darker green;
   How much thy presence beautifies the ground:
How sweet thy modest, unaffected pride
Glows on the sunny bank, and wood's warm side.
   And where thy fairy flowers in groups are found,
The school-boy roams enchantedly along,
   Plucking the fairest with a rude delight:
While the meek shepherd stops his simple song,
   To gaze a moment on the pleasing sight,
O'erjoy'd to see the flowers that truly bring
The welcome news of sweet returning spring.

1816.

HOME

O HOME! however homely—thoughts of thee
   Can never fail to cheer the absent breast;
How oft wild raptures have been felt by me,
   When back returning, weary and distrest;
How oft I've stood to see the chimney pour
   Thick clouds of smoke in columns lightly blue,
And, close beneath, the house-leek's yellow flower,
   While fast approaching to a nearer view,
These, though they're trifles, ever gave delight;
   E'en now they prompt me with a fond desire,
Painting the evening group before my sight
   Of friends and kindred seated round the fire.
O Time! how rapid did thy moments flow,
That chang'd these scenes of joy to scenes of woe.

THE TOMB

ONCE musing o'er an old effaced stone,
   Longing to know whose dust it did conceal,
   I anxious ponder'd o'er what might reveal,
And sought the seeming date with weeds o'ergrown;
   But that prov'd fruitless—both the date and name
Had been for ages in oblivion thrown.
The dim remains of sculptur'd ornament
   Gave proof sufficient 'twas reward for fame:
This did my searching view so much torment,
   That Time I question'd to expose the same;
But soon a check—'And what is it to thee
Whose dust lies here?—since thou wilt quickly be
Forgot like him: then Time shall bid thee go
To heaven's pure bliss, or hell's tormenting woe.'

SORROWS FOR A FRIEND

YE brown old oaks that spread the silent wood,
   How soothing sweet your stillness used to be;
And still could bless, when wrapt in musing mood,
   But now confusion suits the best to me.
'Is it for love,' the breezes seem to say,
   'That you forsake our woodland silence here?
Is it for love, you roam so far away
   From these still shades you valu'd once so dear?'
'No, breezes, no!'—I answer with a sigh,
   'Love never could so much my bosom grieve;
Turnhill, my friend!—alas! so soon to die—
   That is the grief which presses me to leave:
Though noise can't heal, it may some balm bestow;
But silence rankles in the wounds of woe.'

POVERTY

Rank Poverty! dost thou my joys assail,
   And with thy threat'nings fright me from my rest?
I once had thoughts, that with a Bloomfield's tale,
   And leisure hours, I surely should be blest;
But now I find the alterative scene
   From these few days I fondly thought my own,
   Hoping to spend them private and alone,
But, lo! thy troop of spectres intervene:
Want shows his face, with Idleness between,
   Next Shame's approaching step, that hates the throng,
   Comes sneaking on, with Sloth that fetters strong.
Are these the joys my leisure hours must glean?
   Then I decline: but know where'er we meet,
   Ye ne'er shall drive me from the Muses' seat.

TO HOPE

Ah, smiling cherub! cheating Hope, adieu!
   No more I'll listen to your pleasing themes,
No more your flattering scenes with joy review,
   For ah, I've found them all delusive dreams;
Yes, mere delusions all; therefore, adieu!
   No more shall you this aching heart beguile;
No more your fleeting joys will I pursue,
   That mock'd my sorrows when they seem'd to smile,
And flatter'd tales that never will be true:
   Tales, only told to aggravate distress
And make me at my fate the more repine,
   By whispering joys I never can possess,
And painting scenes that never can be mine.

A WINTER SCENE

HAIL, scenes of desolation and despair,
  Keen winter's overbearing sport and scorn!
Torn by his rage, in ruins as you are,
  To me more pleasing than a summer's morn
Your shatter'd state appears—despoil'd and bare,
  Stript of your clothing, naked and forlorn:
Yes, winter's havoc! wretched as you shine,
  Dismal to others as your fate may seem,
Your fate is pleasing to this heart of mine,
  Your wildest horrors I the most esteem.
The ice-bound floods that still with rigour freeze,
  The snow-cloth'd valley, and the naked tree,
These sympathizing scenes my heart can please,
  Distress is theirs—and they resemble me.

                                              1817.

THE MOON

How sweet the Moon extends her cheering ray
  To damp the terrors of the darksome night,
Guiding the lonely traveller on his way,
  Pointing the path that leads his journey right.
  Hail! welcome blessing, to thy silver light,
That charms dull night, and makes its horrors gay.
  So shines the Gospel to the Christian's soul;
So, by its light and inspiration given,
  He (spite of sin and Satan's black control)
Through all obstructions steers his course to heaven.
  So did the Saviour his design pursue,
That we, unworthy sinners, might be blest;
  So suffer'd death, its terrors to subdue,
And made the grave a wish'd-for place of rest.

TO THE GLOW-WORM

TASTEFUL illumination of the night,
  Bright scatter'd, twinkling star of spangled earth!
Hail to the nameless colour'd dark-and-light,
  The witching nurse of thy illumin'd birth.
In thy still hour how dearly I delight
  To rest my weary bones, from labour free;
In lone spots, out of hearing, out of sight,
  To sigh day's smother'd pains; and pause on thee,
  Bedecking dangling brier and ivied tree,
Or diamonds tipping on the grassy spear;
  Thy pale-fac'd glimmering light I love to see,
Gilding and glistering in the dew-drop near:
  O still-hour's mate! my easing heart sobs free,
While tiny bents low bend with many an added tear.

EVENING

NOW glaring daylight's usher'd to a close;
  And nursing eve her soothing care renews,
To welcome weary labour to repose,
  And cherish nature with reviving dews.
Hail, cooling sweets! that breathe so sweetly here;
  Hail, lovely Eve! whose hours so lovely prove;
Thy silent calm! to solitude so dear;
  And oh, this darkness! dearer still to love.
Now the fond lover seeks thy silent plains,
  And with his charmer in fond dalliance strays,
Vowing his love, and telling jealous pains
  Which doubtful fancies in their absence raise.
Ah! though such pleasures centre not in me,
I love to wander and converse with thee.

1818.

TO THE WINDS

HAIL, gentle winds! I love your murmuring sound;
   The willows charm me, wavering to and fro;
And oft I stretch me on the daisied ground,
   To see you crimp the wrinkled flood below:
Delighted more as brisker gusts succeed,
   And give the landscape round a sweeter grace,
Sweeping in shaded waves the ripening mead,
   Puffing their rifled fragrance in my face.
Painters of nature! ye are doubly dear;
   Her children dearly love your whispering charms:
Ah, ye have murmur'd sweet to many an ear
   That now lies dormant in death's icy arms;
And at this moment many a weed ye wave,
That hides the bard in his forgotten grave.

NATIVE SCENES

O NATIVE scenes, for ever, ever dear!
   So blest, so happy as I here have been,
   So charm'd with nature in each varied scene,
To leave you all is cutting and severe.
   Ye hawthorn bushes that from winds would screen,
Where oft I've shelter'd from a threaten'd shower,
In youth's past bliss, in childhood's happy hour,
   Ye woods I've wandered, seeking out the nest,
Ye meadows gay that rear'd me many a flower,
   Where, pulling cowslips, I've been doubly blest,
Humming gay fancies as I pluck'd the prize:
   Oh, fate unkind! beloved scenes, adieu!
Your vanish'd pleasures crowd my swimming eyes,
   And make the wounded heart to bleed anew.

TO A FAVOURITE TREE

OLD, favourite tree! art thou too fled the scene?
  Could not thy 'clining age the axe delay,
And let thee stretch thy shadows o'er the green,
  And let thee die in picturesque decay?
What hadst thou done to meet a tyrant's frown?
  Small value was the ground on which thou stood;
But gain's rude rage it was that cut thee down,
  And dragg'd thee captive from thy native wood.
So gay in summer as thy boughs were dress'd,
  So soft, so cool, as then thy leaves did wave;
I knew thee then, and knowing am distress'd:
  And like as Friendship leaning o'er the grave,
Loving you all, ye trees, ye bushes, dear,
I wander where ye stood, and shed my bosom-tear.

APPROACH OF SPRING

SWEET are the omens of approaching spring,
  When gay the eldern sprouts her winged leaves,
When tootling robins carol-welcomes sing,
  And sparrows chelp glad tidings from the eaves.
What lovely prospects wait each wakening hour,
  When each new day some novelty displays;
How sweet the sunbeam melts the crocus flower,
  Whose borrow'd pride shines dizen'd in his rays:
Sweet, new-laid hedges flush their tender greens;
Sweet peep the arum-leaves their shelter screens;
  Ah! sweet is all which I'm denied to share:
Want's painful hindrance sticks me to her stall—
  But still Hope's smiles unpoint the thorns of Care,
Since Heaven's eternal spring is free for all.

SUMMER

The oak's slow-opening leaf, of deepening hue,
   Bespeaks the power of summer once again;
While many a flower unfolds its charms to view,
   To glad the entrance of his sultry reign.
Where peep the gaping, speckled cuckoo-flowers,
   Sweet is each rural scene she brings to pass;
Prizes to rambling school-boys' vacant hours,
   Tracking wild searches through the meadow grass,
The meadowsweet taunts high its showy wreath,
And sweet the quaking grasses hide beneath.
   Ah, 'barr'd from all that sweetens life below,
Another Summer still my eyes can see
   Freed from the scorn and pilgrimage of woe,
To share the Seasons of Eternity.

THE RIVER GWASH

Where winding Gwash whirls round its wildest scene,
   On this romantic bend I sit me down;
On that side view the meadow's smoothing green,
   Edg'd with the peeping hamlet's chequering brown,
   Here the steep bank, as dropping headling down;
While glides the stream a silver streak between,
   As glide the shaded clouds along the sky,
Bright'ning and deep'ning, losing as they're seen,
In light and shade, to where old willows lean;
   Thus their broad shadow runs the river by,
With tree and bush replete, a wilder'd scene,
   And moss and ivy speckling on my eye.
Oh, thus while musing wild, I'm doubly blest,
My woes unheeding, and my heart at rest.

TO RELIGION

Thou sacred light, that right from wrong discerns;
  Thou safeguard of the soul, thou heaven on earth;
Thou undervaluer of the world's concerns;
  Thou disregarder of its joys and mirth;
Thou only home the houseless wanderers have;
  Thou prop by which the pilgrim's woes are borne;
Thou solace of the lonely hermit's cave,
  That beds him down to rest on fate's sharp thorn;
Thou only hope to sorrow's bosom given;
  Thou voice of mercy when the weary call;
Thou faith extending to thy home in heaven;
  Thou peace, thou rest, thou comfort, all in all:
O sovereign good! on thee all hopes depend,
Till thy grand source unfolds its realizing end.

ANXIETY

One, o'er heaths wandering in a pitch-dark night,
  Making to sounds that hope some village near;
Hermit, retreating to a chinky light,
  Long lost in winding cavern dark and drear;
  A slave, long banish'd from his country dear,
By freedom left to seek his native plains;
  A soldier, absent many a long, long year,
In sight of home ere he that comfort gains;
A thirsty labouring wight, that wistful strains
  O'er the steep hanging bank to reach the stream;
A hope, delay so lingeringly detains,
  We still on point of its disclosure seem:
These pictures weakly 'semble to the eye
A *faint* existence of Anxiety.

126

EXPECTATION

WHEN Expectation in the bosom heaves,
    What longing, anxious views disturb the mind;
What fears, what hopes, distrust and then believe
    That something which the heart expects to find!
How the poor prisoner, ere he's doom'd to die,
    Within his gloomy cell of dreary woe,
How does he watch, with Expectation's eye,
    The lingering, long suspense of fate to know.
Alas, poor soul! though different bonds confine,
The walls his prison is, the world is mine:
    So do I turn my weary eyes above,
So do I look and sigh for peace to come,
    So do I long the grave's dark end to prove,
And anxious wait my long, long journey home.

TO MY OATEN REED

THOU warble wild, of rough, rude melody,
    How oft I've woo'd thee, often thrown thee by!
In many a doubtful rapture touching thee,
    Waking thy rural notes in many a sigh:
    Fearing the wise, the wealthy, proud and high,
Would scorn as vain thy lowly ecstasy,
    Deeming presumptuous thy uncultur'd themes.
Thus vainly courting Taste's unblemish'd eye,
    To list a simple labourer's artless dreams,
    Haply I wander into wide extremes.
But O thou sweet, wild-winding rhapsody,
    Thou jingling charm that dost my heart control,
I take thee up to smother many a sigh,
    And lull the throbbings of a woe-worn soul.

127

TO MY COTTAGE

THOU lowly cot, where first my breath I drew,
  Past joys endear thee, childhood's past delight;
Where each young summer's pictur'd on my view;
  And, dearer still, the happy winter-night,
When the storm pelted down with all his might,
  And roar'd and bellow'd in the chimney-top,
And patter'd vehement 'gainst the window-light,
  And on the threshold fell the quick eaves-drop.
How blest I've listen'd on my corner stool,
  Heard the storm rage, and hugg'd my happy spot,
While the fond parent wound her whirring spool,
  And spar'd a sigh for the poor wanderer's lot.
In thee, sweet hut, this happiness was prov'd,
  And these endear and make thee doubly lov'd.

TO MY MOTHER

WITH filial duty I address thee, Mother,
  Thou dearest tie which this world's wealth possesses;
Endearing name! no language owns another
  That half the tenderness and love expresses;
The very word itself breathes the affection,
  Which heaves the bosom of a luckless child
To thank thee, for that care and that protection,
  Which once, where fortune frowns, so sweetly smil'd.
Ah, oft fond memory leaves its pillow'd anguish,
  To think when in thy arms my sleep was sound;
And now my startled tear oft views thee languish,
  And fain would drop its honey in the wound:
But I am doom'd the sad reverse to see,
Where the worst pain I feel is loss of helping thee.

THE SNOWDROP

Sweet type of innocence, snow-clothed blossom,
  Seemly, though vainly, bowing down to shun
The storm hard-beating on thy wan white bosom,
  Left in the swale, and little cheer'd by sun;
  Resembling that frail jewel, just begun
To ope on vice's eye its witcheries blooming,
  Midst all its storms, with little room to shun—
Ah, thou art winter's snowdrop, lovely Woman!
In this world dropt, where every evil's glooming
  With killing tempests o'er its tender prey,
Watching the opening of thy beauties coming,
  Its every infant charm to snatch away:
Then come the sorrows thou'rt too weak to brave,
And then thy beauty-cheek digs ruin's early grave.

WRITTEN IN AUTUMN

Check'd Autumn, doubly sweet is thy declining,
  To meditate within this wilder'd shade;
To view the wood in its pied lustre shining,
  And catch thy varied beauties as they fade;
Where o'er broad hazel-leaves thy pencil mellows,
  Red as the glow that morning's opening warms,
And ash or maple 'neath thy colour yellows,
  Robbing some sunbeam of its setting charms:
I would say much of what now meets my eye,
But beauties lose me in variety.
  Oh, for the warmth of soul and 'witching measure,
Expressive semblance, Poesy, which is thine,
  And genius' eye to view this transient treasure,
That autumn here might lastingly decline.

LIFE

Life, thou art misery, or as such to me;
One name serves both, or I no difference see;
Tho' some there live would call thee heaven below,
But that's a nickname I've not learn'd to know:
A wretch with poverty and pains replete,
Where even useless stones beneath his feet
Cannot be gather'd up to say 'They're mine,'
Sees little heaven in a life like thine.
Hope lends a sorry shelter from thy storms,
And largely promises, but small performs.
Oh, irksome life! were but this hour my last!
  This weary breath fain sighs for its decay;
Oh, that my soul death's dreary vale had past,
  And met the sunshine of a better day!

POEMS WRITTEN AT HELPSTONE
1819–21

THE VILLAGE MINSTREL

WHILE learned poets rush to bold extremes,
And sunbeams snatch to light the muse's fires,
An humble rustic hums his lowly dreams,
Far in the swale where poverty retires,
And sings what nature and what truth inspires:
The charms that rise from rural scenery,
Which he in pastures and in woods admires;
The sports, the feelings of his infancy,
And such-like artless things, how mean soe'er they be.

Though, far from what the learned's toils requite, .
He unambitious looks at no renown,
Yet little hopes break his oblivious night,
To cheer the bosom of a luckless clown,
Where black neglect spreads one continual frown,
And threats her constant winter cold and chill,
Where toil and slavery bear each fancy down,
That fain would soar and sing 'albeit ill,'
And force him to submit to fate's controlling will.

Young Lubin was a peasant from his birth;
His sire a hind born to the flail and plough,
To thump the corn out and to till the earth,
The coarsest chance which nature's laws allow—
To earn his living by a sweating brow;
Thus Lubin's early days did rugged roll,
And mixt in timely[1] toil—but e'en as now,
Ambitious prospects fired his little soul,
And fancy soared and sung, 'bove poverty's control.

Small joy to him were childhood's tempting tricks,
Which schoolboys look for in their vacant hours;

[1] Clare uses the word in its older meaning, 'early.' Taylor emended to 'untimely.'

With other boys he little cared to mix;
Joy left him lonely in his hawthorn bowers,
As haply binding up his knots of flowers,
Or list'ning unseen birds to hear them sing;
Or gazing downward where the runnel pours
Through the moss'd bridge in many a whirling ring,
How would he muse o'er all on pleasure's fairy wing.

The 'I spy,' 'halloo,' and the marble-ring,
And many a game that infancy employs,
The spinning-top whirl'd from the twitching string,
The boastful jump of strong exulting boys,
Their sports, their pastimes, all their pleasing toys
We leave unsung—though much such rural play
Would suit the theme—yet they're not Lubin's joys:
Truth breathes the song in Lubin's steps to stray,
Through woods and fields and plains, his solitary way;

And tell how vales and shades did please his sight,
And how the wind breath'd music thro' each bough,
And how in rural charms he did delight—
To mark the shepherd's folds, and swains at plough,
And pasture speck'd with sheep, and horse, and cow,
With many a beauty that does intervene,
And steeple peeping o'er the wood's dark brow;
While young hope's fancy popt its smile between,
And wish'd man's days to spend in some such peaceful scene.

Each opening season, and each opening scene,
On his wild view still teem'd with fresh delight;
E'er winter's storms to him have welcome been,
That brought him comfort in its long dark night,
As joyful list'ning, while the fire burnt bright,
Some neighbouring labourer's superstitious tale,
How 'Jinny-burnt-arse,'[1] with her wisp alight,
To drown a 'nighted traveller once did fail,
He knowing well the brook that whimper'd down the vale.

[1] Taylor emended to 'Jack-a-lantern.'

And tales of fairy-land he lov'd to hear,
Those mites of human forms, like skimming bees,
That fly and flirt about but everywhere,
The fly-like tribes of night's un'scerning breeze,
That through a lock-hole even creep with ease:
The freaks and stories of this elfin crew,
Ah, Lubin gloried in such things as these;
How they rewarded industry he knew,
And how the restless slut was pinched black and blue.

How ancient dames a fairy's anger fear'd,
From gossips' stories Lubin often heard;
How they but every night the hearth-stone clear'd,
And 'gainst their visits all things neat prepar'd,
As fays naught more than cleanliness regard;
When in the morn they never fail'd to share
Or gold or silver as their meet reward,
Dropt in the water superstition's care
To make the charm succeed had cautious placed there.

And thousands such the village keeps alive:
Beings that people superstitious earth,
That e'er in rural manners will survive,
As long as wild rusticity has birth
To spread their wonders round the cottage-hearth.
On Lubin's mind these deeply were imprest;
Oft fear forbade to share his neighbour's mirth:
And long each tale, by fancy newly drest,
Brought fairies in his dreams, and broke his infant rest.

He had his dreads and fears, and scarce could pass
A churchyard's dreary mounds at silent night,
But footsteps trampled through the rustling grass,
And ghosts 'hind grave-stones peer'd in sheets of white,
Dread monsters fancy moulded on his sight:
Soft would he step lest they his tread should hear,
And creep and creep till past his wild affright;
Then on wind's wings would rally as it were,
So swift the wild retreat of childhood's fancied fear.

And when fear left him, on his corner-seat,
Much would he chatter o'er each dreadful tale:
Tell how he heard the sound of 'proaching feet,
And warriors jingling in their coats of mail,
And lumping knocks, as one would thump a flail,
Of spirits conjur'd in the charnel floor,
And many a mournful shriek and hapless wail,
Where maids self-murder'd their false loves deplore;
And from that time would vow to tramp on nights no more.

Oh, who can speak his joys when spring's young morn
From wood and pasture open'd on his view,
When tender green buds blush upon the thorn,
And the first primrose dips its leaves in dew:
Each varied charm how joy'd would he pursue,
Tempted to trace their beauties through the day;
Grey-girdled eve and morn of rosy hue
Have both beheld him on his lonely way,
Far, far remote from boys and their unpleasing play.

Sequester'd nature was his heart's delight;
Him would she lead thro' wood and lonely plain,
Searching the pooty from the rushy dyke;
And while the thrush sang her long-silenc'd strain,
He thought it sweet, and mock'd it o'er again;
And while he pluck'd the primrose in its pride,
He ponder'd o'er its bloom 'tween joy and pain,
And a rude sonnet in its praise he tried,
Where nature's simple way the aid of art supplied.

The freshen'd landscapes round his routes unfurl'd,
The fine-ting'd clouds above, the woods below,
Each met his eye a new-revealing world,
Delighting more as more he learn'd to know,
Each journey sweeter, musing to and fro.
Surrounded thus, not paradise more sweet,
Enthusiasm made his soul to glow;
His heart with wild sensations used to beat;
As nature seemly sang, his mutterings would repeat.

Upon a molehill oft he dropt him down,
To take a prospect of the circling scene,
Marking how much the cottage roof's-thatch brown
Did add its beauty to the budding green
Of sheltering trees it humbly peep'd between,
The stone-rock'd wagon with its rumbling sound,
The windmill's sweeping sails at distance seen,
And every form that crowds the circling round,
Where the sky stooping seems to kiss the meeting ground.

And dear to him the rural sports of May,
When each cot-threshold mounts its hailing bough,
And ruddy milkmaids weave their garlands gay,
Upon the green to crown the earliest cow,
When mirth and pleasure wear a joyful brow,
And join the tumult with unbounded glee
The humble tenants of the pale [1] and plough:
He lov'd 'old sports,' by them reviv'd, to see,
But never car'd to join in their rude revelry.

O'er brook-banks stretching, on the pasture-sward,
He gaz'd, far distant from the jocund crew;
'Twas but their feats that claim'd a slight regard;
'Twas his, his pastimes lonely to pursue—
Wild blossoms creeping in the grass to view,
Scarce peeping up the tiny bent as high,
Beting'd with glossy yellow, red, or blue,
Unnam'd, unnotic'd but by Lubin's eye,
That like low genius sprang to bloom their day and die.

Oh, who can tell the sweets of May-day's morn,
To waken rapture in a feeling mind,
When the gilt east unveils her dappled dawn,
And the gay woodlark has its nest resign'd,
As slow the sun creeps up the hill behind,
Morn redd'ning round, and daylight's spotless hue,
As seemly sweet with rose and lily lin'd;
While all the prospect round beams fair to view,
Like a sweet opening flower with its unsullied dew.

[1] Enclosed land. Taylor emended to 'pail.'

Ah, often brushing through the dripping grass
Has he been seen to catch this early charm,
List'ning the 'love song' of the healthy lass
Passing with milk-pail on her well-turn'd arm;
Or meeting objects from the rousing farm,
The jingling plough-teams driving down the steep,
Wagon and cart—and shepherd-dogs' alarm,
Raising the bleatings of unfolding sheep,
As o'er the mountain top the red sun 'gins to peep.

Nor could the day's decline escape his gaze;
He lov'd the closing as the rising day,
And oft would stand to catch the setting rays,
Whose last beams stole not unperceiv'd away;
When, hesitating like a stag at bay,
The bright unwearied sun seem'd loath to drop,
Till chaos' night-hounds hurried him away,
And drove him headlong from the mountain-top,
And shut the lovely scene, and bade all nature stop.

With contemplation's stores his mind to fill,
Oh, doubly happy would he roam as then,
When the blue eve crept deeper round the hill,
While the coy rabbit ventur'd from his den,
And weary labour sought his rest agen;
Lone wanderings led him haply by the stream
Where unperceiv'd he joy'd his hours at will,
Musing the cricket twittering o'er its dream,
Or watching o'er the brook the moonlight's dancing beam.

And here the rural muse might aptly say,
As sober evening sweetly siles along,
How she has chas'd black ignorance away
And warm'd his artless soul with feelings strong
To teach his reed to warble forth a song:
And how it echoed on the even-gale,
All by the brook the pasture-flowers among;
But, ah, such trifles are of no avail:
There's few to notice him, or hear his simple tale.

As most of nature's children prove to be,
His little soul was easy made to smart,
His tear was quickly born to sympathy,
And soon were rous'd the feelings of his heart
In others' woes and wants to bear a part.
Yon parish-huts, where want is shov'd to die,
He never view'd them but his tear would start;
He pass'd not by the doors without a sigh,
And felt for every woe of workhouse-misery.

O Poverty! thy frowns were early dealt
O'er him who mourn'd thee, not by fancy led
To whine and wail o'er woes he never felt,
Staining his rhymes with tears he never shed,
And heaving sighs a mock song only bred:
Alas! he knew too much of every pain
That shower'd full thick on his unshelter'd head;
And as his tears and sighs did erst complain,
His numbers took it up, and wept it o'er again.

Full well might he his early days recall,
When he a thresher with his sire has been,
When he a ploughboy in the fields did maul,
And drudg'd with toil through almost every scene;
How pinch'd with winter's frownings he has been;
And tell of all that modesty conceals,
Of what his friends and he have felt and seen:
But, useless naming what distress reveals,
As every child of want feels all that Lubin feels.

It might be curious here to hint the lad,
How in his earliest days he did appear;
Mean was the dress in which the boy was clad,
His friends so poor, and clothes excessive dear,
They oft were foil'd to rig him once a year;
And housewife's care in many a patch was seen;
Much industry 'gainst want did persevere;
His friends tried all to keep him neat and clean,
Though care has often fail'd, and shatter'd he has been.

Yet oft fair prospects cheer'd his parents' dreams,
Who had on Lubin founded many a joy;
But pinching want soon baffled all their schemes,
And dragg'd him from the school a hopeless boy,
To shrink unheeded under hard employ;
When struggling efforts warm'd him up the while,
To keep the little toil could not destroy;
And oft with books spare hours he would beguile,
And blunder oft with joy round Crusoe's lonely isle.

Folks much may wonder how the thing may be,
That Lubin's taste should seek refined joys,
And court th'enchanting smiles of poesy;
Bred in a village full of strife and noise,
Old senseless gossips, and blackguarding boys,
Ploughmen and threshers, whose discourses led
To nothing more than labour's rude employs,
'Bout work being slack, and rise and fall of bread,
And who were like to die, and who were like to wed:

Housewives discoursing 'bout their hens and cocks,
Spinning long stories, wearing half the day,
Sad deeds bewailing of the prowling fox,
How in the roost the thief had knav'd his way
And made their market-profits all a prey.
And other losses too the dames recite,
Of chick, and duck, and gosling gone astray,
All falling prizes to the swopping kite:
And so the story runs both morning, noon, and night.

Nor sabbath-days much better thoughts instil;
The true-going churchman hears the signal ring,
And takes his book his homage to fulfil,
And joins the clerk his amen-task to sing,
And rarely home forgets the text to bring:
But soon as service ends, he 'gins again
'Bout signs in weather, late or forward spring,
Of prospects good or bad in growing grain;
And if the sermon's long he waits the end with pain.

A more uncouthly lout was hardly seen
Beneath the shroud of ignorance than he;
The sport of all the village he has been,
Who with his simple looks oft jested free;
And gossips, gabbling o'er their cake and tea,
Time after time did prophecies repeat,
How half a ninny he was like to be,
To go so soodling up and down the street
And shun the playing boys whene'er they chanc'd to meet.

Nature look'd on him with a 'witching eye,
Her pleasing scenes were his delightful book,
Were he, while other louts roam'd heedless by,
With wild enthusiasm us'd to look.
The kingcup vale, the gravel-paved brook,
Were paradise with him to muse among;
And haply sheltering in some lonely nook,
He often sat to see it purl along,
And, fir'd with what he saw, humm'd o'er his simple song.

When summer came, how eager has he sped
Where silence reign'd, and the old crowned tree
Bent with its sheltering ivy o'er his head;
And summer-breezes, breathing placidly,
Encroach'd upon the stockdove's privacy,
Parting the leaves that screen'd her russet breast:
'Peace!' would he whisper, 'dread no thief in me,'
And never rose to rob her careless nest;
Compassion's softness reign'd, and warm'd his gentle breast.

And he would trace the stagnant pond or lake,
Where flags sprang up or water-lilies smil'd,
And wipe the boughs aside of bush and brake,
And creep the woods with sweetest scenes beguil'd,
Tracking some channel on its journey wild,
Where dripping blue-bells on the bank did weep:
Oh, what a lovely scene to nature's child,
Through roots and o'er dead leaves to see it creep,
Watching on some moss'd stump in contemplation deep.

'Twas pleasing too, when meadows' browning swath
'Neath sultry sunbeams wither'd on the lea,
To mark the ploughboys at their Sunday bath,
When leisure left them at their wading free
In some clear pit hemm'd round wi' willow tree
And bush and brake to screen the dabbling crew,
Tho' bashful milkmaids couldn't help but see,
And doubtless, blushing by the naked crew,
Their bosoms might be warm'd to wish a nearer view.[1]

And he would mark in July's rosy prime,
Crossing the meadows, how a nameless fly
Of scarlet plumage, punctual to its time,
Perch'd on a flower would always meet his eye;
And plain-drest butterfly of russet dye,
As if awaken'd by the scythe's shrill sound,
Soon as the bent with ripeness 'gan to dye,
Was constant with him in each meadow-ground,
Flirting the withering swath and unmown blossom round.

No insect 'scap'd him, from the gaudy plume
Of dazzling butterflies so fine to view,
To the small midgen that at evening come
Like dust spots dancing o'er the water's blue,
Or, where the spreading oak above-head grew,
Tormenting maidens 'neath their kicking cow;
Who often murmur'd at the elfin crew,
And from th'endanger'd pail, with angry vow
Oft rose, their sport to spoil with switch of murdering bough.

And he has mark'd the curious stained rings,
Though seemly nothing in another's eye,
And bending o'er them thought them wondrous things,
Where nurses' night-fays circling dances hie
And set the cock to watch the morning's eye;
Light soon betrays 'em where their routes have been,
Their printing foot-marks leave a magic dye,
The grass grows gloomy in a darker green,
And look for years to come, and still the place is seen.

[1] Stanza added from MS.

And as declining day his stalking shade
A giant monster stretch'd, in fancy's view,
What bustle to his cottage has he made,
Ere sliving night around his journey threw
Her circling curtains of a grisly hue;
Then of the rings the fairy routs display'd
From gossips' wisdom much he glean'd, who knew
How they were haunts for ghosts as well as fays,
And told what things were seen in granny's younger days.

The verse might tremble with the 'haunted pond,'
And tell of terrors which his heart has found:
How he, to 'scape, shool'd many a pace beyond
Each dreaded, dangerous spot of haunted ground;
Here as he pass'd where Amy's woes were drown'd,
If late at night, his fears would turn him chill;
If naught was seen, he heard a squish-squash sound,
As when one's shoes the drenching waters fill,
And wet and dripping oft he saw her climb the hill.

And round his fields lay many a spot to dread;
'Twould note a history down to mark them all:
Oft monsters have been seen without a head;
And market-men oft got a dangerous fall,
When startled horses saw the sweeping pall
On the cross-roads where 'love-lorn Luce' was lain;
At other spots, like offspring of 'Old Ball,'
Or ploughman's senses often were mista'en,
A shagged foal would fright the early-rising swain.

In autumn-time he often stood to mark
What tumults 'tween the hogs and geese arose
Down the corn-litter'd street, and the rude bark
Of jealous watch-dog on his master's clothes,
E'en rous'd by quawking of the swopping crows,
And every tinkle in that busy toil,
In sultry field and dusty lane that flows:
He glean'd his corn, and lov'd to list the while,
For Lubin mingled there to share of autumn's spoil.

143

And when old women, overpower'd by heat,
   Tuck'd up their clothes and sicken'd at the toil,
Seeking beneath the thorn the mole-hill seat,
   To tell their tales and catch their breath awhile,
   Their gabbling talk did Lubin's cares beguile;
And some would tell their tales, and some would sing,
   And many a dame, to make the children smile,
   Would tell of many a funny laughing thing,
While merrily the snuff went pinching round the ring.

Here Lubin listen'd with awe-struck surprise,
   When 'Hickathrift's' great strength has met his ear,
How he kill'd giants as they were but flies,
   And lifted trees as one would lift a spear,
   Though not much bigger than his fellows were;
He knew no troubles wagoners have known,
   Of getting stall'd, and such disasters drear;
   Up he'd chuck sacks as one would hurl a stone,
And draw whole loads of grain unaided and alone.

And Goody's sympathy would fetch the tear
   From each young list'ner seated by her side,
When 'Cruel Barbara Allen' they did hear,
   The haughty stubbornness of female pride
   To that fond youth who broke his heart and died:
And 'Jack the Giant-killer's' tales she'd say,
   Which still the same enchanting power supplied;
   The stagnant tear amazement wip'd away,
And Jack's exploits were felt for many an after-day.

These were such tales as Lubin did delight;
   But should the muse narrate in Goody's strain,
And tell of all she told from morn till night,
   Fays, ghosts, and giants would her songs detain
   To be at day's return resumed again:
With 'Cinderella' she has charm'd awhile,
   Then 'Thumb's' disasters gave a moment's pain;
   Thus true-thought legends would each soul beguile,
As superstition will'd, to raise the tear or smile.

144

And as the load jogg'd homeward down the lane,
When welcome night shut out the toiling day,
Following he mark'd the simple-hearted swain;
Joying to listen, on his homeward way,
While rest's warm rapture rous'd the rustic's lay,
The threadbare ballad from each quavering tongue,
As 'Peggy Band,' or the 'Sweet Month of May';
Oh, how he joy'd to hear each 'good old song,'
That on night's pausing ear did echo loud and long.

The muse might sing too, for he well did know,
The freaks and plays that harvest-labour end,
How the last load is crown'd with boughs, and how
The swains and maids with fork and rake attend,
With floating ribbons 'dizen'd at the end;
And how the children on the load delight
With shouts of 'Harvest home!' their throats to rend;
And how the dames peep out to mark the sight:
And all the feats that crown the harvest-supper night.

He knew all well, a young familiar there,
And often look'd on all; for he himsen
Join'd with the sun-tann'd group the feast to share,
As years roll'd round him with the change agen,
And brought the masters level with their men,
Who push'd the beer about, and smok'd and drank
With freedom's plenty never shown till then;
Nor labourers dar'd, save now, so free and frank
To laugh, and joke, and play so many a harmless prank.

Much has he laugh'd each rude, rude act to see;
The long-neck'd sheet-clad 'crane' to poke about,
Spoiling each smoker's pipe, and cunningly,
Though blindfold, seen to pick each bald-head out,
And put each bashful maiden to the rout;
The 'fiery parrot' too, a laughing scene,
Where two maids on a sheet invite the lout,
Thrown o'er a water-tub, to sit between,
And as he drops they rise, and let him swearing in.

The 'dusty miller' playing many a rig;
And the 'Scotch pedlars,' with their jokes and fun;
The 'booted hogs drove over Lunnon brig,'
Boys, who had mischief in the harvest done,
As loads o'erturn'd, and foul on posts had run;
And brandy-burning ghosts most deadly blue,
That each old woman did with terror shun;
These with the rest did Lubin yearly view,
And join'd his mirth and fears with the low vulgar crew.

To close the ranting night, the master's health
Went round in bumping horns to every swain,
Who wish'd him best of crops t'increase his wealth,
And's merry sport when harvest came again;
And all in chorus rallied out amain:
The harvest-song (a tugging pull) begun,
Each ere its end the brimming horn must drain,
Or have it fill'd again—there lay the fun,
Till Hodge went drunk to bed, and morts of things were done.

Oh, dear to Lubin autumn's changing cloud,
Where shade and sunshine every minute sees;
And each rude-risen tempest, beetling loud,
Own'd every murmur his wild ear to please,
Sughing its vengeance through the yellow trees,
Pattering the acorns from their cups adown,
Fanning the sere leaf far upon the leas;
And picturesque to him each scrambling clown,
Tearing the woods among to search the nut-bunch brown.

How would he wander round the woods, the plains,
When every flower from nature's wreath had fled;
Tracing the shower-bedimpled sandy lanes,
And winding fountains to their infant bed,
With many a flag and rushy bunch bespread;
Marking each curdle boil and boil away,
And bubbles guggling born, that swell'd and fled
Like changing scenes in life's ephemeron-day:
Thus Lubin paus'd o'er all, and cheer'd his lonely way.

A solitaire through autumn's wan decay,
He heard the tootling robin sound her knell,
Observ'd the sun more coy to slink away,
And lingering oak-shade how it brown'd and fell;
And many a way of nature he could tell,
That secrets are to undiscerning eyes,
As how the bee most careful clos'd her cell,
The mouse with far-fetch'd ear his hole supplies,
And moles root deeper down, from winter's frowning skies,

And he could tell how the shy squirrel far'd,
Who often stood its busy toils to see;
How against winter it was well prepar'd
With many a store in hollow root or tree,
As if being told what winter's wants would be:
Its nuts and acorns he would often find,
And hips and haws too, heaped plenteously
In snug warm corner that broke off the wind,
With leafy nest made nigh, that warm green mosses lin'd.

'Twas thus his fond inquiry us'd to trace
Through nature's secrets with unwearied eye,
And watch the shifting seasons' changing grace:
Spring's first wild flower, and summer's painted sky,
The insect creeping, and the birds that fly,
The autumn's dying breeze, the winter-wind,
That bellow'd round his hut most mournfully:
And as his years increas'd his taste refin'd,
And fancy with new charms enlighten'd up his mind.

Beauty 'gan look too witching on his eye;
The sweetest image seen in nature's glass;
A swelling bosom 'neath its lily dye,
Without admiring, Lubin could not pass;
And downcast eye, and blush of shanny lass,
Had every power his heart to hold in thrall.
O beauteous woman! still thy charms surpass:
In spite of all thy failings and thy fall,
Thou art the comfort still that cheers this earthly ball.

Sure 'twas an oversight in nature's plan,
Such loveliness, that claims the tenderest care,
To leave defenceless with ungrateful man,
Such harden'd brutes as but too many are.
O pleasing flowers! as frail as ye are fair;
Sure some that live have souls to feel and sigh,
When, shrinking 'neath the storms ye cannot bear,
Your beauteous buds bow down to fade and die,
While not one pitying tear melts your seducer's eye.

Full oft, to see their witcheries divine,
He'd mix in circles which their charms did grace,
And merry routs he now began to join;
And though his heart denied to own its case,
It oft was smitten with a beauty's face,
And throbb'd with thrilling aggravating pain;
And many a long, long day has taken place,
Ere he forgot, and met his peace again,
While oft in beauty's praise he humm'd his amorous strain.

He knew the manners too of merry rout;
Statute and feast his village yearly knew;
And glorious revels too without a doubt
Such pastimes were to Hob, and Nell, and Sue,
Milkmaids and clowns that statute-joys pursue,
And rattle off, like hogs to Lunnon mart:
Weary of old, they seek for places new,
Where men hail maidens with a frothing quart,
And Hodge with sweetheart fix'd forgets his plough and
    cart:

Where cakes, and nuts, and gingerbread and all,
Tempt clowns to buy; and far more tempting still,
Where shining ribbons dizen out the stall,
And wenches drag poor sheepish Bob or Bill
Some long, long dallied promise to fulfil,
New wreath or bow for Sunday cap to buy—
'If yah set any store by one yah will!'
Each strings his purse, and makes them no reply,
But thinks returns at night will suit, for clowns are sly.

And there the ballad-singers rave and rant,
And Hodge, whose pockets won't stand treats more high,
Hears which his simpering lass may please to want,
And, brushing through the crowd most manfully,
Outs with his pence the pleasing song to buy,
And crams it in her hand with many a smile;
The trifling present makes the maid comply
To promise him her company the while,
And strutting on at night he hands her o'er the stile.

Here the poor sailor, with his hat in hand,
Hops through the crowd that wonderfully stares
To hear him talk of things in foreign land,
'Bout thundering cannons and most bloody wars;
And as he stops to show his seamy scars,
Pity soon meets the ploughman's penny then:
The sailor heartfelt thankfulness declares,
'God blesses' all, and styles them 'gentlemen,'
And fobs his money up, and 'gins his tale agen.

Here's 'Civil Will' too, with his 'pins and pegs,'
And he makes glorious fun among the chaps:
'Boys, miss my pegs,' he cries, 'and hit my legs,'
'My timbers well can stand your gentle taps,'
Though sure enough he gets most ugly raps,
For here the rustic thinks the sports abound;
Whose aim at 'Civil's' legs his fellows caps
Meets most applause—still 'poor Will' stands his ground,
'Boys, throw your copper salve, and make another wound.'

But soldiers, they're the boys to make a rout,
With boasting bottle brimm'd with gin and rum,
The high-crown'd cap with ribbons hung about,
The tootling fife, and hoarse rap-tapping drum:
Lud, clowns are almost mad where'er they come;
They're like so many kings 'mong country folk,
They push their beer like water round the room,
Who will and welcome there may drink and smoke,
Though chaps have often found they dearly sell a joke.

The bumptious sergeant struts before his men,
And 'Clear the road, young whopstraws!' will he say;
And looks as big as if King George himsen,
And wields his sword around to make a way:
With lace and ribbons dizen'd out so gay,
So flashing smart—full oft, as well's the swain,
The tempted maid his finery does betray,
Who leaves poor slighted Hodge behind in pain,
And many a chiding dame to sorrow and complain.

And Lubin heard the echoing rabble-fight,
When men and maids were hir'd, and sports did close,
And wenches sought their sweethearts up at night,
And found 'em drunk, bedeck'd with soldier's clothes;
As they would pull and scold great tumults rose;
The sergeant's honour totter'd terribly,
From women's threat'nings hardly 'scap'd with blows;
—They 'd box his cap about his ears, if he
Gave not the contest up and set the prisoner free.

Some homeward-bound were coupled, maid and swain,
And Dick from Dolly now for gifts did sue,
He'd giv'n her ribbons, and he deem'd again
Some kind return as nothing but his due;
And he told things that ploughmen little knew,
Of bleeding hearts and pains—she seiz'd the spell,
And though at first she murmur'd 'bout the dew,
Spoiling her Sunday gown, he talk'd so well;
She gave consent at last to what no words dare tell.[1]

The statute nam'd, each servant's day of fun,
The village-feast next warns the muse's song;
'Tis Lubin's sphere, a thresher's lowly son;
Though little used to mix such routs among,
Such fitting subjects to the theme belong:
As pictur'd landscapes, destitute of trees,
Would doubtlessly be fancied painted wrong,
So lowly rural subjects, such as these,
Must have their simple ways discerning eyes to please.

[1] Preceding four lines restored from MS.   Taylor bowdlerized them.

The lovely morn in July's blushes rose,
That brought the yearly feast and holiday,
When villagers put on their bran-new clothes,
And milk-maids, drest like any ladies gay,
Threw 'cotton drabs' and 'worsted hose' away,
And left their pails unscour'd, well pleas'd I ween
To join the dance where gipsy fiddlers play,
Accompanied with thumping tambourine,
From night till morning-light upon the rushy green,

Where the fond swain delighteth in the chance
To meet the sun-tann'd lass he dearly loves;
And, as he leads her down the giddy dance,
With many a token his fond passion proves,
Squeezing her hands, or snatching at her gloves,
And stealing kisses as chance prompts the while,
With eye fixt on her as she graceful moves,
To catch if such fond fancies her beguile,—
When happily her heart confesses in a smile.

O rural love! as spotless as the dove's;
No wealth gives fuel to a borrow'd flame,
To prompt the shepherd where to choose his loves,
And go a forger of that sacred name;
Both hearts in unison here beat the same;
Here nature makes the choice which love inspires;
Far from the wedded lord and haughty dame
This boon of heavenly happiness retires,
Not felon-like law-bound, but wedded in desires.

The woodman and the thresher now are found
Mixing and making merry with their friends;
Children and kin, from neighbouring towns around,
Each at the humble banquet pleas'd attends:
For though no costliness the feast pretends,
Yet something more than common they provide;
And the good dame her small plum-pudding sends
To sons and daughters fast in service tied,
With many a cordial gift of good advice beside.

'Tis pleasing then to view the cotter's cheer,
To mark his gentle and his generous mind;
How free he is to push about his beer;
And well's he knows, with ceremony kind,
Bids help themselves to such as they may find,
Tells them they're welcome as the flowers in May,
And, full of merrimental cheer inclin'd,
Drinks healths and sings when supper's clear'd away
And hopes they all may meet on next year's holiday;

And then for sake of's boys and wenches dear,
Gives leave a dancing in his hut shall be;
While he sits smoking in his elbow-chair,
And pleas'd as Punch his children round to see,
With each a sweetheart frisking merrily.
'God bless ye all!' quoth he, and drinks his beer,
'My boys and wenches, ye're a pride to me:
Lead but an honest life—no matter where,
And do as I have done, and ye'll have naught to fear.

'To bring ye up, from toil I never flinch'd,
Or fail'd to do the thing that's just and right;
Your mother knows ourselves were often pinch'd,
To fill your bellies and to keep ye tight:
May God look down and bless ye all this night!
May wives and husbands here, that are to be,
Instead of sorrows prove your heart's delight!—
I've brought ye up, expect no more from me,
So take your trundle now, and good luck may ye see!'

Thus talk'd the father to his pipe and beer,
For those whom he'd admonish were the while
Too occupied in dancing him to hear;
Yet still with talk and beer he does beguile
His short releasement from his cares and toil;
Then Sir John's spirit stops his merry glee
And lays him quiet down: his children smile,
Break up the dance, and pay the fiddler's fee,
And then the lass he loves each swain pulls on his knee.

152

And the long rural string of merry games,
That at such outings maketh much ado,
All were to Lubin's skill familiar names;
And he could tell each whole performance through,
As plann'd and practis'd by the jovial crew:
—Great sport to them was jumping in a sack,
For beaver hat bedeck'd with ribbons blue;
Soon one bumps down as though he'd broke his neck,
Another tries to rise, and wondrous sport they make.

And monstrous fun it makes to hunt the pig,
As soapt and larded through the crowd he flies:
Thus turn'd adrift he plays them many a rig;
A pig for catching is a wondrous prize,
And every lout to do his utmost tries;
Some snap the ear, and some the tunkey tail,
But still his slippery hide all hold denies,
While old men tumbled down sore hurts bewail,
And boys bedaub'd with muck run home with piteous tale.

And badger-baiting here, and fighting cocks—
But sports too barbarous these for Lubin's strains:
And red-fac'd wenches, for the holland smocks,
Oft puff and pant along the smooth green plains,
Where Hodge feels most uncomfortable pains
To see his love lag hindmost in the throng,
And of unfairness in her cause complains,
And swears and fights the jarring chaps among,
As in her part he'd die, 'fore they his lass should wrong.

And long-ear'd racers, fam'd for sport and fun,
Appear this day to have their swiftness tried;
Where some won't start, and 'Dick,' the race nigh won,
Enamour'd of some 'Jenny' by his side,
Forgets the winning-post to court a bride;
In vain the rout urge on the jockey-clown
To lump his cudgel on his harden'd hide,
Ass after ass still hee-haws through the town,
And in disgrace at last each jockey bumps adown.

And then the noisy rout, their sports to crown,
Form round the ring superior strength to show,
Where wrestlers join to tug each other down,
And thrust and kick with hard revengeful toe,
Till through their worsted hose the blood does flow:
For ploughmen would not wish for higher fame,
Than be the champion all the rest to throw;
And thus to add such honours to his name,
He kicks, and tugs, and bleeds to win the glorious game.

And when the night draws on, each mirthful lout
The ale-house seeks, and sets it in a roar;
And there, while fiddlers play, they rant about,
And call for brimming tankards frothing o'er:
For clouds of smoke ye'd hardly see the door;
No stint they make of 'bacco and of beer;
While money lasts they shout about for more,
Resolv'd to keep it merry when it's here—
As toils come every day, and feasts but once a year.

With village-merriments digress'd awhile,
We now resume poor Lubin's joys again,
And haply find him bending o'er a stile,
Or stretch'd in sabbath-musings on the plain,
Looking around and humming o'er a strain,
Painting the foliage of the woodland trees,
List'ning a bird that's lost its nest complain,
Noting the hummings of the passing bees,
And all the lovely things his musing hears and sees.

Where ling-clad heaths and pastures now may spread,
He oft has heard of castle and of hall;
And curiosity his steps hath led
To gaze on some old arch or fretting wall,
Where ivy scrambles up to stop the fall:
There would he sit him down, and look, and sigh,
And bygone days back to his mind would call,
The bloody-warring times of chivalry,
When Danes' invading routs made unarm'd Britons fly.

He lov'd to view the mossy-arched brigs,
Bending o'er wall or rail, the pits or springs
Below to mark, where willow's dripping twigs
To summer's silken zephyrs' feeblest wings
Bent in the flood, and curv'd its thousand rings;
And where the sunbeam twitter'd on the walls,
And nodding bulrush down its drowk head hings,
And down the rock the shallow water falls,
Wild fluttering through the stones in feeble whimpering
    brawls.

And oft, with shepherds leaning o'er their hooks,
He'd stand conjecturing on the ruins round:
Though little skill'd in antiquated books,
Their knowledge in such matters seem'd profound;
And they would preach of what did once abound,
Castles deep moated round, old haunted hall—
And something like to moats still 'camp the ground
Where beneath Cromwell's rage the towers did fall;
But ivy creeps the hill, and ruin hides it all.

And ancient songs he hung enraptur'd on,
Which herdsmen on a hill have sat to sing,
'Bout feats of Robin Hood and Little John,
Whose might was fear'd by country and by king,
Such strength had they to twitch the thrumming string;
Their darts oft suck'd the life-blood of the deer,
And Sherwood Forest with their horns did ring.
Ah, these were songs which he would joy to hear,
And these were such as warm'd when antique scenes appear.

But who can tell the anguish of his mind,
When reformation's formidable foes
With civil wars 'gainst nature's peace combin'd,
And desolation struck her deadly blows,
As curst improvement 'gan his fields inclose:
O greens, and fields, and trees, farewell, farewell!
His heart-wrung pains, his unavailing woes
No words can utter, and no tongue can tell,
When ploughs destroy'd the green, when groves of
    willows fell.

There once were springs when daisies' silver studs
Like sheets of snow on every pasture spread;
There once were summers when the crow-flower buds
Like golden sunbeams brightest lustre shed;
And trees grew once that shelter'd Lubin's head;
There once were brooks sweet whimpering down the vale:
The brook's no more—kingcup and daisy fled;
Their last fall'n tree the naked moors bewail,
And scarce a bush is left to tell the mournful tale.

Yon flaggy tufts, and many a rushy knot
Existing still in spite of spade and plough,
As seeming fond and loath to leave the spot,
Tell where was once the green—brown fallows now,
Where Lubin often turns a sadden'd brow,
Marks the stopt brook, and mourns oppression's power,
And thinks how once he waded in each slough
To crop the yellow 'horse-blob's' early flower
Or catch the 'miller's-thumb' in summer's sultry hour.

There once were days, the woodman knows it well,
When shades e'en echoed with the singing thrush;
There once were hours, the ploughman's tale can tell,
When morning's beauty wore its earliest blush,
How woodlarks caroll'd from each stumpy bush;
Lubin himself has mark'd them soar and sing:
The thorns are gone, the woodlark's song is hush,
Spring more resembles winter now than spring,
The shades are banish'd all—the birds have took to wing.

There once were lanes in nature's freedom dropt,
There once were paths that every valley wound—
Inclosure came, and every path was stopt;
Each tyrant fix'd his sign where paths were found,
To hint a trespass now who cross'd the ground:
Justice is made to speak as they command;
The high road now must be each stinted bound:
—Inclosure, thou'rt a curse upon the land,
And tasteless was the wretch who thy existence plann'd.

O England! boasted land of liberty,
With strangers still thou mayst thy title own,
But thy poor slaves the alteration see,
With many a loss to them the truth is known:
Like emigrating bird thy freedom's flown,
While mongrel clowns, low as their rooting plough,
Disdain thy laws to put in force their own;
And every village owns its tyrants now,
And parish-slaves must live as parish-kings allow.

Ye fields, ye scenes so dear to Lubin's eye,
Ye meadow-blooms, ye pasture-flowers, farewell!
Ye banish'd trees, ye make me deeply sigh—
Inclosure came, and all your glories fell:
E'en the old oak that crown'd yon rifled dell,
Whose age had made it sacred to the view,
Not long was left his children's fate to tell;
Where ignorance and wealth their course pursue,
Each tree must tumble down—old 'Lea-close Oak,' adieu!

Lubin beheld it all, and, deeply pain'd,
Along the paled road would muse and sigh,
The only path that freedom's rights maintain'd;
The naked scenes drew pity from his eye,
Tears dropt to memory of delights gone by;
The haunts of freedom, cowherd's wattled bower,
And shepherds' huts, and trees that tower'd high,
And spreading thorns that turn'd a summer shower,
All captives lost, and past to sad oppression's power.

And oft with shepherds he would sit, to sigh
O'er past delights of many a bygone day,
And look on scenes now naked to the eye,
And talk as how they once were clothed gay,
And how the runnel wound its weedy way,
And how the willows on its margin grew;
Talk o'er with them the rural feats of May—
Who got the blossoms 'neath the morning dew
That the last garland made, and where such blossoms grew:

And how he could remember well, when he,
Laden with blooming treasures from the plain,
Has mixt with them beneath a dotterel-tree,
Driv'n from his cowslips by a hasty rain,
And heard them there sing each delightful strain;
And how with tales what joys they us'd to wake;
Wishing with them such days would come again:
They lov'd the artless boy for talking's sake,
And said some future day a wondrous man he'd make.

And you, poor ragged outcasts of the land,
That lug your shifting camps from green to green,
He lov'd to see your humble dwellings stand,
And thought your groups did beautify the scene:
Though blam'd for many a petty theft you've been,
Poor wandering souls, to fate's hard want decreed,
Doubtless too oft such acts your ways bemean;
But oft in wrong your foes 'gainst you proceed,
And brand a gipsy's camp when others do the deed.

Lubin would love to list their gibberish talk,
And view the oddity their ways display;
And oft with boys pursued his Sunday walk,
Where warp'd the camp beneath the willows grey,
And its black tenants on the greensward lay;
While, on two forked sticks with cordage tied,
Their pot o'er pilfer'd fuel boils away,
With food of sheep that of red-water died,
Or any nauseous thing their frowning fates provide.

Yet oft they gather money by their trade,
And on their fortune-telling art subsist:
Where her long-hurded groat oft brings the maid,
And secret slives it in the sibyl's fist
To buy good luck and happiness—to list,
What occupies a wench's every thought,
Who is to be the man: while, as she wist,
The gipsy's tale with swains and wealth is fraught,
The lass returns well-pleas'd, and thinks all cheaply bought.

In summer, Lubin oft has mark'd and seen
How eagerly the village-maids pursue
Their Sunday rambles where the camps have been;
And how they give their money to the crew
For idle stories they believe as true;
Crossing their hands with coin or magic stick,
How quak'd the young to hear what things they knew;
While old experienc'd dames saw through the trick,
Who said that all their skill was borrow'd from Old Nick.

And thus the superstitious dread their harm,
And dare not fail relieving the distrest,
Lest they within their cot should leave a charm,
To let naught prosper and bring on some pest:
Of depth of cunning gipsies are possest,
And when such weakness in a dame they find,
Forsooth they prove a terrifying guest;
And though not one to charity inclin'd,
They mutter black revenge, and force her to be kind.

His native scenes! O sweet endearing sound!
Sure never beats a heart, howe'er forlorn,
But the warm'd breast has soft emotions found
To cherish the dear spot where he was born:
E'en the poor hedger, in the early morn
Chopping the pattering bushes hung with dew,
Scarce lays his mitten on a branching thorn,
But painful memory's banish'd thoughts in view
Remind him, when 'twas young, what happy days he knew.

When the old shepherd with his woolly locks
Crosses the green, past joys his eyes will fill,
Where when a boy he us'd to tend his flocks;
Each fringed rushy bed and swelling hill,
Where he has play'd, or stretch'd him at his will,
Freshening anew in life's declining years,
Will jog his memory with its pleasures still.
Oh, how the thought his native scenes endears!
No spot throughout the world so pleasingly appears.

The toil-worn thresher, in his little cot
Whose roof did shield his birth, and still remains
His dwelling-place, how rough soe'er his lot,
His toil though hard, and small the wage he gains
That many a child most piningly maintains;
Send him to distant scenes and better fare,
How would his bosom yearn with parting-pains;
How would he turn and look, and linger there,
And wish e'en now his cot and poverty to share.

How dear the soldier feels the relic prove
Took from his cot or giv'n by love's sweet hand—
A box that bears the motto of true love;
How will he take his quid, and musing stand,
Think on his native lass and native land,
And bring to mind all those past joys again
From which wild youth so foolish was trepann'd,
Kissing the pledge that doth these ways retain,
While fancy points the spot far o'er the barring main.

O dear delightful spots, his native place!
How Lubin look'd upon the days gone by;
How he, though young, would past delights retrace,
Bend o'er gull'd holes where stood his trees, and sigh,
With tears the while bemoist'ning in his eye;
How look'd he for the green, a green no more;
Mourning to scenes that made him no reply,
Save the strong accents they in memory bore,
'Our scenes that charm'd thy youth are dead, to bloom
    no more.'

O samely naked leas, so bleak, so strange!
How would he wander o'er ye to complain,
And sigh, and wish he ne'er had known the change,
To see the ploughshare bury all the plain,
And not a cowslip on its lap remain;
The rush-tuft gone that hid the skylark's nest:
Ah, when will May-morn hear such strains again?
The storms beat chilly on its naked breast,
No shelter grows to shield, no home invites to rest.

'Ah,' would he sigh, 'ye, 'neath the churchyard grass,
Ye sleeping shepherds, could ye rise again,
And see what since your time has come to pass,
See not a bush nor willow now remain,
Looking and list'ning for the brook in vain—
Ye'd little think such was your natal scene;
Ye'd little now distinguish field from plain,
Or where to look for each departed green;
All plough'd and buried now, as though there naught had
    been.'

But still they beam'd with beauties on his eye;
No other scenes were half so sweet to view;
And other flowers but strove in vain to vie
With his few tufts that 'scap'd the wreck and grew;
And skylarks too their singing might pursue,
To claim his praise—he could but only say
Their songs were sweet but not like those he knew
That charm'd his native plains at early day,
Whose equals ne'er were found where'er his steps might
    stray.

When distant village feast or noisy fair
Short absence from his fields did him detain,
How would he feel when home he did repair,
And mix among his joys—the white-spire vane
Meeting his eye above the elms again:
Leaving his friends in the sweet summer-night,
No longer lost on unknown field or plain,
Far from the path with well-known haunts in sight,
He'd stray for scatter'd flowers with added new delight.

As travellers return'd from foreign ground
Feel more endearments for their native earth,
So Lubin cherish'd from each weary round
Still warmer fondness for those scenes of mirth,
Those plains, and that dear cot that gave him birth;
And oft this warmness for his fields he'd own,
Mix'd with his friends around the cottage-hearth,
Relating all the travels he had known,
And that he'd seen no spot so lovely as his own.

Nor has his taste with manhood e'er declin'd:
You still may see him on his lonely way,
O'er stile or gate in thoughtful mood reclin'd;
Or 'long the road with folded arms to stray,
Mixing with autumn's sighs or summer gay;
And curious, nature's secrets to explore,
Brushing the twigs of woods or copse away,
To roam the lonely shade so silent o'er,
Sweet muttering all his joys where clowns intrude no more.

Ah, who can tell the anxiousness of mind,
As now he doth to manhood's cares aspire:
The future blessings which he hopes to find,
The wisht-for prospects of his heart's desire,
And how chill fear oft damps the glowing fire,
And o'er hope's sunshine spreads a cloudy gloom:
Yet foil'd and foil'd, hopes still his songs inspire;
And, like the daisy on the cotter's tomb,
In melancholy scenes he 'joys his cheerless bloom.

He has his friends, compar'd to foes though few,
And like a cornflower in a field of grain
'Mong many a foe his wild weeds ope to view,
And malice mocks him with a rude disdain;
Proving pretensions to the muse as vain,
They deem her talents far beyond his skill,
And hiss his efforts as some forged strain:
But as hopes smile their tongues shall all be still,
E'en envy turns a friend when she's no power to kill.

Ah, as the traveller from the mountain-top
Looks down on misty kingdoms spread below,
And meditates beneath the steepy drop
What life and lands exist, and rivers flow;
How fain that hour the anxious soul would know
Of all his eye beholds—but 'tis in vain:
So Lubin eager views this world of woe,
And wishes time her secrets would explain,
If he may live for joys or sink in 'whelming pain.

162

Fate's close-kept thoughts within her bosom hide;
She is no gossip, secrets to betray:
Time's steady movements must her end decide,
And leave him painful still to hope the day,
And grope through ignorance his doubtful way,
By wisdom disregarded, fools annoy'd.
And if no worth anticipates the lay,
Then let his childish notions be destroy'd,
And he his time employ as erst it was employ'd.

HOLYWELL

NATURE, thou accept the song,
To thee the simple lines belong,
Inspir'd as brushing hill and dell
I stroll'd the way to Holywell.
Though 'neath young April's watery sky,
The sun gleam'd warm, and roads were dry;
And though the valleys, bush, and tree
Still naked stood, yet on the lea
A flush of green, and fresh'ning glow,
In melting patches 'gan to show
That swelling buds would soon again
In summer's livery bless the plain.
The thrushes too 'gan clear their throats,
And got by heart some two'r three notes
Of their intended summer-song,
To cheer me as I stroll'd along.
The wild heath triumph'd in its scenes
Of goss and ling's perpetual greens;
And just to say that spring was come,
The violet left its woodland home,
And, hermit-like, from storms and wind
Sought the best shelter it could find,
'Neath long grass banks, with feeble powers
Peeping faintly purple flowers:
While oft unhous'd from beds of ling

The fluskering pheasant took to wing,
And bobbing rabbits, wild and shy,
Their white tails glancing on the eye,
Just prick'd their long ears list'ning round,
And sought their coverts underground.
The heath was left, and then at will
A road swept gently round the hill,
From whose high crown, as soodling by,
A distant prospect cheer'd my eye,
Of closes green and fallows brown,
And distant glimpse of cot and town,
And steeple beck'ning on the sight,
By morning sunbeams painted white,
And darksome woods with shadings sweet,
To make the landscape round complete,
And distant waters glist'ning by,
As if the ground were patch'd with sky;
While on the blue horizon's line
The far-off things did dimly shine,
Which wild conjecture only sees,
And fancy moulds to clouds and trees,
Thinking, if thither she could fly,
She'd find the close of earth and sky;
But as we turn to look again
On nearest objects, wood and plain,
(So truths than fiction lovelier seem),
One warms as wak'ning from a dream.
From covert hedge, on either side,
The blackbirds flutter'd terrified,
Mistaking me for pilfering boy
That doth too oft their nests destroy;
And 'prink, prink, prink,' they took to wing,
In snugger shades to build and sing.
From tufted grass or bush, the hare
Oft sprung from her endanger'd lair;
Surprise was startled on her rout,
So near one's feet she bolted out.
The sun each tree-top mounted o'er,
And got church-steeple height or more:

And as I soodled on and on,
The ground was warm to look upon,
It e'en invited one to rest,
And have a nap upon its breast:
But thought upon my journey's end,
Where doubtful fancies did depend,
Urg'd on my lazy feet to roam,
Like truant school-boy kept from home,
I oped each gate with idle swing,
And stood to listen ploughmen sing;
While cracking whip and jingling gears
Recall'd the toils of boyish years,
When, like to them, I took my rounds
O'er elting moulds of fallow grounds—
With feet nigh shoeless, paddling through
The bitterest blasts that ever blew,
And napless beaver, weather'd brown,
That want oft wore without its crown:
A poor, unfriended, ragged boy,
Prest ere a child with man's employ.
'Tis past—'tis gone!—in musings lost
So thought I, leaning o'er the post;
And even jump'd with joy to see
Kind fate so highly favour me—
To clear the storms of boyish hours,
And manhood's opening strew with flowers;
To bid such hopes man's summer blow,
As boy's weak spring dare never sow;
And every day desires, at will,
To make each hope bloom brighter still.
With joys as sweet as heart could melt,
With feelings dear as e'er were felt,
I met at last, as like a spell,
The 'witching views of Holywell;
Where hills tower'd high their crowns with pride,
And vales dropp'd headlong by their side,
Bestriped with shades of green and gray,
The firdale and the naked spray;
While, underneath their mingling grains,

The river silver'd down the plains,
And bolted on the stranger's sight,
As stars blink out from clouds at night.
Beside the stream a cotter's shed
Low in the hollow heav'd its head:
Its tenants seem'd as snug to dwell
As lives a bee within its cell;
Its chimney-top high ash embowers;
Beside its wall the river pours
Its guggling sounds in whirling sweep,
That e'en might lull a child to sleep.
Before the door, untrod wi' pads,
The greensward many a beauty adds;
And daisy there, and cowslip too,
And buttercups of golden hue,
The children meet as soon as sought,
And gain their wish as soon as thought;
Who oft, I ween, the children's way,
Will leap the threshold's bounds to play,
And spite of parents' chiding calls
Will straggle where the water falls,
And 'neath the hanging bushes creep
For violet-bud and primrose-peep,
And sigh with anxious, eager dream,
For water-blobs amid the stream;
And up the hill-side turn anon,
To pick the daisies one by one:
Then anxious to their cottage bound,
To show the prize their searches found,
Whose medley flowers, red, white, and blue,
As well can please their parents too;
And as their care and skill contrive,
In flower-pots many a day survive.

Ah, thus conjecturing, musing still,
I cast a look from off the hill,
And loll'd me 'gainst a propping tree,
And thought for them as 'twas with me:
I did the same in April time,

And spoilt the daisy's earliest prime,
Robb'd every primrose root I met,
And oft-times got the root to set,
And joyful home each nosegay bore,
And felt—as I shall feel no more.

DESCRIPTION OF A THUNDERSTORM

SLOW boiling up, on the horizon's brim,
Huge clouds arise, mountainous, dark and grim,
Sluggish and slow upon the air they ride,
As pitch-black ships o'er the blue ocean glide;
Curling and hovering o'er the gloomy south,
As curls the sulphur from the cannon's mouth.
More grisly in the sun the tempest comes,
And through the wood with threatened vengeance hums,
Hissing more loud and loud among the trees:
The frighted wild-wind trembles to a breeze,
Just turns the leaf in terrifying sighs,
Bows to the spirit of the storm, and dies.
In wild pulsations beats the heart of fear,
At the low rumbling thunder creeping near,
Like as I've heard the river's flood, confined
Thro' the gulled locks, hang grumbling on the wind.[1]
The poplar leaf now resteth on its tree;
And the mill-sail, once twirling rapidly,
Lagging and lagging till each breeze had dropt,
Abruptly now in hesitation stopt.
The very cattle gaze upon the gloom,
And seemly dread the threatened fate to come.
The little birds sit mute within the bush,
And nature's very breath is stopt and hush.
The shepherd leaves his unprotected flock,
And flies for shelter in some scooping rock;
There hides in fear from the dread boding wrath,
Lest rocks should tremble when it sallies forth,

[1] Two lines supplied from MS.

And that Almighty Power, that bids it roar,
Hath seal'd the doom when time shall be no more.
The cotter's family cringe round the hearth,
Where all is sadden'd but the cricket's mirth:
The boys through fear in soot-black corner push,
And 'tween their father's knees for safety crush;
Each leaves his plaything on the brick-barr'd floor,
The idle top and ball can please no more,
And oft above the wheel's unceasing thrum
The murmur's heard to whisper—'Is it come?'
The clouds more dismal darken on the eye,
More huge, more fearful, and of deeper dye;
And, as unable to light up the gloom,
The sun drops sinking in its bulging tomb.
Now as one glizes skyward with affright,
Short vivid lightnings catch upon the sight;
While like to rumbling armies, as it were,
Th'approaching thunder mutters on the ear,
And still keeps creeping on more loud and loud,
And stronger lightnings splinter through the cloud.
An awe-struck monument of hope and fear,
Mute expectation waits the terror near,
That dreadful clap, that terminates suspense,
When ruin meets us or is banish'd hence.
The signal's giv'n in that explosive flash—
One moment's pause amid the clouds hell-black,
And then the red fire-bolt and horrid crash: [1]
Almighty, what a shock!—the jostled wrack
Of nature seems in mingled ruins done;
Astounded echo rives the terrors back,
And tingles on the ear a dying swoon.
Flash, peal, and flash still rend the melting cloud;
All nature seems to sigh her race is o'er,
And as she shrinks 'neath chaos' dismal shroud,
Gives meek consent that suns shall shine no more.
Where is the sinner now, with careless eye,
Will look, and say that all is chance's whim;
When hell e'en trembles at God's majesty,

[1] Two lines supplied from MS.

And sullen owns that naught can equal Him?
But clouds now melt like mercy into tears,
And nature's Lord His wrath in kindness stops:
Each trembling cotter now delighted hears
The rain fall down in heavy-pattering drops.
The sun 'gins tremble through the cloud again,
And a slow murmur wakes the delug'd plain;
A murmur of thanksgiving, mix'd with fear,
For God's great power and our deliverance here.

AUTUMN

THE summer-flower has run to seed,
    And yellow is the woodland bough;
And every leaf of bush and weed
    Is tipt with autumn's pencil now.

And I do love the varied hue,
    And I do love the browning plain;
And I do love each scene to view,
    That's mark'd with beauties of her reign.

The woodbine-trees red berries bear,
    That clustering hang upon the bower;
While, fondly lingering here and there,
    Peeps out a dwindling sickly flower.

The trees' gay leaves are turned brown,
    By every little wind undrest;
And as they flap and whistle down,
    We see the birds' deserted nest,

No thrush or blackbird meets the eye,
    Or fills the ear with summer's strain;
They but dart out for worm and fly,
    Then silent seek their rest again.

I—*G   169

Beside the brook, in misty blue,
  Bilberries glow on tendrils weak,
Where many a bare-foot splashes through,
  The pulpy, juicy prize to seek:

For 'tis the rustic boy's delight,
  Now autumn's sun so warmly gleams,
And these ripe berries tempt his sight,
  To dabble in the shallow streams.

And oft his rambles we may trace,
  Delv'd in the mud his printing feet,
And oft we meet a chubby face
  All stained with the berries sweet.

The cow-boy oft slives down the brook
  And tracks for hours each winding round,
While pinders, that such chances look,
  Drive his rambling cows to pound.

The woodland bowers, that us'd to be
  Lost in their silence and their shade,
Are now a scene of rural glee,
  With many a nutting swain and maid.

The scrambling shepherd with his hook,
  'Mong hazel boughs of rusty brown
That overhang some gulphing brook,
  Drags the ripen'd clusters down;

While, on a bank of faded grass,
  Some artless maid the prize receives;
And happy for the sun-tanned lass
  If nuts be all the shepherd gives.[1]

I love the year's decline, and love
  Through rustling yellow shades to range,
O'er stubble land, 'neath willow grove,
  To pause upon each varied change:

[1] MS. reading restored.

And oft have thought 'twas sweet, to list
  The stubbles crackling with the heat,
Just as the sun broke through the mist
  And warm'd the herdsman's rushy seat;

And grunting noise of rambling hogs,
  Where pattering acorns oddly drop;
And noisy bark of shepherds' dogs,
  The restless routs of sheep to stop;

While distant thresher's swingle drops
  With sharp and hollow-twanking raps;
And, nigh at hand, the echoing chops
  Of hardy hedger stopping gaps;

And sportsmen's trembling whistle-calls
  That stay the swift retreating pack;
And cow-boys' whoops, and squawking brawls,
  To urge the straggling heifer back.

Autumn-time, thy scenes and shades
  Are pleasing to the tasteful eye;
Though winter, when the thought pervades,
  Creates an ague-shivering sigh.

Grey-bearded rime hangs on the morn,
  And what's to come too true declares;
The ice-drop hardens on the thorn,
  And winter's starving bed prepares.

No music's heard the fields among;
  Save where the hedge-chats chittering play,
And ploughman drawls his lonely song,
  As cutting short the dreary day.

Now shatter'd shades let me attend,
  Reflecting look on their decline,
Where pattering leaves confess their end,
  In sighing flutterings hinting mine.

For every leaf that twirls the breeze
    May useful hints and lessons give;
The falling leaves and fading trees
    Will teach and caution us to live.

'Wandering clown,' they seem to say,
    'In us your coming end review:
Like you we liv'd, but now decay;
    The same sad fate approaches you.'

Beneath a yellow fading tree,
    As red suns light thee, autumn-morn,
In wildest raptures let me see
    The sweets that most thy charms adorn.

Oh, while my eye the landscape views,
    What countless beauties are display'd;
What varied tints of nameless hues—
    Shades endless melting into shade.

A russet red the hazels gain,
    As suited to their drear decline;
While maples brightest dress retain,
    And in the gayest yellows shine.

The poplar tree hath lost its pride;
    Its leaves in wan consumption pine;
They hoary turn on either side,
    And life to every gale resign.

The stubborn oak, with haughty pride
    Still in its lingering green, we view,
The strength he shows but vainly tried,
    Betinging slow with sickly hue.

The proudest triumph art conceives,
    Or beauties nature's power can crown,
Grey-bearded time in shatters leaves;
    Destruction's trample treads them down.

'Tis lovely now to turn one's eye,
    The changing face of heaven to mind;
How thin-spun clouds glide swiftly by,
    While lurking storms slow move behind.

Now suns are clear, now clouds pervade,
    Each moment chang'd, and chang'd again;
And first a light, and then a shade,
    Swift glooms and brightens o'er the plain.

Poor pussy through the stubble flies
    In vain, o'erpowering foes to shun;
The lurking spaniel points the prize,
    And pussy's harmless race is run.

The crowing pheasant in the brakes
    Betrays his lair with awkward squalls;
A certain aim the gunner takes,
    He clumsy fluskers up, and falls.

But hide thee, muse, the woods among,
    Nor stain thy artless, rural rhymes;
Go leave the murderer's wiles unsung,
    Nor mark the harden'd gunner's crimes.

The fields all clear'd, the labouring mice
    To sheltering hedge and wood patrol,
Where hips and haws for food suffice,
    That chumbled lie about their hole.

The squirrel, bobbing from the eye,
    Is busy now about his hoard,
And in old nest of crow or pie
    His winter-store is oft explor'd.

The leaves forsake the willow grey,
    And down the brook they whirl and wind;
So hopes and pleasures whirl away,
    And leave old age and pain behind.

The thorns and briers, vermilion-hue,
    Now full of hips and haws are seen;
If village-prophecies be true,
    They prove that winter will be keen.

The brook by hasty showers is swelled,
    Nor crumpling gravelly bottom shows;
Each rut, wi' muddy force impelled,
    A dribbling runnel chittering flows.[1]

Hark! started are some lonely strains:
    The robin-bird is urg'd to sing;
Of chilly evening he complains,
    And dithering droops his ruffled wing.

Slow o'er the wood the puddock sails;
    And mournful, as the storms arise,
His feeble note of sorrow wails
    To the unpitying, frowning skies.

More coldly blows the autumn-breeze;
    Old winter grins a blast between;
The north-winds rise and strip the trees,
    And desolation shuts the scene.

COWPER GREEN

Now eve's hours hot noon succeed;
And day's herald, wing'd with speed,
Flush'd with summer's ruddy face,
Hies to light some cooler place.
Now industry her hand has dropt,
And the din of labour's stopt:
Horses jingling in their gears,
Wagons ringing in one's ears,
Lumping flail and smacking whip,

[1] Stanza supplied from MS.

Boys' loud shouts of 'rose' and 'hip': [1]
All is silent, free from care,
The welcome boon of night to share.

Pleas'd I wander from the town,
Pester'd by the selfish clown,
Whose talk, though spun the night about,
Hogs, cows, and horses spin it out.
Far from these, so low, so vain,
Glad I wind me down the lane,
Where a deeper gloom pervades
'Tween the hedges' narrow shades,
Where a mimic night-hour spreads
'Neath the ash-grove's meeting heads.
Onward then I glad proceed,
Where the insect and the weed
Court my eye, as I pursue
Something curious, worthy view:
Chiefly, though, my wanderings bend
Where the ashen groves do end,
And their ceasing lights the scene
Of thy lov'd prospects, Cowper Green!

Though no rills with sandy sweep
Down thy shaggy borders creep,
Save as when thy rut-gull'd lanes
Run little brooks with hasty rains;
Though no yellow plains allow
Food on thee for sheep or cow,
Where on list'ning ears so sweet
Fall the mellow low and bleat,
Greeting, on eve's dewy gale,
Resting-fold and milking-pail;
Though not these adorn thy scene,
Still I love thee, Cowper Green!
Some may praise the grass-plat whims,
Which the gard'ner weekly trims,
And cut hedge and lawn adore,

[1] Preceding four lines added from MS.

175

Which his shears have smoothen'd o'er:
But give me to ponder still
Nature, when she blooms at will,
In her kindred taste and joy,
Wildness and variety;
Where the furze has leave to wreathe
Its dark prickles o'er the heath;
Where the grey-grown hawthorns spread
Foliag'd houses o'er one's head,
By the spoiling axe untouch'd;
Where the oak tree, gnarl'd and notch'd,
Lifts its deep-moss'd furrow'd side,
In nature's grandeur, nature's pride.
Such is still my favour'd scene,
When I seek thee, Cowper Green!
And full pleas'd would nature's child
Wander o'er the narrow wild;
Marking well thy shaggy head,
Where uncheck'd the brambles spread;
Where the thistle meets the sight,
With its down-head, cotton-white,
And the nettle, keen to view,
And hemlock with its gloomy hue;
Where the henbane too finds room
For its sickly-stinking bloom,
And full many a nameless weed,
Neglected, left to run to seed,
Seen but with disgust by those
Who judge a blossom by the nose.
Wildness is my suiting scene,
So I seek thee, Cowper Green!

Still thou oughtst to have thy meed,
To show thy flower as well as weed,
Though no fays from May-day's lap
Cowslips on thee care to drop,
Still does nature yearly bring
Fairest heralds of the spring:
On thy wood's warm sunny side

Primrose blooms in all its pride;
Violets carpet all thy bowers,
And anemone's weeping flowers,
Dyed in winter's snow and rime,
Constant to their early time,
White the leaf-strewn ground agen,
And make each wood a garden then.
Thine's full many a pleasing bloom
Of blossoms lost to all perfume:
Thine the dandelion flowers,
Gilt with dew, like suns with showers;
Hare-bells thine, and bugles blue,
And cuckoo-flowers all sweet to view;
Thy wild-woad on each road we see,
And medicinal betony,
By thy woodside-railing, reeves
With antique mullein's flannel-leaves.
These, though mean, the flowers of waste,
Planted here in nature's haste,
Display to the discerning eye
Her loved, wild variety:
Each has charms in nature's book
I cannot pass without a look.
And thou hast fragrant herbs and seed,
Which only garden's culture need:
Thy horehound tufts I love them well,
And ploughman's spikenard's spicy smell;
Thy thyme, strong-scented 'neath one's feet,
Thy marjoram-beds, so doubly sweet,
And pennyroyal's creeping twine,
These, each succeeding each, are thine,
Spreading o'er thee wild and gay,
Blessing spring, or summer's day.
As herb, flower, weed adorn thy scene,
Pleas'd I seek thee, Cowper Green.

And I oft zigzag me round
Thy uneven, heathy ground;
Here a knoll and there a scoop

Jostling down and clambering up,
Which the sandman's delving spade
And the pitman's picks have made,
Though many a year has o'er thee roll'd,
Since the grass first hid the mould,
And many a hole has delv'd thee still,
Since peace cloth'd each mimic hill:
Where the pitmen often find
Antique coins of various kind,
And, 'neath many a loosen'd block,
Unlid coffins in the rock,
Casting up the skull and bone
Heedless, as one hurls a stone:
Not a thought of battles by,
Bloody times of chivalry,
When each country's kingly lord
'Gainst his neighbour drew his sword,
And on many a hidden scene,
Now a hamlet, field, or green,
Waged his little bloody fight
To keep his freedom and his right:
And doubtless such was once the scene
Of thee, time-shrouded Cowper Green!
O how I love a glimpse to see
Of hoary, bald antiquity;
And often in my musings sigh,
Whene'er such relics meet my eye,
To think that history's early page
Should yield to black oblivion's rage,
And e'er without a mention made,
Resign them to his deadly shade,
Leaving conjecture but to pause,
That such and such might be the cause.

'Tis sweet the fragments to explore,
Time's so kind to keep in store,
Wrecks the cow-boy often meets
On the mole-hills' thymy seats,
When, by careless pulling weeds,

Chance unbares the shining beads,
That to tasteful minds display
Relics of the Druid day,
Opening on conjecturing eyes
Some lone hermit's paradise.
Doubtless oft, as here it might,
Where such relics meet the sight,
On that self-same spot of ground
Where the cow-boy's beads are found,
Hermits, fled from worldly care,
May have moss'd a cottage there,
Liv'd on herbs that there abound,
Food and physic doubly found:
Herbs, that have existence still
In every vale, on every hill—
Whose virtues only in them died,
As rural life gave way to pride.
Doubtless too oblivion's blot
Blacks some sacred lonely spot,
As, Cowper Green, in thee it may,
That once was thine in later day:
Thou mightst hide thy pilgrim then
From the plague of worldly men;
Thou mightst here possess thy cells,
Wholesome herbs, and pilgrim-wells;
And doubtlessly this very seat,
This thyme-capt hill beneath one's feet,
Might be, or nearly so, the spot
On which arose his lonely cot;
And on that existing bank,
Clothed in its sedges rank,
Grass might grow and mosses spread,
That thatch'd his roof and made his bed:
Yes, such might be; and such I love
To think and fancy, as I rove
O'er thy wood-encircled hill,
Like a world-shunning pilgrim still.

Now the dew-mists faster fall,

And the night her gloomy pall
Black'ning flings 'tween earth and sky,
Hiding all things from the eye;
Nor broken seam nor thin-spun screen
The moon can find to peep between:
Now thy unmolested grass,
Untouch'd even by the ass,
Spindled up its destin'd height,
Far too sour for sheep to bite,
Drooping hangs each feeble joint
With a glass knob on its point:
Fancy now shall leave the scene,
And bid good-night to Cowper Green.

THE GIPSY'S CAMP

How oft on Sundays, when I'd time to tramp,
My rambles led me to a gipsy's camp,
Where the real effigy of midnight hags,
With tawny smoked flesh and tatter'd rags,
Uncouth-brimm'd hat, and weather-beaten cloak,
'Neath the wild shelter of a knotty oak,
Along the greensward uniformly pricks
Her pliant bending hazel's arching sticks;
While round-topt bush, or brier-entangled hedge,
Where flag-leaves spring beneath, or ramping sedge,
Keep off the bothering bustle of the wind,
And give the best retreat she hopes to find.
How oft I've bent me o'er her fire and smoke,
To hear her gibberish tale so quaintly spoke,
While the old sibyl forc'd her boding clack,
Twin imps the meanwhile bawling at her back;
Oft on my hand her magic coin's been struck,
And hoping chink, she talk'd of morts of luck:
And still, as boyish hopes did first agree,
Mingled with fears to drop the fortune's fee,
I never fail'd to gain the honours sought,

And Squire and Lord were purchas'd with a groat.
But as man's unbelieving taste came round,
She furious stampt her shoeless foot aground,
Wip'd bye her soot-black hair with clenching fist,
While through her yellow teeth the spittle hist,
Swearing by all her lucky powers of fate,
Which like as footboys on her actions wait,
That fortune's scale should to my sorrow turn,
And I one day the rash neglect should mourn;
That good to bad should change, and I should be
Lost to this world and all eternity;
That poor as Job I should remain unblest;
  (Alas, for fourpence how my die is cast!)
Of not a hoarded farthing be possest,
  And when all's done, be shov'd to hell at last!

RECOLLECTIONS AFTER A RAMBLE

THE rosy day was sweet and young,
  The clod-brown lark that hail'd the morn
Had just his summer anthem sung,
  And trembling dropped in the corn;
The dew-rais'd flower was perk and proud,
  The butterfly around it play'd;
The skies blew clear, save woolly cloud
  That pass'd the sun without a shade.

On the pismire's castle hill,
  While the burnet-buttons quak'd,
While beside the stone-pav'd rill
  Cowslip bunches nodding shak'd,
Bees in every peep did try,
  Great had been the honey shower,
Soon their load was on their thigh,
  Yellow dust as fine as flour.

Brazen magpies, fond of clack,
    Full of insolence and pride,
Chattering on the donkey's back
    Percht, and pull'd his shaggy hide;
Odd crows settled on the pad,
    Dames from milking trotting home
Said no sign was half so sad,
    And shook their heads at ills to come.

While cows restless from the ground
    Plung'd into the stream and drank,
And the rings went whirling round,
    Till they toucht the flaggy bank,
On the arch's wall I knelt,
    Curious, as I often did,
To see the words the sculpture spelt,
    But the moss its letters hid.

Labour sought the water cool,
    And stretching took a hearty sup,
The fish were playing in the pool,
    And turn'd their milk-white bellies up;
Clothes laid down behind a bush,
    Boys were wading near the pad,
Deeply did the maiden blush
    As she pass'd each naked lad.

Some with lines the fish to catch,
    Quirking boys let loose from school,
Others 'side the hedgerow watch,
    Where the linnet took the wool:
'Tending Hodge had slept too fast,
    While his cattle stray'd abroad,
Swift the freed horse gallop'd past,
    Pattering down the stony road.

The gipsies' tune was loud and strong,
    As round the camp they danc'd a jig,
And much I lov'd the brown girl's song,
    While list'ning on the wooden brig;

The shepherd, he was on his rounds,
  The dog stopt short to lap the stream,
And jingling in the fallow grounds
  The ploughman urg'd his reeking team.

Often did I stop to gaze
  On each spot once dear to me,
Known 'mong those remember'd days
  Of banish'd, happy infancy:
Often did I view the shade
  Where once a nest my eyes did fill,
And often mark'd the place I play'd
  At 'roly-poly' down the hill.

In the wood's deep shade did stand,
  As I pass'd, the sticking-troop;
And Goody begg'd a helping hand
  To heave her rotten faggot up:
The riding-gate, sharp jerking round,
  Follow'd fast my heels again,
While echo mockt the clapping sound,
  And 'clap, clap,' sang the woods amain.

The wood is sweet—I love it well,
  In spending there my leisure hours,
To seek the snail its painted shell,
  And look about for curious flowers;
Or 'neath the hazel's leafy thatch,
  On a stulp or mossy ground,
Little squirrel's gambols watch,
  Dancing oak trees round and round.

Green was the shade—I love the woods,
  When autumn's wind is mourning loud,
To see the leaves float on the floods,
  Dead within their yellow shroud:
The wood was then in glory spread—
  I love the browning bough to see
That litters autumn's dying bed—
  Her latest sigh is dear to me.

'Neath a spreading shady oak
    For a while to muse I lay;
From its grains a bough I broke,
    To fan the teasing flies away:
Then I sought the woodland side,
    Cool the breeze my face did meet,
And the shade the sun did hide;
    Though 'twas hot, it seemed sweet.

And as while I clomb the hill,
    Many a distant charm I found,
Pausing on the lagging mill,
    That scarcely mov'd its sails around,
Hanging o'er a gate or stile,
    Till my curious eye did tire,
Leisure was employ'd awhile,
    Counting many a peeping spire.

While the hot sun 'gan to wane,
    Cooling glooms fast deep'ning still,
Refreshing greenness spread the plain,
    As black clouds crept the southern hill;
Labour sought a sheltering place,
    'Neath some thick wood-woven bower,
While odd rain-drops dampt his face,
    Heralds of the coming shower.

Where the oak-plank cross'd the stream,
    Which the early-rising lass
Climbs with milk-pail gathering cream,
    Crook'd paths tracking through the grass:
There, where willows hing their boughs,
    Briers and blackthorns form'd a bower
Stunted thick by sheep and cows—
    There I stood to shun the shower.

Sweet it was to feel the breeze
    Blowing cool without the sun,
Bumming gad-flies ceas'd to tease,
    All seem'd glad the shower to shun:

Sweet it was to mark the flower,
　Rain-drops glist'ning on its head,
Perking up beneath the bower,
　As if rising from the dead.

And full sweet it was to look,
　How clouds misted o'er the hill,
Rain-drops how they dimpt the brook,
　Falling fast and faster still;
While the gudgeons sturting by
　Cring'd 'neath water-grasses' shade,
Startling as each nimble eye
　Saw the rings the dropples made.

And upon the dripping ground,
　As the shower had ceas'd again,
As the eye was wandering round,
　Trifling troubles caus'd a pain;
Overtaken in the shower,
　Bumble-bees I wander'd by,
Clinging to the drowking flower,
　Left without the power to fly:

And full often, drowning wet,
　Scampering beetles rac'd away,
Safer shelter glad to get,
　Drownded out from whence they lay:
While the moth, for night's reprief,
　Waited safe and snug withal
'Neath the plantain's bowery leaf,
　Where not e'en a drop could fall.

Then the clouds dispers'd again,
　And full sweet it was to view
Sunbeams, trembling long in vain,
　Now they 'gan to glimmer through:
And as labour strength regains
　From ale's booning bounty given,
So reviv'd the fresh'ning plains
　From the smiling showers of heaven.

Sweet the birds did chant their songs,
    Blackbird, linnet, lark, and thrush;
Music from a many tongues
    Melted from each dripping bush:
Deafen'd echo, on the plain,
    As the sunbeams broke the cloud,
Scarce could help repeat the strain,
    Nature's anthem flow'd so loud.

What a fresh'ning feeling came,
    As the sun's smile gleam'd again;
Sultry summer wa'n't the same,
    Such a mildness swept the plain;
Breezes, such as one would seek,
    Cooling infants of the shower,
Fanning sweet the burning cheek,
    Trembled through the bramble-bower.

Insects of mysterious birth
    Sudden struck my wondering sight,
Doubtless brought by moisture forth,
    Hid in knots of spittle white;
Backs of leaves the burthen bear,
    Where the sunbeams cannot stray,
'Wood-seers' call'd, that wet declare,
    So the knowing shepherds say.

As the cart-rut rippled down
    With the burden of the rain,
Boys came drabbling from the town,
    Glad to meet their sports again;
Stopping up the mimic rills,
    Till they forc'd their frothy bound,
Then the keck-made water-mills
    In the current whisk'd around.

Once again did memory pain
    O'er the life she once had led;
Once did manhood wish again
    Childish joys had never fled:

'Could I lay these woes aside
    Which I long have murmur'd o'er,
Mix a boy with boys,' I sigh'd,
    'Fate should then be teas'd no more.'

Hot the sun in summer warms,
    Quick the roads dry o'er the plain:
Girls, with baskets on their arms,
    Soon renew'd their sports again;
O'er the green they sought their play,
    Where the cowslip-bunches grew,
Quick the rush-bent fann'd away,
    As they danc'd and bounded through.

Some went searching by the wood,
    Peeping 'neath the weaving thorn,
Where the pouch-lipp'd cuckoo-bud
    From its snug retreat was torn;
Where the ragged-robin grew
    With its pip'd stem streak'd with jet,
And the crow-flower's golden hue
    Careless plenty easier met.

Some, with many an anxious pain
    Childish wishes to pursue,
From the pond-head gaz'd in vain
    On the flag-flower's yellow hue,
Smiling in its safety there,
    Sleeping o'er its shadow'd blow,
While the flood's triumphing care
    Crimpled round its root below.

Then I stood to pause again;
    Retrospection sigh'd and smil'd,
Musing, 'tween a joy and pain,
    How I acted when a child;
When by clearing brooks I've been,
    Where the painted sky was given,
Thinking, if I tumbled in,
    I should fall direct to heaven.

Many an hour had come and gone
    Since the town last met my eye,
Where, huge baskets mauling on,
    Maids hung out their clothes to dry;
Granny there was on the bench,
    Coolly sitting in the swale,
Stopping oft a love-sick wench,
    To pinch her snuff, and hear her tale.

Be the journey e'er so mean,
    Passing by a cot or tree,
In the route there's something seen
    Which the curious love to see;
In each ramble, taste's warm souls
    More of wisdom's self can view
Than blind ignorance beholds
    All life's seven stages through.

SUNDAY

THE Sabbath-day, of every day the best,
The poor man's happiness, a poor man sings;
When labour has no claim to break his rest,
And the light hours fly swift on easy wings.
What happiness this holy morning brings,
How soft its pleasures on his senses steal;
How sweet the village-bells' first warning rings;
And oh, how comfortable does he feel,
When with his family at ease he takes his early meal.

The careful wife displays her frugal hoard,
And both partake in comfort though they're poor;
While love's sweet offsprings crowd the lowly board,
Their little likenesses in miniature.
Though through the week he labour does endure,
And weary limbs oft cause him to complain,
This welcome morning always brings a cure;
It teems with joys his soul to entertain,
And doubly sweet appears the pleasure after pain.

Ah, who can tell the bliss, from labour freed,
His leisure meeteth on a Sunday morn,
Fix'd in a chair, some godly book to read,
Or wandering round to view the crops of corn,
In best clothes fitted out, and beard new shorn,
Dropping adown in some warm shelter'd dell,
With six days' labour weak and weary worn,
List'ning around each distant chiming bell,
That on the soft'ning breeze melodiously doth swell.

And oft he takes his family abroad
In short excursions o'er the field and plain,
Marking each little object on his road,
An insect, sprig of grass, and ear of grain;
Endeavouring thus most simply to maintain
That the same Power that bids the mite to crawl,
That browns the wheat-lands with their summer-stain,
That Power which form'd the simple flower withal,
Form'd all that lives and grows upon this earthly ball.

The bell, when knoll'd its summons once and twice,
Now chimes in concert, calling all to prayers;
The rustic boy that hankers after vice
And of religion little knows or cares
Scrambs up his marbles, and by force repairs,
Though dallying on till the last bell has rung:
The good man there his book devoutly bears,
And often, as he walks the graves among,
Looks on the untravell'd dust from whence his being sprung.

The service ended, boys their play resume
In some snug corner from the parson's view,
And where the searching clerk forgets to come;
There they their games and rural sports pursue,
With chuck and marbles wearing Sunday through;
The poor man seeks his cottage-hearth again,
And brings his family the text to view
From which the parson's good discourse was ta'en,
Which with what skill he may he labours to explain.

Hail, sacred Sabbath! hail, thou poor man's joy!
Thou oft hast been a comfort to my care,
When faint and weary with the week's employ
I met thy presence in my corner-chair,
Musing and bearing up with troubles there;
Thrice hail, thou heavenly boon! by God's decree
At first creation plann'd, that all might share,
Both man and beast, some hours from labour free,
To offer thanks to Him whose mercy sent us thee.

This day the field a sweeter clothing wears,
A Sunday scene looks brighter to the eye;
And hast'ning on to Monday morning's cares
With double speed the wing'd hour gallops by.
How swift the sun streaks down the western sky,
Scarcely perceiv'd till it begins to wane,
When ploughboys mark his setting with a sigh,
Dreading the morn's approaching hours with pain,
When capon's restless calls awake to toil again.

As the day closes on its peace and rest,
The godly man sits down and takes 'the book,'
To close it in a manner deem'd the best;
And for a suiting chapter doth he look,
That may for comfort and a guide be took:
He reads of patient Job, his trials' thrall,
How men are troubled when by God forsook,
And prays with David to bear up with all;
When sleep shuts up the scene, soft as the nightdews fall.

SOLITUDE

Now as even's warning bell
Rings the day's departing knell,
Leaving me from labour free,
Solitude, I'll walk with thee:

Whether 'side the woods we rove,
Or sweep beneath the willow grove;
Whether sauntering we proceed
'Cross the green, or down the mead;
Whether, sitting down, we look
On the bubbles of the brook;
Whether, curious, waste an hour,
Pausing o'er each tasty flower;
Or, expounding nature's spells,
From the sand pick out the shells;
Or, while lingering by the streams,
Where more sweet the music seems,
Listen to the soft'ning swells
Of some distant chiming bells
Mellowing sweetly on the breeze,
Rising, falling by degrees,
Dying now, then wak'd again
In full many a 'witching strain,
Sounding, as the gale flits by,
Flats and sharps of melody.

Sweet it is to wind the rill,
Sweet with thee to climb the hill,
On whose lap the bullock free
Chews his cud most placidly;
Or o'er fallows bare and brown
Beaten sheep-tracks wander down,
Where the mole unwearied still
Roots up many a crumbling hill,
And the little chumbling mouse
Gnarls the dead weed for her house,
While the plough's unfeeling share
Lays full many a dwelling bare;
Where the lark with russet breast
'Hind the big clod hides her nest,
And the black snail's founder'd pace
Finds from noon a hiding-place,
Breaking off the scorching sun
Where the matted twitches run.

Solitude! I love thee well,
Brushing through the wilder'd dell,
Picking from the ramping grass
Nameless blossoms as I pass,
Which the dews of eve bedeck,
Fair as pearls on woman's neck;
Marking shepherds rous'd from sleep
Blundering off to fold their sheep,
And the swain, with toils distrest,
Hide his tools to seek his rest:
While the cows, with hobbling strides,
Twitching slow their fly-bit hides,
Rub the pasture's creaking gate,
Milking maids and boys to wait.
Or as sunshine leaves the sky,
As the daylight shuts her eye,
Sweet it is to meet the breeze
'Neath the shade of hawthorn trees,
By the pasture's wilder'd round,
Where the pismire hills abound,
Where the blushing fin-weed's flower
Closes up at even's hour:
Leaving then the green behind,
Narrow hoof-plod lanes to wind,
Oak and ash embower'd beneath,
Leading to the lonely heath,
Where the unmolested furze
And the burdock's clinging burs,
And the briers, by freedom sown,
Claim the wilder'd spots their own.

There while we the scene survey
Deck'd in nature's wild array,
Swell'd with ling-clad hillocks green
Suiting the disorder'd scene,
Haply we may rest us then
In the banish'd herdsman's den;
Where the wattled hulk is fixt,
Propt some double oak betwixt,

Where the swain the branches lops,
And o'erhead with rushes tops;
Where, with woodbine's sweet perfume,
And the rose's blushing bloom,
Loveliest ceiling of the bower,
Arching in, peeps many a flower;
While a hill of thyme so sweet,
Or a moss'd stone, forms a seat.
There, as 'tween-light hangs the eve,
I will watch thy bosom heave;
Marking then the darksome flows
Night's gloom o'er thy mantle throws;
Fondly gazing on thine eye
As it rolls its ecstasy,
When thy solemn musings caught
Tell thy soul's absorb'd in thought;
When thy finely folded arm
O'er thy bosom beating warm
Wraps thee melancholy round;
And thy ringlets wild unbound
On thy lily shoulders lie,
Like dark streaks in morning's sky.
Peace and silence sit with thee,
And peace alone is heaven to me:
While the moonlight's infant hour
Faint 'gins creep to gild the bower,
And the wattled hedge gleams round
Its diamond shadows on the ground.
Oh, thou soothing Solitude,
From the vain and from the rude,
When this silent hour is come,
And I meet thy welcome home,
What balm is thine to troubles deep,
As on thy breast I sink to sleep;
What bliss on even's silence flows,
When thy wish'd opiate brings repose.

    And I have found thee wondrous sweet,
Sheltering from the noon-day heat,

As 'neath hazels I have stood
In the gloomy hanging wood,
Where the sunbeams, filtering small,
Freckling through the branches fall;
And the flapping leaf the ground
Shadows, flitting round and round:
Where the glimmering streamlets wreathe
Many a crooked root beneath,
Unseen gliding day by day
O'er their solitary way,
Smooth or rough, as onward led
Where the wild-weed dips its head,
Murmuring—dribbling drop by drop
When dead leaves their progress stop—
Or winding sweet their restless way
While the frothy bubbles play.
And I love thy presence drear
In such wildernesses, where
Ne'er an axe was heard to sound,
Or a tree's fall gulsh'd the ground,
Where (as if that spot could be)
First foot-mark'd the ground by me,
All is still, and wild, and gay,
Left as at creation's day.
Pleasant too it is to look
For thy steps in shady nook,
Where, by hedge-side coolly led,
Brooks curl o'er their sandy bed,
On whose tide the clouds reflect,
In whose margin flags are freckt;
Where the waters, winding blue,
Single-arch'd brig flutter through,
While the willow-branches grey
Damp the sultry eye of day,
And in whispers mildly sooth
Chafe the mossy keystone smooth;
Where the banks, beneath them spread,
Level in an easy bed;
While the wild-thyme's pinky bells

Circulate reviving smells;
And the breeze, with feather-feet,
Crimping o'er the waters sweet,
Trembling fans the sun-tann'd cheek,
And gives the comfort one would seek.
Stretching there in soft repose,
Far from peace and freedom's foes,
In a spot, so wild, so rude,
Dear to me is solitude!
Soothing then to watch the ground—
Every insect flitting round,
Such as painted summer brings—
Lady-fly with freckled wings,
Watch her up the tall bent climb;
And from knotted flowers of thyme,
Where the woodland banks are deckt,
See the bee his load collect;
Mark him turn the petals by,
Gold dust gathering on his thigh,
As full many a hum he heaves,
While he pats th'intruding leaves,
Lost in many a heedless spring,
Then wearing home on heavy wing.

But when sorrows more oppress,
When the world brings more distress,
Wishing to despise as then
Brunts of fate, and scorn of men;
When fate's demons thus intrude,
Then I seek thee, Solitude,
Where the abbey's height appears
Hoary 'neath a weight of years;
Where the mouldering walls are seen
Hung with pellitory green;
Where the steeple's taper stretch
Tires the eye its length to reach,
Dizzy, nauntling high and proud,
Top-stone losing in a cloud;
Where the cross, to time resign'd,

Creaking harshly in the wind,
Crowning high the rifted dome,
Points the pilgrim's wish'd-for home;
While the look fear turns away,
Shuddering at its dread decay.
There let me my peace pursue
'Neath the shades of gloomy yew,
Doleful hung with mourning green,
Suiting well the solemn scene;
There, that I may learn to scan
Mites illustrious, called man,
Turn with thee the nettles by
Where the grave-stone meets the eye,
Soon, full soon to read and see
That all below is vanity;
And man, to me a galling thing,
Own'd creation's lord and king,
A minute's length, a zephyr's breath,
Sport of fate, and prey of death,
Tyrant to-day, to-morrow gone,
Distinguish'd only by a stone,
That fain would have the eye to know
Pride's better dust is lodg'd below—
While worms like me are mouldering laid,
With nothing set to say 'they're dead'—
All the difference, trifling thing,
That notes at last the slave and king.
As wither'd leaves, life's bloom when stopt,
That drop in autumn, so they dropt;
As snails, which in their painted shell
So snugly once were known to dwell,
When in the schoolboy's care we view
The pleasing toys of varied hue,
By age or accident are flown,
The shell left empty, tenant gone—
So pass we from the world's affairs,
And careless vanish from its cares;
So leave, with silent, long farewell,
Vain life—as left the snail his shell.

All this when there my eyes behold
On every stone and heap of mould,
Solitude, though thou art sweet,
Solemn art thou then to meet;
When with list'ning pause I look
Round the pillar's ruin'd nook,
Glooms revealing, dim descried,
Ghosts, companion'd by thy side;
Where in old deformity
Ancient arches sweep on high,
And the aisles, to light unknown,
Create a darkness all their own;
Save the moon, as on we pass,
Splinters through the broken glass,
Or the torn roof, patch'd with cloud,
Or the crack'd wall, bulg'd and bow'd—
Glimmering faint along the ground,
Shooting solemn and profound,
Lighting up the silent gloom
Just to read an ancient tomb,
'Neath where, as it gliding creeps
We may see some abbot sleeps;
And as on we mete the aisle,
Daring scarce to breathe the while
Soft as creeping feet can fall,
While the damp green-stained wall
Swift the startled ghost flits by,
Mocking murmurs faintly sigh,
Reminding our intruding fear
Such visits are unwelcome here.
Seemly then, from hollow urn,
Gentle steps our steps return;
E'er so soft and e'er so still,
Check our breath or how we will,
List'ning spirits still reply
Step for step, and sigh for sigh,
Murmuring o'er one's weary woe,
Such as once 'twas theirs to know,
They whisper to such slaves as me,

A buried tale of misery:
'We once had life, ere life's decline,
Flesh, blood, and bones, the same as thine;
We knew its pains, and shar'd its grief,
Till death, long wish'd-for, brought relief;
We had our hopes, and like to thee,
Hoped morrow's better day to see,
But like to thine, our hope the same,
To-morrow's kindness never came:
We had our tyrants, e'en as thou;
Our wants met many a scornful brow;
But death laid low their wealthy powers,
Their harmless ashes mix with ours:
And this vain world, its pride, its form,
That treads on thee as on a worm,
Its mighty heirs—the time shall be
When they as quiet sleep by thee!'

Oh, here's thy comfort, Solitude,
When overpowering woes intrude!
Then thy sad, thy solemn dress
Owns the balm my soul to bless;
Here I judge the world aright,
Here see vain man in his true light,
Learn patience, in this trying hour,
To gild life's brambles with a flower,
Take pattern from the hints thou'st given,
And follow in thy steps to heaven.

THE WOODMAN

DEDICATED TO THE REV. J. KNOWLES HOLLAND

THE beating snow-clad bell, with sounding dead,
Hath clanked four—the woodman's wak'd again;
And, as he leaves his comfortable bed,
Dithers to view the rimy feather'd pane,
And shrugs, and wishes—but 'tis all in vain:

The bed's warm comforts he must now forgo;
His family, that oft till eight hath lain,
Without his labour's wage could not do so,
And glad to make them blest he shuffles through the snow.

The early winter's morn is dark as pitch,
The wary wife, from tinder brought at night,
With flint and steel and many a sturdy twitch,
Sits up in bed to strike her man a light;
And as the candle shows the rapturous sight,
Aside his wife his rosy sleeping boy,
He smacks his lips with exquisite delight,
With all a father's feelings, father's joy,
Then bids his wife good-bye, and hies to his employ.

His breakfast water-porridge, humble food;
A barley crust he in his wallet flings;
On this he toils and labours in the wood,
And chops his faggot, twists his band, and sings,
As happily as princes and as kings
With all their luxury—and blest is he,
Can but the little which his labour brings
Make both ends meet, and from long debts keep free,
And neat and clean preserve his numerous family.

Far o'er the dreary fields the woodland lies,
Rough is the journey which he daily goes;
The woolly clouds, that hang the frowning skies,
Keep winnowing down their drifting sleet and snows,
And thro' his doublet keen the north wind blows;
While hard as iron the cemented ground,
And smooth as glass the glibbed pool is froze;
His nailed boots with clenching tread rebound,
And dithering echo starts, and mocks the clamping sound.

The woods how gloomy in a winter's morn!
The crows and ravens even cease to croak,
The little birds sit chittering on the thorn,
The pies scarce chatter when they leave the oak,

Startled from slumber by the woodman's stroke;
The milkmaid's song is drown'd in gloomy care,
And, while the village chimneys curl their smoke,
She milks, and blows, and hastens to be there;
And nature all seems sad, and dying in despair.

The squirking rabbit scarcely leaves her hole,
But rolls in torpid slumbers all the day;
The fox is loath to 'gin a long patrol,
And scouts the woods, content with meaner prey;
The hare so frisking, timid once, and gay,
'Hind the dead thistle hurkles from the view,
Nor scarce is scar'd though in the traveller's way,
Though waffling curs and shepherd-dogs pursue;
So winter's rugged power affects all nature through.

What different changes winter's frowns supply:
The clown no more a loitering hour beguiles,
Nor gaping tracks the clouds along the sky,
As when buds blossom, and the warm sun smiles,
And 'Lawrence wages bids' on hills and stiles;
Banks, stiles, and flowers, and skies, no longer charm;
Deep drifting snow each summer-seat defiles;
With hasty blundering step and folded arm
He glad the stable seeks, his frost-nipt nose to warm.

The shepherd haunts no more his spreading oak,
Nor on the sloping pond-head lies at lair;
The arbour he once wattled up is broke,
And left unworthy of his future care;
The ragged plundering stickers have been there,
And pilfer'd it away: he passes by
His summer dwelling, desolate and bare,
And ne'er so much as turns a conscious eye,
But gladly seeks his fire, and shuns th'inclement sky.

The scene is cloth'd in snow from morn till night,
The woodman's loath his chilly tools to seize;
The crows, unroosting as he comes in sight,

Shake down the feathery burthen from the trees;
To look at things around he's fit to freeze:
Scar'd from her perch the fluttering pheasant flies;
His hat and doublet whiten by degrees,
He quakes, looks round, and pats his hands and sighs,
And wishes to himself that the warm sun would rise.

And be the winter cutting as it will,
Let north winds winnow fit to nip one through,
In the deep woods hard fate demands him still
To stand the bitterest blasts that ever blew,
When trees instead of leaves and pearly dew
In rime and snow and icicles abound;
The proverb 'use is second nature''s true
It must be so, or how would he be found
To weather out the blast and daily stand his ground?

And yet tho' fortune frowns upon the poor
And dooms their lives to slavish hard employ,
Tho' wealth for ever 'gainst them shuts her door
And strives their fainting wishes to destroy,
Yet still, poor souls, they have a glimpse of joy,
A sugared charm still sweets the sours of fate,
Their sparing bliss, when met, does never cloy,
While overmuch does pall the idly great
As rich and sumptuous food does surfeitings create.

Good luck, it is his providential wealth
That hardy labour and the 'freshing air
Should 'crease his strength and keep entire his health
And ne'er let illness on his soul despair;
Wi' wife and children 'pending on his care,
What would he do a livelihood to gain?
The parish money's but a pining fare;
Such scouts' benevolence he does disdain
Who grudge e'en what they give and mock the poor man's pain.

But if unwell from toil he's forced to stop,
He quickly then repairs to medicine's aid,
Tho' not to nauseates of the druggist's shop

Or cant advice of doctor's mystic trade,
But to such drugs as daily are displayed
E'en round his walks and cottage door profuse—
Self-heal and agrimony which has made
Full many a huswife wondrous cures produce—
These he in summer seeks and hurds up for his use.[1]

The robin, tamest of the feather'd race,
Soon as he hears the woodman's sounding chops,
With ruddy bosom and a simple face
Around his old companion fearless hops,
And there for hours in pleas'd attention stops:
The woodman's heart is tender and humane,
And at his meals he many a crumble drops.
Thanks to thy generous feelings, gentle swain;
And what thy pity gives, shall not be given in vain.

The woodman gladly views the closing day,
To see the sun drop down behind the wood,
Sinking in clouds deep blue or misty grey,
Round as a foot-ball and as red as blood:
The pleasing prospect does his heart much good,
Though 'tis not his such beauties to admire;
He hastes to fill his bags with billet-wood,
Well-pleas'd from the chill prospect to retire,
To seek his corner chair, and warm snug cottage fire.

And soon as dusky even hovers round,
And the white frost 'gins crizzle pond and brook,
The little family are squinting round,
And from the door dart many a wistful look;
The supper's ready stewing on the hook,
And every foot that clampers down the street
Is for the coming father's step mistook;
O'erjoy'd are they when he their eyes does meet,
Bent 'neath his load, snow-clad, as white as any sheet.

I think I see him seated in his chair,
Taking the bellows up the fire to blow;

1 Preceding four stanzas added from MS.

I think I hear him joke and chatter there,
Telling his children news they wish to know;
With leather leggings on, that stopt the snow,
And broad-brimm'd hat uncouthly shapen round:
Nor would he, I'll be bound, if it were so,
Give twopence for the chance, could it be found,
At that same hour to be the king of England crown'd.

The woodman smokes, the brats in mirth and glee
And artless prattle even's hours beguile,
While love's last pledge runs scrambling up his knee,
The nightly comfort from his weary toil,
His chuff cheeks dimpling in a fondling smile;
He claims his kiss, and says his scraps of prayer,
Begging his daddy's pretty song the while,
Playing with his jacket-buttons and his hair—
And thus in wedlock's joys the labourer drowns his care.

His pipe puff'd out, he edges in his chair
And stirs the embers up, his hands to warm;
And with his singing book he does repair
To humming o'er an anthem, hymn, or psalm;
Nor does he think a ballad any harm,
But often carols o'er his cottage hearth
Bold Robin Hood, The Shipwreck, or The Storm.
Oh, where we find this social joy and mirth,
There we may truly say that heaven exists on earth.

The clock when eight warns all for bed prepare;
The children still an extra minute crave
And sawn and stammer longer o'er their prayer;
And they such tempting fond excuses have,
The 'dulging father oft the boon has gave
And sung again the younkers to delight;
And ever hard-earned farthing glad to save,
The careful wife puts out the candle light,
And o'er the fire the song and tale make sweet the winter's
  night.[1]

[1] Preceding two stanzas added from MS.

And as most labourers knowingly pretend
By certain signs to judge the weather right,
As oft from 'Noah's ark' great floods descend,
And burrèd moons foretell great storms at night,
In such-like things the woodman took delight;
And ere he went to bed would always ken
Whether the sky was gloom'd or stars shone bright,
Then went to comfort's arms till morn, and then
As cheery as the sun resum'd his toils agen.

And ere he slept he always breath'd a prayer,
'I thank thee, Lord, that thou to-day didst give
Sufficient strength to toil; I bless thy care,
And thank thee still for what I may receive:
And, O Almighty God! while I still live,
Ere my eyes open on the last day's sun,
Perpare thou me this wicked world to leave,
And fit my passage ere my race is run;
'Tis all I beg, O Lord! thy heavenly will be done.'

Holland! to thee this humble ballad's sent,
Who for the poor man's welfare oft hast pray'd,
Whose tongue did ne'er belie its good intent,
Preacher, as well in practice, as in trade—
Alas, too often money's business made!
Oh, may the wretch, that's still in darkness living,
The Bible's comforts hear by thee display'd;
And many a woodman's family, forgiven,
Have cause for blessing thee that led their way to heaven.

RURAL MORNING

Soon as the twilight through the distant mist
In silver hemmings skirts the purple east,
Ere yet the sun unveils his smiles to view
And dries the morning's chilly robes of dew,
Young Hodge the horse-boy, with a soodling gait,

Slow climbs the stile, or opes the creaky gate,
With willow switch and halter by his side
Prepar'd for Dobbin, whom he means to ride;
The only tune he knows still whistling o'er,
And humming scraps his father sung before,
As 'Wantley Dragon,' and the 'Magic Rose,'
The whole of music that his village knows,
Which wild remembrance, in each little town,
From mouth to mouth through ages handles down.
Onward he jolls, nor can the minstrel-throngs
Entice him once to listen to their songs,
Nor marks he once a blossom on his way;
A senseless lump of animated clay—
With weather-beaten hat of rusty brown,
Stranger to brinks, and often to a crown,
With slop-frock suiting to the ploughman's taste,
Its greasy skirtings twisted round his waist,
And harden'd high-lows clench'd with nails around,
Clamping defiance o'er the stony ground,
The deadly foes to many a blossom'd sprout
That luckless happens in his morning's route,
In hobbling speed he roams the pasture round,
Till hunted Dobbin and the rest are found;
Where some, from frequent meddlings of his whip,
Well know their foe, and often try to slip,
While Dobbin, tam'd by age and labour, stands
To meet all trouble from his brutish hands,
And patient goes to gate or knolly brake,
The teasing burden of his foe to take,
Who, soon as mounted, with his switching weals,
Puts Dob's best swiftness in his heavy heels,
The toltering bustle of a blundering trot
Which whips and cudgels ne'er increas'd a jot,
Though better speed was urged by the clown—
And thus he snorts and jostles to the town.
And now, when toil and summer's in its prime,
In every vill, at morning's earliest time,
To early-risers many a Hodge is seen,
And many a Dob's heard clattering o'er the green.

Now straying beams from day's unclosing eye
In copper-colour'd patches flush the sky,
And from night's prison strugglingly encroach
To bring the summons of warm day's approach,
Till, slowly mounting o'er the ridge of clouds
That yet half shows his face, and half enshrouds,
Th'unfetter'd sun takes his unbounded reign
And wakes all life to noise and toil again:
And while his opening mellows o'er the scenes
Of wood and field their many mingling greens,
Industry's bustling din once more devours
The soothing peace of morning's early hours:
The grount of hogs freed from their nightly dens,
And constant cacklings of new-laying hens,
And ducks and geese that clamorous joys repeat
The splashing comforts of the pond to meet,
And chirping sparrows dropping from the eaves
For offal kernels that the poultry leaves,
Oft signal-calls of danger chittering high
At skulking cats and dogs encroaching nigh,
And lowing steers that hollow echoes wake
Around the yard, their nightly fast to break,
As from each barn the lumping flail rebounds
In mingling concert with the rural sounds;
While o'er the distant fields more faintly creep
The murmuring bleatings of unfolding sheep,
And ploughmen's callings that more hoarse proceed
Where industry still urges labour's speed,
The bellowing of cows with udders full
That wait the welcome halloo of 'come mull,'
And rumbling wagons deafening again,
Rousing the dust along the narrow lane,
And cracking whips, and shepherds' hooting cries,
From woodland echoes urging sharp replies.
Hodge, in his wagon, marks the wondrous tongue,
And talks with echo as he drives along,
Still cracks his whip, bawls every horse's name,
And echo still as ready bawls the same:
The puzzling mystery he would gladly cheat,

And fain would utter what it can't repeat,
Till speedless trials prove the doubted elf
As skill'd in noise and sounds as Hodge himself;
And, quite convinced with the proofs it gives,
The boy drives on and fancies echo lives,
Like some wood-fiend that frights benighted men,
The troubling spirit of a robber's den.

   And now the blossom of the village view,
With airy hat of straw and apron blue
And short-sleev'd gown, that half to guess reveals
By fine-turn'd arms what beauty it conceals,
Whose cheeks health flushes with as sweet a red
As that which stripes the woodbine o'er her head;
Deeply she blushes on her morn's employ,
To prove the fondness of some passing boy,
Who, with a smile that thrills her soul to view,
Holds the gate open till she passes through,
While turning nods beck thanks for kindness done,
And looks—if looks could speak—proclaim her won.
With well-scour'd buckets on proceeds the maid,
And drives her cows to milk beneath the shade,
Where scarce a sunbeam to molest her steals—
Sweet as the thyme that blossoms where she kneels;
And there oft scares the cooing amorous dove
With her own favour'd melodies of love.
Snugly retir'd in yet dew-laden bowers,
This sweetest specimen of rural flowers
Displays, red glowing in the morning wind,
The powers of health and nature when combin'd.

   Last on the road the cow-boy careless swings,
Leading tam'd cattle in their tending strings,
With shining tin to keep his dinner warm
Swung at his back, or tuck'd beneath his arm;
Whose sun-burnt skin, and cheeks chuff'd out with fat,
Are dyed as rusty as his napless hat.
And others, driving loose their herds at will,
Are now heard whooping up the pasture-hill;
Peel'd sticks they bear of hazel or of ash,

The rib-mark'd hides of restless cows to thrash.
In sloven garb appears each bawling boy,
As fit and suiting to his rude employ;
His shoes, worn down by many blundering treads,
Oft show the tenants needing safer sheds:
The pithy bunch of unripe nuts to seek,
And crabs sun-redden'd with a tempting cheek,
From pasture hedges, daily puts to rack
His tatter'd clothes, that scarcely screen the back—
Daub'd all about as if besmear'd with blood,
Stain'd with the berries of the brambly wood
That stud the straggling briers as black as jet,
Which, when his cattle lair, he runs to get;
Or smaller kinds, as if begloss'd with dew,
Shining dim-powder'd with a downy blue,
That on weak tendrils lowly creeping grow
Where, chok'd in flags and sedges, wandering slow,
The brook purls simmering its declining tide
Down the crook'd boundings of the pasture-side.
There they to hunt the luscious fruit delight,
And dabbling keep within their charges' sight;
Oft catching prickly struttles on their rout,
And miller-thumbs and gudgeons driving out,
Hid near the arch'd brig under many a stone
That from its wall rude passing clowns have thrown.
And while in peace cows eat, and chew their cuds,
Moozing cool shelter'd 'neath the skirting woods,
To double uses they the hours convert,
Turning the toils of labour into sport;
Till morn's long streaking shadows lose their tails,
And cooling winds swoon into faltering gales,
And searching sunbeams warm and sultry creep,
Waking the teasing insects from their sleep,
And dreaded gadflies with their drowsy hum
On the burnt wings of midday zephyrs come—
Urging each lown to leave his sports in fear,
  To stop his starting cows that dread the fly;
Droning unwelcome tidings on his ear,
  That the sweet peace of rural morn's gone by.

RURAL EVENING

THE sun now sinks behind the woodland green,
And twittering spangles glow the leaves between;
So bright and dazzling on the eye it plays
As if noon's heat had kindled to a blaze,
But soon it dims in red and heavier hues,
And shows wild fancy cheated in her views.
A mist-like moisture rises from the ground,
And deeper blueness stains the distant round.
The eye each moment, as it gazes o'er,
Still loses objects which it mark'd before;
The woods at distance changing like to clouds,
And spire-points croodling under evening's shrouds;
Till forms of things, and hues of leaf and flower,
In deeper shadows, as by magic power,
With light and all, in scarce-perceiv'd decay,
Put on mild evening's sober garb of grey.

Now in the sleepy gloom that blackens round
Dies many a lulling hum of rural sound,
From cottage door, farm-yard, and dusty lane,
Where home the cart-horse tolters with the swain,
Or padded holm, where village boys resort,
Bawling enraptur'd o'er their evening sport,
Till night awakens superstition's dread
And drives them prisoners to a restless bed.
Thrice happy eve of days no more to me!
Who ever thought such change belong'd to thee?
When, like to boys whom now thy gloom surrounds,
I chas'd the stag, or shouted fox-and-hounds,
Or wander'd down the lane with many a mate
To play at swee-swaw on the pasture-gate,
Or on the threshold of some cottage sat
To watch the flittings of the shrieking bat,
Who, seemly pleas'd to mock our treacherous view,
Would even swoop and touch us as he flew,
And vainly still our hopes to entertain
Would stint his route, and circle us again—

Till, wearied out with many a coaxing call
Which boyish superstition loves to bawl,
His shrill song shrieking he betook to flight,
And left us puzzled in short-sighted night.
Those days have fled me, as from them they steal,
And I've felt losses they must shortly feel;
But sure such ends make every bosom sore,
To think of pleasures we must meet no more.

   Now from the pasture milking-maidens come,
With each a swain to bear the burden home,
Who often coax them on their pleasant way
To soodle longer out in love's delay;
While on a mole-hill, or a resting stile,
The simple rustics try their arts the while
With glegging smiles, and hopes and fears between,
Snatching a kiss to open what they mean:
And all the utmost that their tongues can do,
The honey'd words which nature learns to woo,
The wild-flower sweets of language, 'love' and 'dear,'
With warmest utterings meet each maiden's ear;
Who as by magic smit, she knows not why,
From the warm look that waits a wish'd reply
Droops fearful down in love's delightful swoon,
As slinks the blossom from the suns of noon;
While sighs half-smother'd from the throbbing breast,
And broken words sweet trembling out the rest,
And cheeks, in blushes burning, turn'd aside,
Betray the plainer what she strives to hide.
The amorous swain sees through the thin disguise,
Discerns the fondness she at first denies,
And with all passions love and truth can move
Urges more strong the simpering maid to love;
More freely using toying ways to win—
Tokens that echo from the soul within—
Her soft hand nipping, that with ardour burns,
And, timid, gentlier presses its returns;
Then stealing pins with innocent deceit,
To loose the kerchief from its envied seat;

Then unawares her bonnet he'll untie,
Her dark-brown ringlets wiping gently by,
To steal a kiss in seemly feign'd disguise,
As love yields kinder taken by surprise:
While, nearly conquer'd, she less disapproves,
And owns at last, mid tears and sighs, she loves.
With sweetest feelings that this world bestows
Now each to each their inmost souls disclose,
Vow to be true; and to be truly ta'en,
Repeat their loves, and vow it o'er again;
And pause at loss of language to proclaim
Those purest pleasures, yet without a name:
And while, in highest ecstasy of bliss
The shepherd holds her yielding hand in his,
He turns to heaven to witness what he feels,
And silent shows what want of words conceals;
Then ere the parting moments hustle nigh,
    And night in deeper dye his curtain dips,
Till next day's evening glads the anxious eye,
    He swears his truth, and seals it on her lips.

    At even's hour, the truce of toil, 'tis sweet
The sons of labour at their ease to meet,
On piled bench, beside the cottage door,
Made up of mud and stones and sodded o'er;
Where rustic taste at leisure trimly weaves
The rose and straggling woodbine to the eaves,
And on the crowded spot that pales enclose
The white and scarlet daisy rears in rows,
Training the trailing peas in bunches neat,
Perfuming evening with a luscious sweet,
And sun-flowers planting for their gilded show,
That scale the window's lattice ere they blow,
Then, sweet to habitants within the sheds,
Peep through the diamond pane their golden heads:
Or at the shop where ploughs and harrows lie,
Well known to every child that passes by
From shining fragments littering on the floor,
And branded letters burnt upon the door;

Where meddling boys, the torment of the street,
In hard-burnt cinders ready weapons meet,
To pelt the martins 'neath the eves at rest,
That oft are wak'd to mourn a ruin'd nest,
Or sparrows, that delight their nests to leave,
In dust to flutter at the cool of eve.
For such-like scenes the gossip leaves her home,
And sons of labour light their pipes, and come
To talk of wages, whether high or low,
And mumble news that still as secrets go;
When, heedless then to all the rest may say,
The beckoning lover nods the maid away,
And at a distance many an hour they seem
In jealous whisperings o'er their pleasing theme;
While children round them teasing sports prolong,
To twirl the top, or bounce the hoop along,
Or shout across the street their 'one catch all,'
Or prog the hous'd bee from the cotter's wall.

Now at the parish cottage wall'd with dirt,
Where all the cumber-grounds of life resort,
From the low door that bows two props between,
Some feeble tottering dame surveys the scene;
By them reminded of the long-lost day
When she herself was young, and went to play;
And, turning to the painful scenes again,
The mournful changes she has met since then,
Her aching heart, the contrast moves so keen,
E'en sighs a wish that life had never been.
Still vainly sinning, while she strives to pray,
Half-smother'd discontent pursues its way
In whispering Providence, how blest she'd been,
If life's last troubles she'd escap'd unseen;
If, ere want sneak'd for grudg'd support from pride,
She had but shar'd of childhood's joys, and died.
And as to talk some passing neighbours stand,
And shove their box within her tottering hand,
She turns from echoes of her younger years,
And nips the portion of her snuff with tears.

RUSTIC FISHING

On Sunday mornings, freed from hard employ,
How oft I mark the mischievous young boy
With anxious haste his pole and lines provide,
For makeshifts oft crook'd pins to thread were tied;
And delve his knife with wishes ever warm
In rotten dunghills for the grub and worm,
The harmless treachery of his hooks to bait;
Tracking the dewy grass with many a mate,
To seek the brook that down the meadows glides,
Where the grey willow shadows by its sides,
Where flag and reed in wild disorder spread,
And bending bulrush bows its taper head;
And, just above the surface of the floods,
Where water-lilies mount their snowy buds,
On whose broad swimming leaves of glossy green
The shining dragon-fly is often seen;
Where hanging thorns, with roots wash'd bare, appear,
That shield the moor-hen's nest from year to year;
While crowding osiers mingling wild among
Prove snug asylums to her brood when young,
Who, when surpris'd by foes approaching near,
Plunge 'neath the weeping boughs and disappear.
There far from terrors that the parson brings,
Or church bell hearing when its summons rings,
Half hid in meadow-sweet and keck's high flowers,
In lonely sport they spend the Sunday hours.
Though ill supplied for fishing seems the brook,
That breaks the mead in many a stinted crook,
Oft chok'd in weeds, and foil'd to find a road,
The choice retirement of the snake and toad,
Then lost in shallows dimpling restlessly,
In fluttering struggles murmuring to be free—
O'er gravel stones its depth can scarcely hide
It runs the remnant of its broken tide,
Till, seemly weary of each chok'd control,
It rests collected in some gulled hole
Scoop'd by the sudden floods when winter's snow

Melts in confusion by a hasty thaw;
There bent in hopeful musings on the brink
They watch their floating corks that seldom sink,
Save when a wary roach or silver bream
Nibbles the worm as passing up the stream,
Just urging expectation's hopes to stay
To view the dodging cork, then slink away;
Still hopes keep burning with untir'd delight,
Still wobbling curves keep wavering like a bite:
If but the breezy wind their floats should spring,
And move the water with a troubling ring,
A captive fish still fills the anxious eyes
And willow-wicks lie ready for the prize;
Till evening gales awaken damp and chill,
And nip the hopes that morning suns instil,
And resting flies have tired their gauzy wing,
Nor longer tempt the watching fish to spring,
Who at the worm no nibbles more repeat,
But lunge from night in sheltering flag-retreat.
Then disappointed in their day's employ,
They seek amusement in a feebler joy.
Short is the sigh for fancies prov'd untrue:
With humbler hopes still pleasure they pursue
Where the rude oak-bridge scales the narrow pass,
Half hid in rustling reeds and scrambling grass,
Or stepping-stones stride o'er the narrow sloughs
Which maidens daily cross to milk their cows;
There they in artless glee for minnows run,
And wade and dabble past the setting sun,
Chasing the struttle o'er the shallow tide,
And flat stones turning up where gudgeons hide.
All former hopes their ill success delay'd,
In this new change they fancy well repaid.
And thus they wade, and chatter o'er their joys
Till night, unlook'd-for, young success destroys,
Drives home the sons of solitude and streams,
And stops uncloy'd hope's ever-fresh'ning dreams.
They then, like schoolboys that at truant play,
In sloomy fear lounge on their homeward way,

And inly tremble, as they gain the town,
Where chastisement awaits with many a frown,
And hazel twigs, in readiness prepar'd,
For their long absence bring a meet reward.

SUNDAY WALKS

How fond the labourer's ear at leisure dwells
On the soft soundings of his village bells,
As on a Sunday morning at his ease
He takes his rambles, just as fancies please,
Down narrow balks that intersect the fields,
Hid in profusion that its produce yields:
Long twining peas, in faintly misted greens,
And wing'd-leaf multitudes of crowding beans,
And flighty oatlands of a lighter hue,
And speary barley bowing down with dew,
And browning wheat-ear, on its taper stalk,
With gentle breezes bending o'er the balk,
Greeting the parting hand that brushes near
With patting welcomes of a plenteous year;
Or narrow lanes, where cool and gloomy-sweet
Hedges above-head in an arbour meet,
Meandering down, and resting for a while
Upon a moss-clad mole-hill or a stile;
While every scene that on his leisure crowds,
Wind-waving valleys and light passing clouds,
In brighter colours seems to meet the eye,
Than in the bustle of the days gone by.
A peaceful solitude around him creeps,
And nature seemly o'er her quiet sleeps;
No noise is heard, save sutherings through the trees
Of brisk wind gushes, or a trembling breeze,
And song of linnets in the hedgerow thorn,
Twittering their welcomes to the day's return,
And hum of bees, where labour's doom'd to stray
In ceaseless bustle on his weary way,

And low of distant cattle here and there,
Seeking the stream, or dropping down to lair,
And bleat of sheep, and horses' playful neigh,
From rustics' whips, and plough, and wagon, free,
Biting in careless freedom o'er the leas,
Or turn'd to knap each other at their ease.
While 'neath the bank on which he rests his head
The brook mourns drippling o'er its pebbly bed,
And whimpers soothingly a calm serene
O'er the lull'd comforts of a Sunday scene,
He ponders round, and muses with a smile
On thriving produce of his earlier toil;
What once were kernels from his hopper sown,
Now browning wheat-ears and oat-bunches grown,
And pea-pods swell'd, by blossoms long forsook,
And nearly ready for the scythe and hook:
He pores with wonder on the mighty change
Which suns and showers perform, and thinks it strange;
And though no philosophic reasoning draws
His musing marvels home to nature's cause,
A simple feeling in him turns his eye
To where the thin clouds smoke along the sky;
And there his soul consents the power must reign
Who rules the year, and shoots the spindling grain,
Lights up the sun, and sprinkles rain below—
The fount of nature whence all causes flow.
Thus much the feeling of his bosom warms,
Nor seeks he farther than his soul informs.

A six-days' prisoner, life's support to earn
From dusty cobwebs and the murky barn,
The weary thresher meets the rest that's given,
And thankful soothes him in the boon of heaven;
But happier still in Sabbath-walks he feels,
With love's sweet pledges poddling at his heels,
That oft divert him with their childish glee
In fruitless chases after bird and bee;
And, eager gathering every flower they pass
Of yellow lambtoe and the totter-grass,

Oft whimper round him disappointment's sigh
At sight of blossom that's in bloom too high,
And twitch his sleeve with all their coaxing powers
To urge his hand to reach the tempting flowers:
Then as he climbs, their eager hopes to crown,
On gate or stile to pull the blossoms down
Of pale hedge-roses straggling wild and tall,
And scrambling woodbines that outgrow them all,
He turns to days when he himself would tease
His tender father for such toys as these,
And smiles with rapture, as he plucks the flowers,
To meet the feelings of those lovely hours,
And blesses Sunday's rest, whose peace at will
Retains a portion of those pleasures still.

But when the duty of the day's expir'd,
And priest and parish offer what's requir'd,
When godly farmer shuts his book again
To talk of profits from advancing grain,
Short memory keeping what the parson read,
Prayers 'neath his arm, and business in his head,
And, dread of boys, the clerk is left to close
The creaking church-door on its week's repose,
Then leave me Sunday's remnant to employ
In seeking sweets of solitary joy,
And lessons learning from a simple tongue,
Where nature preaches in a cricket's song;
Where every tiny thing that flies and creeps
   Some feeble language owns, its prayer to raise;
Where all that lives, by noise or silence, keeps
   A homely sabbath in its Maker's praise.

There, free from labour, let my musings stray
Where footpaths ramble from the public way
In quiet loneliness o'er many a scene,
Through grassy close, or grounds of blossom'd bean;
Oft winding balks where groves of willows spread
Their welcome waving shadows overhead,
And thorns beneath in woodbines often drest

Inviting strongly in their peace to rest;
Or wildly left to follow choice at will
O'er many a trackless vale and pathless hill,
Or, nature's wilderness, o'er heaths of goss,
Each footstep sinking ankle-deep in moss,
By pleasing interruptions often tied
A hedge to clamber or a brook to stride;
Where no approaching feet or noises rude
Molest the quiet of one's solitude,
Save birds, their song broke by a false alarm,
Through branches fluttering from their fancied harm;
And cows and sheep with startled low and bleat
Disturb'd from lair by one's unwelcome feet—
The all that's met in Sunday's slumbering ease,
That adds to, more than checks, the power to please.
And sweet it is to creep one's blinded way
Where woodland boughs shut out the smiles of day,
Where, hemm'd in glooms that scarce give leave to spy
A passing cloud or patch of purple sky,
We track, half hidden from the world besides,
Sweet hermit-nature that in woodlands hides;
Where nameless flowers that never meet the sun,
Like bashful modesty, the sight to shun,
Bud in their snug retreat, and bloom, and die,
Without one notice of a passing eye;
There, while I drop me in the woody waste
'Neath arbours Nature fashions to her taste,
Entwining oak-trees with the ivy's gloom
And woodbines propping over boughs to bloom,
And scallop'd bryony mingling round her bowers
Whose fine bright leaves make up the want of flowers—
With nature's minstrels of the woods let me,
Thou Lord of sabbaths, add a song to thee,
An humble offering for the holy day
    Which thou most wise and graciously hast given,
As leisure dropt in labour's rugged way
    To claim a passport with the rest to heaven.

Soon as the spring its earliest visit pays,
And buds with March and April's lengthen'd days
Of mingled suns and shades and snow and rain,
Forcing the crackling ice to melt again,
Oft sprinkling from their bosoms, as they come,
A dwindling daisy here and there to bloom,
I mark the widow, and her orphan boy,
In preparation for their old employ.
The cloak and hat that had for seasons past
Repell'd the rain and buffeted the blast,
Though worn to shreddings, still are occupied
In make-shift way their nakedness to hide;
For since her husband died her hopes are few,
When time's worn out the old, to purchase new.
Upon the green they're seen by rising sun,
To sharp winds croodling they would vainly shun,
With baskets on their arm and hazel crooks
Dragging the sprouting cresses from the brooks;
A savoury salad sought for Luxury's whim,
Though small reward her labours meet from him,
When, parcell'd out, she humbly takes for sale
The simple produce of the water'd vale
In yearly visits to some market town,
Meeting by turns a penny and a frown.
Of all the masks deception ever weaves,
Life, thine's the visage that the most deceives;
One hour of thine an emperor's glory greets,
Another turns him begging in the streets:
E'en this poor wretch, thy meanest link, who lives
On scantiest sustenance that labour gives,
Has known her better days, whom thou, times gone,
E'en condescended to look kindly on.
Things went not thus, when abler hands supplied
The calls of hunger ere her husband died,
Who various ways a living did pursue,
Clerk of the parish, and schoolmaster too.
He punctual always rang the evening bell,

And sang 'Amen' on Sundays loud and well;
And though not nice in this and that respect,
Was rarely found his duty to neglect.
His worldly ways religions ne'er perplext,
He never fail'd to recollect the text,
Or quote the sermon's passages by heart
In warm devotion o'er an honest quart;
And, as a brother of those subtle tools
That make such figuring in our country schools,
He lov'd his skill to flourish, and to show
As well as godly he was learned too;
Though, with the boast most common to his kin,
The use of figures he knew little in—
By far too puzzling for his head were they,
He sought fame's purchase by an easier way;
And, like his scholars, with his A, B, C
Was found more ready, than with 'rule of three.'
He 'd many things to crack on with his ale,
For clowns less learn'd to wonder at the tale;
And o'er his pot he'd take the news and preach,
And observations make from speech to speech,
Till those around him swore each wise remark
Show'd him more fit for parson than for clerk.
To minutes he would tell when moons were new,
And of eclipses talk the seasons through,
Run o'er as ready as he'd read his prayers
All the saint-days the calendar declares,
Mystic conclusions draw from many a sign
Which made him judge of weather foul or fine,
And dripping moons, or suns in crimson set,
To him sure tokens were of fair or wet.
Of wonders he knew all the yearly store
That fill the learned almanacks of Moore:
Earthquakes, and plagues, and floods, when they befell,
From second father Noah's days, could tell;
Till most gave out, had he divulg'd his trade,
The best of almanacks he would have made;
And much they wonder'd, when he died, to find
He left no fragment of his art behind.

And as he always, for the sake of fame,
Conceal'd the sources whence his learning came,
His artless list'ners, who of books none knew
'Sides the large Bible in the parson's pew,
Thought he more things than lawful understood,
And knowledge got from helpers not too good.

When he was living she had food on shelf,
And knew no trials to support herself,
Though industry would oft from leisure steal
Odd hours to knit, or turn the humming wheel:
Choice is not misery; she had neighbour's fare,
Got hand to mouth, and decent clothes to wear.
Though joys fall sparing in this chequer'd life,
Wide difference parts the widow from the wife:
Encroaching want show'd not such frightful form,
Nor drove her dithering in the numbing storm,
Picking half naked round the brooks for bread,
To earn her penny ere she can be fed,
In grief pursuing every chance to live,
That timely toils in seasons please to give,
Through hot and cold, come weather as it will,
Striving with pain, and disappointed still,
Just keeping from expiring life's last fire,
That pining lingers ready to expire:
The winter through, near barefoot, left to pull
From bushes hung with snow her mites of wool,
A hard-earn'd sixpence when her mops are spun,
By many a walk and aching finger won,
And seeking, hirpling round from time to time,
Her harmless sticks from hedges hung with rime,
The daily needings want's worst shifts require,
To hunt her fuel ere she makes her fire;
Where she, while grinning to the hissing blast,
With buds or berries often breaks her fast.
All summer, too, the little rest of care
Is every morning cheated of its share,
And ere one sunbeam glistens in the dew
The long wet pasture grass she dabbles through,

Where sprout the mushrooms in the fairy-rings,
Which night's black mystery to perfection brings;
And these she seeks, ere 'gin her early toils,
As extra gains to labour's scanty spoils:
By every means thus ling'ring life along,
Continual struggling 'gainst a stream too strong.

THE LAST OF MARCH

WRITTEN AT LOLHAM BRIGS

Though o'er the darksome northern hill
    Old ambush'd winter frowning flies,
And faintly drifts his threatenings still
    In snowy sleet and blackening skies;
    Yet where the willow leaning lies
And shields beneath the budding flower,
    Where banks to break the wind arise,
'Tis sweet to sit and spend an hour.

Though floods of winter bustling fall
    Adown the arches bleak and blea,
Though snow-storms clothe the mossy wall,
    And hourly whiten o'er the lea;
    Yet when from clouds the sun is free
And warms the learning bird to sing,
    'Neath sloping bank and sheltering tree
'Tis sweet to watch the creeping spring.

Though still so early, one may spy
    And track her footsteps every hour;
The daisy with its golden eye,
    And primrose bursting into flower;
    And snugly, where the thorny bower
Keeps off the nipping frost and wind,
    Excluding all but sun and shower,
There children early violets find.

Here 'neath the shelving bank's retreat
    The horse-blob swells its golden ball;
Nor fear the lady-smocks to meet
    The snows that round their blossoms fall:
    Here by the arch's ancient wall
The antique eldern buds anew;
    Again the bulrush sprouting tall
The water wrinkles, rippling through.

As spring's warm herald April comes,
    As nature's sleep is nearly past,
How sweet to hear the wakening hums
    Of aught beside the winter blast!
    Of feather'd minstrels first and last,
The robin's song's again begun;
    And, as skies clear when overcast,
Larks rise to hail the peeping sun.

The stirtling peewits, as they pass,
    Scream joyous whizzing overhead,
Right glad the fields and meadow grass
    Will quickly hide their careless shed:
    The rooks, where yonder witchens spread,
Quawk clamorous to the spring's approach;
    Here silent, from its watery bed,
To hail its coming, leaps the roach.

While stalking o'er the fields again
    In stripp'd defiance to the storms,
The hardy seedsman spreads the grain,
    And all his hopeful toil performs:
    In flocks the timid pigeon swarms,
For scatter'd kernels chance may spare;
    And as the plough unbeds the worms,
The crows and magpies gather there.

Yon bullocks low their liberty,
    The young grass cropping to their fill;
And colts, from straw-yards neighing free,
    Spring's opening promise 'joy at will:

Along the bank, beside the rill
The happy lambkins bleat and run,
    Then weary, 'neath a sheltering hill
Drop basking in the gleaming sun.

At distance from the water's edge,
    On hanging sallow's farthest stretch,
The moor-hen 'gins her nest of sedge
    Safe from destroying schoolboy's reach.
    Fen-sparrows chirp and fly to fetch
The wither'd reed-down rustling nigh,
    And, by the sunny side the ditch,
Prepare their dwelling warm and dry.

Again a storm encroaches round,
    Thick clouds are darkening deep behind;
And, through the arches, hoarsely sound
    The risings of the hollow wind:
    Spring's early hopes seem half resign'd,
And silent for a while remain;
    Till sunbeams broken clouds can find,
And brighten all to life again.

Ere yet a hailstone pattering comes,
    Or dimps the pool the rainy squall,
One hears, in mighty murmuring hums,
    The spirit of the tempest call:
    Here sheltering 'neath the ancient wall
I still pursue my musing dreams,
    And as the hailstones round me fall
I mark their bubbles in the streams.

Reflection here is warm'd to sigh,
    Tradition gives these brigs renown,
Though heedless Time long pass'd them by
    Nor thought them worthy noting down:
    Here in the mouth of every clown
The 'Roman road' familiar sounds;
    All else, with everlasting frown,
Oblivion's mantling mist surrounds.

224

These walls the work of Roman hands!
　　How may conjecturing Fancy pore,
As lonely here one calmly stands,
　　On paths that age has trampled o'er.
　　The builders' names are known no more;
No spot on earth their memory bears;
　　And crowds, reflecting thus before,
Have since found graves as dark as theirs.

The storm has ceas'd—again the sun
　　The ague-shivering season dries;
Short-winded March, thou'lt soon be done,
　　Thy fainting tempest mildly dies.
　　Soon April's flowers and dappled skies
Shall spread a couch for lovely May,
　　Upon whose bosom Nature lies
And smiles her joyous youth away.

THE WILD-FLOWER NOSEGAY

In life's first years as on a mother's breast,
　　When Nature nurs'd me in her flowery pride,
I cull'd her bounty, such as seemed best,
　　And made my garlands by some hedgerow side:
With pleasing eagerness the mind reclaims
　　From black oblivion's shroud such artless scenes,
And cons the calendar of childish names
　　With simple joy, when manhood intervenes.

From the sweet time that spring's young thrills are born,
　　And golden catkins deck the sallow tree,
Till summer's blue-caps blossom mid the corn,
　　And autumn's ragwort yellows o'er the lea,
I roam'd the fields about, a happy child,
　　And bound my posies up with rushy ties,
And laugh'd and mutter'd o'er my visions wild,
　　Bred in the brain of pleasure's ecstasies.

Crimp-frilled daisy, bright bronze buttercup,
    Freckt cowslip-peeps, gilt whins of morning's dew,
And hooded arum early sprouting up
    Ere the whitethorn bud half unfolds to view,
And wan-hued lady-smocks, that love to spring
    'Side the swamp margin of some plashy pond;
And all the blooms that early Aprils bring,
    With eager joy each fill'd my playful hand:

The jaundice-tinctur'd primrose, sickly sere,
    Mid its broad curled leaves of mellow green,
Hemm'd in with relics of the 'parted year,
    The mournful wrecks of summers that have been—
Dead leaves of ash, and oak, and hazel tree,
    The constant covering of all woody land;
With tiny violets, creeping plenteously,
    That one by one entic'd my patient hand.

As shadowy April's suns and showers did pass,
    And summer's wild profusions plenteous grew,
Hiding the spring-flowers in long weeds and grass,
    What meads and copses would I wander thro'!
When on the water op'd the lily buds,
    And fine long purples shadow'd in the lake,
When freckled cuckoos peeped in the woods
    'Neath darkest shades that boughs and leaves could make.

Then did I wear day's many hours away
    In gathering blooms of seemly sweetest kinds,
Scrambling for blossoms of the whitethorn may,
    Ere they fell victims to unfeeling winds;
And twisted woodbines, and the flusht brier rose,
    How sweet remembrance on the mind doth rise
As they bow'd arching where the runnel flows,
    To think how oft I waded for the prize.

The ragged-robins by the spinney lake,
    And flag-flower bunches deeper down the flood,
And, snugly hiding 'neath the feather'd brake,
Full many a blue-bell frond and cuckoo-bud,

And old man's beard, that wreath'd along the hedge
    Its oddly rude misshapen tawny flowers,
And prickly burs that crowd the leaves of sedge,
    Have claim'd my pleasing search for hours and hours.

And down the hay-fields, wading 'bove the knees
    Through seas of waving grass, what days I've gone,
Cheating the hopes of many labouring bees
    By cropping blossoms they were perch'd upon;
As thyme along the hills, and lambtoe knots,
    And the wild stalking Canterbury bell,
By hedgerow side or bushy bordering spots,
    That loves in shade and solitude to dwell.

And when the summer's swarms, half-nameless, fled,
    And autumn's landscape faded bleak and wild,
When leaves 'gan fall and show their berries red,
    Still with the season would I be beguil'd
Lone spots to seek, home leaving far behind—
    Where wildness rears her lings and teazle-burs,
And where, last lingering of the flowery kind,
    Blue heath-bells tremble 'neath the shelt'ring furze.

Sweet were such walks on the half-barren wild,
    Which ploughs leave quiet with their briers and brakes,
Prospects of freedom pleasing from a child,
    To track the crook'd pads which the rabbit makes!
On these past times one loves to look behind;
    Nor lives a soul, mere trifles as they be,
But feels a joy in bringing to his mind
    The wild-flower rambles of his infancy.

'Tis sweet to view, as in a favour'd book,
    Life's rude beginning page long turned o'er;
'Tis nature's common feeling, back to look
    On things that pleas'd us, when they are no more:
Pausing on childish scenes a wish repeat,
    Seeming more sweet to value when we're men,
As one, awaken'd from a vision sweet,
    Wishes to sleep and dream it o'er agen.

EFFUSION

Aʜ, little did I think in time that's past,
By summer burnt, or numb'd by winter's blast,
Delving the ditch a livelihood to earn,
Or lumping corn out in a dusty barn,
With aching bones returning home at night,
And sitting down with weary hand to write,
Ah, little did I think, as then unknown,
Those artless rhymes I even blush'd to own
Would be one day applauded and approv'd,
By learning notic'd, and by genius lov'd.
God knows, my hopes were many, but my pain
Damp'd all the prospects which I hop'd to gain;
I hardly dar'd to hope.   Thou corner-chair,
In which I've oft slung back in deep despair,
Hadst thou expression, thou couldst easy tell
The pains and all that I have known too well:
'Twould be but sorrow's tale, yet still 'twould be
A tale of truth, and passing sweet to me.
How oft upon my hand I've laid my head,
And thought how poverty deform'd our shed;
Look'd on each parent's face I fain had cheer'd,
Where sorrow triumph'd, and pale want appear'd;
And sigh'd, and hop'd, and wish'd some day would come,
When I might bring a blessing to their home—
That toil and merit comforts had in store,
To bid the tear defile their cheeks no more.
Who that has feelings would not wish to be
A friend to parents, such as mine to me,
Who in distress broke their last crust in twain,
And though want pinch'd, the remnant broke again,
And still, if craving of their scanty bread,
Gave their last mouthful that I might be fed?
Nor for their own wants tear-drops follow'd free,
Worse anguish stung—they had no more for me.
And now hope's sun is looking brighter out,
And spreading thin the clouds of fear and doubt,
That long in gloomy sad suspense to me

Hid the long-waited smiles I wish'd to see.
And now, my parents, helping you is sweet—
The rudest havoc fortune could complete;
A piteous couple, little blest with friends,
Where pain and poverty have had their ends.
I'll be thy crutch, my father, lean on me;
Weakness knits stubborn while it's bearing thee:
And hard shall fall the shock of fortune's frown,
To eke thy sorrows, ere it breaks me down.
My mother, too, thy kindness shall be met,
And ere I'm able will I pay the debt;
For what thou'st done, and what gone through for me,
My last-earn'd sixpence will I break with thee:
And when my dwindled sum won't more divide,
   Then take it all—to fate I'll leave the rest;
In helping thee I'll always feel a pride,
   Nor think I'm happy till ye both are blest.

ADDRESS TO MY FATHER

CALM resignation meets a happy end;
And Providence, long trusted, brings a friend.
God's will be done, be patient and be good;
Elisha was, and ravens brought him food:
And so wast thou, my father—fate's decree
Doom'd many evils should encompass thee;
And, like Elisha, though it met thee late,
Patience unwearied did not vainly wait.
Thou hast, my father, long been us'd to pine,
And patient borne thy pain; great pain was thine.
Thou hast submitted, ah, and thou hast known
The roughest storms that life has ever blown,
Yet met them like a lamb: thou wert resign'd,
And though thou pray'dst a better place to find,
'Twas naught presumptuous—meekly wouldst thou crave,
When pains rack'd sore, some easement in the grave;
To lay thy aching body down in peace.

Where want and pain, poor man's tormentors, cease.
'Twas all thy wish—and not till lately wish'd,
When age came on, and pain thy strength had crush'd.
There stood thy childern: 'Ah,' thou oft wouldst sigh,
'Let's see my babes brought up, and let me die.
Though what I do brings them but little food,
It better keeps them than a workhouse would.
I've small enticement in this world to find,
But could not rest if they were left behind.'
Bless thee, my father! thou'st been kind to me,
And God, who saw it, will be kind to thee.
Now pain has mark'd thee long with age's scars,
And age with double blow thy end prepares—
A crooked wreck, the trace of what has been,
Toil, want, and pain, now but too plainly seen—
Thou'st met with friends who joy to damp despair,
And when most needed brought thy easy chair;
An easy seat thy wasted form to bless,
And make thy useless limbs to pain thee less:
Oh, mayst thou long enjoy the comfort given,
  Live long to bless them who the deed have done;
Then change thy earthly pains for joys in heaven!—
  So beats the bosom of thy only son,
Whose bliss is at its height, whose long hope's crown'd,
To prove, when wanted most, thy friends are found.

TO AN INFANT DAUGHTER

SWEET gem of infant fairy-flowers!
Thy smiles on life's unclosing hours,
Like sunbeams lost in summer showers,
        They wake my fears;
When reason knows its sweets and sours,
        They'll change to tears.

God help thee, little senseless thing!
Thou, daisy-like of early spring,

Of ambush'd winter's hornet sting
      Hast yet to tell;
Thou know'st not what to-morrows bring:
      I wish thee well.

But thou art come, and soon or late
'Tis thine to meet the frowns of fate,
The harpy grin of envy's hate,
      And mermaid-smiles
Of worldly folly's luring bait,
      That youth beguiles.

And much I wish, whate'er may be
The lot, my child, that falls to thee,
Nature may never let thee see
      Her glass betimes,
But keep thee from my failings free—
      Nor itch at rhymes.

Lord help thee in thy coming years
If thy mad father's picture 'pears
Predominant!—his feeling fears
      And jingling starts;
I'd freely now gi' vent to tears
      To ease my heart.

May thou, unknown to rhyming bother,
Be ignorant as is thy mother,
And in thy manners such another,
      Save sin's nigh quest;
And then with 'scaping this and t'other
      Thou mayst be blest.[1]

Lord knows my heart, it loves thee much;
And may my feelings, aches, and such,
The pains I meet in folly's clutch
      Be never thine:
Child, it's a tender string to touch,
      That sounds 'Thou'rt mine.'

[1] Preceding two verses added from MS.

PROPOSALS FOR BUILDING A COTTAGE

BESIDE a runnel build my shed,
    With stubbles cover'd o'er;
Let broad oaks o'er its chimney spread,
    And grass-plats grace the door.

The door may open with a string,
    So that it closes tight;
And locks would be a wanted thing,
    To keep out thieves at night.

A little garden, not too fine,
    Inclose with painted pales;
And woodbines, round the cot to twine,
    Pin to the wall with nails.

Let hazels grow, and spindling sedge,
    Bent bowering overhead;
Dig old man's beard from woodland hedge,
    To twine a summer shade.

Beside the threshold sods provide,
    And build a summer seat;
Plant sweetbrier bushes by its side,
    And flowers that blossom sweet.

I love the sparrows' ways to watch
    Upon the cotters' sheds,
So here and there pull out the thatch,
    That they may hide their heads.

And as the sweeping swallows stop
    Their flights along the green,
Leave holes within the chimney-top
    To paste their nest between.

Stick shelves and cupboards round the hut,
    In all the holes and nooks;

Nor in the corner fail to put
   A cupboard for the books.

Along the floor some sand I'll sift,
   To make it fit to live in;
And then I'll thank ye for the gift,
   As something worth the giving.

ON THE SIGHT OF SPRING

How sweet it us'd to be, when April first
Unclos'd the arum-leaves, and into view
Its ear-like spindling flowers their cases burst,
Beting'd with yellowish white or lushy hue:
Though manhood now with such has small to do,
Yet I remember what delight was mine
When on my Sunday walks I us'd to go,
Flower-gathering tribes in childish bliss to join,
Peeping and searching hedgerow side or woods,
When thorns stain green with slow unclosing buds.
Ah, how delighted, humming on the time
Some nameless song or tale, I sought the flowers,
Some rushy dyke to jump, or bank to climb,
Ere I obtain'd them; while from hasty showers
Oft under trees we nestled in a ring,
Culling our 'lords and ladies.'—O ye hours!
I never see the broad-leav'd arum spring
Stained with spots of jet, I never see
Those dear delights which April still does bring,
But memory's tongue repeats it all to me.
I view her pictures with an anxious eye,
I hear her stories with a pleasing pain:
Youth's wither'd flowers, alas! ye make me sigh,
To think in me ye'll never bloom again.

TO A BOWER

THREE times, sweet hawthorn, I have met thy bower,
  And thou hast gain'd my love, and I do feel
An aching pain to leave thee: every flower
  Around thee opening doth new charms reveal,
And binds my fondness stronger.—Wild wood bower,
  In memory's calendar thou'rt treasur'd up:
And should we meet in some remoter hour,
  When all thy bloom to winter-winds shall droop,
Ah, in life's winter, many a day to come,
  Should my grey wrinkles pass thy spot of ground,
And find it bare—with thee no longer crown'd,
  Within the woodman's faggot torn from hence,
Or chopt by hedgers up for yonder fence,
  Ah, should I chance by thee as then to come,
I'll look upon thy nakedness with pain,
  And, as I view thy desolated doom,
In fancy's eye I'll fetch thy shade again,
  And of this lovely day I'll think and sigh,
And ponder o'er this sweetly-passing hour,
  And feel as then the throes of joys gone by,
When I was young, and thou a blooming bower.

TO POESY

O SWEETLY wild and witching Poesy!
  Thou light of this world's hermitage I prove thee;
And surely none helps loving thee that knows thee,
  A soul of feeling cannot help but love thee.
I would say how thy secret wonders move me,
  Thou spell of loveliness!—but 'tis too much:
Had I the language of the gods above me
  I might then venture thy wild harp to touch,
And sing of all thy thrilling pains and pleasures,
  The flowers I meet in this world's wilderness,

234

The comforts rising from thy spell-bound treasures,
  Thy cordial balm that softens my distress:
I would say all, but thou art far above me;
  Words are too weak, expression can't be had;
I can but say I love, and dearly love thee,
  And that thou cheer'st me when my soul is sad.

TO THE CLOUDS

O PAINTED clouds! sweet beauties of the sky,
  How have I view'd your motion and your rest,
When like fleet hunters ye have left mine eye,
  In your thin gauze of woolly-fleecing drest;
Or in your threaten'd thunder's grave black vest,
  Like black deep waters slowly moving by,
Awfully striking the spectator's breast
  With your Creator's dread sublimity,
As admiration mutely views your storms.
  And I do love to see you idly lie,
Painted by heav'n as various as your forms,
  Pausing upon the eastern mountain high,
As morn awakes with spring's wood-harmony;
  And sweeter still, when in your slumbers sooth
You hang the western arch o'er day's proud eye,
  Still as the even-pool, uncurv'd and smooth,
My gazing soul has look'd most placidly,
  And higher still devoutly wish'd to strain,
To wipe your shrouds and sky's blue blinders by,
  With all the warmness of a moon-struck brain—
To catch a glimpse of Him who bids you reign,
  And view the dwelling of all majesty.

TO A DEAD TREE

OLD tree, thou art wither'd—I pass'd thee last year,
  And the blackbird snug hid in thy branches did sing,
Thy shadow stretch'd dark o'er the grass sprouting near,
  And thou wert as green as thy mates of the spring.

How alter'd since then! not a leaf hast thou got,
  Thy honours brown round thee that clothed the tree;
The clown passeth by thee and heedeth thee not,
  But thou'rt a warm source of reflection for me.

I think, while I view thee and rest on the stile,
  Life's bloom is as frail as the leaves thou hast shed;
Like thee I may boast of my honours awhile,
  But new springs may blossom, and mine may be fled:
Fond friends may bend o'er the rais'd turf where I'm laid,
  And warm recollection the past may look o'er,
And say by my life, as I say by thy shade,
  'Last spring he was living, but now he's no more.'

LANGLEY BUSH

O Langley Bush! the shepherd's sacred shade,
  Thy hollow trunk oft gain'd a look from me;
Full many a journey o'er the heath I've made,
  For such-like curious things I love to see.
What truth the story of the swain allows,
  That tells of honours which thy young days knew,
Of 'Langley Court' being kept beneath thy boughs,
  I cannot tell—thus much I know is true,
That thou art reverenc'd: even the rude clan
  Of lawless gipsies, driven from stage to stage,
Pilfering the hedges of the husbandman,
  Spare thee, as sacred, in thy withering age.
Both swains and gipsies seem to love thy name,
  Thy spot's a favourite with the sooty crew,
And soon thou must depend on gipsy-fame,
  Thy mouldering trunk is nearly rotten through.
My last doubts murmur on the zephyr's swell,
  My last look lingers on thy boughs with pain;
To thy declining age I bid farewell,
  Like old companions, ne'er to meet again.

A LOOK AT THE HEAVENS

Oh, who can witness with a careless eye
The countless lamps that light an evening sky,
And not be struck with wonder at the sight!
To think what mighty Power must there abound,
That burns each spangle with a steady light,
And guides each hanging world its rolling round.
What multitudes my misty eyes have found!
The countless numbers speak a Deity:
In numbers numberless the skies are crown'd,
And still they're nothing which my sight can see,
When science, searching through her aiding glass,
In seeming blanks to me can millions trace;
While millions more, that every heart impress,
Still brighten up throughout eternal space.
O Power Almighty! whence these beings shine,
All wisdom's lost in comprehending thine.

WINTER RAINBOW

Thou Winter, thou art keen, intensely keen;
    Thy cutting frowns experience bids me know,
For in thy weather days and days I've been,
    As grinning north-winds horribly did blow,
And pepper'd round my head their hail and snow:
    Throughout thy reign 'tis mine each year to prove thee;
And, spite of every storm I've beetled in,
    With all thy insults, Winter, I do love thee,
Thou half enchantress, like to pictur'd Sin!
    Though many frowns thy sparing smiles deform,
Yet when thy sunbeam shrinketh from its shroud,
    And thy bright rainbow gilds the purple storm,
I look entranced on thy painted cloud:
    And what wild eye with nature's beauties charm'd,
That hangs enraptur'd o'er each witching spell,
    Can see thee, Winter, then, and not be warm'd
To breathe thy praise, and say, 'I love thee well!'

CHILDISH RECOLLECTIONS

Perhaps it is foolish to remark it, but there are times and places
when I am a child at those things.—MACKENZIE.

Each scene of youth to me's a pleasing toy,
  Which memory, like a lover, dotes upon;
And mix'd with them I am again a boy,
  With tears and sighs regretting pleasures gone.

Ah! with enthusiast excesses wild
  The scenes of childhood meet my moist'ning eye,
With all the foibled weakness of a child
  I feel the raptures of delights gone by.

And still I fancy, as around I stroll
  Each boyish scene, to mark the sport and game,
Others are living with a self-like soul,
  That think, and love such trifles, just the same.

An old familiar spot I witness here,
  With young companions where we oft have met:
Tho' since we play'd 'tis bleach'd with many a year,
  The sports as warmly thrill my bosom yet.

Here winds the dyke where oft we jump'd across,
  'Tis just as if it were but yesternight;
There hangs the gate we call'd our wooden horse,
  Where we in swee-swaw riding took delight.

And everything shines round me just as then,
  Mole-hills, and trees, and bushes speckling wild,
That freshen all those pastimes up agen—
  Oh, grievous day that chang'd me from a child!

To seek the plaything and the pleasing toy,
  The painted pooty-shell and summer-flowers,
How blest was I when I was here a boy;
  What joys were mine in those delightful hours!

On this same bank I bound my posies up,
　And cull'd the sweetest blossoms one by one;
The cowslips still entice me down to stoop,
　But all the feelings they inspir'd are gone.

Though in the midst of each endear'd delight,
　Where still the cowslips to the breezes bow,
Though all my childish scenes are in my sight,
　Sad manhood marks me an intruder now.

Here runs the brook which I have damm'd and stopt
　With choking sods, and water-weeds, and stones,
And watch'd with joy till bursting off it plopt,
　In rushing gushes of wild murmuring groans.

Here stands the tree with clasping ivy bound,
　Which oft I've climb'd, to see the men at plough,
And chequer'd fields for many a furlong round,
　Rock'd by the winds upon its topmost bough.

Ah, on this bank how happy have I felt,
　When here I sat and mutter'd nameless songs,
And with the shepherd-boy and neatherd knelt
　Upon yon rush-beds, plaiting whips and thongs.

Fond memory warms, as when with gravel-shells
　I pil'd my fancied cots and walled rings,
And scoop'd with wooden knife my little wells,
　And fill'd them up with water from the springs.

Ah, memory sighs, now hope my heart beguiles
　To build as yet snug cots to cheer despair,
While fate at distance mocks with girning smiles,
　And calls my structures castles in the air.

Now e'en the thistles quaking in the wind,
　The very rushes nodding o'er the green,
Hold each expressive language to my mind,
　And, like old comrades, tell of what has been.

O sweet the joys from infancy that flow!
　　When can we witness joys so sweet as then?
Might I but have my choice of bliss below,
　　I 'd only ask to be a boy agen.

Life owns no joy so pleasant as the past,
　　That banish'd pleasure, wrapt in memory's womb:
It leaves a flavour sweet to every taste,
　　Like the sweet substance of the honeycomb.

TO THE RIGHT HONORABLE ADMIRAL LORD RADSTOCK

'Tis sweet to recollect life's past controls,
　　And turn to days of sorrow when they're by,
And think of gentle friends and feeling souls
　　That offered shelter when the storm was high.
It thrills one's heart: as mariners have turn'd,
　　When 'scap'd from shipwreck 'mid the billows' roar,
To look on fragments that the tempest spurn'd,
　　On which they clung, and struggled to the shore,
So sweet it is to turn. And, hour by hour,
　　Reflection muses on the good and great,
That lent a portion of their wealthy power,
　　And sav'd a wormling from destruction's fate.
Oft to the patron of her first essays
　　The rural muse, O Radstock, turns her eye,
Not with the fulsome noise of fawning praise,
　　But soul's deep gushings in a silent sigh;
As drooping blossoms, dwindling deep in shade,
　　Should e'er a sunbeam to their lot be given,
Perk up in hopeful bloom their feeble head,
　　And seemly offer silent thanks to heaven.

TO THE RURAL MUSE

Simple enchantress! wreath'd in summer blooms
　　Of slender bent-stalks topt with feathery down,
Heath's creeping vetch, and glaring yellow brooms,

With ash-keys nodding on thy rushy crown;
Simple enchantress! how I've woo'd thy smiles,
  How often sought thee far from flush'd renown,
Sought thee unseen where fountain-waters fell,
  Touch'd thy wild reed unheard, in weary toils;
And though my heavy hand thy song defiles,
  'Tis hard to leave thee, and to bid farewell.

Simple enchantress! ah, from all renown
  Far off, my soul hath warm'd in bliss to see
The varied figures on thy summer-gown,
  That nature's finger works so 'witchingly;
The colour'd flower, the silken leaves that crown
  Green nestling bower-bush and high towering tree;
Brooks of the sunny green and shady dell:
  Ah, sweet full many a time they've been to me;
And though my weak song falters, sung to thee,
  I cannot, wild enchantress, bid farewell.

Still must I seek thee, though I wind the brook
  When morning sunbeams o'er the waters glide,
And trace thy footsteps in the lonely nook
  As evening moists the daisy by thy side;
Ah, though I woo thee on thy bed of thyme—
  If courting thee be deem'd ambition's pride,
It is so passing sweet with thee to dwell—
  If love for thee in clowns be call'd a crime,
Forgive presumption, O thou queen of rhyme!
  I've lov'd thee long, I cannot bid farewell.

IN AUTUMN

THE fields all cleared, the labouring mice
  To sheltering hedge and wood patrol,
Where hips and haws for food suffice
  That chumbled lie about the hole.

241

And squirrel, bobbing from the eye,
    Is busy now about its hoard,
And in old nest of crow and pie
    Its winter store is oft explored.

The leaves now leave the willows grey
    And down the brook they wind:
So hopes and pleasures whirl away
    And vanish from the mind.

FRAGMENT

How eager doth he eddy round
    To seek his peace and rest,
And blest to know where peace is found
    Drops happy in his nest.

Ah, pleasure's but in vain display'd
    My lot to discommode,
Where hope but checkers up the shade
    To show my gloomy road.

Alas, to me no home belongs
    But what my dreams create;
Vain cuckoo-like, I sing my songs,
    And leave the rest to fate.

AN AFTER-REPENTANCE

I SEEK the shop that's full of noise,
    Where signs in gay temptations hing,
And join the ranting, roaring boys,
To blunt old memory's hornet sting.

Past is the scene of love's delights,
    Curst bitter dregs the sweet succeed;
Gone are my honeymooning nights;
    How hard love's sweets should prove a deed!

But parsons' lessons fools deceive;
    Their pocket fees their preachings suit;
Without we wed, they'd make's believe
    To taste of love 's forbidden fruit.
Good Lord! I tremble at the crime,
    A sinful, sad, unruly lout;
I quake, I quake at gossip time,
    Whose tongue blabs every secret out.

TO AN EARLY COWSLIP

Cowslip bud, so early peeping,
　　Warm'd by April's hazard hours;
O'er thy head though sunshine's creeping,
　　Close the threatening tempest lowers:
Trembling blossom, let me bear thee
　　To a better, safer home;
Though a fairer blossom wear thee,
　　Never tempest there shall come:

Mary's bonny breast to charm thee,
　　Bosom soft as down can be,
Eyes like any suns to warm thee,
　　And scores of sweets unknown to me;
Ah! for joys thou'lt there be meeting,
　　In a station so divine,
I could wish, what's vain repeating,
　　Cowslip bud, thy life were mine.

A PASTORAL

Surely Lucy love returns,
　　Though her meaning's not reveal'd;
Surely love her bosom burns,
　　Which her coyness keeps conceal'd:
Else what means that flushing cheek,
　　When with her I chance to be?
And those looks, that almost speak
　　A secret warmth of love for me?

Would she, where she valued not,
　　Give such proofs of sweet esteem?
Think what flowers for me she's got—
　　What can this but fondness seem?

When, to try their pleasing powers,
    Swains for her cull every grove,
When she takes my meaner flowers,
    What can guide the choice but love?

Was not love seen yesternight,
    When two sheep had rambled out?
Who but Lucy set them right?
    The token told, without a doubt.
When others stare, she turns and frowns;
    When I but glance, a smile I see;
When others talk, she calls them clowns;
    But never says such words to me.

And when, with swains to love inclin'd,
    To bear her milk I often go;
Though they beg first, she turns behind,
    And lingers till I ask her too:
O'er stepping-stones that cross the brooks,
    Who mind such trifles plainly see,
In vain the shepherds prop their hooks,
    She always gi'es her hand to me.

To-day, while chaps were standing by,
    She wish'd for roses from the bower;
The man too wish'd was in her eye,
    Though others flew to get the flower:
And striving all they could to please,
    When prickt with thorns they left the tree,
She never seem'd concern'd at these,
    But only turn'd to caution me.

To-day she careless view'd the bark
    Where many a swain had cut her name,
Till whisper'd which was Colin's mark,
    Her cheek was instant in a flame:
In blushing beckons love did call,
    And courage seiz'd the chance the while;
And though I kiss'd her 'fore them all,
    Her worst rebukings wore a smile.

TO A CITY GIRL

Sweet Mary, though nor sighs nor pains
   Impassion'd courtship prove,
My simple song the truth ne'er feigns
   To win thee to my love:
I ask thee from thy bustling life,
   Where naught can pleasing prove,
From city noise, and care, and strife
   Oh, come, and be my love!

If harmless mirth delight thine eyes,
   Then make my cot thy home;
The country life abounds with joys,
   And whispers thee to come;
Here fiddles urge thy nimble feet
   Adown the dance to move,
Here pleasures in continuance meet—
   Oh, come, and be my love!

If music's charm, that all delights,
   Has witcheries for thee,
The country then my love invites,
   In echoed melody;
Here thrushes chant their madrigals,
   Here breathes the ringed dove
Soft as day's closing murmur falls—
   Oh, come, and be my love!

If nature's prospects, wood, and vale,
   Thy visits can entice,
The country's scenes thy coming hail,
   To meet a paradise;
Here pride can raise no barring wall
   To hide the flower and grove,
Here fields are gardens, free for all—
   Oh, come, and be my love!

If music, mirth, and all combine
    To make my cot thy home,
To tempt thee, Mary, to be mine,
    Then why delay to come?
Here night-birds sing my love to sleep,
    Here sweet thy dreams shall prove,
Here in my arms shall Mary creep—
    Oh, come, and be my love!

IMPROMPTU

'WHERE art thou wandering, little child?'
    I said to one I met to-day—
She push'd her bonnet up and smil'd,
    'I'm going upon the green to play:
Folks tell me that the may's in flower,
    That cowslip-peeps are fit to pull,
And I've got leave to spend an hour
    To get this little basket full.'

—And thou'st got leave to spend an hour!
    My heart repeated—she was gone;
—And thou hast heard the thorn's in flower,
    And childhood's bliss is urging on:
Ah, happy child! thou mak'st me sigh,
    This once as happy heart of mine,
Would nature with the boon comply,
    How gladly would I change for thine.

TO . . . . .

MY love, thou'rt like yon morning bed
      The hills above
        In yonder east we see;
Thy breasts so white, thy cheeks so red,
    Oh, sweet the morning wakes in thee,
      My witching love.

247

My love, thou'rt like the summer's day
That wakes the dove
And smiles so sweet we see;
Thy looks so smiling, dress so gay,
Oh, sweet the summer shines in thee,
My witching love.

My love, thou'rt like the evening scene,
As sweet to prove,
Oh, passing sweet to me;
So meek, so gentle in thy mien,
Oh, sweet the evening meets in thee,
My witching love.

COUNTRY SWEETHEARTS

'I'LL ne'er walk at even grim
When the night is glimpt wi' grey;
When the light is waxing dim;
Deeds are done at closing day.
Ever sin' by blossom'd bean
While the gnats were dancing by,
Ye did on my bosom lean,
Aye the tear's bin in my eye.

'Ever sin' ye pass'd the morn
When ye little dreamt a spy,
Meeting Dolly 'hind the thorn,
Aye the tear's bin in my eye.
Ever sin' ye vow'd to wed,
And I prov'd wi' heavy sigh
Ye'd the vow to many made,
Aye the tear's bin in my eye.'

'Sweet the tear shines on thee, love,
Which I soon will wash away;
Tenderness has won me, love,
Fear thou not the even grey.
Sin' we sat by beans in bloom,
I have bin the ring to buy;
Think no harm from that shall come,
Wipe the tear from either eye.'

BALLAD

A WEEDLING wild, on lonely lea,
My evening rambles chanc'd to see;
And much the weedling tempted me
        To crop its tender flower:
Expos'd to wind and heavy rain,
Its head bow'd lowly on the plain;
And silently it seem'd complain
        Of life's endanger'd hour.

'And wilt thou bid my bloom decay,
And crop my flower, and me betray,
And cast my injur'd sweets away,'
        Its silence seemly sigh'd—
'A moment's idol of thy mind?
And is a stranger so unkind,
To leave a shameful root behind,
        Bereft of all its pride?'

And so it seemly did complain;
And beating fell the heavy rain;
And low it droop'd upon the plain,
        To fate resign'd to fall:
My heart did melt at its decline,
And 'Come,' said I, 'thou gem divine,
My fate shall stand the storm with thine';
        So took the root and all.

BALLAD

Where the dark ivy the thorn-tree is mounting,
 Sweet shielding in summer the nest of the dove,
There lies the sweet spot, by the side of the fountain,
 That's dear to all sweetness that dwells upon love:
For there setting sunbeams, ere even's clouds close 'em,
 Once stretch'd a long shadow of one I adore;
And there did I meet the sweet sighs of the bosom
 Of one ever dear, though I meet her no more.

And who with a soul and a share of warm feeling,
 And who with a heart that owns love for the fair,
Can pass by the spot where his first look was stealing,
 Or first fondness ventur'd love-tales to declare?
Ah, who can pass by it, and notice it never?
 Can long days forget on first fondness to call?
Sure time kindles love to burn brighter than ever,
 And nature's first choice must be sweetest of all.

I prove it, sweet Mary, I prove it too truly;
 That fountain, once sweeten'd with presence of thee,
As oft as I pass it at eve, and as duly
 As May brings the time round, I think upon thee:
I go and I sit on the soft bed of rushes,
 As nigh as remembrance the spot can decide;
There lonely I whisper, in sorrow's warm gushes,
 That bliss when my Mary was plac'd by my side.

It grieves me to see the first open may-blossom;
 For, Mary, if still 'tis remember'd by thee,
'Twas just then thou wish'd one to place in thy bosom,
 When scarce a peep show'd itself open to me.
Each May with a tear are that flower and I parted,
 As near that lov'd spot it first peeps on the bower;
'I've no cause to pluck thee,' I sigh broken-hearted,
 'There's no Mary nigh to be pleas'd with the flower.'

250

BALLAD

When nature's beauty shone complete,
　　With summer's lovely weather,
And even, shadowing day's retreat,
　　Brought swains and maids together;
Then I did meet a charming face,
　　But who—I'll be discreet:
Though lords themselves without disgrace
　　Might love whom I did meet.

'Good evening, lovely lass,' said I,
　　To make her silence break;
The instant evening's blushing sky
　　Was rivall'd in her cheek;
Her eyes were turn'd upon the ground,
　　She made me no reply,
But downward looks my bosom found:
　　'You've won me,' whisper'd I.

And I did try all love could do,
　　And she tried all to fly,
Now lingering slow to let me go,
　　Then hurrying to pass by:
'My love,' said I, 'you've me mistook,
　　No harm from me you'll meet';
She only answer'd with a look,
　　But it was 'witching sweet.

I own'd my love, and prais'd her eyes,
　　Whose power she little knew;
And doubtless then she fancied lies
　　What since she's proved true;
Confusion mingling fear and shame,
　　Between the 'Yes' and 'No,'
Oh, when I mention'd love's soft name
　　How sweet her cheeks did glow!

I told her all the open truth,
　'Bout being a labouring swain,
With not one groat to boast, forsooth,
　But what hard work did gain,
And begg'd excuse in such-like clothes
　Within her way to fall;
Wenches are ta'en with flashy beaus—
　But she excus'd it all.

As near the humble cot we came,
　Her fears did meet alarm
Lest friends imprudent ways should blame,
　And think I meant her harm:
So there I prest her to my heart,
　And there a kiss was ta'en,
And there I vow'd, ere we did part,
　To meet her soon again.

BALLAD

I LOVE thee, sweet Mary, but love thee in fear;
　Were I but the morning breeze, healthy and airy,
As thou goest a-walking I'd breathe in thine ear,
　And whisper and sigh how I love thee, my Mary!

I wish but to touch thee, but wish it in vain;
　Wert thou but a streamlet a-winding so clearly,
And I little globules of soft dropping rain,
　How fond would I press thy white bosom, my Mary!

I would steal a kiss, but I dare not presume;
　Wert thou but a rose in thy garden, sweet fairy,
And I a bold bee for to rifle its bloom,
　A whole summer's day would I kiss thee, my Mary!

I long to be with thee, but cannot tell how;
　　Wert thou but the eldern that grows by thy dairy,
And I the blest woodbine to twine on the bough,
　　I'd embrace thee and stick to thee ever, my Mary!

SONG

Swamps of wild rush-beds, and sloughs' squashy traces,
　　Grounds of rough fallows with thistle and weed,
Flats and low valleys of kingcups and daisies,
　　Sweetest of subjects are ye for my reed:
Ye commons left free in the rude rags of nature,
　　Ye brown heaths beclothed in furze as ye be,
My wild eye in rapture adores every feature,
　　Ye are dear as this heart in my bosom to me.

O native endearments! I would not forsake ye,
　　I would not forsake ye for sweetest of scenes;
For sweetest of gardens that nature could make me,
　　I would not forsake ye, dear valleys and greens:
Tho' nature ne'er dropt ye a cloud-resting mountain,
　　Nor waterfalls tumble their music so free;
Had nature denied ye a bush, tree, or fountain,
　　Ye still had been lov'd as an Eden by me.

And long, my dear valleys, long, long may ye flourish,
　　Though rush-beds and thistles make most of your pride;
May showers never fail the green's daisies to nourish,
　　Nor suns dry the fountain that rills by its side.
Your skies may be gloomy, and misty your mornings,
　　Your flat swampy valleys unwholesome may be;
Still, refuse of nature, without her adornings
　　Ye are dear as this heart in my bosom to me.

SONG

THE sultry day it wears away,
 And o'er the distant leas
The mist again, in purple stain,
 Falls moist on flower and trees:
His home to find, the weary hind
 Glad leaves his carts and ploughs;
While maidens fair, with bosoms bare,
 Go coolly to their cows.

The red round sun his work has done,
 And dropt into his bed;
And sweetly shines, the oaks behind,
 His curtains fring'd with red:
And step by step the night has crept,
 And day, as loath, retires;
But clouds, more dark, night's entrance mark,
 Till day's last spark expires.

Pride of the vales, the nightingales
 Now charm the oaken grove;
And loud and long, with amorous tongue,
 They try to please their love:
And where the rose reviving blows
 Upon the swelter'd bower,
I'll take my seat, my love to meet,
 And wait th'appointed hour.

And like the bird, whose joy is heard
 Now he his love can join,
Who hails so loud the even's shroud,
 I'll wait as glad for mine:
As weary bees o'er parched leas
 Now meet reviving flowers;
So on her breast I'll sink to rest,
 And bless the evening hours.

SONG

One gloomy eve I roam'd about
    'Neath Oxey's hazel bowers,
While timid hares were daring out,
    To crop the dewy flowers;
And soothing was the scene to me,
    Right placid was my soul,
My breast was calm as summer's sea
    When waves forget to roll.

But short was even's placid smile,
    My startled soul to charm,
When Nelly lightly skipt the stile,
    With milk-pail on her arm:
One careless look on me she flung,
    As bright as parting day;
And like a hawk from covert sprung,
    It pounc'd my peace away.

SONG

A beautiful flower, that bedeck'd a mean pasture,
    In virgin perfection I found;
Its fair bloom stood naked to every disaster,
    And deep the storm gather'd around:
The rose in the midst of its brambles is blooming,
    Whose weapons intruders alarm,
But sweetest of blossoms, fond, fair, and weak woman
    Has nothing to guard her from harm.

Each stranger seem'd struck with a blossom so lovely,
    In such a lone valley that grew;
The clown's admiration was cast on it roughly,
    While blushing it shrank from his view:

Oh, sweet was the eve when I found the fair blossom,
  Sure never seem'd blossom so fair,
I instant transplanted its charms to my bosom,
  And deep has the root gather'd there.

SONG

There was a time when love's young flowers
  With many a joy my bosom prest:
Sweet hours of bliss!—but short are hours,
  Those hours are fled—and I'm distrest.
I would not wish, in reason's spite,
  I would not wish new joy to gain;
I only wish for one delight—
  To see those hours of bliss again.

There was a day when love was young
  And naught but bliss did there belong,
When blackbirds nestling o'er us sung,
  Ah me! what sweetness wak'd his song.
I wish not springs for ever fled;
  I wish not birds' forgotten strain;
I only wish for feelings dead
  To warm, and wake, and feel again.

But, ah! what once was joy is past:
  The time's gone by; the day and hour
Are whirring fled on trouble's blast,
  As winter nips the summer flower.
A shadow is but left the mind,
  Of joys that once were real to view;
An echo only fills the wind,
  With mocking sounds that once were true.

SONG

THERE's the daisy, the woodbine,
  And crow-flower so golden;
There's the wild rose, the eglantine,
  And May-buds unfolding;
There are flowers for my fairy,
  And bowers for my love:
Wilt thou gang with me, Mary,
  To the banks of Broomsgrove?

There's the thorn-bush and the ash-tree
  For to shield from the heat,
While the brook to refresh thee
  Runs close by thy feet;
The thrushes are chanting clear,
  In the pleasures of love;
Thou'rt the only thing wanting here
  Mid the sweets of Broomsgrove.

Then come ere a minute's gone,
  Since the long summer's day
Puts her wings swift as linnets' on
  For hieing away.
Then come with no doubtings near,
  To fear a false love;
For there's nothing without thee, dear,
  Can please in Broomsgrove.

The woodbine may nauntle here,
  In blossoms so fine,
The wild roses mantling near
  In blushes may shine;
Mary queen of each blossom proves,
  She's the blossom I love,
She's the all that my bosom loves
  'Mong the sweets of Broomsgrove.

SONG

MARY, the day of love's pleasures has been,
  And the day is o'erclouded and gone;
These eyes all their fullness of pleasure have seen,
  What they never again shall look on.
The sun has oft risen and shrunk from the heaven,
  And flowers with the night have been wet;
And many a smile on another's been given,
  Since the first smile of Mary I met.

And eyes have been won with thy charms when thou smil'd,
  As ripe blossoms tempting the bee;
And kisses the sweets of thy lips have defil'd,
  Since last they breath'd heaven on me.
Their honey's first tasting was lovely and pleasant,
  But others have rifled the cell:
Love sickens to think of the past and the present,
  Bidding all that was Mary farewell.

The blushes of rose-blossoms shortly endure,
  Though sweet is their unbudding gem;
But love in long absence may often keep pure,
  If jealousy blight not the stem.
We look o'er the doubts of our minds, and we sicken,
  And hope what we think is a dream;
We turn to the past, and love's jealousies quicken—
  We cannot first pleasures redeem.

The sun will rise bright, though in night it be set;
  And the dew-drop from blossoms will sever;
But the doubtfulness, Mary, that rose since we met,
  Is pain to this bosom for ever.
The beauty of things raises constant desire;
  The gem rarely 'scapeth the view;
In the fears of a second first love doth expire,
  And biddeth false Mary adieu!

SONG

MARY, leave thy lowly cot
  When thy thickest jobs are done;
When thy friends will miss thee not,
  Mary, to the pastures run.
Where we met the other night
  'Neath the bush upon the plain,
Be it dark or be it light,
  Ye may guess we'll meet again.

Should ye go or should ye not,
  Never shilly-shally, dear.
Leave your work and leave your cot,
  Nothing need ye doubt or fear:
Fools may tell ye lies in spite,
  Calling me a roving swain;
Think what passed the other night—
  I'll be bound ye'll meet again.

SONNETS

ON DEATH

O Life, thy name to me's a galling sound,
　　A sound I fain would wish to breathe no more;
One only peace for me my hopes have found,
　　When thy existence and wild race is o'er;
When Death, with one, heals every other wound,
And lays my aching head in the cold ground.
　　O happy hour!　I only wish to have
　　Another moment's gasp, and then the grave.
I only wish for one departing sigh,
A welcome farewell take of all, and die.
　　Thou'st given me little, world, for thanks' return,
Thou tempt'st me little with thee still to bide:
　　One only cause in leaving thee I mourn,
That I had e'er been born, nor in the cradle died.

NATIVE SCENES

O native scenes, naught to my heart clings nearer
　　Than you, ye Edens of my youthful hours;
Naught in this world warms my affections dearer
　　Than you, ye plains of white and yellow flowers,
　　Ye hawthorn hedgerows, and ye woodbine bowers,
Where youth has rov'd, and still where manhood roves
The pasture-pathway 'neath the willow groves.
　Ah, as my eye looks o'er those lovely scenes,
All the delights of former life beholding;
　　Spite of the pain, the care that intervenes—
When lov'd remembrance is her bliss unfolding,
　　Picking her childish posies on your greens—
My soul can peer o'er its distress awhile,
And sorrow's cheek find leisure for a smile.

PEACE

I SEEK for peace—I care not where 'tis found:
   On this rude scene in briers and brambles drest,
If peace dwells here, 'tis consecrated ground,
   And owns the power to give my bosom rest;
To soothe the rankling of each bitter wound,
   Gall'd by rude envy's adder-biting jest,
And worldly strife—ah, I am looking round
For peace's hermitage, can it be found?—
Surely that breeze that o'er the blue wave curl'd
Did whisper soft, 'Thy wanderings here are blest.'
How different from the language of the world!
Nor jeers nor taunts in this still spot are given:
Its calm's a balsam to a soul distrest;
And, where peace smiles, a wilderness is heaven.

MORNING

OH, now the crimson east, its fire-streak burning,
   Tempts me to wander 'neath the blushing morn,
Winding the zig-zag lane, turning and turning,
   As winds the crooked fence's wilder'd thorn.
Where is the eye can gaze upon the blushes,
Unmov'd, with which yon cloudless heaven flushes?
   I cannot pass the very bramble, weeping
'Neath dewy tear-drops that its spears surround,
   Like harlot's mockery on the wan cheek creeping,
Gilding the poison that is meant to wound—
   I cannot pass the bent, ere gales have shaken
Its transient crowning off, each point adorning—
   But all the feelings of my soul awaken,
To own the witcheries of most lovely morning.

TO AN HOUR-GLASS

OLD-FASHIONED uncouth measurer of the day,
  I love to watch thy filtering burthen pass;
Though some there are that live would bid thee stay;
  But these view reasons through a different glass
From him, time's meter, who addresses thee.
  The world has joys which they may deem as such;
The world has wealth to season vanity,
  And wealth is theirs to make their vainness much:
But small to do with joys and fortune's fee
Hath he, time's chronicler, who welcomes thee.
  So jog thou on, through hours of doom'd distress;
So haste thou on the glimpse of hopes to come,
  As every sand-grain counts a trouble less,
As every drain'd glass leaves me nearer home.

TO AN ANGRY BEE

MALICIOUS insect, little vengeful bee,
  With venom-sting thou'rt whirling round and round
A harmless head that ne'er meant wrong to thee,
  And friendship's hand it is thou'dst wish to wound:
Cool thy revenge, and judge thy foes aright;
  The harden'd neatherd and the sweet-tooth'd boy—
Thy moss-wrapp'd treasures, if but in their sight,
  Soon would they all thy honey'd lives destroy:
But delve the cowslip-peep in labour free,
And dread no pilferer of thy hoards in me.
  Thus man to man oft takes a friend for foe,
And spurns a blessing when it's in his power,
  Mistakes real happiness for worldly woe,
Crops sorrow's weed, and treads on pleasure's flower.

DAYBREAK

THE red east glows, the dewy cheek of day
  Has not yet met the sun's o'erpowering smile;
The dew-drops in their beauty still are gay,
  Save those the shepherd's early steps defile.
  Pleas'd will I linger o'er the scene awhile;
The black clouds melt away, the larks awaken—
  Sing, rising bird, and I will join with thee:
With daybreak's beauties I have much been taken,
  As thy first anthem breath'd its melody.
  I've stood and paus'd the varied cloud to see,
And warm'd in ecstasy, and look'd and warm'd,
  When day's first rays, the far hill-top adorning,
Fring'd the blue clouds with gold. Oh, doubly charm'd
  I hung in raptures then on early morning.

TO THE IVY

DARK creeping Ivy, with thy berries brown,
  That fondly twists on ruins all thine own,
Old spire-points studding with a leafy crown
  Which every minute threatens to dethrone;
With fearful eye I view thy height sublime,
  And oft with quicker step retreat from thence
Where thou, in weak defiance, striv'st with Time,
  And hold'st his weapons in a dread suspense.
But, bloom of ruins, thou art dear to me,
  When, far from danger's way, thy gloomy pride
Wreathes picturesque around some ancient tree
  That bows his branches by some fountain-side:
Then sweet it is from summer suns to be,
With thy green darkness overshadowing me.

HOPE

THIS world has suns, but they are overcast;
　　This world has sweets, but they're of ling'ring bloom;
Life still expects, and empty falls at last;
　　Warm Hope on tiptoe drops into the tomb.
Life's journey's rough—Hope seeks a smoother way,
　　And dwells on fancies which to-morrow see :
To-morrow comes, true copy of to-day,
　　And empty shadow of what is to be;
Yet cheated Hope on future still depends,
And ends but only when our being ends.
　　I long have hoped, and still shall hope the best
Till heedless weeds are scrambling over me,
　　And hopes and ashes both together rest
At journey's end, with them that cease to be.

THE ARBOUR

THERE is a wilder'd spot delights me well,
　　Pent in a corner of my native vale,
Where tiny blossoms with a purple bell
　　Shiver their beauties to the autumn gale.
　　'Tis one of those mean arbours that prevail
With manhood's weakness, still to seek and love
　　For what is past.　Destruction's axe did fail
To maul it down with its companion grove.
　　Though but a trifling thorn, oft shelt'ring warm
A brood of summer birds, by nature led
　　To seek for covert in a hasty storm,
I often think it lifts its lonely cares,
　　In piteous bloom where all the rest are fled,
Like a poor warrior the rude battle spares.

NATURE

O SIMPLE Nature, how I do delight
  To pause upon thy trifles—foolish things,
As some would call them.   On the summer night,
  Tracing the lane-path where the dog-rose hings
  With dew-drops seeth'd, while chick'ring cricket sings,
My eye can't help but glance upon its leaves,
  Where love's warm beauty steals her sweetest blush,
When, soft the while, the even silent heaves
  Her pausing breath just trembling thro' the bush,
  And then again dies calm, and all is hush.
Oh, how I feel, just as I pluck the flower
  And stick it to my breast—words can't reveal;
But there are souls that in this lovely hour
  Know all I mean, and feel whate'er I feel.

A WISH

BE where I may when Death brings in his bill,
  Demanding payment for life's ling'ring debt,
Or in my native village nestling still,
  Or tracing scenes I've never known as yet,
Oh, let one wish, go where I will, be mine—
  To turn me back and wander home to die,
'Mong nearest friends my latest breath resign,
  And in the churchyard with my kindred lie,
'Neath the thick-shaded sycamore's decay,
  Its broad leaves trembling to the breeze of day:
  To see its shadow o'er my ashes wave,
How soothing will it be, while, hovering near,
  My unseen spirit haunts its daisied grave,
Pausing on scenes in life once lov'd so dear.

THE LAST OF APRIL

OLD April wanes, and her last dewy morn
 Her death-bed steeps in tears: to hail the May
New blooming blossoms 'neath the sun are born,
 And all poor April's charms are swept away.
 The early primrose, peeping once so gay,
Is now chok'd up with many a mounting weed,
 And the poor violet we once admired
Creeps in the grass unsought for—flowers succeed,
 Gaudy and new, and more to be desired,
 And of the old the schoolboy seemeth tired.
So with us all, poor April, as with thee!
 Each hath his day; the future brings my fears:
Friends may grow weary, new flowers rising be,
 And my last end, like thine, be steep'd in tears.

HEREAFTER

AH, when this world and I have shaken hands,
 And all the frowns of this sad life got through,
When from pale care and sorrow's dismal lands
 I turn a welcome and a wish'd adieu;
How blest and happy, to eternal day,
 To endless happiness without a pain,
Will my poor weary spirit sail away,
 That long long look'd-for 'better place' to gain:
How sweet the scenes will open on her eye,
 Where no more troubles, no more cares annoy;
All the sharp brambles of this life torn by,
 And safely moor'd in heaven's eternal joy:
Sweet will it seem to Fate's oppressed worm,
As trembling sunbeams creeping from the storm.

EARLY SPRING

Winter is past—the little bee resumes
    Her share of sun and shade, and o'er the lea
Hums her first hymnings to the flowers' perfumes,
    And wakes a sense of gratefulness in me:
The little daisy keeps its wonted pace;
    Ere March by April gets disarm'd of snow,
A look of joy opes on its smiling face,
    Turn'd to that Power that suffers it to blow.
Ah, pleasant time, as pleasing as you be,
One still more pleasing Hope reserves for me;
    Where suns, unsetting, one long summer shine,
Flowers endless bloom, where winter ne'er destroys:
    Oh, may the good man's righteous end be mine,
That I may witness these unfading joys.

SUMMER

How sweet, when weary, dropping on a bank,
    Turning a look around on things that be!
E'en feather-headed grasses, spindling rank,
    A-trembling to the breeze one loves to see;
    And yellow buttercup, where many a bee
Comes buzzing to its head and bows it down;
    And the great dragon-fly with gauzy wings,
In gilded coat of purple, green, or brown,
    That on broad leaves of hazel basking clings,
    Fond of the sunny day—and other things
Past counting, please me while thus here I lie.
    But still reflective pains are not forgot:
Summer sometime shall bless this spot, when I,
    Hapt in the cold dark grave, can heed it not.

THE ANTS

WHAT wonder strikes the curious, while he views
   The black ant's city, by a rotten tree
Or woodland bank!   In ignorance we muse:
   Pausing, annoy'd, we know not what we see,
   Such government and thought there seem to be;
Some looking on, and urging some to toil,
   Dragging their loads of bent-stalks slavishly;
And what's more wonderful, when big loads foil
One ant or two to carry, quickly then
A swarm flock round to help their fellow-men.
   Surely they speak a language whisperingly,
Too fine for us to hear; and sure their ways
   Prove they have kings and laws, and that they be
Deformed remnants of the fairy-days.

MILTON ABBEY

HERE grandeur triumphs at its topmost pitch
   In gardens, groves, and all that life beguiles;
Here want, too, meets a blessing from the rich,
   And hospitality for ever smiles;
Soldier or sailor, from his many toils,
   Here finds no cause to rail at pomp and pride;
He shows his scars, and talks of battle's broils,
   And wails his poverty, and is supplied.
No dogs bark near, the fainting wretch to chide,
   That bows to misery his aged head,
And tells how better luck did once betide,
   And how he came to beg his crust of bread:
   Here he but sighs his sorrows and is fed—
Mansion of wealth, by goodness dignified!

IN HILLY WOOD

How sweet to be thus nestling deep in boughs,
  Upon an ashen stoven pillowing me;
Faintly are heard the ploughmen at their ploughs,
  But not an eye can find its way to see.
The sunbeams scarce molest me with a smile,
  So thick the leafy armies gather round;
And where they do, the breeze blows cool the while,
  Their leafy shadows dancing on the ground.
Full many a flower, too, wishing to be seen,
Perks up its head the hiding grass between.
  In mid-wood silence, thus, how sweet to be;
Where all the noises that on peace intrude
  Come from the chittering cricket, bird, and bee,
Whose songs have charms to sweeten solitude.

A COPSE IN WINTER

SHADES, though you're leafless, save the bramble-spear,
  Whose weather-beaten leaves, of purple stain,
In hardy stubbornness cling all the year
  To their old thorns, till spring buds new again;
Shades, still I love you better than the plain,
  For here I find the earliest flowers that blow,
While on the bare blea bank do yet remain
  Old winter's traces, little heaps of snow.
  Beneath your ashen roots, primroses grow
From dead grass tufts and matted moss, once more;
  Sweet beds of violets dare again be seen
In their deep purple pride; and, gay display'd,
  The crow-flowers, creeping from the naked green,
Add early beauties to your sheltering shade.

269

TO A RED CLOVER BLOSSOM

SWEET bottle-shaped flower of lushy red,
  Born when the summer wakes her warmest breeze,
Among the meadow's waving grasses spread,
  Or 'neath the shade of hedge or clumping trees,
Bowing on slender stem thy heavy head;
In sweet delight I view thy summer bed,
  And list the drone of heavy humble-bees
Along thy honey'd garden gaily led,
  Down cornfield, striped balks, and pasture leas.
Fond warmings of the soul, that long have fled,
  Revive my bosom with their kindlings still,
As I bend musing o'er thy ruddy pride;
  Recalling days when, dropt upon a hill,
I cut my oaten trumpets by thy side.

NIGHT

NIGHT spreads upon the plain her ebon pall,
  Day seems unable to wash out the stain;
A pausing truce kind nature gives to all,
  And fairy nations now have leave to reign:
So may conjecturing fancy think, and feign.
  Doubtless in tiny legions, now unseen,
They venture from their dwellings once again:
  From keck-stalk cavity, or hollow bean,
  Or perfum'd bosom of pea-flower between,
They to the dark green rings now haste, to meet,
  To dance, or pay some homage to their queen;
Or journey on, some pilgrim-friend to greet.
  With rushy switch they urge some beetle's flight,
  And ride to revel, ere 'tis morning light.

NOON

THE midday hour of twelve the clock counts o'er,
 A sultry stillness lulls the air asleep;
The very buzz of flies is heard no more,
 Nor faintest wrinkles o'er the waters creep.
Like one large sheet of glass the pool does shine,
 Reflecting in its face the burnt sunbeam:
The very fish their sturting play decline,
 Seeking the willow-shadows 'side the stream.
And, where the hawthorn branches o'er the pool,
 The little bird, forsaking song and nest,
Flutters on dripping twigs his limbs to cool,
 And splashes in the stream his burning breast.
Oh, free from thunder, for a sudden shower,
To cherish nature in this noonday hour!

AUTUMN

THE spring is gone, the summer-beauty wanes,
 Like setting sunbeams, in their last decline;
As evening shadows, lingering on the plains,
 Gleam dim and dimmer till they cease to shine:
The busy bee hath humm'd himself to rest;
 Flowers dry to seed, that held the sweets of spring;
Flown is the bird, and empty is the nest,
 His broods are rear'd, no joys are left to sing.
There hangs a dreariness about the scene,
A *present* shadow of a bright *has been*.
 Ah, sad to prove that pleasure's golden springs,
Like common fountains, should so quickly dry,
 And be so near allied to vulgar things!
The joys of this world are but born to die.

TO TIME

In fancy's eye, what an extended span,
 Time, hoary herald, has been stretch'd by thee:
Vain to conceive where thy dark burst began,
 Thou birthless, boundless, vast immensity!
Vain all conceptions of weak-minded man
 Thee to unravel from thy mystery!
In mortal wisdom, thou'st already ran
 A circled travel of eternity;
Still, but a moment of thy mighty plan
 Seems yet unwound, from what thy age shall see,
Consuming tyrant of all mortal kind!
 And what thou art, and what thou art to be,
Is known to none but that Immortal Mind
 Who reigns alone superior to thee.

WINTER

The small wind whispers through the leafless hedge
 Most sharp and chill, where the light snowy flakes
Rest on each twig and spike of wither'd sedge,
 Resembling scatter'd feathers; vainly breaks
The pale split sunbeam through the frowning cloud,
 On Winter's frowns below—from day to day
Unmelted still he spreads his hoary shroud,
 In dithering pride on the pale traveller's way,
Who, croodling, hastens from the storm behind
Fast gathering deep and black, again to find
 His cottage fire and corner's sheltering bounds;
Where, haply, such uncomfortable days
 Make musical the wood-sap's frizzling sounds,
And hoarse loud bellows puffing up the blaze.

TWILIGHT

The setting sun withdraws his yellow light,
    A gloomy staining shadows over all,
While the brown beetle, trumpeter of night,
    Proclaims his entrance with a droning call.
    How pleasant now, where slanting hazels fall
Thick o'er the woodland stile, to muse and lean;
    To pluck a woodbine from the shade withal,
And take short snatches o'er the moisten'd scene;
While deep and deeper shadows intervene,
    And leave fond Fancy moulding to her will
The cots, and groves, and trees so dimly seen,
    That die away more undiscerned still;
Bringing a sooty curtain o'er the sight,
And calmness in the bosom still as night.

SPRING

What charms does Nature at the spring put on,
    When hedges unperceiv'd get stain'd in green;
When even moss, that gathers on the stone,
    Crown'd with its little knobs of flowers is seen;
And every road and lane, through field and glen,
    Triumphant boasts a garden of its own.
In spite of nipping sheep, and hungry cow,
    The little daisy finds a place to blow:
And where old Winter leaves her splashy slough,
    The lady-smocks will not disdain to grow;
And dandelions like to suns will bloom,
    Aside some bank or hillock creeping low;
Though each too often meets a hasty doom
    From trampling clowns, who heed not where they go.

EARLY SORROWS

FULL many a sharp, sad, unexpected thorn
   Finds room to wound life's lacerated flower,
Which subtle fate, to every mortal born,
   Guides unprevented in an early hour.
   Ah, cruel thorns, too soon I felt your power;
Your throbbing shoots of never-ceasing pain
   Hope's blossoms in their bud did long devour,
And left continued my sad eyes to strain
   On wilder'd spots chok'd up with sorrow's weeds,
   Alas, that's shaken but too many seeds
To leave me room for hopes to bud again,
   But fate may torture, while it is decreed,
Where all my hopes' unblighted blooms remain,
   That Heaven's recompense shall this succeed.

EVENING

WHAT time the cricket unmolested sings,
And blundering beetles try their clumsy wings,
Leave me to meet the sweets of even's hour
By hawthorn hedges when the may's in flower,
With light enough to guard my cautious tread
As not to trample on the daisy's head,
Down beaten pathways of a wish'd extent,
Ev'n unimpeded by the bending bent
That, night and morning, bowing down with dew,
Sullies the brightness of the maiden's shoe:
There leave me musing 'neath the bow'ring ash,
Counting the knoll of bells, or spurting dash
Of muttering fountain-fall, with wild delight,
Till even loses in the blank of night.

EXPRESSION

EXPRESSION, throbbing utterance of the soul,
　　Born in some bard, when with the muses' fires
His feeling bursts unaw'd, above control,
　　And to the topmost height of heaven aspires,
Stealing the music of some angel's song
　　To tell of all he sees and all admires,
Which fancy's colours paint so sweet, so strong!
And to far humbler scenes thou dost belong:
　　In sorrow thou art warm, when speaking tears
Down some sad cheek in silence wail their wrong;
　　And, ah, most sweet, Expression, then appears
Thy smile of gratitude, where bosoms bleed.
　　Through high the lofty poet's frenzy steers,
In nature's simplest garb thou'rt sweet indeed.

CHILDHOOD

WHAT trifles touch our feelings, when we view
　　The simple scenes of childhood's early day,
Pausing on spots where gather'd blossoms grew,
　　Or favour'd seats of many a childish play;
Bush, dyke, or wood, where painted pooties lay,
　　Where oft we've crept and crept the shades among,
Where ivy hung old roots bemoss'd with grey,
　　Where nettles oft our infant fingers stung,
And tears would weep the gentle wounds away:
Ah, gentle wounds indeed, I well may say,
　　To those sad manhood's tortur'd passage found,
Where naked fate each day new pangs doth feel,
　　Clearing away the brambles that surround,
Inflicting tortures death can only heal.

A LAIR AT NOON

THE hawthorn gently stopt the sun, beneath,
  The ash above its quiv'ring shadows spread,
And downy bents, that to the air did wreathe,
  Bow'd 'neath my pressure in an easy bed;
The water whirled round each stunted nook,
  And sweet the splashings on the ear did swim
Of fly-bit cattle gulshing in the brook,
  Nibbling the grasses on the fountain's brim:
The little minnows, driv'n from their retreat,
Still sought the shelving bank to shun the heat,
  I fain had slept, but flies would buzz around;
I fain had looked calmly on the scene,
  But the sweet snug retreat my search had found
Waken'd the muse to sing the woody screen.

WRITTEN IN NOVEMBER

AUTUMN, I love thy parting look to view
  In cold November's day, so bleak and bare,
When thy life's dwindled thread worn nearly thro',
  With ling'ring, pott'ring pace, and head bleach'd bare,
Thou, like an old man, bidd'st the world adieu.
  I love thee well: and often, when a child,
Have roam'd the bare brown heath a flower to find;
  And in the moss-clad vale, and wood-bank wild,
Have cropt the little bell-flowers, paly blue,
  That trembling peept the shelt'ring bush behind.
When winnowing north-winds cold and blealy blew,
  How have I joy'd, with dithering hands, to find
Each fading flower; and still how sweet the blast,
Would bleak November's hour restore the joy that's past.

SUMMER TINTS

How sweet I've wander'd bosom-deep in grain,
   When Summer's mellowing pencil sweeps his shade
Of ripening tinges o'er the chequer'd plain:
   Light tawny oat-lands with a yellow blade,
   And bearded corn, like armies on parade,
Beans lightly scorch'd, that still preserve their green,
   And nodding lands of wheat in bleachy brown,
   And streaking banks, where many a maid and clown
Contrast a sweetness to the rural scene—
   Forming the little haycocks up and down:
While o'er the face of nature softly swept
   The ling'ring wind, mixing the brown and green
So sweet, that shepherds from their bowers have crept,
   And stood delighted musing o'er the scene.

SUMMER MORNING

I LOVE to peep out on a summer's morn,
   Just as the scouting rabbit seeks her shed,
And the coy hare squats nestling in the corn,
   Frit at the bow'd ear tott'ring o'er her head;
And blund'ring pheasant, that from covert springs,
   His short sleep broke by early trampling feet,
Makes one to startle with his rustling wings,
   As through the boughs he seeks more safe retreat.
The litlte flower, begemm'd around with drops
   That shine at sunrise like to burnish'd gold,
'Tis sweet to view: the milk-maid often stops,
   And wonders much such spangles to behold;
The hedger, too, admires them deck the thorn,
And thinks he sees no beauties like the morn.

JOYS OF YOUTH

How pleasing simplest recollections seem!
   Now summer comes, it warms me to look back
   On the sweet happiness of youth's wild track,
Varied and fleeting as a summer dream:
   Here have I paus'd upon the sweeping rack
That specks like wool-flocks through the purple sky;
   Here have I careless stooped down to catch
The meadow flower that entertain'd my eye;
And as the butterfly went whirring by,
   How anxious for its settling did I watch;
And oft long purples on the water's brink
   Have tempted me to wade, in spite of fate,
To pluck the flowers.   Oh, to look back and think,
   What pleasing pains such simple joys create!

WILD NOSEGAY

THE yellow lambtoe I have often got,
   Sweet creeping o'er the banks in summer-time,
And totter-grass, in many a trembling knot;
   And robb'd the mole-hill of its bed of thyme:
   And oft with anxious feelings would I climb
The waving willow-row, a stick to trim,
   To reach the water-lily's tempting flower
That on the surface of the pool did swim:
   I've stretch'd, and tried vain schemes for many an hour;
   And scrambled up the hawthorn's prickly bower,
For ramping woodbines and blue bitter-sweet.
   Still summer blooms, these flowers appear again;
But, ah, the question's useless to repeat,
   When will the feelings come I witness'd then?

SABBATH WALKS

Upon the sabbath, sweet it is to walk
   'Neath wood-side shelter of oak's spreading tree,
Or by a hedgerow trace a padded balk,
   Or stretch 'neath willows on the meadow lea,
   List'ning, delighted, hum of passing bee,
And curious pausing on the blossom's head;
   And mark the spider at his labour free,
Spinning from bent to bent his silken thread,
   And lab'ring ants, by careful nature led
To make the most of summer's plenteous stay,
   And lady-cow, beneath its leafy shed,
Call'd, when I mix'd with children, 'clock-a-clay,'
   Pruning its red wings on its pleasing bed,
Glad like myself to shun the heat of day.

ON TASTE

——————————Taste is from heaven,
   An inspiration nature can't bestow;
Though nature's beauties, where a taste is given,
   Warm the ideas of the soul to flow
   With that intense, enthusiastic glow
That throbs the bosom, when the curious eye
   Glances on beauteous things that give delight,
Objects of earth, or air, or sea, or sky,
   That bring the very senses in the sight
   To relish what we see : but all is night
To the gross clown—nature's unfolded book,
   As on he blunders, never strikes his eye;
Pages of landscape, tree, and flower, and brook,
   Like bare blank leaves, he turns unheeded by.

MAY NOON

How sweet it is, when suns get warmly high,
   In the mid-noon, as May's first cowslip springs,
   And the young cuckoo his soft ditty sings,
To wander out, and take a book, and lie
    'Neath some low pasture-bush, by guggling springs
That shake the sprouting flag leaf crimpling by;
   Or where the sunshine freckles on the eye
Through the half-clothed branches in the woods;
   Where airy leaves of woodbines, scrambling nigh,
Are earliest venturers to unfold their buds;
And little rippling runnels curl their floods,
   Bathing the primrose-peep, and strawberry wild,
And cuckoo-flowers just creeping from their hoods,
   With the sweet season, like their bard, beguil'd.

SUMMER EVENING

How pleasant, when the heat of day is by,
   And seething dew empurples round the hill
Of the horizon, sweeping with the eye
   In easy circles, wander where we will!
While o'er the meadow's little fluttering rill
   The twittering sunbeam weakens cool and dim,
And busy hum of flies is hush'd and still.
   How sweet the walks by hedgerow bushes seem,
On this side wavy grass, on that the stream;
   While dog-rose, woodbine, and the privet-spike,
On the young gales their rural sweetness teem,
   With yellow flag-flowers rustling in the dyke;
Each mingling into each, a ceaseless charm
To every heart that nature's sweets can warm.

TO PATTY

THOU lovely bud, with many weeds surrounded,
  I once again address thee with a song,
  To cheer thee up 'gainst envy's adder-tongue
That deeply oft thy reputation wounded,
  And did thy tender blossom mickle wrong.
But, look thou up!—'tis known in nature's law
  That serpents seek the honey-hoarding bee,
Rosemary's sweets the loathsome toad will draw,
  So beauty curdles envy's look on thee.
Fain would the peacock's tail the bow express
  Which paints the clouds so sweet in April's rain,
And just the same, that imp of ugliness
  Mimics thy lovely blossom—but in vain;
And fain would poison what she can't possess.

PLEASURES PAST

SPRING's sweets they are not fled, though summer's blossom
  Has met its blight of sadness, drooping low;
Still flowers gone by find beds in memory's bosom,
  Life's nursling buds among the weeds of woe.
Each pleasing token of spring's early morning
  Warms with the pleasures which we once did know;
Each little stem the leafy bank adorning,
  Reminds of joys from infancy that flow.
Spring's early heralds on the winter smiling,
  That often on their errands meet their doom,
Primrose and daisy, dreary hours beguiling,
  Smile o'er my pleasures past whene'er they come;
And the speckt throstle never wakes his song,
But life's past spring seems melting from his tongue.

HELPSTONE CHURCHYARD

WHAT makes me love thee now, thou dreary scene,
   And see in each swell'd heap a peaceful bed?
I well remember that the time has been,
   To walk a churchyard when I us'd to dread;
And shudder'd, as I read upon the stone
Of well-known friends and next-door neighbours gone.
   But then I knew no cloudy cares of life,
Where ne'er a sunbeam comes to light me thorough;
   A stranger then to this world's storms and strife,
Where ne'er a calm is met to lull my sorrow:
   I then was blest, and had not eyes to see
Life's future change, and Fate's severe to-morrow;
   When all those ills and pains should compass me,
   With no hope left but what I meet in thee.

TO AN EARLY BUTTERFLY

THRICE welcome here again, thou flutt'ring thing,
   That gaily seek'st about the opening flower,
And op'st and shutt'st thy gaudy-spangled wing
   Upon its bosom in the sunny hour;
Fond grateful thoughts from thy appearance spring:
To see thee, Fly, warms me once more to sing
   His universal care who hapt thee down,
And did thy winter-dwelling please to give.
   That Being's smiles on me dampt winter's frown,
And snatch'd me from the storm, and bade me live.
   And now again the welcome season's come,
'Tis thine and mine, in nature's grateful pride,
   To thank that Good who snatch'd us from the tomb,
And stood our prop, when all gave way beside.

TO THE MEMORY OF JOHN KEATS

THE world, its hopes, and fears, have pass'd away;
   No more its trifling thou shalt feel or see;
Thy hopes are ripening in a brighter day,
   While these left buds thy monument shall be.
When Rancour's aims have past in naught away,
   Enlarging specks discern'd in more than thee,
And beauties 'minishing which few display—
   When these are past, true child of Poesy,
Thou shalt survive.   Ah, while a being dwells,
   With soul, in nature's joys, to warm like thine,
With eye to view her fascinating spells,
   And dream entranced o'er each form divine,
Thy worth, Enthusiast, shall be cherish'd here,
Thy name with him shall linger, and be dear.

TO AUTUMN

COME, pensive Autumn, with thy clouds, and storms,
   And falling leaves, and pastures lost to flowers;
A luscious charm hangs on thy faded forms,
   More sweet than Summer in her loveliest hours,
Who, in her blooming uniform of green,
   Delights with samely and continued joy:
But give me, Autumn, where thy hand hath been,
   For there is wildness that can never cloy—
The russet hue of fields left bare, and all
The tints of leaves and blossoms ere they fall.
   In thy dull days of clouds a pleasure comes,
Wild music softens in thy hollow winds;
   And in thy fading woods a beauty blooms,
That's more than dear to melancholy minds.

WINTER SONG

I HEAR the redbreast's faint and feeble note,
    As on the thorn he prunes his drooping wing:
His song scarce warbles from his whispering throat,
    He sings like one that's little cheer'd to sing.
Ah, little bird, thy song is like my sigh,
    It warbles not on happiness to come:
It's not prophetic news of summer nigh,
    It's not excited by the daisy's bloom.
The sad reverse! thy song's a solemn dirge
    That rings the dying year its passing bell,
As friendship bends o'er death's departing verge
    And weeping takes his leave, farewell! farewell!
Still, redbreast, dear to me thy mournful lay
That mourns the memory of past pleasure's day.

POEMS WRITTEN AT HELPSTONE
1821–4

THE SHEPHERD'S CALENDAR

JANUARY

I

WITHERING and keen the winter comes,
While Comfort flies to close-shut rooms,
And sees the snow in feathers pass
Winnowing by the window-glass;
Whilst unfelt tempests howl and beat
Above his head in chimney-seat.

Now, musing o'er the changing scene,
Farmers behind the tavern-screen
Collect; with elbow idly press'd
On hob, reclines the corner's guest,
Reading the news, to mark again
The bankrupt lists, or price of grain;
Or old Moore's annual prophecies
Of flooded fields and clouded skies;
Whose Almanac's thumb'd pages swarm
With frost and snow, and many a storm,
And wisdom, gossip'd from the stars,
Of politics and bloody wars.
He shakes his head, and still proceeds,
Nor doubts the truth of what he reads:
All wonders are with faith supplied—
Bible, at once, and weather-guide.
Puffing the while his red-tipt pipe,
He dreams o'er troubles nearly ripe;
Yet, not quite lost in profit's way,
He'll turn to next year's harvest-day,
And, winter's leisure to regale,
Hope better times, and sip his ale.

The schoolboy still, with dithering joys,
In pastime leisure hours employs,
And, be the weather as it may,
Is never at a loss for play:

287

Making rude forms of various names,
Snow-men, or aught his fancy frames;
Till, numb'd and shivering, he resorts
To brisker games and warmer sports—
Kicking, with many a flying bound,
The football o'er the frozen ground,
Or seeking bright glib ice, to play
And slide the wintry hours away,
As quick and smooth as shadows run,
When clouds in autumn pass the sun.
Some, hurrying rambles eager take
To skate upon the meadow lake,
Scaring the snipe from her retreat,
From shelving bank's unfrozen seat,
Or running brook, where icy spars,
Which the pale sunlight specks with stars,
Shoot crizzling o'er the restless tide,
To many a likeness petrified.
The moor-hen, too, with fear opprest,
Starts from her reedy shelter'd rest,
As skating by, with curving springs,
And arms outspread like heron's wings,
They race away, for pleasure's sake,
With hunter's speed along the lake.

Blackening through the evening sky,
In clouds the starnels daily fly
To Whittlesea's reed-wooded mere,
And osier holts by rivers near;
Whilst many a mingled swarthy crowd—
Rook, crow, and jackdaw—noising loud,
Fly to and fro to dreary fen,
Dull winter's weary flight again;
They flop on heavy wings away
As soon as morning wakens grey,
And, when the sun sets round and red,
Return to naked woods to bed.
Wood pigeons too in flocks appear,
By hunger tamed from timid fear;

They mid the sheep unstartled steal
And share with them a scanty meal,
Picking the green leaves want bestows
Of turnips sprouting thro' the snows.[1]

The sun is creeping out of sight
Behind the woods —whilst running night
Hastens to shut the day's dull eye,
And grizzle o'er the chilly sky,
Dark, deep and thick, by day forsook,
As cottage chimney's sooty nook.[2]
Now maidens, fresh as summer roses,
Journeying from the distant closes,
Haste home with yokes and swinging pail;
The thresher, too, sets by his flail,
And leaves the mice at peace again
To fill their holes with stolen grain;
Whilst owlets, glad his toils are o'er,
Swoop by him as he shuts the door.

Bearing his hook beneath his arm,
The shepherd seeks the cottage warm;
And, weary in the cold to roam,
Scenting the track that leads him home,
His dog goes swifter o'er the mead,
Barking to urge his master's speed;
Then turns, and looks him in the face,
And trots before with mending pace,
Till, out of whistle from the swain,
He sits him down and barks again,
Anxious to greet the open'd door,
And meet the cottage fire once more.

The robin, that with nimble eye
Glegs round a danger to espy,
Now pops from out the open door
From crumbs half left upon the floor,
Nor wipes his bill on perching chair,
Nor stays to clean a feather there,

[1] Six lines added from MS.   [2] Two lines added from MS.

Scared at the cat that slinketh in
A chance from evening's glooms to win,
To jump on chairs or tables nigh,
Seeking what plunder may supply,
The children's littered scraps to thieve
Or aught that negligence may leave,
Creeping, where housewives cease to watch
Or dairy doors are off the latch,
On cheese or butter to regale
Or new milk reeking in the pail.
The hedger now in leather coat,
From woodland wilds and fields remote,
After a journey far and slow,
Knocks from his shoes the caking snow
And opes the welcome creaking door,
Throwing his faggot on the floor;
And at his listening wife's desire
To eke afresh the blazing fire
With sharp bill cuts the hazel bands,
Then sits him down to warm his hands
And tell in labour's happy way
His story of the passing day;
While as the warm blaze cracks and gleams
The supper reeks in savoury steams
Or kettle murmurs merrily
And tinkling cups are set for tea;
Thus doth the winter's dreary day
From morn to evening wear away.[1]

II

The shutter closed, the lamp alight,
The faggot chopt and blazing bright—
The shepherd now, from labour free,
Dances his children on his knee;
While, underneath his master's seat,
The tired dog lies in slumbers sweet,

[1] Thirty-four lines added from MS. *January* appears in the MSS. as two poems; the second begins here.

Starting and whimpering in his sleep,
Chasing still the straying sheep.
The cat's roll'd round in vacant chair,
Or leaping children's knees to lair,
Or purring on the warmer hearth,
Sweet chorus to the cricket's mirth.

The redcap, hanging overhead,
In cage of wire is perch'd abed;
Slumbering in his painted feathers,
Unconscious of the outdoor weathers;
Ev'n things without the cottage walls
Meet comfort as the evening falls,
As happy in the winter's dearth
As those around the blazing hearth.
The ass (frost-driven from the moor,
Where storms through naked bushes roar,
And not a leaf or sprig of green,
On ground or quaking bush, is seen,
Save grey-vein'd ivy's hardy pride,
Round old trees by the common side),
Litter'd with straw, now dozes warm,
Beneath his shed, from snow and storm:
The swine are fed and in the sty;
And fowls snug perch'd in hovel nigh,
With head in feathers safe asleep,
Where foxes cannot hope to creep,
And geese are gabbling in their dreams
Of litter'd corn and thawing streams.
The sparrow, too, a daily guest,
Is in the cottage eaves at rest;
And robin small, and smaller wren,
Are in their warm holes safe agen
From falling snows, that winnow by
The hovels where they nightly lie,
And ague winds, that shake the tree
Where other birds are forc'd to be.

The housewife, busy night and day,
Clears the supper-things away;

The jumping cat starts from her seat;
And stretching up on weary feet,
The dog wakes at the welcome tones
That call·him up to pick the bones.

On corner walls, a glittering row,
Hang fire-irons—less for use than show,
With horse-shoe brighten'd, as a spell,
Witchcraft's evil powers to quell,
And warming-pan, reflecting bright
The crackling blaze's flickering light,
That hangs the corner wall to grace,
Nor oft is taken from its place:
There in its mirror, bright as gold,
The children peep, and straight behold
Their laughing faces, whilst they pass,
Gleam on the lid as plain as glass.

Supper removed, the mother sits,
And tells her tales by starts and fits.
Not willing to lose time or toil,
She knits or sews, and talks the while—
Something that may be warnings found
To the young listeners gaping round—
Of boys who in her early day
Stroll'd to the meadow-lake to play,
Where willows, o'er the bank inclined,
Shelter'd the water from the wind,
And left it scarcely crizzled o'er—
When one plopt in, to rise no more!
And how, upon a market-night,
When not a star bestow'd its light,
A farmer's shepherd, o'er his glass,
Forgot that he had woods to pass:
And having sold his master's sheep,
Was overta'en by darkness deep.
How, coming with his startled horse,
To where two roads a hollow cross,
Where, lone guide when a stranger strays,
A white post points four different ways,

Beside the woodride's lonely gate
A murdering robber lay in wait.
The frighten'd horse, with broken rein
Stood at the stable-door again;
But none came home to fill his rack,
Or take the saddle from his back:
The saddle—it was all he bore;
The man was seen alive no more!
In her young days, beside the wood,
The gibbet in his terror stood:
Though now decay'd, 'tis not forgot,
But dreaded as a haunted spot.

She from her memory oft repeats
Witches' dread powers and fairy feats:
How one has oft been known to prance
In cowcribs, like a coach, to France,
And ride on sheep-trays from the fold
A race-horse speed to Burton-hold,
To join the midnight mystery's rout,
Where witches meet the yews about:
And how, when met with unawares,
They turn at once to cats or hares,
And race along with hellish flight,
Now here, now there, now out of sight!
And how the other tiny things
Will leave their moonlight meadow-rings,
And, unperceiv'd, through key-holes creep,
When all around have sunk to sleep,
And crowd in cupboards as they please,
As thick as mites in rotten cheese,[1]
To feast on what the cotter leaves—
Mice are not reckon'd greater thieves.
They take away, as well as eat,
And still the housewife's eye they cheat,
In spite of all the folks that swarm
In cottage small and larger farm;
They through each key-hole pop and pop,

[1] Two lines added from MS.

293

Like wasps into a grocer's shop,
With all the things that they can win
From chance to put their plunder in;
As shells of walnuts, split in two
By crows, who with the kernels flew;
Or acorn-cups, by stock-doves pluck'd,
Or egg-shells by a cuckoo suck'd;
With broad leaves of the sycamore
They clothe their stolen dainties o'er,
And when in cellar they regale,
Bring hazel-nuts to hold their ale,
With bung-holes bor'd by squirrels well,
To get the kernel from the shell,
Or maggots a way out to win,
When all is gone that grew within;
And be the key-holes e'er so high,
Rush poles a ladder's help supply,
Where soft the climbers fearless tread
On spindles made of spiders' thread.
And foul, or fair, or dark the night,
Their wild-fire lamps are burning bright,
For which full many a daring crime
Is acted in the summer-time;
When glow-worm found in lanes remote
Is murder'd for its shining coat,
And put in flowers, that Nature weaves
With hollow shapes and silken leaves,
Such as the Canterbury bell,
Serving for lamp or lantern well;
Or, following with unwearied watch
The flight of one they cannot match,
As silence sliveth upon sleep,
Or thieves by dozing watch-dogs creep,
They steal from Jack-a-lantern's tails
A light, whose guidance never fails
To aid them in the darkest night
And guide their plundering steps aright,
Rattling away in printless tracks.
Some, housed on beetles' glossy backs,

Go whisking on —and others hie
As fast as loaded moths can fly:
Some urge, the morning cock to shun,
The hardest gallop mice can run,
In chariots, lolling at their ease,
Made of whate'er their fancies please;
Things that in childhood's memory dwell—
Scoop'd crow-pot-stone, or cockle-shell,
With wheels at hand of mallow seeds,
Where childish sport was stringing beads;
And thus equipp'd, they softly pass
Like shadows on the summer-grass,
And glide away in troops together
Just as the spring-wind drives a feather.
As light as happy dreams they creep,
Nor break the feeblest link of sleep:
A midgeon in their road abed,
Feels not the wheels run o'er his head,
But sleeps till sunrise calls him up,
Unconscious of the passing troop.

Thus dame the winter-night regales
With wonder's never-ceasing tales;
While in a corner, ill at ease,
Or crushing 'tween their father's knees,
The children—silent all the while—
And e'en repressed the laugh or smile—
Quake with the ague chills of fear,
And tremble though they love to hear,
Starting, while they the tales recall,
At their own shadows on the wall:
Till the old clock, that strikes unseen
Behind the picture-pasted screen
Where Eve and Adam still agree
To rob Life's fatal apple-tree,
Counts over bed-time's hour of rest,
And bids each be sleep's fearful guest.
She then her half-told tales will leave
To finish on to-morrow's eve.

The children steal away to bed,
And up the ladder softly tread,
Scarce daring—from their fearful joys—
To look behind or make a noise;
Nor speak a word, but still as sleep
They secret to their pillows creep,
And whisper o'er, in terror's way,
The prayers they dare no louder say,
Then hide their heads beneath the clothes,
And try in vain to seek repose;
While yet, to fancy's sleepless eye,
Witches on sheep-trays gallop by,
And fairies, like a rising spark,
Swarm twittering round them in the dark;
Till sleep creeps nigh to ease their cares,
And drops upon them unawares.

Oh, spirit of the days gone by—
Sweet childhood's fearful ecstasy!
The witching spells of winter nights,
Where are they fled with their delights?
When list'ning on the corner seat,
The winter evening's length to cheat,
I heard my mother's memory tell
Tales superstition loves so well:
Things said or sung a thousand times,
In simple prose or simpler rhymes.
Ah! where is page of poesy
So sweet as this was wont to be?
The magic wonders that deceived,
When fictions were as truths believed,
The fairy feats that once prevailed,
Told to delight, and never failed,
Where are they now, their fears and sighs,
And tears from founts of happy eyes?
I read in books, but find them not,
For poesy hath its youth forgot:
I hear them told to children still,
But fear numbs not my spirits chill:

I still see faces pale with dread,
While mine could laugh at what is said,
See tears imagined woes supply,
While mine with real cares are dry.
Where are they gone—the joys and fears,
The links, the life of other years?
I thought they twined around my heart
So close, that we could never part;
But Reason, like a winter's day,
Nipp'd childhood's visions all away,
Nor left behind one withering flower
To cherish in a lonely hour.
Memory may yet the themes repeat,
But childhood's heart hath ceased to beat
At tales, which Reason's sterner lore
Turns like weak gossips from her door:
The Magic Fountain, where the head
Rose up, just as the startled maid
Was stooping from the weedy brink
To dip her pitcher in to drink,
That did its half-hid mystery tell
To smooth its hair, and use it well;
Which, doing as it bade her do,
Turn'd to a king and lover too.
The tale of Cinderella, told
The winter through, and never old:
The pumpkin that, at her approach,
Was turn'd into a golden coach;
The rats that fairies' magic knew,
And instantly to horses grew;
The coachmen ready at her call,
To drive her to the Prince's ball,
With fur-changed jackets silver lined,
And tails hung 'neath their hats behind;
The golden glove, with fingers small,
She lost while dancing in the hall,
That was on every finger tried,
And fitted hers, and none beside,
When Cinderella, soon as seen,

Was woo'd and won, and made a Queen.
The Boy that did the Giant slay,
And gave his mother's cows away
For magic mask, that day or night,
When on, would keep him out of sight.
The running bean—not such as weaves
Round poles the height of cottage eaves,
But magic one—that travell'd high
Some steeple's journey up the sky,
And reach'd a giant's dwelling there,
A cloud-built castle in the air:
Where, venturing up the fearful height,
That serv'd him climbing half the night,
He search'd the giant's coffers o'er,
And never wanted riches more;
While, like a lion scenting food,
The giant roar'd, in hungry mood,
A storm of threats that might suffice
To freeze the hottest blood to ice.

I hear it now, nor dream of woes;
The storm is settled to repose.
Those fears are dead! What will not die
In fading Life's mortality?
Those truths have fled, and left behind
A real world and doubting mind.

FEBRUARY

The snow has left the cottage top;
    The thatch-moss grows in brighter green;
And eaves in quick succession drop,
    Where grinning icicles have been,
Pit-patting with a pleasant noise
    In tubs set by the cottage-door;
While ducks and geese, with happy joys,
    Plunge in the yard-pond brimming o'er.

The sun peeps through the window-pane;
　Which children mark with laughing eye,
And in the wet street steal again
　To tell each other spring is nigh:
Then, as young hope the past recalls,
　In playing groups they often draw,
To build beside the sunny walls
　Their spring-time huts of sticks or straw.

And oft in pleasure's dreams they hie
　Round homesteads by the village side,
Scratching the hedgerow mosses by,
　Where painted pooty shells abide,
Mistaking oft the ivy spray
　For leaves that come with budding spring,
And wond'ring, in their search for play,
　Why birds delay to build and sing.

The milkmaid singing leaves her bed,
　As glad as happy thoughts can be,
While magpies chatter o'er her head
　As jocund in the change as she:
Her cows around the closes stray,
　Nor ling'ring wait the foddering-boy,
Tossing the molehills in their play,
　And staring round with frolic joy.

The shepherd now is often seen
　Near warm banks o'er his hook to bend,
Or o'er a gate or stile to lean,
　Chattering to a passing friend:
Ploughmen go whistling to their toils,
　And yoke again the rested plough;
And, mingling o'er the mellow soils,
　Boys shout, and whips are noising now.

The barking dogs, by lane and wood,
　Drive sheep afield from foddering ground;
And Echo, in her summer mood,
　Briskly mocks the cheering sound.

The flocks, as from a prison broke,
　　Shake their wet fleeces in the sun,
While, following fast, a misty smoke
　　Reeks from the moist grass as they run.

No more behind his master's heels
　　The dog creeps on his winter-pace;
But cocks his tail, and o'er the fields
　　Runs many a wild and random chase,
Following, in spite of chiding calls,
　　The startled cat with harmless glee,
Scaring her up the weed-green walls,
　　Or mossy mottled apple-tree.

As crows from morning perches fly,
　　He barks and follows them in vain;
E'en larks will catch his nimble eye,
　　And off he starts and barks again,
With breathless haste and blinded guess,
　　Oft following where the hare hath gone,
Forgetting, in his joy's excess,
　　His frolic puppy-days are done.

The hedgehog, from his hollow root,
　　Sees the wood-moss clear of snow,
And hunts the hedge for fallen fruit—
　　Crab, hip, and winter-bitten sloe;
But often check'd by sudden fears,
　　As shepherd-dog his haunt espies,
He rolls up in a ball of spears,
　　And all his barking rage defies.

The gladden'd swine bolt from the sty,
　　And round the yard in freedom run,
Or stretching in their slumbers lie
　　Beside the cottage in the sun.
The young horse whinnies to his mate,
　　And, sickening from the thresher's door,
Rubs at the straw-yard's banded gate,
　　Longing for freedom on the moor.

The small birds think their wants are o'er,
  To see the snow-hills fret again,
And, from the barn's chaff-litter'd door,
  Betake them to the greening plain.
The woodman's robin startles coy,
  Nor longer to his elbow comes,
To peck, with hunger's eager joy,
  'Mong mossy stulps the litter'd crumbs.

'Neath hedge and walls that screen the wind,
  The gnats for play will flock together;
And e'en poor flies some hope will find
  To venture in the mocking weather;
From out their hiding-holes again,
  With feeble pace, they often creep
Along the sun-warm'd window-pane,
  Like dreaming things that walk in sleep.

The mavis thrush with wild delight,
  Upon the orchard's dripping tree,
Mutters, to see the day so bright,
  Fragments of young Hope's poesy:
And oft dame stops her buzzing wheel
  To hear the robin's note once more,
Who tootles while he pecks his meal
  From sweetbrier hips beside the door.

The sunbeams on the hedges lie,
  The south wind murmurs summer-soft;
The maids hang out white clothes to dry
  Around the elder-skirted croft:
A calm of pleasure listens round,
  And almost whispers winter by;
While Fancy dreams of summer's sound,
  And quiet rapture fills the eye.

Thus Nature of the spring will dream
  While south winds thaw; but soon again
Frost breathes upon the stiff'ning stream,
  And numbs it into ice: the plain

Soon wears its mourning garb of white;
    And icicles, that fret at noon,
Will eke their icy tails at night
    Beneath the chilly stars and moon.

Nature soon sickens of her joys,
    And all is sad and dumb again.
Save merry shouts of sliding boys
    About the frozen furrow'd plain.
The foddering-boy forgets his song,
    And silent goes with folded arms;
And croodling shepherds bend along,
    Crouching to the whizzing storms.

MARCH

MARCH, month of 'many weathers,' wildly comes
In hail, and snow, and rain, and threatening hums,
And floods; while often at his cottage-door
The shepherd stands, to hear the distant roar
Loosed from the rushing mills and river-locks,
With thundering sound and overpowering shocks.
From bank to bank, along the meadow lea,
The river spreads, and shines a little sea;
While, in the pale sunlight, a watery brood
Of swopping white birds flock about the flood.

    Yet Winter seems half weary of his toil;
And round the ploughmen, on the elting soil,
Will thread a minute's sunshine wild and warm,
Through the ragg'd places of the swimming storm;
And oft the shepherd in his path will spy
The little daisy in the wet grass lie,
That to the peeping sun uncloses gay,
Like Labour smiling on a holiday;
And where the steep bank fronts the southern sky,
By lanes or brooks where sunbeams love to lie,
A cowslip-peep will open faintly coy,
Soon seen and gather'd by a wondering boy.

A tale of spring around the distant haze
Seems muttering pleasures with the lengthening days;
Morn wakens, mottled oft with May-day stains;
And shower-drops hang the grassy sprouting plains,
Or on the naked thorns of brassy hue
Drip glistening, like a summer-dream of dew.
The woodman, in his pathway down the wood,
Crushes with hasty feet full many a bud
Of early primrose; yet if timely spied,
Shelter'd some old half-rotten stump beside,
The sight will cheer his solitary hour,
And urge his feet to stride and save the flower.
Muffled in baffles, leather coat and gloves,
The hedger toils, oft scaring rustling doves
From out the hedgerows, who in hunger browze [1]
The chocolate berries on the ivy boughs,
Or flocking fieldfares, speckled like the thrush,
Picking the red haw from the sweeing bush,
That come and go on winter's chilling wing,
And seem to share no sympathy with spring.
The stooping ditcher in the water stands,
Letting the [flooding] lakes from off the lands,
Or splashing cleans the pasture brooks of mud,
Where many a wild weed freshens into bud;
And sprouting from the bottom purply green,
The water-cresses 'neath the waves are seen,
Which the old woman gladly drags to land
With reaching long rake in her tottering hand. [2]
The ploughmen maul along the doughy sloughs
And often stop their songs, to clean their ploughs
From teasing twitch, that in the spongy soil
Clings round the coulter, interrupting toil.
The sower, striding o'er his dirty way,
Sinks ankle deep in pudgy sloughs and clay,
And o'er his heavy hopper stoutly leans, [3]
Strewing with swinging arms the pattering beans,
Which, soon as April's milder weather gleams,

[1] Three lines added from MS.   [2] Eight lines added from MS.
[3] Three lines added from MS.

Will shoot up green between the furrow'd seams.
The driving boy, glad when his steps can trace
The swelling edding as a resting-place,
Slings from his clotted shoes the dirt around,
And fain would rest him on the solid ground,
And sings when he can meet the parting green
Of rushy balks that bend the land between.[1]
Not far behind them struts the nauntly crow,
And daw, whose head seems powder'd o'er with snow,
Seeking the worms: the rook, a noisy guest,
That on the wind-rock'd elms prepares her nest,
On the fresh furrow often drops, to pull
The twitching roots, or gather sticks and wool
From trees whose dead twigs litter to the wind
And gaps where stray sheep left their coats behind;
While ground-larks, on a sweeing clump of rushes,
Or on the top twigs of the oddling bushes,
Chirp their 'cree-creery' note, that sounds of spring;
And sky-larks meet the sun with fluttering wing.
Soon as the morning opes its brightning eye
Large troops of starnels blacken thro' the sky
From osier holts about the misty fen
And reed-shaw borders by the river Nen;
And wild geese regiments now again repair
To the wet bosom of broad marshes there,
In marching columns and attentive all,
Listening and following their ringleader's call.[2]

    The shepherd-boy, that hastens now and then
From hail and snow beneath his sheltering den
Of flags, or file-leaved sedges tied in sheaves,
Or stubble shocks, oft as his eye perceives
Sun-threads shrink out in momentary smiles,
With fairy thoughts his loneliness beguiles;
Thinking the struggling winter howling by,
As down the edges of the distant sky
The hail-storm sweeps; and while he stops to strip
The stooping hedgebrier of its lingering hip,

[1] Two lines added from MS.   [2] Eight lines added from MS.

He hears the wild geese gabble o'er his head;
Then, pleased with fancies in his musings bred,
He marks the figured forms in which they fly,
And pausing, follows with a wondering eye,
Likening their curious march, in curves or rows,
To every letter which his memory knows;
While, far above, the solitary crane
Swings lonely to unfrozen dykes again,
Cranking a jarring melancholy cry
Through the wild journey of the cheerless sky.

Often, at early seasons, mild and fair
March bids farewell, with garlands in her hair
Of hazel tassels, woodbine's bushy sprout,
And sloe and wild-plum blossoms peeping out
In thick-set knots of flowers, preparing gay,
For April's reign, a mockery of May,
That soon will glisten on the earnest eye
Like snow-white cloaks hung in the sun to dry.[1]
The old dame then oft stills her humming wheel—
When the bright sunbeams through the windows steal
And gleam upon her face, and dancing fall
In diamond shadows on the pictur'd wall;
While the white butterfly, as in amaze,
Will settle on the glossy glass to gaze—
And smiling, glad to see such things once more,
Up she will get and totter to the door,
And look upon the trees beneath the eaves—
Sweetbrier and lad's-love—swelling into leaves;
And, stooping down, cull from her garden beds
The early blossoms perking out their heads,
In flower-pots on the window-board to stand,
Where the old hour-glass spins its thread of sand.
And while the passing clown remarks, with pride,
Days lengthen in their visits a 'cock's stride,'
She cleans her candlesticks and sets them by,
Glad of the makeshift light that eves supply.

[1] Two lines added from MS.

The boy, retiring home at night from toil,
Down lane and close, o'er footbrig, gate, and stile,
Oft trembles into fear, and stands to hark
The waking fox renew his short gruff bark;
And shepherds—that within their hulks remain
Night after night upon the chilly plain,
To watch the dropping lambs, that at all hours
Come in the quaking blast like tender flowers—
When in the nightly watch they chance to hear
The badger's shrieks, can hardly stifle fear;
Likening the cry, from woodland's dark recess,
To that of helpless woman in distress:
For Superstition hath a thousand tales
To people all her midnight woods and vales;
And the dread spot from whence the dismal noise
Mars the night-musings of their dark employs,
Owns its sad tale to realize their fear—
A tale their hearts in boyhood ached to hear.
A maid, at night, by treacherous love decoy'd,
Was in that shrieking wood, years past, destroy'd.
She went, 'twas said, to meet the waiting swain;
But home and friends ne'er saw her face again!
Mid brake and thorns that crowded round the dell,
And matting weeds that had no tongue to tell,
He murder'd her alone at dead midnight,
While the pale moon threw round her sickly light.
Loud screams assail'd the thicket's slumbers deep,
But only scar'd the little birds from sleep,
When the pale murderer's terror-frowning eye
Told its dread errand—that the maid should die.
Mid thick blackthorns her secret grave was made;
And there the unresisting corpse was laid,
When no one saw the deed but God and he,
And moonlight sparkling through the sleeping tree.
The robin redbreast might at morning steal
There, for the worm to meet his early meal,
In fresh-turn'd moulds which first beheld the sun—
Nor know the deed that dismal night had done.
Such is the tale that Superstition gives,

Which in her midnight memory ever lives,
Which makes the boy run by with wild affright,
And shepherds startle on their rounds at night.

Now love-teased maidens, from the droning wheel,
At the red hour of sunset, slyly steal
From scolding dames, to meet their swains again;
Though water checks their visits o'er the plain:
They slive where no one sees, some wall behind,
Or orchard apple-tree that stops the wind,
To talk about spring's pleasures hovering nigh,
And happy rambles when the roads get dry.

The insect-world, now sunbeams higher climb,
Oft dream of spring, and wake before their time.
Bees stroke their little legs across their wings,
And venture short flights where the snowdrop hings
Its silver bell, and winter aconite
Its buttercup-like flowers that shut at night,
With green leaf furling round its cup of gold,
Like tender maiden muffled from the cold:
They sip, and find their honey-dreams are vain,
Then feebly hasten to their hives again.
The butterflies, by eager hopes undone,
Glad as a child come out to greet the sun,
Beneath the shadow of a sudden shower
Are lost—nor see to-morrow's April flower.

APRIL

Now infant April joins the spring,
    And views the watery sky,
As youngling linnet tries its wing,
    And fears at first to fly;
With timid step she ventures on,
    And hardly dares to smile,
Till blossoms open one by one,
    And sunny hours beguile.

But finer days are coming yet,
    With scenes more sweet to charm,
And suns arrive that rise and set
    Bright strangers to a storm:
Then, as the birds with louder song
    Each morning's glory cheer,
With bolder step she speeds along,
    And loses all her fear.

In wanton gambols, like a child,
    She tends her early toils,
And seeks the buds along the wild,
    That blossoms while she smiles;
Or, laughing on, with naught to chide,
    She races with the Hours,
Or sports by Nature's lovely side,
    And fills her lap with flowers.

The shepherd on his pasture walks
    The first fair cowslip finds,
Whose tufted flowers, on slender stalks,
    Keep nodding to the winds.
And though the thorns withhold the may,
    Their shades the violets bring,
Which children stoop for in their play
    As tokens of the spring.

Those joys which childhood calls its own,
    Would they were kin to men!
Those treasures to the world unknown,
    When known, are wither'd then!
But hovering round our growing years,
    To gild Care's sable shroud,
Their spirit through the gloom appears
    As suns behind a cloud.

Since thou didst meet my infant eyes,
    As through the fields I flew,
Whose distance, where they meet the skies,
    Was all the world I knew;

That warmth of fancy's wildest hours,
    Which fill'd all things with life,
Which heard a voice in trees and flowers,
    Has swoon'd in reason's strife.

Sweet month! thy pleasures bid thee be
    The fairest child of spring;
And every hour, that comes with thee,
    Comes some new joy to bring:
The trees still deepen in their bloom,
    Grass greens the meadow-lands,
And flowers with every morning come,
    As dropt by fairy hands.

The field and garden's lovely hours
    Begin and end with thee;
For what's so sweet, as peeping flowers
    And bursting buds to see,
What time the dew's unsullied drops,
    In burnish'd gold, distil
On crocus flowers' unclosing tops,
    And drooping daffodil?

To see thee come, all hearts rejoice;
    And, warm with feelings strong,
With thee all Nature finds a voice,
    And hums a waking song.
The lover views thy welcome hours,
    And thinks of summer come,
And takes the maid the early flowers,
    To tempt her steps from home.

Along each hedge and sprouting bush
    The singing birds are blest,
And linnet green and speckled thrush
    Prepare their mossy nest;
On the warm bed thy plains supply,
    The young lambs find repose,
And mid thy green hills basking lie
    Like spots of ling'ring snows.

Thy open'd leaves and ripen'd buds
　　The cuckoo makes his choice,
And shepherds in thy greening woods
　　First hear his cheering voice:
And to thy ripen'd blooming bowers
　　The nightingale belongs,
And, singing to thy parting hours,
　　Keeps night awake with songs.

With thee the swallow dares to come,
　　And primes his sooty wing;
And, urged to seek his yearly home,
　　Thy suns the martin bring.
O lovely month! be leisure mine
　　Thy yearly mate to be;
Though May-day scenes may brighter shine,
　　Their birth belongs to thee.

I waked me with thy rising sun,
　　And thy first glories viewed,
And, as thy welcome hours begun,
　　Their sunny steps pursued.
And now thy sun is on thee set,
　　Like to a lovely eve,
I view thy parting with regret,
　　And linger loath to leave.

Though at her birth the northern gale
　　Come with its withering sigh,
And hopeful blossoms, turning pale,
　　Upon her bosom die,
Ere April seeks another place,
　　And ends her reign in this,
She leaves us with as fair a face
　　As e'er gave birth to bliss.

MAY

Come, Queen of Months! in company
With all thy merry minstrelsy:
The restless cuckoo, absent long,
And twittering swallows' chimney-song;
With hedgerow crickets' notes, that run
From every bank that fronts the sun;
And swarthy bees, about the grass,
That stop with every bloom they pass,
And every minute, every hour,
Keep teasing weeds that wear a flower;
And toil, and childhood's humming joys,
For there is music in the noise
When village children, wild for sport,
In school-time's leisure, ever short,
Alternate catch the bounding ball,
Or run along the churchyard wall,
Capp'd with rude figured slabs, whose claims
In time's bad memory have no names,
Or race around the nooky church,
Or raise loud echoes in the porch,
Throw pebbles o'er the weathercock,
Viewing with jealous eyes the clock,
Or leap o'er grave-stones' leaning heights,
Uncheck'd by melancholy sights,
Though green grass swells in many a heap
Where kin, and friends, and parents sleep.
They think not, in their jovial cry,
The time will come when they shall lie
As lowly and as still as they,
While other boys above them play,
Heedless, as they are now, to know
The unconscious dust that lies below.

The driving boy, beside his team,
Of May-month's beauty now will dream,
And cock his hat, and turn his eye
On flower, and tree, and deepening sky;

And oft burst loud in fits of song,
And whistle as he reels along,
Cracking his whip in starts of joy—
A happy, dirty, driving boy.
The youth, who leaves his corner stool
Betimes for neighbouring village-school,
Where, as a mark to guide him right,
The church spire's all the way in sight,
With cheerings from his parents given,
Beneath the joyous smiles of heaven
Saunters, with many an idle stand,
With satchel swinging in his hand,
And gazes, as he passes by,
On everything that meets his eye.
Young lambs seem tempting him to play,
Dancing and bleating in his way;
With trembling tails and pointed ears
They follow him, and lose their fears;
He smiles upon their sunny faces,
And fain would join their happy races.
The birds, that sing on bush and tree,
Seem chirping for his company;
And all—in fancy's idle whim—
Seem keeping holiday, but him.
He lolls upon each resting stile,
To see the fields so sweetly smile,
To see the wheat grow green and long;
And lists the weeder's toiling song,
Or short note of the changing thrush
Above him in the whitethorn bush,
That o'er the leaning stile bends low
Its blooming mockery of snow.

Each hedge is cover'd thick with green;
And where the hedger late hath been,
Young tender shoots begin to grow
From out the mossy stumps below.
But woodmen still on spring intrude,
And thin the shadow's solitude;

With sharpen'd axes felling down
The oak-trees budding into brown,
Which, as they crash upon the ground,
A crowd of labourers gather round.
These, mixing 'mong the shadows dark,
Rip off the crackling, staining bark,
Depriving yearly, when they come,
The green woodpecker of his home,
Who early in the spring began,
Far from the sight of troubling man,
To bore his round holes in each tree
In fancy's sweet security;
Now, startled by the woodman's noise,
He wakes from all his dreary joys.
The blue-bells too, that thickly bloom
Where man was never known to come;
And stooping lilies of the valley,
That love with shades and dews to dally,
And bending droop on slender threads,
With broad hood-leaves above their heads,
Like white-robed maids, in summer hours,
Beneath umbrellas shunning showers;
These, from the bark-men's crushing treads,
Oft perish in their blooming beds.
Stripp'd of its boughs and bark, in white
The trunk shines in the mellow light
Beneath the green surviving trees,
That wave above it in the breeze,
And, waking whispers, slowly bend,
As if they mourn'd their fallen friend.

Each morning, now, the weeders meet
To cut the thistle from the wheat,
And ruin, in the sunny hours,
Full many a wild weed with its flowers;
Corn-poppies, that in crimson dwell,
Call'd 'headaches,' from their sickly smell;
And charlocks, yellow as the sun,
That o'er the May-fields quickly run;

And 'iron-weed,' content to share
The meanest spot that spring can spare—
E'en roads, where danger hourly comes,
Are not without its purple blooms,
Whose leaves, with threat'ning thistles round
Thick set, that have no strength to wound,
Shrink into childhood's eager hold
Like hair; and, with its eye of gold
And scarlet-starry points of flowers,
Pimpernel, dreading nights and showers,
Oft call'd 'the shepherd's weather-glass,'
That sleeps till suns have dried the grass,
Then wakes, and spreads its creeping bloom
Till clouds with threatening shadows come—
Then close it shuts to sleep again:
Which weeders see, and talk of rain;
And boys, that mark them shut so soon,
Call them 'John-go-to-bed-at-noon.'
And fumitory too—a name
That superstition holds to fame—
Whose red and purple mottled flowers
Are cropp'd by maids in weeding hours,
To boil in water, milk, and whey,
For washes on a holiday,
To make their beauty fair and sleek,
And scare the tan from summer's cheek;
And simple small 'forget-me-not,'
Eyed with a pin's-head yellow spot
I' the middle of its tender blue,
That gains from poets notice due:
These flowers, that toil by crowds destroys,
Robbing them of their lowly joys,
Had met the May with hopes as sweet
As those her suns in gardens meet;
And oft the dame will feel inclined,
As childhood's memory comes to mind,
To turn her hook away, and spare
The blooms it loved to gather there.
—Now young girls whisper things of love,

And from the old dames' hearing move;
Oft making 'love-knots' in the shade,
Of blue-green oat or wheaten blade;
Or, trying simple charms and spells
Which rural superstition tells,
They pull the little blossom threads
From out the knotweed's button heads,
And put the husk, with many a smile,
In their white bosoms for a while—
Then, if they guess aright the swain
Their loves' sweet fancies try to gain,
'Tis said, that ere it lies an hour,
'Twill blossom with a second flower,
And from their bosom's handkerchief
Bloom as it ne'er had lost a leaf.
—But signs appear that token wet,
While they are 'neath the bushes met;
The girls are glad with hopes of play,
And harp upon the holiday:
A high blue bird is seen to swim
Along the wheat, when skies grow dim
With clouds; slow as the gales of spring
In motion, with dark-shadow'd wing
Beneath the coming storm he sails:
And lonely chirp the wheat-hid quails,
That come to live with spring again,
But leave when summer browns the grain;
They start the young girls' joys afloat,
With 'wet my foot'—their yearly note:
So fancy doth the sound explain,
And oft it proves a sign of rain!

The thresher, dull as winter days,
And lost to all that spring displays,
Still mid his barn-dust forced to stand,
Swings round his flail with weary hand;
While o'er his head shades thickly creep,
That hide the blinking owl asleep,
And bats, in cobweb-corners bred,

Sharing till night their murky bed.
The sunshine trickles on the floor
Through ev'ry crevice of the door:
This makes his barn, where shadows dwell,
As irksome as a prisoner's cell;
And, whilst he seeks his daily meal,
As schoolboys from their task will steal,
So will he stand with fond delay
To see the daisy in his way,
Or wild weeds flowering on the wall;
For these to memory still recall
The joys, the sports that come with spring—
The twirling top, the marble ring,
The jingling halfpence hustled up
At pitch-and-toss, the eager stoop
To pick up *heads*, the smuggled plays
'Neath hovels upon sabbath-days,
The sitting down, when school was o'er,
Upon the threshold of the door,
Picking from mallows, sport to please,
Each crumpled seed he call'd a cheese,
And hunting from the stack-yard sod
The stinking henbane's belted pod,
By youth's warm fancies sweetly led
To christen them his loaves of bread.
He sees, while rocking down the street
With weary hands and crimpling feet,
Young children at the self-same games,
And hears the self-same boyish names
Still floating on each happy tongue:
Touch'd with the simple scene so strong,
Tears almost start, and many a sigh
Regrets the happiness gone by;
Thus, in sweet Nature's holiday,
His heart is sad while all is gay.

How lovely now are lanes and balks,
For lovers in their Sunday walks!
The daisy and the buttercup—

For which the laughing children stoop
A hundred times throughout the day,
In their rude romping summer play—
So thickly now the pasture crowd,
In a gold and silver sheeted cloud,
As if the drops of April showers
Had woo'd the sun, and changed to flowers.
The brook resumes her summer dresses,
Purling 'neath grass and water-cresses,
And mint and flagleaf, swording high
Their blooms to the unheeding eye,
And taper, bow-bent, hanging rushes,
And horsetail, children's bottle-brushes; [1]
The summer tracks about its brink
Are fresh again where cattle drink;
And on its sunny bank the swain
Stretches his idle length again;
While all that lives enjoys the birth
Of frolic summer's laughing mirth.

JUNE

Now summer is in flower, and Nature's hum
Is never silent round her bounteous bloom;
Insects, as small as dust, have never done
With glitt'ring dance, and reeling in the sun;
And green wood-fly, and blossom-haunting bee,
Are never weary of their melody.
Round field and hedge, flowers in full glory twine,
Large bindweed bells, wild hop, and streak'd woodbine,
That lift athirst their slender-throated flowers,
Agape for dew-falls, and for honey showers;
These o'er each bush in sweet disorder run,
And spread their wild hues to the sultry sun.
The mottled spider, at eve's leisure, weaves
His webs of silken lace on twigs and leaves,

[1] Two lines added from MS.

Which every morning meet the poet's eye,
Like fairies' dew-wet dresses hung to dry.
The wheat swells into ear, and hides below
The May-month wild flowers and their gaudy show,
Leaving a schoolboy's height, in snugger rest,
The leveret's seat, and lark and partridge nest.

The mowers now bend o'er the beaded grass,
Where oft the gipsy's hungry journeying ass
Will turn his wishes from the meadow paths,
List'ning the rustle of the falling swaths.
The ploughman sweats along the fallow vales,
And down the sun-crack'd furrow slowly trails,
Oft seeking, when athirst, the brook's supply,
Where, brushing eagerly the bushes by
For coolest water, he disturbs the rest
Of ring-dove, brooding o'er its idle nest.
The shepherd's leisure hours are over now;
No more he loiters 'neath the hedgerow bough,
On shadow-pillowed banks and lolling stile;
The wilds must lose their summer friend awhile.
With whistle, barking dogs, and chiding scold,
He drives the bleating sheep from fallow fold
To wash-pits, where the willow shadows lean,
Dashing them in, their stained coats to clean;
Then, on the sunny sward, when dry agen,
He brings them homeward to the clipping pen,
In hurdles pent, where elm or sycamore
Shut out the sun—or to some threshing-floor.
There with the scraps of songs, and laugh, and tale,
He lightens annual toil, while merry ale
Goes round, and glads some old man's heart to praise
The threadbare customs of his early days:
How the high bowl was in the middle set
At breakfast time, when clippers yearly met,
Fill'd full of furmety, where dainty swum
The streaking sugar and the spotting plum.
The maids could never to the table bring
The bowl, without one rising from the ring

To lend a hand; who, if 'twere ta'en amiss,
Would sell his kindness for a stolen kiss.
The large stone pitcher in its homely trim,
And clouded pint-horn with its copper rim,
Were there; from which were drunk, with spirits high,
Healths of the best the cellar could supply;
While sung the ancient swains, in uncouth rhymes,
Songs that were pictures of the good old times.
Thus will the old man ancient ways bewail,
Till toiling shears gain ground upon the tale,
And break it off—then from the timid sheep
The fleece is shorn, and with a fearful leap
He starts, while with a pressing hand
His sides are printed by the tarry band,[1]
Shaking his naked skin with wond'ring joys,
And others are tugged in by sturdy boys.

Though fashion's haughty frown hath thrown aside
Half the old forms simplicity supplied,
Yet there are some pride's winter deigns to spare,
Left like green ivy when the trees are bare.
And now, when shearing of the flocks is done,
Some ancient customs, mix'd with harmless fun,
Crown the swain's merry toils. The timid maid,
Pleased to be praised, and yet of praise afraid,
Seeks the best flowers; not those of woods and fields,
But such as every farmer's garden yields—
Fine cabbage-roses, painted like her face,
The shining pansy, trimm'd with golden lace,
The tall-topp'd larkheels, feather'd thick with flowers,
The woodbine, climbing o'er the door in bowers,
The London tufts, of many a mottled hue,
The pale pink pea, and monkshood darkly blue,
The white and purple gilliflowers, that stay
Ling'ring, in blossom, summer half away,
The single blood-walls, of a luscious smell,
Old-fashion'd flowers which housewives love so well,
The columbines, stone-blue, or deep night-brown,

[1] Three lines added from MS.

Their honeycomb-like blossoms hanging down,
Each cottage-garden's fond adopted child,
Though heaths still claim them, where they yet grow wild
'Mong their old wild companion summer blooms—
Furze brake and mozzling ling and golden broom;
Snapdragons gaping like to sleepy clowns
And 'clipping pinks' (which maidens' Sunday gowns
Full often wear, catched at by teasing chaps),
Pink as the ribbons round their snowy caps;
'Bess in her bravery' too, of glowing dyes
As deep as sunset's crimson pillowed skies,[1]
With marjoram knots, sweetbrier, and ribbon-grass,
And lavender, the choice of ev'ry lass,
And sprigs of lad's-love—all familiar names,
Which every garden through the village claims.
These the maid gathers with a coy delight,
And ties them up, in readiness for night;
Then gives to every swain, 'tween love and shame,
Her 'clipping posies' as his yearly claim.
He rises, to obtain the custom'd kiss:
With stifled smiles, half hankering after bliss,
She shrinks away, and blushing, calls it rude;
Yet turns to smile, and hopes to be pursued;
While one, to whom the hint may be applied,
Follows to claim it, and is not denied.
The rest the loud laugh raise, to make it known—
She blushes silent, and will not disown.
Thus ale, and song, and healths, and merry ways,
Keep up a shadow still of former days;
But the old beechen bowl, that once supplied
The feast of furmety, is thrown aside,
And the old freedom that was living then,
When masters made them merry with their men,
When all their coats alike were russet brown,
And his rude speech was vulgar as their own—
All this is past, and soon will pass away
The time-torn remnant of the holiday.

[1] Eight lines added from MS.

JULY

July, the month of summer's prime,
Again resumes his busy time;
Scythes tinkle in each grassy dell,
Where solitude was wont to dwell;
And meadows, they are mad with noise
Of laughing maids and shouting boys,
Making up the withering hay
With merry hearts as light as play.
The very insects on the ground
So nimbly bustle all around,
Among the grass, or dusty soil,
They seem partakers in the toil.
The landscape even reels with life,
While mid the busy stir and strife
Of industry, the shepherd still
Enjoys his summer dreams at will,
Bent o'er his hook, or listless laid
Beneath the pasture's willow shade,
Whose foliage shines so cool and grey
Amid the sultry hues of day,
As if the morning's misty veil
Yet linger'd in its shadows pale;
Or lolling in a musing mood
On mounds where Saxon castles stood,
Upon whose deeply-buried walls
The ivied oak's dark shadow falls,
He oft picks up with wond'ring gaze
Some little thing of other days,
Saved from the wrecks of time—as beads,
Or broken pots among the weeds,
Of curious shapes—and many a stone
From Roman pavements thickly strown,
Oft hoping, as he searches round,
That buried riches may be found,
Though, search as often as he will,
His hopes are disappointed still;
Or watching, on his mossy seat,

The insect world beneath his feet,
In busy motion here and there
Like visitors to feast or fair,
Some climbing up the rush's stem,
A steeple's height or more to them,
With speed, that sees no fear to stop,
Till perch'd upon its spiry top,
Where they awhile the view survey,
Then prune their wings, and flit away;
And others journeying to and fro
Among the grassy woods below,
Musing, as if they felt and knew
The pleasant scenes they wander'd through,
Where each bent round them seems to be
Huge as a giant timber-tree.
Shaping the while their dark employs
To his own visionary joys,
He pictures such a life as theirs,
As free from summer's sweating cares,
And only wishes that his own
Could meet with joys so thickly sown:
Sport seems the all that they pursue,
And play the only work they do.

The cow-boy still cuts short the day,
By mingling mischief with his play;
Oft in the pond, with weeds o'ergrown,
Hurling quick the plashing stone
To cheat his dog, who watching lies,
And instant plunges for the prize;
And though each effort proves in vain,
He shakes his coat, and dives again,
Till, wearied with the fruitless play,
He drops his tail, and sneaks away,
Nor longer heeds the bawling boy,
Who seeks new sports with added joy:
Now on some bank's o'erhanging brow
Beating the wasp's nest with a bough,
Till armies from the hole appear,

And threaten vengeance in his ear
With such determined hue-and-cry
As makes the bold besieger fly;
Then, pelting with excessive glee
The squirrel on the woodland-tree,
Who nimbles round from grain to grain,
And cocks his tail, and peeps again,
Half-pleased, as if he thought the fray
Which mischief made was meant for play,
Till scared and startled into flight,
He instant tumbles out of sight.
Thus he his leisure hour employs,
And feeds on busy meddling joys,
While in the willow-shaded pool
His cattle stand, their hides to cool.

   Loud is the summer's busy song;
The smallest breeze can find a tongue;
While insects of each tiny size
Grow teasing with their melodies,
Till noon burns with its blistering breath
Around, and day dies still as death.
The busy noise of man and brute
Is on a sudden lost and mute;
Even the brook that leaps along
Seems weary of its bubbling song,
And, so soft its waters creep,
Tired silence sinks in sounder sleep.
The cricket on its banks is dumb,
The very flies forget to hum;
And, save the wagon rocking round,
The landscape sleeps without a sound.
The breeze is stopt, the lazy bough
Hath not a leaf that dances now;
The totter-grass upon the hill,
And spiders' threads, are standing still;
The feathers dropt from moor-hen's wing,
Which to the water's surface cling,
Are steadfast, and as heavy seem

As stones beneath them in the stream;
Hawkweed and groundsel's fanning downs
Unruffled keep their seedy crowns;
And in the oven-heated air,
Not one light thing is floating there,
Save that to the earnest eye,
The restless heat seems twittering by.
Noon swoons beneath the heat it made,
And flowers e'en wither in the shade,
Until the sun slopes in the west,
Like weary traveller, glad to rest
On pillowed clouds of many hues;
Then nature's voice its joy renews,
And chequer'd field and grassy plain
Hum, with their summer songs again,
A requiem to the day's decline,
Whose setting sunbeams coolly shine,
As welcome to day's feeble powers
As falling dews to thirsty flowers.

Now to the pleasant pasture dells,
Where hay from closes sweetly smells,
Adown the pathway's narrow lane
The milking maiden hies again,
With scraps of ballads never dumb,
And rosy cheeks of happy bloom,
Tann'd brown by summer's rude embrace,
Which adds new beauties to her face,
And red lips never pale with sighs,
And flowing hair, and laughing eyes
That o'er full many a heart prevailed,
And swelling bosom loosely veiled,
White as the love it harbours there,
Unsullied with the taunts of care.

The mower now gives labour o'er,
And on his bench beside the door
Sits down to see his children play,
Smoking a leisure hour away:

While from her cage the blackbird sings,
That on the woodbine arbour hings;
And all with soothing joys receive
The quiet of a summer's eve.

AUGUST

HARVEST approaches with its busy day;
The wheat tans brown, and barley bleaches grey;
In yellow garb the oatland intervenes,
And tawny glooms the valley throng'd with beans.
Silent the village grows—wood-wandering dreams
Seem not so lonely as its quiet seems;
Doors are shut up as on a winter's day,
And not a child about them lies at play;
The dust that winnows 'neath the breeze's feet
Is all that stirs about the silent street:
Fancy might think that desert-spreading Fear
Had whisper'd terrors into Quiet's ear,
Or plundering armies past the place had come
And drove the lost inhabitants from home.
The fields now claim them, where a motley crew
Of old and young their daily tasks pursue.
The reapers leave their rest before the sun,
And gleaners follow in the toils begun
To pick the litter'd ear the reaper leaves,
And glean in open fields among the sheaves.
The ruddy child, nursed in the lap of Care,
In Toil's rude strife to do its little share,
Beside its mother poddles o'er the land,
Sunburnt, and stooping with a weary hand,
Picking its tiny glean of corn or wheat,
While crackling stubbles wound its little feet;
Full glad it often is to sit awhile
Upon a smooth green balk to ease its toil,
And fain would spend an idle hour in play
With insects, strangers to the moiling day,
Creeping about each rush and grassy stem,

325

And often wishes it were one of them.
Meanwhile the expecting mother stops to tie
Her handful up, and, waiting his supply,
Misses the idle younker from her side;
Then shouts of rods, and morts of threats beside,
Picture harsh truths in his unpractised breast—
How they who idle in the harvest rest
Shall well-deserving in the winter pine,
Or hunt the hedges with the birds and swine.
In vain he wishes that the rushes' height
Were tall as trees to hide him from her sight.
Leaving his pleasant seat, he sighs and rubs
His legs, and shows scratch'd wounds from piercing stubs,
To make excuse for play; but she disdains
His little wounds, and smiles while he complains;
And as he stoops adown in troubles sore,
She sees his grief, and bids him mourn no more,
For by and by, on the next sabbath-day,
He shall have well-earn'd pence as well as play,
When he may buy, almost without a stint,
Sweet candied horehound, cakes, and peppermint,
At the gay shop, within whose window lie
Things of all sorts to tempt his eager eye:
Rich sugar-plums in phials shining bright,
In every hue, young fancies to delight,
Coaches and ladies of gilt gingerbread,
And downy plums, and apples streak'd with red.
Such promises all sorrow soon displace,
And smiles are instant kindled in his face;
Scorning the troubles which he felt before,
He picks the trailing ears, and mourns no more.

The fields are all alive with sultry noise
Of labour's sounds, and insects' busy joys.
The reapers o'er their glittering sickles stoop,
Startling full oft the partridge coveys up;
Some o'er the rustling scythe go bending on;
And shockers follow where their toils have gone,
Heaping the swaths that rustle in the sun,

Where mice from terror's dangers nimbly run,
Leaving their tender young in fear's alarm
Lapt up in nests of chimbled grasses warm,
Hoping for safety from their flight in vain;
While the rude boy, or churlish-hearted swain,
Pursues with lifted weapons o'er the ground,
And spreads an instant murder all around.
In vain the anxious maiden's tender prayer
Urges the clown their little lives to spare;
She sighs, while trailing the long rake along,
At scenes so cruel, and forgets her song.
When the sun stoops to meet the western sky,
And noon's hot hours have wander'd weary by,
Seeking a hawthorn bush or willow-tree
For resting-places that the coolest be,
Where baskets heaped and unbroached bottle lie,
Which dogs in absence watched with wary eye,
They catch their breath awhile, and share the boon
Which bevering-time allows their toil at noon.
Next to her favour'd swain the maiden steals,
Blushing at kindness which his love reveals;
Making a seat for her of sheaves around,
He drops beside her on the naked ground.
Then from its cool retreat the beer they bring,
And hand the stout-hoop'd bottle round the ring.
Each swain soaks hard; the maiden, ere she sips,
Shrieks at the bold wasp settling on her lips,
That seems determined only hers to greet,
As if it fancied they were cherries sweet!
The dog forgoes his sleep awhile, or play,
Springing at frogs that rustling jump away,
To watch each morsel carelessness bestows,
Or wait the bone or crust the shepherd throws;
For shepherds are no more of ease possest,
But share in harvest-labours with the rest.

When day declines and others meet repose,
The bawling boy his evening journey goes;
At toil's unwearied call the first and last,

He drives his horses to their night's repast,
In dewy close or meadow to sojourn;
And often ventures, on his still return,
O'er garden pales, or orchard walls, to hie,
When sleep's safe key hath lock'd up danger's eye,
All but the mastiff watching in the dark,
Who snuffs and knows him, and forbears to bark.
With fearful haste he climbs each loaded tree,
And picks for prizes, that the ripest be;
While the pale moon, creeping with jealous light,
Fills empty shadows with the power to fright,
And, from the barn-hole, pops and hurries by
The grey owl, screaming with a fearful cry;
He hears the noise, and, hastening to escape,
Thinks each thing grows around a dismal shape.
Quick tumbling o'er the mossy mould'ring wall,
He loses half his booty in the fall;
Where, soon as ever morning opes its eyes,
The restless hogs will happen on the prize,
And crump adown the mellow and the green,
Making all seem as nothing e'er had been.

Amid the broils of harvest's weary reign,
How sweet the Sabbath wakes its rest again!
And on each weary mind what rapture dwells,
To hear once more the pleasant chiming bells,
That from each steeple, peeping here and there,
Murmur a soothing lullaby to care.
The shepherd, journeying on his morning rounds,
Pauses awhile to hear the pleasing sounds,
While the glad children, free from toil's employ,
Mimic the 'ding-dong' hums, and laugh for joy.
The fields themselves seem happy to be free,
Where insects chatter with unusual glee;
While Solitude, the grass and stubs among,
Appears to muse and listen to the song.
In quiet peace awakes the welcome morn;
Men tired, and children with their gleaning worn,
Weary and stiff, lie round the doors all day,

To rest themselves, with little heart for play.
In calm delight the Sabbath wears along;
Yet round the Cross, at noon, a tempted throng
Of little younkers, with their pence, repair
To buy the downy plum and luscious pear
That melts i' the mouth, which gardeners never fail,
For gain's strong impulse, to expose for sale,
Placed on the circling Cross-steps in the sun,
What time the parson has his sermon done.
There, soon the boy his sore-earn'd penny spends;
And he the while that penniless attends,
In sullen, silent mood, approaching nigh,
Full often drops a keen, desiring eye
Upon each loaded basket, to perceive
What makes his little fingers itch to thieve;
But, close at hand, the stocks in terror shine,
And temptings strong to stronger fears resign.
Thus Sunday's leisure passes swiftly by
In rest, soft peace, and home-tranquillity,
Till Monday morning doth its cares pursue,
Rousing the harvest's busy toils anew.

SEPTEMBER

HARVEST awakes the morning still,
And toil's rude groups the valleys fill;
Deserted is each cottage hearth
To all life, save the cricket's mirth;
Each burring wheel its sabbath meets,
Nor walks a gossip in the streets;
The bench beneath the eldern bough,
Lined o'er with grass, is empty now,
Where blackbirds, caged from out the sun,
Would whistle while their mistress spun:
All haunt the throngèd fields, to share
The harvest's lingering bounty there.

As yet, no meddling boys resort
About the streets in idle sport;
The butterfly enjoys its hour,
And flirts, unchased, from flower to flower;
The humming bees, which morning calls
From out the low hut's mortar walls,
And passing boy no more controls,
Fly undisturb'd about their holes;
The sparrows in glad chirpings meet,
Unpelted in the quiet street.
None but imprison'd children now
Are seen, where dames with angry brow
Threaten each younker to his seat,
Who, through the window, eyes the street,
Or from his hornbook turns away,
To mourn for liberty and play.

Yet loud are morning's early sounds;
The farm or cottage yard abounds
With creaking noise of opening gate,
And clanking pumps, where boys await
With idle motion, to supply
The thirst of cattle crowding nigh.
Upon the dovecote's mossy slates,
The pigeons coo around their mates;
And close beside the stable wall,
Where morning sunbeams earliest fall,
The basking hen, in playful rout,
Flaps the powdery dust about.
Within the barn-hole sits the cat
Watching to seize the thirsty rat,
Who oft at morn its dwelling leaves
To drink the moisture from the eaves;
The redbreast, with his nimble eye,
Dares scarcely stop to catch the fly,
That, tangled in the spider's snare,
Mourns in vain for freedom there.
The dog beside the threshold lies,
Mocking sleep, with half-shut eyes—

With head crouch'd down upon his feet,
Till strangers pass his sunny seat—
Then quick he pricks his ears to hark,
And bustles up to growl and bark;
While boys in fear stop short their song,
And sneak in startled speed along;
And beggar, creeping like a snail,
To make his hungry hopes prevail
O'er the warm heart of charity,
Leaves his lame halt and hastens by.

The maid afield now leaves the farm,
With dinner-basket on her arm,
Loitering unseen in narrow lane,
To be o'ertook by following swain,
Who, happy thus her truth to prove,
Carries the load and talks of love.
Soon as the dew is off the ground,
Rumbling like distant thunder round,
The wagons haste the corn to load,
And hurry down the dusty road;
While driving boy with eager eye
Watches the church clock passing by—
Whose gilt hands glitter in the sun—
To see how far the hours have run;
Right happy, in the breathless day,
To see time wearing fast away.
But now and then a sudden shower
Will bring to toil a resting hour;
Then, under sheltering shocks, a crowd
Of merry voices mingle loud,
Draining, with leisure's laughing eye,
Each welcome, bubbling bottle dry;
Till peeping suns dry up the rain,
Then off they start to toil again.

Anon the fields are getting clear,
And glad sounds hum in labour's ear;
When children halloo, 'Here they come!'
And run to meet the Harvest Home,

Covered with boughs, and thronged with boys,
Who mingle loud a merry noise,
And, when they meet the stack-thronged yard
Cross-buns and pence their shouts reward.
Then comes the harvest-supper night,
Which rustics welcome with delight;
When merry game and tiresome tale,
And songs, increasing with the ale,
Their mingled uproar interpose,
To crown the harvest's happy close;
While Mirth, that at the scene abides,
Laughs, till she almost cracks her sides.

Now harvest's busy hum declines,
And labour half its help resigns.
Boys, glad at heart, to play return;
The shepherds to their peace sojourn,
Rush-bosom'd solitudes among,
Which busy toil disturb'd so long.
The gossip, happy all is o'er,
Visits again her neighbour's door,
On scandal's idle tales to dwell,
Which harvest had no time to tell;
And free from all its sultry strife,
Enjoys once more her idle life.
A few, whom waning toil reprieves,
Thread the forest's sea of leaves,
Where the pheasant loves to hide,
And the darkest glooms abide,
Beneath the old oaks moss'd and grey,
Whose shadows seem as old as they;
Where time hath many seasons won,
Since aught beneath them saw the sun;
Within these brambly solitudes,
The ragged, noisy boy intrudes,
To gather nuts, that, ripe and brown,
As soon as shook will patter down.

Thus harvest ends its busy reign,
And leaves the fields their peace again,

Where autumn's shadows idly muse
And tinge the trees in many hues:
Amid whose scenes I'm fain to dwell,
And sing of what I love so well.
But hollow winds, and tumbling floods,
And humming showers, and moaning woods,
All startle into sadden strife,
And wake a mighty lay to life,
Making, amid their strains divine,
Unheard a song so mean as mine.

OCTOBER

NATURE now spreads around, in dreary hue,
A pall to cover all that summer knew;
Yet, in the poet's solitary way,
Some pleasing objects for his praise delay,
Something that makes him pause and turn again,
As every trifle will his eye detain:
The free horse rustling through the stubble field,
And cows at lair in rushes, half conceal'd,
With groups of restless sheep who feed their fill,
O'er clear'd fields rambling wheresoe'er they will;
The hedger stopping gaps, amid the leaves,
Which time, o'erhead, in every colour weaves;
The milkmaid stepping with a timid look,
From stone to stone, across the brimming brook;
The cotter journeying with his noisy swine,
Along the wood-side where the brambles twine,
Shaking from mossy oaks the acorns brown,
Or from the hedges red haws dashing down;
The nutters, rustling in the yellow woods,
Who tease the wild things in their solitudes;
The hunters, from the thicket's avenue,
In scarlet jackets, startling on the view,
Skimming a moment o'er the russet plain,
Then hiding in the motley woods again;
The plopping guns' sharp, momentary shock,

Which Echo bustles from her cave to mock;
The bawling song of solitary boys,
Journeying in rapture o'er their dreaming joys.
Haunting the hedges in their reveries,
For wilding fruit that shines upon the trees;
The wild wood music from the lonely dell,
Where merry gipsies o'er their raptures dwell,
Haunting each common's wild and lonely nook,
Where hedges run as crooked as the brook,
Shielding their camps beneath some spreading oak,
And but discovered by the circling smoke
Puffing, and peeping up, as wills the breeze,
Between the branches of the coloured trees:
Such are the pictures that October yields,
To please the poet as he walks the fields;
While Nature—like fair woman in decay,
Whom pale consumption hourly wastes away—
Upon her waning features, winter chill,
Wears dreams of beauty that seem lovely still.
Among the heath-furze still delights to dwell,
Quaking, as if with cold, the harvest bell;
And mushroom-buttons each moist morning brings,
Like spots of snow-shine in dark fairy rings.
Wild shines each hedge in autumn's gay parade;
And, where the eldern trees to autumn fade,
The glossy berry picturesquely cleaves
Its swarthy bunches mid the yellow leaves,
On which the tootling robin feeds at will
And coy hedge-sparrow stains its little bill.
The village dames, as they get ripe and fine,
Gather the bunches for their 'eldern wine,'
Which, bottled up, becomes a rousing charm,
To kindle winter's icy bosom warm,
And, with its merry partner, nut-brown beer,
Makes up the peasant's Christmas-keeping cheer.

   Like to a painted map the landscape lies;
And wild above, shine the cloud-thronged skies,
That chase each other on with hurried pace,

Like living things, as if they ran a race.
The winds, that o'er each sudden tempest brood,
Waken like spirits in a startled mood,
Flirting the sear leaves on the bleaching lea,
That litter under every fading tree,
And pausing oft, as falls the patting rain,
Then gathering strength, and twirling them again,
Till drops the sudden calm: the hurried mill
Is stopt at once, and every noise is still;
Save crows, that from the oak-trees quawking spring,
Dashing the acorns down with beating wing,
Waking the wood's short sleep in noises low,
Patting the crimpt brakes withering brown below;
And whirr of starling crowds, that dim the light
With mimic darkness, in their numerous flight;
Or shrilly noise of puddocks' feeble wail,
As in slow circles round the woods they sail;
While huge black beetles, revelling alone,
In the dull evening hum their heavy drone.
These trifles linger through the shortening day,
To cheer the lone bard's solitary way;
Till surly winter comes with biting breath,
And strips the woods, and numbs the scene with death;
Then all is still o'er wood and field and plain,
As naught had been, and naught would be again.

NOVEMBER

THE landscape sleeps in mist from morn till noon;
And, if the sun looks through, 'tis with a face
Beamless and pale and round, as if the moon,
When done the journey of her nightly race,
Had found him sleeping, and supplied his place.
For days the shepherds in the fields may be,
Nor mark a patch of sky—blindfold they trace
The plains, that seem without a bush or tree,
Whistling aloud by guess to flocks they cannot see.

335

The timid hare seems half its fears to lose,
  Crouching and sleeping 'neath its grassy lair,
And scarcely startles, tho' the shepherd goes
  Close by its home, and dogs are barking there;
The wild colt only turns around to stare
  At passer by, then knaps his hide again;
And moody crows beside the road, forbear
  To fly, tho' pelted by the passing swain;
Thus day seems turn'd to night, and tries to wake in vain.

The owlet leaves her hiding-place at noon,
  And flaps her grey wings in the doubting light;
The hoarse jay screams to see her out so soon,
  And small birds chirp and startle with affright;
Much doth it scare the superstitious wight,
  Who dreams of sorry luck, and sore dismay;
While cow-boys think the day a dream of night,
  And oft grow fearful on their lonely way,
Fancying that ghosts may wake, and leave their graves by day.

Yet but awhile the slumbering weather flings
  Its murky prison round—then winds wake loud;
With sudden stir the startled forest sings
  Winter's returning song—cloud races cloud,
And the horizon throws away its shroud,
  Sweeping a stretching circle from the eye;
Storms upon storms in quick succession crowd,
  And o'er the sameness of the purple sky
Heaven paints, with hurried hand, wild hues of every dye.

At length it comes among the forest oaks,
  With sobbing ebbs, and uproar gathering high;
The scared, hoarse raven on its cradle croaks,
  And stockdove-flocks in hurried terrors fly,
While the blue hawk hangs o'er them in the sky.
  The hedger hastens from the storm begun,
To seek a shelter that may keep him dry;
  And foresters, low bent the wind to shun,
Scarce hear amid the strife the poacher's muttering gun.

The ploughman hears its humming rage begin,
And hies for shelter from his naked toil;
Buttoning his doublet closer to his chin,
He bends and scampers o'er the elting soil,
While clouds above him in wild fury boil,
And winds drive heavily the beating rain;
He turns his back to catch his breath awhile,
Then ekes his speed and faces it again,
To seek the shepherd's hut beside the rushy plain.

The boy, that scareth from the spiry wheat
The melancholy crow, in hurry weaves,
Beneath an ivied tree, his sheltering seat
Of rushy flags and sedges tied in sheaves,
Or from the field a shock of stubble thieves.
There he doth dithering sit, and entertain
His eyes with marking the storm-driven leaves;
Oft spying nests where he spring eggs had ta'en,
And wishing in his heart 'twas summer-time again.

Thus wears the month along, in chequer'd moods,
Sunshine and shadows, tempests loud and calms;
One hour dies silent o'er the sleepy woods,
The next wakes loud with unexpected storms;
A dreary nakedness the field deforms—
Yet many a rural sound and rural sight
Lives in the village still about the farms,
Where toil's rude uproar hums from morn till night,
Noises in which the ears of Industry delight.

At length the stir of rural labour's still,
And Industry her care awhile forgoes;
When Winter comes in earnest to fulfil
His yearly task, at bleak November's close,
And stops the plough, and hides the field in snows;
When frost locks up the stream in chill delay,
And mellows on the hedge the jetty sloes
For little birds—then Toil hath time for play,
And naught but threshers' flails awake the dreary day.

DECEMBER

GLAD Christmas comes, and every hearth
   Makes room to give him welcome now,
E'en want will dry its tears in mirth,
   And crown him with a holly bough;
Though tramping 'neath a winter sky,
   O'er snowy paths and rimy stiles,
The housewife sets her spinning by
   To bid him welcome with her smiles.

Each house is swept the day before,
   And windows stuck with evergreens,
The snow is besom'd from the door,
   And comfort crowns the cottage scenes.
Gilt holly, with its thorny pricks,
   And yew and box, with berries small,
These deck the unused candlesticks,
   And pictures hanging by the wall.

Neighbours resume their annual cheer,
   Wishing, with smiles and spirits high,
Glad Christmas and a happy year
   To every morning passer-by;
Milkmaids their Christmas journeys go,
   Accompanied with favour'd swain;
And children pace the crumping snow,
   To taste their granny's cake again.

The shepherd, now no more afraid,
   Since custom doth the chance bestow,
Starts up to kiss the giggling maid
   Beneath the branch of misletoe
That 'neath each cottage beam is seen,
   With pearl-like berries shining gay;
The shadow still of what hath been,
   Which fashion yearly fades away.

The singing waits, a merry throng,
   At early morn, with simple skill,
Yet imitate the angels' song,
   And chant their Christmas ditty still;

And, mid the storm that dies and swells
　　By fits, in hummings softly steals
The music of the village bells,
　　Ringing round their merry peals.

When this is past, a merry crew,
　　Bedeck'd in masks and ribbons gay,
The 'Morris-dance,' their sports renew,
　　And act their winter evening play.
The clown turn'd king, for penny-praise,
　　Storms with the actor's strut and swell;
And Harlequin, a laugh to raise,
　　Wears his hunchback and tinkling bell.

And oft for pence and spicy ale,
　　With winter nosegays pinn'd before,
The wassail-singer tells her tale,
　　And drawls her Christmas carols o'er.
While prentice boy, with ruddy face,
　　And rime-bepowder'd, dancing locks,
From door to door with happy pace,
　　Runs round to claim his 'Christmas box.'

The block upon the fire is put,
　　To sanction custom's old desires;
And many a faggot's bands are cut,
　　For the old farmers' Christmas fires;
Where loud-tongued Gladness joins the throng,
　　And Winter meets the warmth of May,
Till feeling soon the heat too strong,
　　He rubs his shins, and draws away.

While snows the window-panes bedim,
　　The fire curls up a sunny charm,
Where, creaming o'er the pitcher's rim,
　　The flowering ale is set to warm;
Mirth, full of joy as summer bees,
　　Sits there, its pleasures to impart,
And children, 'tween their parents' knees,
　　Sing scraps of carols o'er by heart.

And some, to view the winter weathers,
  Climb up the window-seat with glee,
Likening the snow to falling feathers,
  In fancy's infant ecstasy;
Laughing, with superstitious love,
  O'er visions wild that youth supplies,
Of people pulling geese above,
  And keeping Christmas in the skies.

As tho' the homestead trees were drest,
  In lieu of snow, with dancing leaves,
As tho' the sun-dried martin's nest,
  Instead of ickles, hung the eaves,
The children hail the happy day—
  As if the snow were April's grass,
And pleas'd, as 'neath the warmth of May,
  Sport o'er the water froze to glass.

Thou day of happy sound and mirth,
  That long with childish memory stays,
How blest around the cottage hearth
  I met thee in my younger days!
Harping, with rapture's dreaming joys,
  On presents which thy coming found,
The welcome sight of little toys,
  The Christmas gift of cousins round:

The wooden horse with arching head,
  Drawn upon wheels around the room,
The gilded coach of gingerbread,
  And many-colour'd sugar-plum,
Gilt-cover'd books for pictures sought,
  Or stories childhood loves to tell,
With many an urgent promise bought,
  To get to-morrow's lesson well;

And many a thing, a minute's sport,
  Left broken on the sanded floor,
When we would leave our play, and court
  Our parents' promises for more.

Tho' manhood bids such raptures die,
    And throws such toys aside as vain,
Yet memory loves to turn her eye,
    And count past pleasures o'er again.

Around the glowing hearth at night,
    The harmless laugh and winter tale
Go round, while parting friends delight
    To toast each other o'er their ale;
The cotter oft with quiet zeal
    Will musing o'er his Bible lean;
While in the dark the lovers steal
    To kiss and toy behind the screen.

Old customs! Oh! I love the sound,
    However simple they may be:
Whate'er with time hath sanction found,
    Is welcome and is dear to me.
Pride grows above simplicity,
    And spurns them from her haughty mind,
And soon the poet's song will be
    The only refuge they can find.

WANDERINGS IN JUNE

THE season now is all delight,
    Sweet smile the passing hours,
And Summer's pleasures, at their height,
    Are sweet as are her flowers;
The purple morning waken'd soon,
    The midday's gleaming din,
Grey evening with her silver moon,
    Are sweet to mingle in.

While waking doves betake to flight
    From off each roosting bough,
While Nature's locks are wet with night,
    How sweet to wander now!

341

Fast fade the vapours cool and grey,
    The red sun waxes strong,
And streaks on labour's early way
    His shadows lank and long.

Serenely sweet the Morning comes
    O'er the horizon's sweep,
And calmly breaks the wakening hums
    Of Nature's nightly sleep.
What rapture swells with every sound
    Of Morning's maiden hours!
What healthful feelings breathe around!
    What freshness opes the flowers!

Each tree and flower, in every hue
    And varied green, are spread,
As fair and frail as drops the dew
    From off each blooming head;
Like to that beauty which beguiles
    The eyes of wondering men,
Led blushing to perfection's smiles
    And left to wither then.

How strange a scene has come to pass
    Since Summer 'gan its reign!
Spring flowers are buried in the grass,
    To sleep till spring again:
Her dew-drops Evening still receives
    To gild the morning hours;
But dew-drops fall on open'd leaves
    And moisten stranger-flowers.

The artless daisies' smiling face
    My wanderings find no more;
The kingcups that supplied their place,
    Their golden race is o'er;
And clover bottles' ruddy bloom,
    That blossom where these fell,
Ere autumn's fading mornings come
    Shall meet their grave as well.

342

Life's every beauty fades away,
    And short its worldly race;
Change leads us round its varied day,
    And strangers take our place:
On summers past, how many eyes
    Have waken'd into bliss,
That death's eclipsing hand denies
    To view the charms of this!

The open flower, the loaded bough,
    The fields of spindling grain,
Were blooming then the same as now,
    And so will bloom again:
When with the past my being dies,
    Still summer suns shall shine,
And other eyes shall see them rise
    When death has darkened mine.

Reflection, with thy mortal shrouds
    When thou dost interfere,
Though all is gay, what gloomy clouds
    Thy musings shadow here!
To think of summers yet to come
    That I am not to see,
To think a weed is yet to bloom
    From dust that I shall be!

The misty clouds of purple hue
    Are fading from the eye,
And ruddy streaks, which morning drew,
    Have left a dappled sky;
The sun has call'd the bees abroad,
    Wet with the early hour,
By toiling for the honey'd load
    Ere dews forsake the flower.

O'er yonder hill, a dusty rout
    Wakes solitude from sleep;
Shepherds have wattled pens about,
    To shear their bleating sheep;

Less pleasing is the public way,
 Traced with awaken'd toil;
And sweet are woods shut out from day,
 Where sunbeams never smile.

The woodbines, fresh with morning hours,
 Are what I love to see;
The ivy-spreading darksome bowers
 Is where I love to be:
Left there, as when a boy, to lie
 And talk to flower and tree,
And fancy, in my ecstasy,
 Their silence answers me.

While some desire tumultuous joys,
 And shun what nature wears,
Give me the choice which they despise,
 And I'll not sigh for theirs:
The shady wild, the summer dreams
 Enjoying there at will,
The whispering voice of woods and streams
 That breathe of Eden still.

How sweet the fanning breeze is felt,
 Breathed through the dancing boughs!
How sweet the rural noises melt
 From distant sheep and cows!
The lovely green of wood and hill,
 The hummings in the air,
Serenely in my breast instil
 The rapture reigning there.

To me how sweet the whispering winds,
 The woods again how sweet,
To find the peace which freedom finds,
 And from the world retreat;
To stretch beneath a spreading tree,
 That far its shadow shoots,
While by its side the water free
 Curls through its twisted roots.

Such silence oft be mine to meet
  In leisure's musing hours;
Oft be a fountain's brink my seat—
  My partners, birds and flowers:
No tumult here creates alarm,
  No pains our follies find;
Peace visits us in every calm,
  Health breathes in every wind.

Now cool the wood my wanderings shrouds,
  'Neath arbours Nature weaves,
Shut up from viewing fields and clouds,
  And buried deep in leaves;
The sounds without amuse me still,
  Mixt with the sounds within—
The scythe with sharpening tinkles shrill,
  The cuckoo's soothing din.

The eye, no longer left to range,
  Is pent in narrowest bound,
Yet Nature's works, unnamed and strange,
  My every step surround;
Things small as dust, of every dye,
  That scarce the sight perceives,
Some clad with wings fly droning by,
  Some climb the grass and leaves.

And flowers these darksome woodlands rear,
  Whose shades they yearly claim,
That Nature's wond'rous mystery wear,
  And bloom without a name:
What different shapes in leaves are seen
  That o'er my head embower,
Clad in as many shades of green
  As colours in the flower!

My path now gleams with fairer light,
  The side approaches near,
A heath now bolts upon the sight,
  And rabbit-tracks appear:

I love the heath, though mid the brakes
   Fear shudders, trampling through,
Oft check'd at things she fancies snakes
   Quick nestling from the view.

Yet where the ground is nibbled bare
   By rabbits and by sheep,
I often fearless loiter there,
   And think myself to sleep.
Dear are the scenes which Nature loves,
   Where she untamed retires,
Far from the stretch of planted groves
   Which polish'd taste admires.

Here oft, though grass and moss are seen
   Tann'd brown for want of showers,
Still keeps the ling its darksome green,
   Thick set with little flowers;
And yonder, mingling o'er the heath,
   The furze delights to dwell,
Whose blossoms steal the summer's breath,
   And shed a sultry smell.

Here threat'ning ploughs have tried in vain
   To till the sandy soil;
Yon slope, already sown with grain,
   Shows Nature mocks the toil;
The wild weeds choke the straggling ears,
   And motley gardens spread;
The blue-cap there in bloom appears,
   And poppies, lively red.

But now my footsteps sidle round
   The gently sloping hill,
Now falter over marshy ground,
   Yet Nature charms me still:
Here moss, and grass, and flowers appear
   Of different forms and hues;
And insects too inhabit here,
   Which still my wonder views.

Here horsetail round the water's edge
    In bushy tufts is spread,
With rush, and cutting leaves of sedge
    That children learn to dread;
Its leaves, like razors, mingling there
    Oft make the youngster turn,
Leaving his rushes in despair,
    A wounded hand to mourn.

What wonders strike my idle gaze,
    As near the pond I stand!
What life its stagnant depth displays,
    As varied as the land:
All forms and sizes swimming there,
    Some, sheath'd in silvery den,
Oft siling up as if for air,
    Then nimbling down agen.

Now rising ground permits the plain
    To change the restless view,
The pathways leading down the lane
    My pleasures still renew.
The osier's slender shade is by,
    And bushes thickly spread;
Again the ground is firm and dry,
    Nor trembles 'neath the tread.

On this side, ash or oak embowers;
    There, hawthorns humbler grow,
With goatsbeard wreath, and woodbine flowers,
    That shade a brook below,
Which feebly purls its rippling moans
    With summer draining dry,
Till struttles, as I step the stones,
    Can scarcely struggle by.

Now soon shall end these musing dreams
    In solitude's retreat;
The eye that dwelt on woods and streams
    The village soon shall meet:

Nigh on the sight the steeple towers;
  The clock, with mellow hum,
Counts out the day's declining hours,
  And calls my ramblings home.

I love to visit Spring's young blooms
  When wet with April showers;
Nor feel less joy, when Summer comes,
  To trace her darker bowers;
I love to meet the Autumn winds
  Till they have mourn'd their last;
Nor less delight my journey finds
  In Winter's howling blast.

THE APPROACH OF SPRING

Now once again, thou lovely Spring,
  Thy sight the day beguiles;
For fresher greens the fairy ring,
  The daisy brighter smiles:
The winds, that late with chiding voice
  Would fain thy stay prolong,
Relent, while little birds rejoice,
  And mingle into song.

Undaunted maiden, thou shalt find
  Thy home in gleaming woods,
Thy mantle in the southern wind,
  Thy wreath in swelling buds:
And may thy mantle wrap thee round,
  And hopes still warm and thrive,
And dews with every morn be found
  To keep thy wreath alive.

May coming suns, that tempt thy flowers,
  Smile on as they begin;
And gentle be succeeding hours
  As those that bring thee in:

Full lovely are thy dappled skies,
  Pearl'd round with promised showers,
And sweet thy blossoms round thee rise
  To meet the sunny hours.

The primrose bud, thy early pledge,
  Sprouts 'neath each woodland tree,
And violets under every hedge
  Prepare a seat for thee:
As maids just meeting woman's bloom
  Feel love's delicious strife,
So Nature warms to find thee come,
  And kindles into life.

Through hedgerow leaves, in drifted heaps
  Left by the stormy blast,
The little hopeful blossom peeps,
  And tells of winter past;
A few leaves flutter from the woods,
  That hung the season through,
Leaving their place for swelling buds
  To spread their leaves anew.

'Mong wither'd grass upon the plain,
  That lent the blast a voice,
The tender green appears again,
  And creeping things rejoice;
Each warm bank shines with early flowers,
  Where oft a lonely bee
Drones, venturing on in sunny hours,
  Its humming song to thee.

The birds are busy on the wing,
  The fish play in the stream;
And many a hasty curdled ring
  Crimps round the leaping bream;
The buds unfold to leaves apace,
  Along the hedgerow bowers,
And many a child with rosy face
  Is seeking after flowers.

349

The soft wind fans the violet blue,
　　Its opening sweets to share,
And infant breezes, waked anew,
　　Play in the maidens' hair—
Maidens that freshen with thy flowers,
　　To charm the gentle swain,
And dally, in their milking hours,
　　With lovers' vows again.

Bright dews illume the grassy plain,
　　Sweet messengers of morn,
And drops hang glistening after rain
　　Like gems on every thorn;
What though the grass is moist and rank
　　Where dews fall from the tree,
The creeping sun smiles on the bank
　　And warms a seat for thee.

The eager morning earlier wakes
　　To glad thy fond desires,
And oft its rosy bed forsakes
　　Ere night's pale moon retires;
Sweet shalt thou feel the morning sun
　　To warm thy dewy breast,
And chase the chill mist's purple dun
　　That lingers in the west.

Her dresses Nature gladly trims,
　　To hail thee as her queen,
And soon shall fold thy lovely limbs
　　In modest garb of green:
Each day shall like a lover come
　　Some gifts with thee to share,
And swarms of flowers shall quickly bloom
　　To dress thy golden hair.

All life and beauty warm and smile
　　Thy lovely face to see,
And many a hopeful hour beguile
　　In seeking joys with thee:

The sweetest hours that ever come
    Are those which thou dost bring,
And sure the fairest flowers that bloom
    Are partners of the Spring.

I've met the Winter's biting breath
    In Nature's wild retreat,
When Silence listens as in death,
    And thought its wildness sweet;
And I have loved the Winter's calm
    When frost has left the plain,
When suns that morning waken'd warm
    Left eve to freeze again.

I've heard in Autumn's early reign
    Her first, her gentlest song;
I've mark'd her change o'er wood and plain,
    And wish'd her reign were long;
Till winds, like armies, gather'd round,
    And stripp'd her colour'd woods,
And storms urged on, with thunder-sound,
    Their desolating floods.

And Summer's endless stretch of green,
    Spread over plain and tree,
Sweet solace to my eyes has been,
    As it to all must be;
Long I have stood his burning heat,
    And breathed the sultry day,
And walk'd and toil'd with weary feet,
    Nor wish'd his pride away.

But oft I've watch'd the greening buds
    Brush'd by the linnet's wing,
When, like a child, the gladden'd woods
    First lisp the voice of Spring;
When flowers, like dreams, peep every day,
    Reminding what they bring,
I've watch'd them, and am warn'd to pay
    A preference to Spring.

TO THE COWSLIP

Once more, thou flower of childish fame,
    Thou meet'st the April wind;
The selfsame flower, the very same
    As those I used to find.
Thy peeps, tipt round with ruddy streak,
    Again attract mine eye,
As they were those I used to seek
    Full twenty summers by.

But I'm no more akin to thee,
    A partner of the spring;
For time has had a hand with me,
    And left an alter'd thing:
A thing that's lost thy golden hours,
    And all I witness'd then,
Mix'd in a desert, far from flowers,
    Among the ways of men.

Thy blooming pleasures, smiling, gay,
    The seasons still renew;
But mine were doom'd a stinted stay,
    Ah, they were short and few!
The every hour that hurried by,
    To eke the passing day,
Lent restless pleasures wings to fly
    Till all were flown away.

Blest flower! with spring thy joy's begun,
    And no false hopes are thine;
One constant cheer of shower and sun
    Makes all thy stay divine.
But my May-morning quickly fled,
    And dull its noon came on—
And happiness is past and dead
    Ere half that noon is gone.

Ah! smile and bloom, thou lovely thing!
    Though May's sweet days are few,

Still coming years thy flowers shall bring,
　　And bid them bloom anew.
Man's Life, that bears no kin to them,
　　Past pleasures well may mourn:
No bud clings to its withering stem—
　　No hope for Spring's return.

THE LAST OF AUTUMN

COME, bleak November, in thy wildness come:
　　Thy mornings clothed in rime, thy evenings chill—
E'en these have power to tempt me from my home,
　　E'en these have beauty to delight me still.
Though Nature lingers in her mourning weeds,
　　And wails the dying year in gusty blast,
Still added beauty to the last proceeds,
　　And wildness triumphs when her bloom is past.

Though long grass all the day is drench'd in dew,
　　And splashy pathways lead me o'er the greens,
Though naked fields hang lonely on the view,
　　Long lost to harvest and its busy scenes,
Yet in the distance shines the painted bough,
　　Leaves changed to every colour ere they die,
And through the valley rivers widen now,
　　Once little brooks which summer dribbled dry.

Here ragged boys, pleased with the change of scene,
　　Try new inventions of their infant skill,
Leaving their leap-frog races on the green,
　　To watch the waves and build the dashing mill;
Or where the molehill island lifts its head,
　　There form the castle with its guarding moat,
And o'er the jumping waves, with little dread,
　　Turn nutshell boats and paper ships afloat.

On bridge-wall sitting, by such scenes as these,
　　I meet with pleasures that can please for hours;
Mix'd in the uproar of those little seas,
　　That roll their floods where summer left her flowers.

A wild confusion hangs upon the ear,
  And something half romantic meets the view;
Arches half fill'd with wither'd leaves appear,
  Where white foam stills the billow boiling through.

Those yellow leaves that litter on the grass,
  'Mong dry brown stalks that lately blossom'd there,
Instil a mournful pleasure as they pass:
  For melancholy has its joy to spare—
A joy that dwells in autumn's lonely walks,
  And whispers, like a vision, what shall be,
How flowers shall blossom on those wither'd stalks,
  And green leaves clothe each nearly naked tree.

Oft in the woods I hear the thundering gun;
  And, through the brambles as I cautious creep,
A bustling hare, the threatening sound to shun,
  Oft skips the pathway in a fearful leap;
And spangled pheasant, scared from stumpy bush,
  Oft blunders rustling through the yellow boughs;
While farther off, from beds of reed and rush,
  The startled woodcock leaves its silent sloughs.

Here Echo oft her autumn ditty sings,
  Mocking the cracking whip and yelping hounds,
While through the woods the wild disorder rings,
  Chorus'd with hunter's horns of mellower sounds,
And bawling halloos of the sporting train,
  Who dash through woodland, in their gay parade,
And leap the ditch, and sweep the level plain,
  Fresh wildness adding to the chequer'd shade.

The timid sheep that huddled from the wind
  'Neath the broad oaks, beside the spinney rails,
Half mad with fear such hue and cry to find,
  In rattling motion chase adown the vales:
And, falsely startled by unheeding dogs,
  From where the acorns patter bright and brown,
Through the thorn hedges burst the random hogs,
  Who grunt and scamper till they reach the town.

The playing boys, to eke the rude uproar,
  Turn hunters some, some mock the yelping hounds,
Whose real barkings urge their noise the more,
  And keck-made bugles spout their twanging sounds,
But soon foot-foundered, youngster hunters lag,
  By mounted sportsmen distanced far away,
Yet still they chase the fancied fox or stag,
  And feel as happy in the cheat as they.

Ah! sweet is boyish joy in memory's eye;
  An artless tale with no attending pains,
Save the sad thought—to feel such pleasures fly;
  And the vain hope—-to wish them back again.
How many autumns brought the woods their guest,
  With mimic horns, in hunting sports to join!
How many autumns since that time have past,
  Stretching the distance when such joys were mine!

Still joys are mine, uncertain paths to take
  Through the wild woods, to hide and walk at will,
Rustling aside the brown and wither'd brake,
  To rest on roots, and think, and linger still.
Though trumpet-kecks are passed unheeded by,
  Whose hollow stalks inspired such eager joy,
Still other trifles other sports supply,
  Which manhood seeks as eager as the boy.

To meanest trifles pleasure's hold will cling;
  'Tis even felt to view that greening moss;
These simple wrecks of summer and of spring—
  Like other children I regret their loss.
But there is something in that wind that mourns,
  And those black clouds that hide the heav'n as well,
And in that sun, that gilds and glooms by turns,
  Which leaves a pleasure that's unspeakable.

Though nuts have long been glean'd by many crews
  Of shatter'd poor, who daily rambled there,
And squirrels claim'd the remnant as their dues,
  Still to the woods the hungry boys repair,

Brushing the long dead grass with anxious feet,
  While round their heads the stirr'd leaves patter down,
To seek the bramble's jet-fruit, lushy sweet,
  Or climbing service-berries ripe and brown.

Amidst the wreck of perishable leaves,
  How fresh and fine appears the evergreen!
How box, or holly, garden-walks relieves!
  How bright the ivy round the oak is seen!
And on old thorns the long-leaved mistletoe
  Regains fresh beauties as its parent dies;
While dark spurge-laurel, on the banks below,
  In stubborn bloom the autumn blight defies.

But garden shades have long been doom'd to fall,
  Where naked fruit-trees drop their constant showers:
All blooms are fled, save on the wet moss'd wall
  As yet may peep some faded gilliflowers.
The mist and smoke, in shadows mingling deep,
  Around each cottage hover all the day;
Through the dim panes the prison'd children peep,
  And look in vain for summer and for play.

Now this heath's eminence extends the views,
  How sweet yon hill-tops on the distance rise,
Crowned with stretched woods of many-coloured hues,
  And wildly hung with autumn's changing skies,
Where dark black clouds come slowly rolling on,
  By others close pursued of lighter stain,
Dull shadows glooming dreary: and anon
  Blue skies and sunlight brighten up again.

Light streaks yon sandy road far o'er the grounds,
  Lost in the vales and peeping with the hills,
While in the mist the distance daily bounds,
  Spires dimly rise and turning sails of mills.
And near at hand, aside yon spreading oak,
  Midst furze and ling and tufts of withered grass
The gipsy's dwelling curls its feeble smoke,
  Where its scant bounty nips the weary ass.

O'er yon brown stubble-field which nature shuns,
   What gaudy views the year did once command
When yellow carlock glittered in the sun
   And crimson cornflowers blazed about the land
For furlongs round! when tufty blades of wheat
   Hid the coy wanderings of the timid hare,
That now for furlongs vainly seeks a seat
   And flies to woods to skulk from danger there.

And in the lane, along its hedgerow bank,
   Where naught shines now but littered yellow leaves,
And withered weeds, which summer spindled rank—
   Save round old stulps, where ivy wildly weaves—
There once the spring one's pleasant walks beguiled
   With swarms of violet flowers both white and blue;
There mid broad leaves the primrose meekly smiled,
   And cowslip roots, less plenteous, often grew.

Dull seems the town which one's return receives,
   Where naught is heard around but twanking flails,
Save chirping sparrows on our cottage eaves
   Or twittering robins on some garden pales.
There's nothing there one's bounded views can meet
   But gabbling geese and battling swine's uproar,
Where stepping-stones along the dirty street
   Are laid as bridges to each cottage door.[1]

WINTER

From nuddling night's embrace now chill
   The winter's waxing days begin,
Dull reddening o'er the east's blea hill
   And creeping sad and shyly in!
Now gilds the sun each bare tree-top
   And pale peeps thro' each window light,
While from the eaves the ickles drop,
   That eke afresh their tails at night.

[1] Last five stanzas added from MS.

The snows and rime lodge everywhere;
　　Each cot in dazzling white is drest;
Nor thatch nor wither'd weeds appear
　　Where birds their numbing feet may rest.
And every twig thro' wood and plain
　　Where summer hung her greening bough,
Wild winter's mockery clothes again
　　With hoary shapes and shadows now.

The street is throng'd with bawling boys,
　　Who pat their redden'd fingers warm,
And, eager after dithering joys,
　　Unheeding brave each pelting storm,
To roll their giant forms of snow,
　　Or slide—or seeking rude repast,
Hirpling by hedges where the sloe
　　Hangs mellow'd by the biting blast.

Past noon's thaw'd snow along the street,
　　Stiffen'd to ice now night has been,
Oft balks the maiden's stepping feet,
　　Who falls and blushes to be seen,
While amorous feelings inly warm
　　Some passing clown who turns to steal
A glimpse of modesty's alarm
　　Which such-like accidents reveal.

In winter's surly depth how sweet
　　To meet those comforts we desire,
Possessing some snug corner seat
　　Where blazes nigh the welcome fire;
Warming one's toes upon the hearth
　　And reading poems not too long,
While basks the cat in purring mirth,
　　While crickets sing their winter song:

And, winter's tiresome hours to cheat,
　　Have means to visit now and then,
Where neighbours o'er their tankard meet
　　And there the corner share agen:

Each comfort suiting best to choose,
  To sit and crump warm penny rolls,
Or take short snatches o'er the news
  While warms the nappy on the coals.

And when suns creep the warmest height
  And north winds whisper nearly still,
When greening patches meet the sight
  On southward slant of bank or hill,
And berries freed from rime awhile
  Shine red on hedgerow twigs again,
One may a midday hour beguile
  To walk in shielding wood and plain:

To track some woodland's gentle ride,
  Where hanging branches lend a screen
On banks slop'd down on either side,
  Where sheltering valleys creep between.
As down such hollows one proceeds,
  We instant feel a warmer day,
While 'mong each bank-top's rustling weeds
  Winds noise their unfelt rage away.

Each twig when touch'd, tho' hardly stirr'd
  Its white shower litters to the ground,
And from the shake of startled bird
  The rime like powder puthers round:
And as one fails those tracks to meet
  By shepherds made and foddering boys,
The snow shrinks from one's hast'ning feet,
  Harsh crumping with incessant noise.

Now, view the prospect where we will,
  On woods above or vales below,
Or nigh or distant, winter still
  Stretches his dazzling scene of snow.
The very spire-points catch the eye
  As chang'd with winter's frowning pride,
And where a sunbeam cannot lie
  Shine whiten'd on their northern side.

The arch of light around us bowed
    Stretches for days its cloudless sky,
Save freckling shadows of a cloud
    That lose to nothing passing by.
The clouds oft darken closing day
    And round the north disordered lie,
Like rocks with bases torn away,
    On nothing hung 'tween earth and sky.

Nature, that pauses nearly dumb,
    But startles some complaint to make,
Not like the buried busy hum
    Which vanish'd summer kept awake:
Where sheep their bleating wants reveal,
    And hollow noise of bawling cow
That waits the fodderer's stinted meal
    Is all one's walks can listen now:

Save when some clown with beetle breaks
    The pond's thick ice for stock to drink;
Wild noises round the village wakes
    From geese that gabble on the brink,
Who mope and brood about the snows
    When frost their plashy sport destroys,
Till such scant chance relief bestows
    To urge afresh their squalling joys.

Oft o'er one flies the chirping lark
    With rime hung round his chilly breast,
Complaining of some dog's rude bark
    That scared him from his chilly rest.
And oft from snow-bank's ridgy edge
    The hare steps hirpling o'er the plain,
Till found a bush or bunch of sedge—
    Then drops its ears and squats again.

And feebly whines the puddock's wail,
    Slow circling naked woods around,
And wild geese ranks that swifter sail
    Oft start one with a hoarser sound;

While, towering at the farthest height,
  The heron drawls its lonely cry,
Who intercepts the dazzled light
  And looks a cloud-speck in the sky.

The herdboy's drawling noise is o'er,
  And all the scenes his summer saw;
His cows now haunt each thresher's door
  And pick in sullen mood the straw.
The ploughman's song is vanish'd now,
  And quawking rooks and chattering pies
Are silent all—each idle plough
  Froze in the snow-hid furrow lies.

Made bold by want, in many a flock,
  The ringdoves fly from solitude,
And mingling share with friendly stock
  A portion of their winter food—
A meal which providence bestows
  Where hardy turnip-roots abound,
And oft one sees upon the snows
  Their little footmarks dinted round.

Cold woods the blackbirds gladly shun,
  Where round their perch the ickles freeze,
And court, less shy, the noonday sun,
  And hop about our garden trees;
And little birds with hunger tame
  To cottage yards undaunted go,
Where pity warms some gentle dame
  To scatter crumbles round the snow.

Yet all, save robin, will retreat
  And shun rude man's forbidding sight—
Who seemly welcomes trampling feet
  And ruffs its feathers in delight,
Brisk hopping from its shielding thorn
  As one who would our steps detain—
Then droops its wing and sits forlorn
  When left to solitude again.

In blackening droves, the rook and crow
　　Flap the cold air with heavy wings,
To seek what home will not bestow
　　As soon as morn the summons brings.
Full many a weary mile they fly
　　To try what stranger fields will spare,
Till eve returns her freezing sky—
　　Then wearied to their homes repair.

Tho' doled about, reserv'd and shy,
　　As one who hates to please us—still
Beauty will often catch the eye
　　From snow surrounding wood and hill.
Those drops which night's chill finger hings,
　　Froze on the point of every thorn,
Are trifles kin to lovely things
　　When gilt by slanting beams of morn.

And where in midway ripples still
　　The brook boils on its hasty tides,
And slides the touch of winter chill
　　Save on its calmer sleeping sides,
There frost, his quiet toil resumed,
　　Shoots streaking spars that wildly run
From weed to weed and shine illumed
　　Like glittering stars before the sun:

Where, as one steps its oaken plank,
　　The hollow frozen sounding noise
From flags and sedge beside the bank
　　The wild duck's brooding peace destroys;
And snipes, with long misshapen bill,
　　Oft startle from intruding fears,
Who haunt the brooks in winter chill,
　　And vanish as the spring appears.

The ivy greens in brightness now
　　And round the tree its beauty weaves,
With chocolate berries on its bough
　　And shoots of paler-veined leaves:

362

And beech-trees, tho' their bloom is flown,
    Still fragments of the autumn wear;
Muffled in leaves of rustling brown,
    Coy beauty's wildness lingers there.

And, milking hovels passing by,
    In some close nook, where shelter dwells,
And cows at quiet musing lie,
    Whose breath steams up in savoury smells,
One often meets the healthy lass,
    As fair and fresh as summer flowers,
Which leaves a pleasure as we pass
    That gladdens winter's lonely hours.

And when a sudden thaw comes on,
    And floods like autumn roll and noise,
When hills of snow are sunk and gone,
    Then winter has her added joys.
Banks, where the north wind never comes,
    Then green as with the hopes of spring,
And birds fly round their changing homes,
    Chirping as tho' they tried to sing.

Woodpecker, too, whose glossy wings
    Seem leaves upon each wither'd oak,
Where lured by suns it often clings
    And taps for hours its gentle stroke;
And ravens, croaking on the wing,
    And crows will clamorous ditties raise,
All busied with the hopes of spring
    When thaws mock winter's warmest days.

The stock, now huddled side to side,
    From winter's nipping age to brood,
Will then disperse and wander wide
    Nor wait the fodderer's call to food.
Yon sullen steed, that hangs his head,
    Will prick his ears in pleasure then,
And by the pasture's promise fed
    Will plunge in frolic joys agen.

The swain then whistles to his sheep,
  Nor plods his dog behind his heels,
As he was wont, from winds to creep,
  But runs at random o'er the fields,
Chasing the startled hare by guess,
  Then stops and barks his master on,
And in his antic joy's excess
  Forgets his puppy days are gone.

Each bank smiles in the sunny hours
  As sweet as those the spring provides,
Save that they want the daisy flowers
  And white lambs basking by their sides.
May's mildness mocks the gladden'd sky,
  And clouds as swiftly clouds pursue,
Save that no swallow cares to fly,
  Nor cuckoo sings the story true.

Thus some few days may idly dwell
  And hold the tempting season still,
And tempt the early buds to swell
  For lurking winter's blast to kill;
And many a flower on sunny slopes,
  That startles up the spring to see,
Is doomed to lose their early hopes
  And perish in their infancy.

And oft one views the hairy leaves
  Of woodbines in the shelter'd plain,
Sprouting when winter's thaw deceives—
  To perish when he frowns again.
And pity often mourns to meet
  A daisy smiling to the sun,
Unconscious of the tempting cheat,
  That fancies gentle spring begun.

But short is nature's waking hope;
  A frowning cloud may cross the skies—
When sun and warmth and all elope,
  And shrivell'd leaf and daisy dies;

As cuckoos' songs in summer cease,
    As swallows from the autumn flew,
So flies in mystery winter's peace,
    And storms steal on to frown anew.

And give me, then as now, at eve
    The chimney-corner's idle joys,
As day's cold scenes my rambles leave,
    To list the kettle's simmering noise;
And while the chimney mocks the blast,
    And windows quake with jarring din,
Let doors and shutters tightened fast
    Keep cold night out and comfort in.

PASTIME IN SUMMER

GIVE me the leisure of a summer's day,
With one old friend to loiter it away
Where level meadows stretch their green domains,
Alive with joys of laughing maids and swains;
Some making hay beside our pleasant paths
And mowers sweeping with their even swaths;
'Neath sheltering haycocks some, and willow bowers,
Soaking the bottle in their booning hours—
Discoursing onward with our lines and hooks,
With some refreshments nor without some books;
Cheer'd by the rural objects as we pass
To where trees' shadow keepeth green the grass,
Checking intrusions of the summer suns.
Then drop us down close where the river runs
In sight of rural rounds and pleasing strife
That warms the laughing landscape into life.
And while in cheerful mirth as we prepare
Our sporting things, and bait our angles there
With fly or fish of artificial forms,
To shun the anguish of the wreathing worms,

Feel warm hopes glow with earnest eagerness
To mark the signs that promise us success—
As gleaming suns that twitter while they gleam,
And dance their blazing shadows in the stream,
Where small black moths dip light their fluttering wings,
And heedless fishes leap in bouncing springs,
Curving the flood, tho' winds withhold their breath,
In ceaseless eddies with their playful mirth.
Then, free from bother of entangling weeds,
As we throw in where clear the stream proceeds,
Watch for the trembling float that shows a bite
And follow'd jerks that dodge it out of sight,
While taper angles, as we eager rise,
Bend as we pull and prophesy the prize:
Thus sporting on, till, weary with the cheat,
The fish get wise, and sicken, and retreat,
Our quiet floats more shyly sliding by,
To jump at distance for the dancing fly;
Leaving us then our leisure to regale,
To sip refreshment from our hoarded ale,
And loll upon the grass 'neath willows grey,
To view the scene or talk the hours away;
Or with my Thomson added joys engage,
Reading the season in his blooming page,
Where budding springs eternally appear
And fragrant summers freshen all the year.

There while the willow o'er the water spreads
And bushes throw dark shadows o'er our heads,
We'll fancy Damons rapt in daring dreams
And Musidoras shrinking to the streams,
With flowing hair let loose upon the breeze,
O'er maddening charms a Damon only sees,
White breasts, and burning cheeks that redder glow
To see the image in the flood below.
Tho' our real scenes perfection fail to give,
Where Musidoras of less beauty live,
Yet there are Damons that as warmly burn
And maidens lov'd that make as kind return.

And then, as weary of our reading hours,
We'd shut our books and look upon the flowers,
Or any scene that might engage the eye,
As booming by us went the dragon-fly,
In wonder's admiration often led
To mark confusions nature round us spread;
Insects on constant travel as they past
Show each new-comer different to the last,
And butterflies whose varied painted wings
Boast every hue that summer's glory brings;
Like the gilt eyes in peacocks' feathers some,
Some hued like flowers, to which their wanderings come;
In nameless colours others sport the plains,
Hued as mysterious as their birth remains:
Then cropping flowers that round our sitting dwells
Nor marvel less to meet so many smells,
Each different scent possest by different tribes,
Sense easy feels, but ignorance describes.
For like the mystery wonder left before,
We know we feel it, and we know no more.

Thus would we muse o'er nature's varied book
Where fresh enchantments rose at every look,
That with new wonders on our senses come
And still delight us till we ramble home,
When suns sink downward with a reddening face,
And blue clouds fringe as if with golden lace,
Sunk 'hind the meadows' bridges calm and chill,
And thro' the arches peep'd upon us still,
While blue cool haziness approach'd us round
And misty patches smok'd about the ground;
When reeds and flags, that rustled by our seat
As if their bloom was wither'd by the heat,
Now green'd agen from gifts which night receives,
As forming dewdrops moisten on the leaves;
When laughing labour left its toils and glee,
And sought its dwelling with the 'housing bee,'
Whose mournful hum bewails declining day
While waking crickets welcome it away;

And fluttering larks betook themselves to rest
And with less caution pass'd us to their nest.
Then would we leave what leisure had pursued
And in our memories feel the joy renewed.

THE LAST OF SUMMER

A BEAUTY on the scene attends
Ere autumn comes and summer ends,
When summer's glory first we see
As stained with its mortality.
Each morn wakes wan, its sunlight wanes
On yellowing leaves and fading plains;
Green fields no more the summer views,
All sickened into ripened hues
Of brown and grey and darksome glooms
That mark the path where autumn comes;
And in each woodland's buried way
The dewdrop lives for half the day.
Dank mists oft creep 'twixt earth and sky,
And dreaming dim the morning's eye,
And dullness wears along the while
As if the sun was loath to smile.
Yet at midday his feebled powers
Will brighten up in sultry hours,
And sweating toil, that often stops
To wipe aside the falling drops,
Pierced with his downward daily ray,
Wishes the lagging hours away.
By swallows we may plain perceive
When summer's on the point to leave,
Who skim the pond and rippling spring
Where oft they dipt their sutty wing,
And green lanes where from morn till night
They joyed to wheel their curling flight;
Now perched on cottage tops to rest,
They twit and prime each dingy breast,
Or flock together in the sky

As if to learn their young to fly,
Preparing each unpractised wing
For flight, to seek another spring.
Each orchard now is smiling gay,
Glittering in the morning ray:
Rich clustering plums of varied hue,
Of freckled red and misty blue,
And sun-tanned pears with ruddy streak,
Brown as was summer's lusty cheek,
And blushing apples round and red,
Whose loaded branches pat the head
Of longing maid who hither goes
To hang on lines the bleaching clothes.
And boys will often slive from play
And in the orchard find a way,
Hurling up stones with jerking spring,
Or sticks with many a sturdy swing,
Till on the foot-marked, battered ground
The pears and apples patter round.
And truant schoolboy, stealing play,
Oft sneaks along some secret way;
Though ne'er a nest his eye perceives,
Though pooties hide in falling leaves,
Yet are there hips and haws to seek,
And sun-tanned crabs with ruddy cheek,
And with harsh grin and wrinkled frown
He chews the unpleasant prizes down;
And arching o'er the woodland way,
Blackberries tempt his thoughts astray.
Sloes, powdered o'er with misty down,
From hedges too he scrambles down,
By shepherds deemed a pleasant treat,
Though not till winter makes them sweet;
When frost-nipped, they awake desire,
And anxious to his cottage fire
On the clear blaze each branch he throws,
And roasts the hissing, spluttering sloes.
Now mushrooms with the morning light
Above the wet grass glisten white;

Nor are the summer's farewell hours
Always left without their flowers;
The marjoram oft in shady lane
Night's plenteous dews revive again;
Long scorched in summer's earlier hours,
It now will freshen into flowers.
On hills and roads and everywhere,
The ragwort blossoms half the year,
And thistles on each rushy balk
Are constant blushing in our walk,
That tower in scornful majesty
O'er oddling daisies peeping nigh,
Untouched by sheep that hither stray,
Who from its prickles sneak away;
And endive flowering closely by,
That steals its colours from the sky.
The old man's beard too in its prime
Covers the hedges like a rime,
With downy flowers that, thickly twined,
Oft shield the swain from rain and wind.
These live till summer's last decay,
And lingering oft in fond delay
With autumn, if she enters mild,
Are sought and found by many a child,
Who sort their blooms in posies fair,
And garlands glad her yellow hair.
O Autumn, now thy reign is nigh,
I fain would hail thy majesty,
But hollow winds and tumbling floods,
And surging showers and yellow woods,
These are thy mighty minstrelsy,
Who, maddening into life with thee,
Would make, amid their strains divine,
Unheard the song so tame as mine.

THE RIVER GWASH

WHILE swift the mail coach rattles up the hill,
   Nearly unseen beneath a cloud of dust,
And the poor beggar, pined and weary still,
   Drops on the bank to rest and eat his crust,

Upon thy winding side, wild Gwash, I lie,
   Viewing with curious eye the silver bream
Take vaunting springs to trap the thoughtless fly,
   That heedless dances on thy gentle stream.

The black snail wakens from the swoons of day;
   And from the boughs that nestle by thy side
The light-winged moths steal out again to play,
   Crossing with hasty wing thy rippling tide.

How sweet the blackbird chaunts her evening song,
   While the shrill larks in twittering chorus join;
And oh, sad deed! while boys thy shades among
   With hardened hearts her unfledged young purloin.

The cows stand loitering by thy flaggy brink,
   Free from noon's sultry flies, and in delight
The weary cart-horse hastens in to drink,
   Then knaps the moist grass with a keener bite.

The singing milkmaid, journeying from the town,
   Skips o'er the stones that stride the meadow slough,
And on thy banks she sets her bucket down
   To reach a wild rose ere she calls her cow.

With heedless step the homeward journeying boys
   Climb the rude plank that totters o'er thy deeps,
And pelt the fish, while startled at the noise,
   From hollow tree the plunging otter leaps.

Cooling and pleasant to the river-side,
   The skipping breezes o'er the waters run,
That sweetly curl along the gentle tide
   And swell in spangles to the setting sun,

Which now, as clouds brood round and breezes drop,
    In reddening lustre siles and slinks from view,
And on the village steeple's peeping top
    Hangs faint and weary in a last adieu.

The slender rush in idle motion bows
    With meek obedience to the floods below,
Where jostling reeds and willows' dangling boughs
    Impede their gurgling progress as they flow.

On the thorn bush that overhangs the streams,
    The moorhen slumbers in her nest of sedge;
While the shrill dormouse in its summer dreams
    Chitters unceasing from the water's edge.

Sheep seek their folds in many a hurried troop,
    Frit by the dogs that bark them to their rest,
Who with their noises often startle up
    The partridge coveys from their grassy nest.

The weary mower on the meadow path
    With wallets o'er his shoulders rocks along,
Leaving the cricket in the moistening swath
    To brood in quiet o'er its evening song.

And pleased to watch the summer evening's birth,
    I linger here, wild Gwash, thy quiet guest,
And from reposing nature's sober mirth
    Catch these soft sounds that lull my cares to rest.

A SUNDAY WITH SHEPHERDS AND HERDBOYS

    THE shepherds and the herding swains
    Keep their sabbaths on the plains;
    For them the church bells vainly call;
    Fields are their church and house and all;
    They'll lie and catch the passing sound
    That comes from steeples shining round,

Enjoying in the service time
The happy bells' delightful chime,
And, if they sit on rising ground,
To view the landscape spreading round,
Swimming from the following eye
In greens and stems of every dye
O'er wood and vale and fen's smooth lap
Like a richly coloured map;
Square plots of clover red and white
Scented with summer's warm delight,
And cinquefoil of a fresher stain,
And different greens of warmèd grain;
Wheat spindles bursting into ear
And browning gently; grasses sere
In swathy seed-pods dried by heat,
Rustling when brushed by passing feet;
And beans and peas of deadening green,
And cornland's ribbon strips between,
And stretching villages that lie
Like light spots in a deeper sky.

. . . . .

And from the fields they'll often steal
The green peas for a Sunday meal,
And in snug nooks, their huts beside,
The gipsy blazes they provide,
Shaking the rotten from the trees,
While some sit round to shell the peas,
Or pick from hedges pilfered wood
To boil on props their stolen food;
Sitting on stones or heaps of brakes,
Each of the wild repast partakes,
Telling to pass the hours along
Tales that to fitter days belong,
While one within his scrip contains
A shattered Bible's thumbed remains,
O'er whose blank leaf with pious care
A host of names is scribbled there.

. . . . .

373

The herdboys, anxious after play,
Find sports to pass the time away,
Fishing for struttles in the brooks
With thread for lines and pins for hooks,
And stripping 'neath the willow shade
In warm muddy ponds to bathe,
And pelting with unerring eye
The heedless swallows slanting by;
Oft breaking boughs from trees to kill
The nest of wasps beside a hill,
Till one gets stung, then they resort
And follow to less dangerous sport
(Leaving to chance their sheep and cows),
To thread the brakes and forest boughs
To scare the squirrel's lively joys
With stones and sticks and shouting noise,
That sat within its secret place
Upon its tail to clean its face;
When found, they shout with joy to see
It hurly-burly round a tree;
And as they turn in sight again,
It peeps and squats behind a grain;
And oft they'll cut up sticks to try
The holes where badgers darkling lie,
Looking for footmark prints about
The fresh mounds not long rooted out;
And peep in burrows newly done
Where rabbits from their noises run;
Where oft in terror's wild affright
They spy—and startle at the sight—
Rolled like a whipthong round and round,
Asleep upon the sunny ground,
A snake, that wakens at their play
And starts as full of fear as they;
And newt-shaped swifts that nimbly pass
And rustle in the brown, lank grass.

.   .   .   .   .

The herder too is peeping round

To find a tenant for his ground;
Heedless of rest or parson's prayers,
He seldom to the church repairs,
But thinks religion hath its due
In paying yearly for his pew.
Soon as fair morn puts night away
And has put on her mantle grey,
Before one sunbeam o'er the ground
Spindles its light and shadow round,
He's o'er the fields as soon as morn
To see what stock are in the corn:
A neighing colt that tries to catch
A gate at night left off the latch
By traveller seeking home in haste
Or the clown by fancies chased,
That, lasting while he made a stand,
Opens each gate with fearful hand,
Fearing a minute to remain
And put it on the latch again;
And cows, who often with their horns
Toss from the gaps the stuffing thorns—
These, like a fox upon the watch,
He in the morning tries to catch
And drives them to the pound for pay,
Careless about the sabbath day.

THE INSECT WORLD

The insect world amid the suns and dew
Awake and hum their tiny songs anew,
And climb the totter-grass and blossom's stem
As huge in size as mighty oaks to them;
And rushy burnets on the pasture rise
As tall as castles to their little eyes;
Each leaf's a town and the smooth meadow grass
A mighty world whose bounds they never pass;
E'en spots no bigger than the husbandman's
Or shepherd's noontide dwarf-shrunk shadow spans

—Or e'en the milkmaid tripping through the dew,
Each space she covers with her slender shoe—
Seem to their view high woods in which they roam
As lorn, lost wanderers many miles from home,
Creeping up bents and down whole weary hours
And resting oft on the soft breasts of flowers;
Till age, in minutes long as years, creeps on,
Or waning summer warns them to be gone.

FLOWERS

ERE yet the year is one month old,
    In spite of frost and wind and snow,
Bare-bosomed to the quaking cold,
    Spring's little selfsown flowers will blow;
And ever kin to early hours
    Peep aconites in cups of gold,
With frilled leaves muffled round their flowers
    Like tender maidens shunning cold;

And then as winter's parting pledge,
    Like true love in his crabbed reign,
The violets 'neath the naked hedge
    Peep thro' the rustling leaves again,
Soon as from off the thicket's moss
    The sunshine clears the doubting snow,
And the o'erjoyed and neighing horse
    Can find a patch of green to blow.

Like jewels brought by early hours,
    These little littered blossoms come;
Like wanderers from fairy bowers,
    They smile and gladly find a home;
And on the threshold of the spring,
    Like timid children out of doors,
They lie and wait the birds to sing,
    And laugh upon the splashy moors.

In April's smiling-frowning weather,
    Like younkers to a holiday,
The young flowers bud in troops together
    To wait the feast of merry May;
In sunny nooks and shelter nurst,
    Buds all their early blooms display,
Where sunbeams show their faces first
    And make when there the longest stay.

TO THE SNIPE

LOVER of swamps
    And quagmire overgrown
With hassock-tufts of sedge, where fear encamps
    Around thy home alone,

The trembling grass
    Quakes from the human foot,
Nor bears the weight of man to let him pass
    Where thou, alone and mute,

Sittest at rest
    In safety, near the clump
Of huge flag-forest that thy haunts invest
    Or some old sallow stump,

Thriving on seams
    That tiny islands swell,
Just hilling from the mud and rancid streams,
    Suiting thy nature well;

For here thy bill,
    Suited by wisdom good,
Of rude unseemly length, doth delve and drill
    The jellied mass for food;

And here, mayhap,
    When summer suns have drest
The moor's rude, desolate and spongy lap,
    May hide thy mystic nest—

Mystic indeed;
For isles that oceans make
Are scarcely more secure for birds to build
Than this flag-hidden lake.

Boys thread the woods
To their remotest shades;
But in these marshy flats, these stagnant floods,
Security pervades.

From year to year
Places untrodden lie,
Where man nor boy nor stock hath ventured near,
Naught gazed on but the sky

And fowl that dread
The very breath of man,
Hiding in spots that never knew his tread,
A wild and timid clan,

Widgeon and teal
And wild duck—restless lot,
That from man's dreaded sight will ever steal
To the most dreary spot.

Here tempests howl
Around each flaggy plot,
Where they who dread man's sight, the water fowl,
Hide and are frightened not.

'Tis power divine
That heartens them to brave
The roughest tempest and at ease recline
On marshes or the wave.

Yet instinct knows
Not safety's bounds:—to shun
The firmer ground where skulking fowler goes
With searching dogs and gun,

By tepid springs
Scarcely one stride across
(Though bramble from its edge a shelter flings
Thy safety is at loss)

—And never choose
The little sinky foss,
Streaking the moors whence spa-red water spews
From pudges fringed with moss;

Freebooters there,
Intent to kill or slay,
Startle with cracking guns the trepid air,
And dogs thy haunts betray.

From danger's reach
Here thou art safe to roam,
Far as these washy flag-sown marshes stretch
A still and quiet home.

In these thy haunts
I've gleaned habitual love;
From the vague world where pride and folly taunts
I muse and look above.

Thy solitudes
The unbounded heaven esteems,
And here my heart warms into higher moods
And dignifying dreams.

I see the sky
Smile on the meanest spot,
Giving to all that creep or walk or fly
A calm and cordial lot.

Thine teaches me
Right feelings to employ—
That in the dreariest places peace will be
A dweller and a joy.

SUMMER IMAGES [1]

Now swarthy summer, which rude health embrowns,
Takes precedence of rosy-fingered spring
    And litters from her lap
    A world of varied hues.

Joy, never silent with her laugh and song,
And health robust with bosom soft as down,
    And patient industry
    Still plying busy toils—

These in her merry path run jovial on,
Or hang upon her arm in smiling guise,
    And from her happy face
    Steal smiles that grace their own.

Thee with thy sultry locks all loose and rude,
And mantle laced with gems of tawdry hues,
    I love thee, and as wont
    Win pleasure from thy smiles.

And thus delighted, on I thread with thee
Rude wood, wild heath, and cornfield laced with
       streams,
    And feel life's stirring pulse
    Throb into genial song.

Me not the noise of brawling pleasure cheers,
In mighty revels or in city streets,
    But joys which soothe
    And not distract mine ear,

That one at musing leisure ever meets
In the green woods and meadows summer-shorn,
    Or fields where gadfly sounds
    Its small and tiresome horn.

Jet-black and shining, from the dripping hedge
Slow peeps the fearful snail,
    And from each tiny bent
    Withdraws his timid horn.

[1] This is the first rough draft of the *Summer Images* in Volume ii.

The yellow frog from underneath the swath
Leaps startling as the dog with heavy feet
    Brushes across the path
    And runs the timid hare.

And mark the bird-boy peep from out the corn,
Bawling aloud to know the passing hour,
    And at the lessening day
    To list his louder song.

The aspen leaves, enamoured of the wind,
Turn up their silver lining to the sun,
    And rustle on the ear
    Like fast-approaching showers.

The south-west wind—I love the sudden sound,
And then to feel it gush upon my cheek,
    And then with weary pause
    Await the creeping storm.

To me right luscious sing the stirring leaves,
Just bade to dance attendance on the storm,
    That blackens in the south
    And threatens hasty showers.

I love the wizard noise, and rave in turn,
Half-vacant thoughts in self-imagined rhymes,
    Then hide me from the shower,
    And mutter to the winds.

Now sound the village bells; how musical,
Across the valley of that winding flood,
    Upon the listening ear
    Comes the soft pealing chime;

As glad and healthful as the morning sun,
The shepherd boy leans o'er the meadow bridge
    To list their mellow sounds
    And muse in vacant joy.

Woods, meadows, cornfields, all around
Glow in their harmony of varied greens,
While o'er them, lost in light,
Far spreads the laughing sky.

EMMONSALE'S HEATH

In thy wild garb of other times
I find thee lingering still;
Furze o'er each lazy summit climbs,
At nature's easy will.

Grasses that never knew a scythe
Wave all the summer long;
And wild weed blossoms waken blithe,
That ploughmen never wrong.

Stern industry, with stubborn toil
And wants unsatisfied,
Still leaves untouched thy maiden soil
In its unsullied pride.

The birds still find their summer shades
To build their nests agen,
And the poor hare its rushy glade,
To hide from savage men.

Nature its family protects
In thy security,
And blooms, which love what man neglects,
Find peaceful homes in thee.

The wild rose scents the summer air,
And woodbines weave in bowers,
To glad the swain sojourning there
And maidens gathering flowers.

Creation's steps one wandering meets
Untouched by those of man:
Things seem the same in such retreats
As when the world began.

Furze, ling, and brake, all mingling free,
  And grass for ever green—
All seem the same old things to be
  As they have ever been.

The brook o'er such neglected ground,
  One's weariness to soothe,
Still wildly winds its lawless bound
  And chafes the pebble smooth;

Crooked and rude, as when at first
  Its waters learned to stray,
And, from their mossy fountain burst,
  It washed itself a way.

I've often met with places rude,
  Nor failed their sweets to share,
But passed an hour with solitude
  And left my blessing there.

He that can meet the morning wind
  And o'er such places roam,
Nor leave a lingering wish behind
  To make their peace his home—

His heart is dead to quiet hours,
  Nor love his mind employs,
Nor poesy shares with him its flowers,
  Nor solitude its joys.

I've stretched my boyish walks to thee
  When May-day's paths were dry,
When leaves had nearly hid each tree,
  And grass greened ankle high;

And mused the sunny hours away,
  And thought of little things
That children mutter o'er their play
  When fancy tries its wings.

Joy nursed me in her happy mood,
    And all life's little crowd
That haunt the valley, field, and wood,
    Would sing their joys aloud.

I thought how kind that mighty Power
    Must in his splendour be,
Who spread around my boyish hour
    Such gleams of harmony,

Who did with joyous rapture fill
    The low as high degree,
And made the pismires round the hill
    Seem full as blest as me.

Hope's sun is seen of every eye;
    The halo that it gives
In nature's wide and common sky
    Cheers everything that lives.

THE COTTAGER

TRUE as the church clock hand the hour pursues,
He plods about his toils and reads the news,
And at the blacksmith's shop his hour will stand
To talk of 'Lunun' as a foreign land.
For from his cottage door in peace or strife
He ne'er went fifty miles in all his life.
His knowledge with old notions still combined
Is twenty years behind the march of mind.
He views new knowledge with suspicious eyes
And thinks it blasphemy to be so wise.
On steam's almighty tales he wondering looks
As witchcraft gleaned from old blackletter books.
Life gave him comfort but denied him wealth,
He toils in quiet and enjoys his health,
He smokes a pipe at night and drinks his beer,
And runs no scores on tavern screens to clear.

384

He goes to market all the year about
And keeps one hour and never stays it out.
E'en at St. Thomastide old Rover's bark
Hails Dapple's trot an hour before it's dark.
He is a simple-worded plain old man
Whose good intents take errors in their plan.
Oft sentimental and with saddened vein
He looks on trifles and bemoans their pain,
And thinks the angler mad, and loudly storms
With emphasis of speech o'er murdered worms,
And hunters cruel—pleading with sad care
Pity's petition for the fox and hare,
Yet feels self-satisfaction in his woes
For war's crushed myriads of his slaughtered foes.
He is right scrupulous in one pretext
And wholesale errors swallows in the next.
He deems it sin to sing, yet not to say
A song—a mighty difference in his way.
And many a moving tale in antique rhymes
He has for Christmas and such merry times,
When 'Chevy Chase,' his masterpiece of song,
Is said so earnest none can think it long.
'Twas the old vicar's way who should be right,
For the late vicar was his heart's delight;
And while at church he often shakes his head
To think what sermons the old vicar made,
Downright and orthodox, that all the land
Who had their ears to hear might understand,
But now such mighty learning meets his ears
He thinks it Greek or Latin which he hears,
Yet church receives him every sabbath day,
And, rain or snow, he never keeps away.
All words of reverence still his heart reveres,
Low bows his head when Jesus meets his ears,
And still he thinks it blasphemy as well
Such names without a capital to spell.
In an old corner cupboard by the wall
His books are laid, though good, in number small;
His Bible first in place, from worth and age,

Whose grandsire's name adorns the title page,
And blank leaves once, now filled with kindred claims,
Display a world's epitome of names.
Parents and children and grandchildren all
Memory's affections in the lists recall.
And prayer-book next, much worn though strongly bound,
Proves him a churchman orthodox and sound.
The *Pilgrim's Progress* and the *Death of Abel*
Are seldom missing from his reading table,
And prime old Tusser in his homely trim,
The first of bards in all the world with him,
And only poet which his leisure knows;
Verse deals in fancy, so he sticks to prose.
These are the books he reads and reads again,
And weekly hunts the almanacks for rain.
Here and no further learning's channels ran;
Still, neighbours prize him as the learned man.
His cottage is a humble place of rest
With one spare room to welcome every guest,
And that tall poplar pointing to the sky
His own hand planted when an idle boy,
It shades his chimney while the singing wind
Hums songs of shelter to his happy mind.
Within his cot the largest ears of corn
He ever found his picture-frames adorn:
Brave Granby's head, De Grasse's grand defeat;
He rubs his hands and shows how Rodney beat.
And from the rafters upon strings depend
Beanstalks beset with pods from end to end,
Whose numbers without counting may be seen
Wrote on the almanack behind the screen.
Around the corner upon worsted string
Pooties in wreaths above the cupboard hing.
Memory at trifling incidents awakes
And there he keeps them for his children's sakes,
Who when as boys searched every sedgy lane,
Traced every wood and sheltered close again,
Roaming about on rapture's easy wing
To hunt those very pooty shells in spring.

And thus he lives too happy to be poor
While strife ne'er pauses at so mean a door.
Low in the sheltered valley stands his cot,
He hears the mountain storm and feels it not;
Winter and spring, toil ceasing ere 'tis dark,
Rests with the lamb and rises with the lark,
Content his helpmate to the day's employ,
And care ne'er comes to steal a single joy.
Time, scarcely noticed, turns his hair to grey,
Yet leaves him happy as a child at play.

HELPSTONE STATUTE *or* THE RECRUITING PARTY

UNCLOUDED rose the morning sun
  Through autumn's pleasant weather,
In promise of some glorious fun
  When all were got together;
There wa'n't a road led to the town
  But ye'd see clowns by dozens,
For masters some, and some for sport,
  And some to see their cousins;

And skipping girls as sweet and fair
  As smiles and dress could make 'em,
With pattens in their sweethearts' care,
  Who thought it pride to take 'em;
They graceful lifted up their gowns
  To show a taper ankle,
Which made the hearts of following clowns
  With beauty's visions rankle.

In gladdened speed awoke the morn
  With holiday caresses;
Young laughing clowns with beards new shorn,
  And girls in Sunday dresses,
And children peeping in the street
  For sisters and for brothers,
And maids their coming swains to meet
  And anxious watching mothers.

Horses and gigs went whisking by
   With farming gent and lady,
Although 'twas autumn's cloudy sky
   Joys blossomed as at May Day;
And soldiers 'gan their drums to rap
   When near the town advancing,
Which set like magic every chap
   To capering and to dancing.

Ah, Helpstone, thou art droning dull
   Till Statutes yearly find thee,
And then thou'rt mad as any bull
   And care is cast behind thee;
Each house where lorn the year about
   Signs creak to wind and weather,
Relieved by thee and barmy stout,
   Draws scores of lads together.

Thy fame with vigour yearly blooms
   Through all the neighbouring towns,
Renowned for cakes well stored with plums,
   And fun that pleases clowns;
For Civil Wills and winking jades
   And E-O tables turning,
Where gamesters oft are beggars made,
   And mirth is changed to mourning.

There merry Punch displays his pranks
   In squeaking jokes and blunders,
And there the pale-faced mountebanks
   Spout loud their tale of wonders,
Of balsams that will blooms secure
   In fading belles and madams,
And, for the aged, lives ensure
   As long as father Adam's.

The place now thronged with young and old,
   For labour had its leisure,
While every face its errand told
   As seeking mirth and pleasure;

Sweet beauty now displayed its bloom,
　　Red cheeks and lily bosoms;
Mirth buzzed like wild bees' merry hum
　　Round fields of clover blossoms.

With sweethearts hanging on their arms,
　　In blushes softly blooming,
Each maiden smiled in witching charms,
　　Just blossoming to woman;
And redcoat gentry soon in style
　　For liquor 'gan a-calling,
And where their winks could meet a smile
　　Set maids in corners squalling.

And loose-laced Sergeant Macaroon,
　　A hogshead sort of dandy,
With visage like a harvest moon,
　　And nose as burnt as brandy,
He strutted round the room with ale
　　And drank to tittering wenches,
Making clowns stare at valour's tale
　　Of storming towers and trenches.

He jested o'er the battle's strife
　　As play when they'd been schooled to't,
And swore that to a soldier's life
　　King William's were a fool to't;
He bragged about their mints of cash,
　　And swaggered and insisted,
Till boys that scarcely reached his sash
　　Bawled, teasing to be 'listed.

Some listened and believed it true,
　　And some, disposed to quarrel,
Swore he of valour never knew
　　A gunshot from the barrel;
But he bragged on and spent his crowns
　　And tossed off foaming glasses,
A very hero with the clowns
　　And Cupid with the lasses.

The alehouse room was in a rout,
    And all was helter-skelter,
And Molly Meek came puffing out—
    She said 'twas fit to melt her;
The truth on't was that Corporal Sly
    Had won her with his feather,
And secret whispered by and by
    To trample out together.

A sweetheart she to Booby Briggs,
    Who, soon's he cleared the trick up,
Cursed all the redcoats' roguish rigs
    And rumptions 'gan to kick up.
They cocked their consequential caps
    And sneering filled their glasses,
Saying they'd make lords of straw-yard chaps
    And ladies of the lasses.

But Booby's heart was bad for fight;
    He could but rave and rattle;
And, when he'd broke the peace, his spite
    Most coolly shunned the battle.
The row got high, boards 'gan to fall
    Where stood the pipes and cans on,
And alewife swore revenge on all
    She e'er could lay her hands on.

And in she bounced with face as red
    As if 'twas daubed with riddle,
And first 'gan thump the fiddler's head—
    O fun protect the fiddle!
The scraper's fist was soon for blows,
    Ale's courage rarely failed him,
And woe'd been to her brandy nose
    If lasses hadn't quailed him.

He loved the wenches monstrous well
    And never wished to tease 'em,
But gloried in his fiddling skill,
    That had the power to please 'em;

And when he'd found his trampled hat
    Mid broken pipes and glasses,
With vengeance half appeased he sat
    And struck up 'Bonny Lasses.'

She soon broke up the fighting rout,
    By soldier lads assisted,
And sharply played the sticks about
    The rebels that resisted;
She boldly shoved and showed the door
    In spite of oaths and cavil;
Some cursed, and staggered while they swore,
    And wished her to the devil.

But broken pots and broken pipes,
    All that were slain in battle,
Made her for vengeance fury-ripe
    And loud her tongue did rattle;
Till brawlings loud for quarts of ale
    And sound of money chinking
Did by and by her vengeance quail,
    And peace was signed by drinking.

The Statute now was all in mobs;
    Each maiden interposes,
Swooning with heart-bursting sobs
    O'er sweethearts' bloody noses;
E'en boys bethought 'em men that day,
    As high's one's knee and hardly,
And stript and bruised amid the fray
    And acted most blackguardly.

At length, with bruising softened down,
    Those not so full of mettle
Got weary trying for renown,
    And battle 'gan to settle;
And soon the aid of pipe and pot
    Made up for hits and misses;
In corners some with sweethearts got
    To cure black eyes with kisses.

And Corporal Sly had played his rigs,
  And Moll had proved his jesting,
Who sneaked agen to Booby Briggs,
  Her innocence protesting;
No maid could simper more demure
  And keep such meek parade up;
Poor Booby thought it true besure
  And matters soon were made up.

To put a soldier's heart in thrall
  He thought her mighty clever,
And then—prize Booby after all—
  He loved her more than ever;
And while his purse had sixpence in't
  With kindnesses he paid her,
And gifts, almost without a stint,
  Of nuts and cakes he made her.

The soldiers now began to drum,
  And gaping stood the ninnies
To see the sergeant 'neath his thumb
  Hold out the tempting guineas;
And rustics tempted at the sight
  Their parents' tears were scorning,
And ranting o'er their quarts till night
  Left sorrow for the morning.

Some ere the daylight wore away
  Went home with lovers happy,
And others still inclined to stay
  Sat ranting o'er their nappy;
Some drunk and weary sunk to rest
  On leaning chairs reposing,
And others, they more haply blest,
  On sweethearts' bosoms dozing.

Soul-stirring ale, thy laurelled brow
  Blooms an immortal fairly,
Or long as England yokes a plough
  And summers ripen barley;

And curse the wretch who, craving chink,
    Thy fame with drugs defaces;
I wish him hell denied of drink
    Who thus thy worth debases.

Thus passed the day, and weary night
    Found some with empty purses,
And some that 'scaped with hasty flight
    From bottles, blows, and curses,
And some with headache's shoots severe
    Felt the last tankard's drainings,
While maidens wept with secret fear
    Uncurable complainings.

ST. MARTIN'S EVE *or* THE COTTAGE FESTIVAL

Now that the year grows wearisome with age,
And days grow short and nights excessive long,
No outdoor sports the village hands engage;
Still is the meadow romp and harvest song
That wont to echo from each merry throng.
At dinner hours beneath huge spreading tree
Rude winds hath done the landscape mickle wrong,
That nature in her mirth did ill foresee,
Who clingeth now to hope like shipwrecked folks at sea.

The woods are desolate of song—the sky
Is all forsaken of its joyous crowd;
Martin and swallow there no longer fly;
Huge seeming rocks and deserts now enshroud
The sky for aye with shadow-shaping cloud.
None there of all those busy tribes remain;
No song is heard save one that wails aloud
From the all lone and melancholy crane,
Who, like a traveller lost, the right road seeks in vain.

The children, hastening in from threatening rain,
No longer round the fields for wild fruit run,
But at their homes from morn to night remain,
And wish in vain to see the welcome sun.
Winter's imprisonment is all begun;
Yet when the wind grows troublous and high,
Pining for freedom like a love-sick nun,
Around thy garden's little bounds they fly
Beneath the roaring trees fall'n apples to espy.

But spite of all the melancholy moods
That out of doors poor pleasure's heart alarm,
Flood-bellowing rivers and wind-roaring woods,
The fireside evening owns increasing charm;
What with the tale and eldern wine that warms
In purple bubbles by the blazing fire
Of simple cots and rude old-fashioned farms,
They feel as blest as joys can well desire,
And midnight often joins before the guests retire.

And such a group on good St. Martin's Eve
Was met together upon pleasure bent,
Where tales of fun did cares so well deceive
That the old cottage rung with merriment,
And even the very rafters groaned and bent;
Not so much, it would seem, from tempest's din,
That roared without in howling discontent,
As from the merry noise and laugh within,
That seemed as summer's sports had never absent bin.

Beside the fire, large apples lay to roast,
And in a huge brown pitcher creaming ale
Was warming, seasoned with a nutmeg toast,
The merry group of gossips to regale.
Around her feet the glad cat curled her tail,
Listening the cricket's song with half-shut eyes;
While in the chimney-top loud roared the gale
Its blustering howl of outdoor symphonies
That round the cottage hearth bade happier moods arise.

And circling round the fire the merry folks
Brought up all sports their memories could devise,
Playing upon each other merry jokes;
And now one shuts his hands and archly cries,
'Come, open wide your mouth and shut your eyes
And see what gifts are sent you.'   Foolish thing,
He doth as he is bid; and quickly rise
The peals of laughter when they up and fling
The ashes in, while he goes spitting from the ring.

And the old dame, though not in laughing luck—
For that same night, at one fell sweeping stroke,
Mischievous cat that at a mouse had struck
Upon the shelf her best blue china broke—
Yet spite of fate, so funny was the joke,
She laughed until her very sides did shake;
And some so tittled were they could not smoke,
Laying down their pipes lest they their pipes should break,
And laughed and laughed again until their ribs did ache.

Then deftly one with cunning in his eyes,
With outstretched hand walks backward in the dark,
Encouraged to the feat with proffered prize
If so he right can touch pretended mark
Made on the wall;—and happy as a lark
He chuckles o'er success, by hopes prepared,
While one with open mouth like greedy shark
Glides in the place and bites his finger hard;
He bawls for freedom loud, and shame's his whole reward.

Then come more games of wonderment and fun,
Which set poor Hodge's wisdom all aghast,
Who sought three knives to hide them one by one,
While one, no conjuror to reveal the past,
Blindfold would tell him where he hid the last.
Hodge, hiding two, did for the third inquire;
All tittered round and bade him hold it fast;
But oh, he shook it from his hand in ire,
For while he hid the two they warmed it in the fire.

Then to appease him with his burning hand
They bade him hide himself, and they would tell
The very way in which he chose to stand;
Hodge thought the matter most impossible,
And on his knees behind the mash-tub fell
And muttering said, 'I'll beat 'em now or never,'
Crying out, 'How stand I?' just to prove the spell;
They answered, 'Like a fool!' and trick so clever
Raised laughter against Hodge more long and loud than ever.

Nor can the aged in their boisterous glee
Escape the tricks for laugh and jest designed;
The old dame takes the bellows on her knee
And puffs in vain, to tricks of roguery blind,
Nor heeds the urchin who lets out the wind
With crafty finger and such cunning skill
That for her life the cause she cannot find,
Until the group, unable to be still,
Laugh out, and dame, though trickt, smiles too against her will.

Yet mid this strife of joy, on corner stool
One sits all silent, doomed to worst of fate,
Who made one slip in love and played the fool,
And since, condemned to live without a mate,
No youth again courts once-beguilèd Kate;
Tho' hopes of sweethearts yet perplex her head,
And charms to try by gipsies told of late,
Beneath her pillow lays an onion red,
To dream on this same night with whom she is to wed;

And hopes that like to sunshine warming fall
Being all the solace to her withering mind,
When they for dancing rise, old, young, and all,
She in her corner musing stays behind,
Her pallid cheek upon her hand reclined,
Nursing rude melancholy like a child
Who sighs in silence to the sobbing wind
That in the chimney roars with fury wild,
While every other heart to joy is reconciled.

One thumps the warming-pan with merry glee,
That bright as is a mirror decks the cot;
Another, droning as an humble bee,
Plays on the muffled comb till piping hot
With overstrained exertion;—yet the lot
Is such an happy one that still he plays,
Fatigue and all its countless ills forgot,
All that he wants he wins, for rapture pays
To his unwearied skill right earnest words of praise.

Ah, happy hearts, how happy can't be told,
To fancy music in such clamorous noise;
Like those converting all they touched to gold,
These all they hearken to convert to joys.
Thrice happy hearts, old men as wild as boys
Feel naught of age creep o'er their ecstasies;
Old women whom no care of life destroys
Dance with the girls: true did the bard surmise,
'Where ignorance is bliss, 'tis folly to be wise.'

When weary of the dance, one reads a tale,
Tho' puzzled oft to spell a lengthy word;
Stories—tho' often read yet never stale,
But gaining interest every time they're heard
With morts of wonderment—that ne'er occurred.
Yet, simple souls, their faith it knows no stint;
Things least to be believed are most preferred;
All counterfeits as from truth's sacred mint
Are readily believed if once put down in print.

Bluebeard and all his murders' dread parade
Are listened to and mourned for; and the tear
Drops from the blue eye of the listening maid,
Warm as it fell upon her lover's bier.
None in the circle doubt of what they hear;
It were a sin to doubt o'er tales so true:
So say the old, whose wisdom all revere,
And unto whom such reverence may be due
For honest good intents—praise that belongs to few.

And 'Tib, a Tinker's Daughter,' is the tale
That doth by wonder their rude hearts engage;
O'er young and old its witchcraft scenes prevail
In the rude legend of her pilgrimage:
How she in servitude did erst engage
To live with an old hag of dreadful fame,
Who often fell in freaks of wondrous rage
And played with Tib full many a bitter game,
Till e'en the children round cried out for very shame.

They read how once to thrash her into chaff
The fearful witch tied Tibby in a sack,
And hied her to the wood to seek a staff
That might be strong enough her bones to whack;
But lucky Tib escaped ere she came back
And tied up dog and cat her doom to share,
And pots and pans—and loud the howl and crack
That rose when the old witch with inky hair
Began the sack to thrash with no intent to spare.

And when she found her unrevenged mistake,
Her rage more fearful grew, but all in vain;
For fear no more caused Tibby's heart to ache;
She far away from the old hag's domain
Ran heartsomely, a better place to gain:
And here the younkers' tongues grew wonder glib
With gladness, and the reader stopt again,
Declaring all too true to be a fib
And urged full glasses round to drink success to Tib.

And when her sorrows and her pilgrimage,
The plot of most new novels and old tales,
Grew to a close, her beauty did presage
Luck in the wind—and fortune spread her sails
In favouring bounty to Tib's summer gales.
All praised her beauty, and the lucky day
At length its rosy smiling face unveils,
When Tib of course became a lady gay,
And loud the listeners laughed while children turned to play.

Anon the clock counts twelve; amid their joys
The startled blackbird smooths its feathers down,
That in its cage grew weary of their noise.
The merry maiden and the noisy clown
Prepare for home; and down the straggling town
To seek their cottages they twittering go,
Heartened with sports and stout ale berry-brown;
Beside their dames like chanticleer they crow,
While every lanthorn flings long gleams along the snow.

THE DREAM

Thou scarest me with dreams.—JOB.

WHEN night's last hours, like haunting spirits, creep
With listening terrors round the couch of sleep,
And midnight, brooding in its deepest dye,
Seizes on fear with dismal sympathy,
'I dreamed a dream' something akin to fate,
Which superstition's blackest thoughts create—
Something half natural to the grave that seems,
Which death's long trance of slumber haply dreams;
A dream of staggering horrors, and of dread,
Whose shadows fled not when the vision fled,
But clung to memory with their gloomy view,
Till doubt and fancy half believed it true.

That time was come, or seemed as it was come,
When Death no longer makes the grave his home;
When waking spirits leave their earthly rest
To mix for ever with the damned or blest;
When years, in drowsy thousands counted by,
Are hung on minutes with their destiny:
When Time in terror drops his draining glass,
And all things mortal, like to shadows, pass,
As 'neath approaching tempests sinks the sun—
When Time shall leave Eternity begun.
Life swoon'd in terror at that hour's dread birth
As in an ague, shook the fearful Earth;

And shuddering Nature seemed herself to shun;
Whilst trembling Conscience felt the deed was done.

A gloomy sadness round the sky was cast,
Where clouds seemed hurrying with unusual haste;
Winds urged them onward, like to restless ships,
And light dim faded in its last eclipse,
And Agitation turned a straining eye,
And Hope stood watching like a bird to fly,
While suppliant Nature, like a child in dread,
Clung to her fading garments till she fled.

Then awful sights began to be revealed,
Which Death's dark dungeons had so long concealed;
Each grave its doomsday-prisoner resigned,
Bursting in noises like a hollow wind;
And spirits, mingling with the living then,
Thrilled fearful voices with the cries of men.
All flying furious, grinning deep despair,
Shaped dismal shadows on the troubled air:
Red lightning shot its flashes as they came,
And passing clouds seemed kindling into flame;
And strong and stronger came the sulphury smell,
With demons following in the breath of hell,
Laughing in mockery as the doomed complained,
Losing their pains in seeing others pained.

Fierce raged destruction, sweeping o'er the land,
And the last counted moment seemed at hand:
As scales near equal hang the earnest eyes
In doubtful balance which shall fall or rise,
So, in the moment of that crashing blast,
Eyes, hearts, and hopes paused trembling for the last.
Loud burst the thunder's clap, and yawning rents
Gashed the frail garments of the elements;
Then sudden whirlwinds, winged with purple flame
And lightnings' flash, in stronger terrors came;
Burning all life and nature where they fell,
And leaving earth as desolate as hell.

The pleasant hues of woods and fields were past,
And nature's beauties had enjoyed their last:
The coloured flower, the green of field and tree,
What they had been for ever ceased to be:
Clouds, raining fire, scorched up the hissing dews;
Grass shrivelled brown in miserable hues;
Leaves fell to ashes in the air's hot breath,
And all awaited universal death.
The sleepy birds, scared from their mossy nest,
Beat through the evil air in vain for rest;
And many a one, the withering shades among,
Wakened to perish o'er its brooded young.
The cattle, startled with the sudden fright,
Sickened from food, and maddened into flight;
And steed and beast in plunging speed pursued
The desperate struggle of the multitude.
The faithful dogs yet knew their owners' face,
And cringing followed with a fearful pace,
Joining the piteous yell with panting breath,
While blasting lightnings followed fast with death;
Then, as destruction stopt the vain retreat,
They dropped, and dying licked their masters' feet.

When sudden thunders paused, loud went the shriek,
And groaning agonies, too much to speak,
From hurrying mortals, who, with ceaseless fears,
Recalled the errors of their vanished years,
Flying in all directions, hope-bereft,
Followed by dangers that would not be left,
Offering wild vows, and begging loud for aid,
Where none was nigh to help them when they prayed.
None stood to listen, or to soothe a friend,
But all complained, and sorrow had no end.
Sons from their fathers, fathers sons did fly,
The strongest fled, and left the weak to die;
Pity was dead: none heeded for another;
Brother left brother; and the frantic mother
For fruitless safety hurried east and west,
And dropped the babe to perish from her breast;

All howling prayers that would be noticed never,
And craving mercy that was fled for ever.
While earth, in motion like a troubled sea,
Opened in gulphs of dread immensity,
Amid the wild confusions of despair,
And buried deep the howling and the prayer
Of countless multitudes, and closed—and then
Opened, and swallowed multitudes agen.

Stars drunk with dread rolled giddy from the heaven,
And staggering worlds like wrecks in storms were driven;
The pallid moon hung fluttering on the sight,
As startled bird whose wings are stretched for flight;
And o'er the east a fearful light begun
To show the sun rise—not the morning sun,
But one in wild confusion, doomed to rise
And drop again in horror from the skies;
To heaven's midway it reeled, and changed to blood,
Then dropped, and light rushed after like a flood.
The heaven's blue curtains rent and shrank away,
And heaven itself seem'd threaten'd with decay;
While hopeless distance with a boundless stretch
Flashed on despair the joy it could not reach,
A moment's mockery—ere the last dim light
Vanished, and left an everlasting night:
And with that light Hope fled, and shrieked farewell,
And hell in yawning echoes mocked that yell.

Now Night resumed her uncreated vest,
And chaos came again, but not its rest;
The melting glooms, that spread perpetual stains,
Kept whirling on in endless hurricanes;
And tearing noises, like a troubled sea,
Broke up that silence which no more would be.

The reeling earth sank loosened from its stay,
And nature's wrecks all felt their last decay.
The yielding, burning soil, that fled my feet,
I seemed to feel, and struggled to retreat;

And midst the dreads of horror's mad extreme
I lost all notion of its being a dream:
Sinking, I fell through depths that seemed to be
As far from fathom as Eternity;
While dismal faces on the darkness came,
With wings of dragons, and with fangs of flame,
Writhing in agonies of wild despairs,
And giving tidings of a doom like theirs.
I felt all terrors of the damned, and fell
With conscious horror that my doom was hell:
And Memory mocked me, like a haunting ghost,
With light and life and pleasures that were lost.
As dreams turn night to day, and day to night,
So Memory flashed her shadows of that light
That once bade morning suns in glory rise,
To bless green fields and trees and purple skies,
And wakened life its pleasures to behold;—
That light flashed on me, like a story told;
And days misspent with friends and fellow men,
And sins committed—all were with me then.
The boundless hell, where tortures never tire,
Glimmered beneath me like a world on fire:
That soul of fire, like to its souls entombed,
Consuming on, and ne'er to be consumed,
Seemed nigh at hand—where oft the sulphury damps
O'er-awed its light, as glimmer dying lamps,
Spreading a horrid gloom from side to side,
A twilight scene of terrors half descried.
Sad boiled the billows of that burning sea,
And Fate's sad yellings dismal seemed to be;
Blue rolled its waves with horrors uncontrolled,
And its live wrecks of souls dashed howling as they rolled.

    Again I struggled, and the spell was broke,
And midst the laugh of mocking ghosts I woke;
My eyes were opened on an unhoped sight—
The early morning and its welcome light,
And, as I pondered o'er the past profound,
I heard the cock crow, and I blest the sound.

THE NIGHTMARE

Her steps take hold of hell.—SOLOMON.

MY dream began in bliss and lifted high
My sleeping feelings into fancy's joy;
Though like one wandering in a sweet far land
I seemed to hear and could not understand
Among the many voices humming by,
Nor knew one face where many met my eye.
That dim-seen mystery which in dreams appears
Was mine, a feeling of joy, hopes, and fears,
Mingling together; yet I knew not why,
Where all was beauty, trouble should be by.
The place was light—and yet no sun was there
To cause it—pale and beautifully fair,
Nor glare nor gloom but like eternity
Mild, like what spirits may expect to see;
But there was earth and sky and trees and flowers,
Different in kind and yet resembling ours;
And mightiest objects that the eye surveyed,
No light they clouded and they cast no shade;
But in that sky no cloud crossed east and west,
No storm crept frowning o'er its crystal rest.

.   .   .   .   .

At length a mighty mansion gathered high,
Whose bounds seemed almost boundless to the eye,
A place that wakened fancy's wonders there,
As mystery's mask left half her shadow bare;
A shapeless shape and semblance faint of things
That earth calls palaces, the place of kings.
Here all seemed entering; yet there was no crowd,
No anxious rushing, and no noises loud.
All seemed intent on matters yet unknown,
And every other's interest seemed their own,
Like as a brook pursues its gliding way,
Urged by an impulse which they could not stay.
Fear shrank to silence now and hovered round,
Till wandering steps seemed listening for their sound.

Restless as waves in their eternal race,
Where one crowd passed another took its place.
The gathering throngs that seemed to make one spot,
I seemed to know some and then knew them not;
Some more familiar seemed; I turned again
And they were strange and left a lonely pain;
And other eyes on my inquiries came
And seemed they knew me, but to feel the same;
As birds seek nests which idle boys have got,
They sought what had been and they found it not;
What memory's shadows dimly might display—
Friends, loves, and kin—found none and turned away.
At length one singled from the mighty throng
Where I had gazed on vacant looks so long,
With flowing robes, blue eyes, and face divine,
Came forth and fixed her tender gaze on mine.
It looked familiar as I'd seen the same;
But recollections of her earthly name
Were lost, if e'er she had a claim to one;
She joined my steps and seemed to lead me on.
We entered with the rest, and by my side
She stood, my all companion, friend, and guide.
Arches empillared like the rainbow's height
Went sweeping up and almost left the sight;
And yet o'er them a covering met the eye,
As earth seems covered with surrounding sky.
At last the silence with a murmur broke
Like the first hum when organs are awoke,
And every face seemed turned towards the sound
Where hope would soothe and mystery would confound;
Fate seemed as writing upon every brow
A fearful question, 'Who'll be summoned now?'
Yet woman seemed (though beauty's face beguiles
One's heart to favour) checking fears with smiles;
And my companion seated by my side
Seemed checking mine and strove her own to hide;
Her long white hand pressed mine with cheering power
As offering safety in a dangerous hour;
She looked and spake not yet, her lips the while

Closed mid the tumult in a timid smile;
And as the mystery waking gathered near,
Looked as one dares a danger, 'Never fear.'
More loud the music rose and yet more loud
Chorused with humming of a mighty crowd;
And through the mild light that at first clothed all
A brighter streamed, like sunbeams on a wall,
Growing more bright and losing it away
Like creeping sunrise on a summer's day;
A light that dazzled not, and yet it threw
Around o'erpowering splendour as it grew;
More high the music seemed, more strong the fear,
And awful symptoms rousing gathered near;
Voices awoke from many a troubling tongue,
But no words came distinctly from the throng;
Fears grew within me, and I fain had tried
To search the purpose of my angel guide.
Anxiety turned on her quiet face,
And recollections would [old] memories trace,
As one I'd witnessed once or else the same,
The looks of one I had not power to name;
She seemed at first as living beauty seems,
Then changed more lovely in the shade of dreams;
Then faded dim, confused, and hurrying by
Like memory waning into vacancy.
The music rose in terror's ecstasies,
In gradual swells like winds in summer trees,
Gathering and gathering to its highest bound,
And burst at last in mystery's mightiest sound.

Millions of hopes, hung on a spider's tie
'Tween time's suspense and fate's eternity,
Seemed cut at once, and all around the host
Felt at that moment if his own was lost;
And in a moment sudden changes rang
Confusion's uproar—discord's jarring clang,
Harsh noises, stunning crush, and thrilling yell,
As the whole mansion on their shoulders fell.
A light glowed round with horror's staggering sound,

And all seemed giddy, reeling, sinking round;
A weight plopt on me with a sudden crush,
A noise like waters that for freedom rush;
I could not move, nor speak; yet reason's power
Seemed wide awake in that spell-prisoning hour;
I felt as tried, whate'er the lot might be,
And strove and struggled with my destiny;
And then my eyes in hopeless wandering spied
That lovely shadow which had been my guide,
Seemly bent o'er me, offering mercy's plea,
'Tween death's dark hell and life's eternity.
Her face grew pale and awful, yet a shade
Of beauty hung in every change it made.
Her eyes o'er mine hung beautiful and bright,
Like the sun setting upon deepening night;
And love, fear, hope—all mortals can recall—
I felt none separate, but I felt them all.
Her white round arms threw back her streaming hair,
And smiles hung o'er me as in death's despair.

   Something drew near me and my guide withdrew,
Beauteous as ever but in terror too;
Her bright eyes lessened dim but not with tears,
Heavy with sorrows and the gloom of fears;
And scarce I turned her desert flight to trace
Ere a foul fiend seemed standing in her place.
'Twas Mary's voice that hung in her farewell;
The sound that moment on my memory fell—
A sound that held the music of the past;
But she was blest and I alone was cast;
My dangers dimmed the glory of her eyes,
And turned her smiling and her hopes to sighs.
The gloomiest pictures fear could ever make,
The fiend drew near to make my terrors ache—
Huge circles lost to eyes, and rotten hulls
Raised with dead groans from the dread 'place of skulls',—
Then turned with horrid laugh its haggard head
To where the earth-loved shadow dimly fled,
As mockery—waking hell with horrid sound

Like many murmurs moving underground.
I shuddering struggled from his horrid glare
And snapped my bonds and ended my despair,
And—as woke reason from the vision crept,
She seemed to start as one that ne'er had slept;
Horror and joy and mystery when by
Seemed less of vision than reality,
A nightmare mystery of a sealing doom,
A feeble picture of the dread to come.[1]

THE ROBBER

YET what am I? A robber: and why bring
In robbers' haunts so fair and sweet a thing?
Men who will steal a purse a heart will steal,
And beauty wakes the roughest hearts to feel.
Why did I wrong her with the name of wife
And hate her as the dearest thing in life?
For love like mine is nothing else but hate—
To link bright beings to so dark a fate;
Who if she knew one link that holds that tie,
Her heart would chill with terrors all and die,
Her ears would grow too adamant to hear
One word related of that tale of fear,
Her soul would be on fire could she but see
One shadow of a robber's history.

'Tis night, 'tis midnight!—hark, the horse's tramp
Comes plashing through the old heath's hollow swamp.
We tied the gate—and ere that gate we tied,
Or held that weapon, would that I had died!
The traveller heard one whistle shrill and clear,
And muttered: 'Poachers! come on, Dobbin, never fear!'
The horse could see us at the wood gate stand
And snorted at the weapon in my hand;

[1] CLARE'S NOTE. I wish to acknowledge that whatsoever merit this and *The Dream* may be thought to possess they owe it in part to the *English Opium Eater*, as they were written after (though actual dreams) the perusal of that singular and interesting production.

But the old farmer checked the trembling steed
To try the gate—and midnight knew the deed.
The shot was fired—dead silence paused—then groans
That would have fretted human hearts to stones;
And that last groan of uttermost despair,
I hear it now—or did I stir the chair?
That last groan waked an echo which I hear
Now and for ever, here and everywhere—
A howl—a shriek—a hoarse unearthly call—
'Twas this and that and all made up of all;
Just from our lair it came within the wood:
'They're mine; they've sealed the bond in death and blood.'
The gun dropt from my hand, and where it fell
The ground seemed opening like the mouth of hell.
I was not drunk but sober all, yet fear
Could see that sight and still that sound could hear;
And though I stopt my ears and held my breath,
The wind and grass and bushes muttered 'Death!'
'Do good and good shall come,' the parson said;
But I was poaching while he preached or prayed.
And when he read his lessons and his prayers,
My mind was busy after dogs and hares.
'Do good and good shall come.' I know it now.
Oh, could I wipe this murther from my brow!
And good had come, but harm blocks all the way,
And I must suffer, for I cannot pray.
Look! there's the wood gate—don't you see it tied?
Untie it now—and throw that gun aside!
No; all's too late—you help me all in vain;
Blood will for ever on its bands remain.
I hear the groan again, the midnight yell;
Guns may go off half cocked—but ere mine fell
The shot was fired; yet when it met the ground
A sputtering fire one moment blazed around;
Trees trembled to their trunks, a dreadful sign,
When that unearthly hoarseness muttered 'Mine!'
I hear't again! Oh, wipe that stain away,
That stains that dreadful place this very day.
Nay, chop the bushes up, they speak so loud.

Look! now 'tis there upon that dismal cloud:
A giant—no a monster—sails; look there!
He'll swallow up the moon, stars, all—beware!
He hears the muttering guns; well, never fear;
'Tis but a hare—the crime is not severe.
There, now 'tis changed!—a dragon from his hole,
His body black, his head a burning coal:
Oh, what a horrid picture! don't you see?
He darts his venom fangs and mocks at me.
Ah, that's the horrid demon of the heath!
Chop down those trees—I choke for want of breath.
Nay, take that bullet out—'twill burst the gun!
The gun's not bursted, but the deed is done.
Grub up the bushes! 'Death,' they sighed and sighed.
I stopt my ears to hear; he groaned—and died.

The robber's wife had all that women heir,
A form all lovely, and a face so fair
In nature's sunny lap she seemed as nursed,
Until the robber into misery cursed
Her poor forsaken presence.   Wonder stared
On that sweet face that sorrow sadly marred,
And marvelled how a flower of winning grace
Could trust itself in such a dangerous place
As the affections of a robber's heart.
But in love's faith suspicion bears no part;
They could not feel, while wasting idle breath,
That love like ivy clings to life and death.
Yet when the law's decision met her ears,
The last hope [fell] that propt up all her fears;
So young, so beautiful, she was not born
To stand against the world's down-trampling scorn.
Rich beauty ne'er was made for thorny ways,
That only blooms and thrives on smiles and praise.
It could not bear the withering frowns of scorn;
As well might blossoms bear a frosty morn.
She withered into death for nothing done,
And shunned her life that had no sin to shun.
Then pity's hand was held before its eyes,

410

And scorn itself grew tender in disguise;
'So young, so beautiful, and thus to die!'—
So pity sighed; scorn uttered no reply.

LIFE, DEATH, AND ETERNITY

A SHADOW moving by one's side,
    That would a substance seem—
That is, yet is not—though descried
    Like skies beneath the stream;
A tree that's ever in the bloom,
    Whose fruit is never rife;
A wish for joys that never come—
    Such are the hopes of Life.

A dark, inevitable night,
    A blank that will remain;
A waiting for the morning light,
    Where waiting is in vain;
A gulph, where pathway never led
    To show the depth beneath;
A thing we know not, yet we dread—
    The hornèd thing—'tis Death.

The vaulted void of purple sky
    That everywhere extends,
That stretches from the dazzled eye,
    In space that never ends;
A morning whose uprisen sun
    No setting e'er shall see;
A day that comes without a noon—
    Such is Eternity.[1]

[1] Another MS. reads:

    A morn where night's for ever gone,
        A never-setting sun,
    A day where ne'er a noon comes on
        But keeps as it begun;
    Wave chasing wave, unceasing never,
        Along the mighty sea
    That rolls in majesty for ever—
        Such is Eternity.

ANTIQUITY

ANTIQUITY, thou dark sublime,
  Though mystery wakes thy song,
Thou dateless child of hoary Time,
  Thy name shall linger long!
In vain Age bared Destruction's arm
  To blight thy strength and fame;
Learning still keeps thy embers warm,
  And kindles them to flame.

Nay, learning's self may turn to dust,
  And ignorance again
May leave its glimmering lamp to rust;
  Antiquity shall reign!
Creation's self thy date shall be,
  And Earth's age be as thine;
The sun and moon are types of thee,
  Nor shall they longer shine.

Though Time may o'er thy memory leap,
  And Ruin's frowns encroach;
Eternity shall start from sleep
  To hear thy near approach.
Though bounds are for thy station set,
  Still, ere those bounds are past,
Thy fame with Time shall struggle yet,
  And die with Time the last.

Whene'er I walk where thou hast been,
  And still art doomed to be,
Reflection wakens at the scene,
  As at eternity;
To think what days in millions by
  Have bade suns rise and set
On thy unwearied gazing eye,
  And left thee looking yet!

While those that raised thy early fame
  With hope's persisting hand,
During as marble left thy name
  And graved their own on sand:

That same sun did its smiles impart,
In that same spreading sky,
When thou wert left; and here thou art,
Like one that cannot die!

On the first page that Time unfurled,
Thy childhood did appear,
And now thy volume is the world,
And thou art everywhere.
Each leaf is filled with many a doom
Of kingdoms past away,
Where tyrant power in little room
Records its own decay.

Thy Roman fame o'er England still
Swells many a lingering scar,
Where Caesars led, with conquering skill,
Their legions on to war:
And camps and stations still abide
On many a sloping hill;
Though Time hath done its all to hide—
Thy presence guards them still.

The moss that crowns the mountain stone,
The grass that greens the plain,
All love to make thy haunts their own,
And with thy steps remain.
And ivy, as thy lasting bower,
In gloomy grandeur creeps,
And, careless of life's passing hour,
Its endless summer keeps.

I walk with thee my native plains,
As in a nobler clime,
Rapt where thy memory still remains,
Disciple unto Time,
Whose foot in ruins crushed Power's fame,
And left its print behind,
Till Ruin, weary of its name,
Their fate to thee resigned.

And 'neath thy care, in mist sublime,
    They reign and linger still;
Though ivy finds no wall to climb,
    Grass crowns each swelling hill;
Where slumbering Time will often find
    His rebel deeds again,
And turn a wondering look behind
    To see them still remain.

Thus through the past thy name appears,
    All hoary and sublime,
Unburied in the grave of years,
    To run its race with Time;
While men, as sunbeams gild the brook,
    Shine till a cloud comes on,
And then, ere Time a stride hath took,
    Their name and all is gone.

Temple and tower of mighty name,
    And monumental bust,
Neglect the errands of their fame,
    And mingle with the dust:
The clouds of ruin soon efface
    What pride had told in vain;
But still thy genius haunts the place,
    And long thy steps remain.

Lorn Silence o'er their mystery dreams,
    And round them Nature blooms
Sad, as a May-flower's dwelling seems
    With solitary tombs!
Round where their buried memory sleeps,
    Spring spreads its dewy sky
In tender mood, as one that weeps
    Life's faded majesty.

Time's frost may crumble stubborn towers,
    Fame once believed its own;
Thou still art reigning, past his powers,
    And ruin builds thy throne:

When all is past, the very ground
  Is sacred unto thee;
When dust and weeds hide all around,
  That dust thy home shall be.

ON SEEING A BEAUTIFUL STATUE

Thou lovely shade of heavenly birth—
  Aught else thou canst not be,
The copy of the loves on earth
  Were never types of thee;
Where is the face can looks impart
  So heavenly-born as thine?
Rude nature tam-ed with studied art
  Owns nothing so divine.

Thou type of beauty's reigning flower,
  To form thee thus was given
A soul that spurned at earthly power
  And grasped the fire of heaven.
Of faded Greece the goddess still,
  Formed from eternity,
'Twere hard to deem it heathen-ill
  To worship such as thee.

For love might yet with bended knee
  Urge its Promethean prayer
And worship in its ecstasy
  The soul thought kindles there;
Beauty's the type of heaven above
  Where sinless praise is given,
Nor is it vain for earth to love
  Aught that resembles heaven.

THE CALM

BENEATH my feet the very dust
   Up with the whirlwind's summons flies
To tell the doubting and the just
   That even dust shall greet the skies;
Beside my path the flowers and grass
   In trembling joy their praises pay,
Yet unobserving man goes by
   Nor gleans a lesson in his way.

Though Nature breathes in quiet moods
   And woos the heart in gentle ways,
A sterner power with time intrudes,
   Shall waken all to fear and praise,
When Death shall rise on every eye
   And blend his voice with every call,
When all but Nature's debt shall die
   And man the debtor pay for all.

That day shall come; in mighty storms
   Each year its coming typifies;
For what are thunder's dread alarms
   To that shall bid the dead to rise?
The wind, the water, fire and all
   As actors in that dreadful play
Make ready in their parts to fall,
   Rehearsing portions every day.

Yet man, ordained in every scene
   To act the first and chiefest part,
Neglects to feel the part he's in
   Nor gets a single page by heart,
Although the stage be worlds destroyed,
   The curtains, torn unpillared skies,
The actor, man by God employed
   To do his part of smiles or sighs,
Life everlastingly enjoyed
   Or pain's unceasing sacrifice.
And I, by idle things employed,
   Dread what the finale typifies.

THE MILKING HOUR

THE sun had grown on lessening day
   A table, large and round,
And in the distant vapours grey
   Seemed leaning on the ground;
When Mary, like a lingering flower,
   Did tenderly agree
To stay beyond her milking hour,
   And talk awhile with me.

We wandered till the distant town
   Was silenced nearly dumb,
And lessened on the quiet ear,
   Small as a beetle's hum.
She turned her milkpails upside down,
   And made us each a seat,
And there we talked the evening brown,
   Beneath the rustling wheat.

And while she milked her breathing cows
   I sat beside the streams,
In musing o'er our evening joys,
   Like one in pleasant dreams:
The bats and owls, to meet the night,
   From hollow trees had gone,
And e'en the flowers had shut for sleep,
   Yet still she lingered on.

We mused in raptures side by side,
   Our wishes seemed as one;
We talked of Time's retreating tide,
   And sighed to find it gone.
And we had sighed more deeply still
   O'er all our pleasures past,
If we had known what now we know,
   That we had met the last.

THE TOPER'S RANT

GIVE me an old crone of a fellow
   Who loves to drink ale in a horn,
And sing racy songs when he's mellow,
   Which topers sung ere he was born.
For such a friend fate shall be thankèd,
   And, line but our pockets with brass,
We'd sooner suck ale through a blanket
   Than thimbles of wine from a glass.

Away with your proud thimble-glasses
   Of wine foreign nations supply,
A toper ne'er drinks to the lasses
   O'er a draught scarce enough for a fly.
Club me with the hedger and ditcher
   Or beggar that makes his own horn,
To join o'er an old gallon pitcher
   Foaming o'er with the essence of corn.

I care not with whom I get tipsy
   Or where with brown stout I regale,
I'll weather the storm with a gipsy
   If he be a lover of ale.
I'll weather the toughest storm weary
   Altho' I get wet to the skin,
For my outside I never need fear me
   While warm with real stingo within.

We'll sit till the bushes are dropping
   Like the spout of a watering pan,
And till the cag's drained there's no stopping,
   We'll keep up the ring to a man.
We'll sit till Dame Nature is feeling
   The breath of our stingo so warm,
And bushes and trees begin reeling
   In our eyes like to ships in a storm.

We'll start it three hours before seven,
   When larks wake the morning to dance,

And we'll stand it till night's black eleven,
   When witches ride over to France;
And we'll sit it in spite of the weather
   Till we tumble dead drunk on the plain,
When the morning shall find us together,
   All willing to stand it again.

ENCLOSURE

FAR spread the moory ground, a level scene
Bespread with rush and one eternal green,
That never felt the rage of blundering plough,
Though centuries wreathed spring blossoms on its brow.
Autumn met plains that stretched them far away
In unchecked shadows of green, brown, and grey.
Unbounded freedom ruled the wandering scene;
No fence of ownership crept in between
To hide the prospect from the gazing eye;
Its only bondage was the circling sky.
A mighty flat, undwarfed by bush and tree,
Spread its faint shadow of immensity,
And lost itself, which seemed to eke its bounds,
In the blue mist the horizon's edge surrounds.

Now this sweet vision of my boyish hours,
Free as spring clouds and wild as forest flowers,
Is faded all—a hope that blossomed free,
And hath been once as it no more shall be.
Enclosure came, and trampled on the grave
Of labour's rights, and left the poor a slave;
And memory's pride, ere want to wealth did bow,
Is both the shadow and the substance now.
The sheep and cows were free to range as then
Where change might prompt, nor felt the bonds of men.
Cows went and came with every morn and night
To the wild pasture as their common right;
And sheep, unfolded with the rising sun,
Heard the swains shout and felt their freedom won,

Tracked the red fallow field and heath and plain,
Or sought the brook to drink, and roamed again;
While the glad shepherd traced their tracks along,
Free as the lark and happy as her song.
But now all's fled, and flats of many a dye
That seemed to lengthen with the following eye,
Moors losing from the sight, far, smooth, and blea,
Where swopt the plover in its pleasure free,
Are banished now with heaths once wild and gay
As poet's visions of life's early day.
Like mighty giants of their limbs bereft,
The skybound wastes in mangled garbs are left,
Fence meeting fence in owner's little bounds
Of field and meadow, large as garden-grounds,
In little parcels little minds to please,
With men and flocks imprisoned, ill at ease.
For with the poor scared freedom bade farewell,
And fortune-hunters totter where they fell;
They dreamed of riches in the rebel scheme
And find too truly that they did but dream.

THE LAMENT OF SWORDY WELL

I'M Swordy Well, a piece of land
   That's fell upon the town,
Who worked me till I couldn't stand
   And crush me now I'm down.

There was a time my bit of ground
   Made freeman of the slave,
The ass no pounder'd dare to pound
   When I his supper gave.

The gipsy's camp was not afraid,
   I made his dwelling free,
Till vile enclosure came, and made
   A parish slave of me.

Alas, dependence, thou'rt a brute
    Want only understands;
His feelings wither branch and root
    Who falls in parish hands.

The muck that clouts the ploughman's shoe,
    The moss that hides the stone,
Now I'm become the parish due,
    Is more than I can own.

The silver springs are naked dykes,
    With scarce a clump of rushes;
When gain got nigh, the tasteless tykes
    Grubbed up trees, banks, and bushes.

Though I'm no man, yet any wrong
    Some sort of right may seek,
And I am glad if e'en a song
    Give me the room to speak.

I've got among such grubbling gear
    And such a hungry pack,
If I brought harvests twice a year,
    They'd bring me nothing back.

And should the price of grain get high
    —Lord help and keep it low!—
I shan't possess a butterfly
    Nor get a weed to grow,

I shan't possess a yard of ground
    To bid a mouse to thrive;
For gain has put me in a pound,
    I scarce can keep alive.

Ah me!—they turned me inside out
    For sand and grit and stones,
And turned my old green hills about
    And picked my very bones.

The bees fly round in feeble rings
    And find no blossom by,
Then thrum their almost weary wings
    Upon the moss, and die.

Rabbits that find my hills turned o'er
    Forsake my poor abode;
They dread a workhouse like the poor,
    And nibble on the road.

If with a clover bottle now
    Spring dares to lift her head,
The next day brings the hasty plough
    And makes me misery's bed.

I've scarce a nook to call my own
    For things that creep or fly;
The beetle hiding 'neath a stone
    Does well to hurry by.

And if I could but find a friend
    With no deceit to sham,
Who'd send me some few sheep to tend,
    And leave me as I am,

To keep my hills from cart and plough
    And strife of mongrel men,
And as spring found me find me now,
    I should look up agen.

And save his Lordship's woods, that past
    The day of danger dwell,
Of all the fields I am the last
    That my own face can tell;

Yet what with stone-pits' delving holes,
    And strife to buy and sell,
My name will quickly be the whole
    That's left of Swordy Well.

TO ANNA, THREE YEARS OLD

My Anna, summer laughs in mirth,
    And we will of the party be,
And leave the crickets in the hearth
    For green fields' merry minstrelsy.

I see thee now with little hand
    Catch at each object passing by,
The happiest thing in all the land
    Except the bee and butterfly.

The weed-based arches' walls that stride
    O'er where the meadow water falls
Will turn thee from thy path aside
    To gaze upon the mossy walls.

And limpid brook that leaps along,
    Gilt with the summer's burnished gleam,
Will stop thy little tale or song
    To gaze upon its crimping stream.

Thou'lt leave my hand with eager speed
    The new-discovered things to see—
The old pond with its water-weed
    And danger-daring willow-tree,
Who leans, an ancient invalid,
    O'er spots where deepest waters be.

In sudden shout and wild surprise
    I hear thy simple wonderment,
As new things meet thy childish eyes
    And wake some innocent intent;

As bird or bee or butterfly
    Bounds through the crowd of merry leaves
And starts the rapture of thine eye
    To run for what it ne'er achieves;

The simple reasoning arguments
   Shaped to thy fancy's little view,
The joys and rapturous intents
   That everywhere pursue.

So dreamed I over hope's young boon,
   When merry summer was returning,
And little thought that time so soon
   Would change my early hope to mourning.

I thought to have heard thee mid the bowers
   To mock the cuckoo's merry song,
And see thee seek thy daisy flowers
   That's been thy anxious choice so long.

But thou art on the bed of pain,
   So tells each poor forsaken toy.
Ah, could I see that happy hour
   When these shall be thy heart's employ,
And see thee toddle o'er the plain,
   And stoop for flowers, and shout for joy.

A DAYDREAM IN SUMMER

Wearied with his lonely walk,
Hermit-like with none to talk,
And cloyed with often-seen delight,
His spirits sickened at the sight
Of life's realities and things
That spread around his wanderings,
Of wood and heath in brambles clad,
That seemed like him in silence sad,
The lone enthusiast, weary worn,
Sought shelter from the heats of morn,
And in a cool nook by the stream,
Beside a bridge-wall, dreamed a dream;
And instant from his half-closed eye
Reality seemed fading by;

424

Dull fields and woods that round him lay
Like curtains to his dreaming play
All slided by, and on his sight
New scenes appeared in fairy light;
The skies lit up a brighter sun,
The birds a cheery song begun,
And flowers bloomed fair and wildly round
As ever grow on dreaming ground;
And mid the sweet enchanting view,
Created every minute new,
He swooned at once from care and strife
Into the poesy of life.
A stranger to the thoughts of men,
He felt his boyish limbs agen
Revelling in all the glee
Of life's first fairy infancy;
Chasing by the rippling spring
Dragon-flies of purple wing,
Or setting mushroom tops afloat,
Mimicking the sailing boat;
Or vainly trying by surprise
To catch the settling butterflies;
And oft with rapture driving on
Where many partner boys had gone,
Wading through the rustling wheat,
Red and purple flowers to meet,
To weave and trim a wild cockade
And play the soldiers' gay parade;
Now tearing through the clinging thorns,
Seeking kecks for bugle horns.
Thus with a schoolboy's heart again
He chased and hallo'd o'er the plain,
Till the church clock counted one
And told them freedom's hour was gone;
In its dull, humming, drowsy way,
It called them from their sports and play.
How different did the sound appear
To that which brought the evening near,
That lovely, humming, happy strain,

That brought them liberty again.
The desk, the books, were all the same,
Marked with each well-known little name,
And many a cover blotched and blurred
With shapeless forms of beast and bird;
And the old master, white with years,
Sat there to waken boyish fears,
While the tough sceptre of his sway,
That awed to silence all the day,
The peeled wand, acting at his will,
Hung o'er the smoke-stained chimney still.
The churchyard still its trees possessed,
And jackdaws sought their boughs to rest,
In whose old trunks they did acquire
Homes safe as in the mossy spire.
The school they shadowed as before,
With its white dial o'er the door,
And bees hummed round in summer's pride,
In its time-creviced walls to hide.
The gravestones childhood eager reads
Peeped o'er the rudely clambering weeds,
Where cherubs gilt, that represent
The slumbers of the innocent,
Smiled glittering to the slanting sun,
As if death's peace with heaven was won.
All, all was blest, and peace and plays
Brought back the enthusiast's fairy days;
And leaving childhood unperceived,
Scenes sweeter still his dream relived,
Life's calmest spot that lingers green
Manhood and infancy between,
When youth's warm feelings have their birth,
Creating angels upon earth,
And fancying woman born for joy,
With naught 'to wither and destroy.'
That picture of past youth's delight
Was swimming now before his sight,
And love's soft thrill of pleasant pain
Was whispering its deceits again,

And Mary, pride of pleasures gone,
Was at his side to lead him on.
And on they went through field and lane,
Haunts of their loves to trace again;
Clung to his arm, she skipt along
With the same music on her tongue,
The selfsame voice as soft and dear
As that which met his youthful ear;
The sunny look, the witching grace
Still blushed upon her angel face,
As though one moment's harmless stay
Had never stole a charm away,
The selfsame bloom—and in her eye
That blue of thirteen summers by.
The pleasant spots where they had met
All shone as naught had faded yet;
The sun was setting o'er the hill,
The thorn-bush it was blooming still,
As it was blooming on the day
When last he reached her boughs of may,
And pleased he clomb the thorny grain
To crop its firstling buds again,
And claimed in eager ecstasies
Love's favours as he reached the prize.
Objects of summer all the same
Were nigh, her gentle praise to claim.
The lark was rising from his nest
To sing the setting sun to rest,
And her fair hand was o'er her eyes
To see her favourite to the skies;
And oft his look was turned to see
If love still felt that melody;
And blooming flowers were at her feet,
Her bending lovely looks to meet,
The blooms of spring and summer days,
Lingering as to wait her praise;
And though she showed him weeds the while,
He praised and loved them for a smile.
The cuckoo sang in soft delight

Its ditty to departing light,
And murmuring children far away
Mocked the music in their play;
And in the ivied tree the dove
Breathed its soothing song to love.
He loved to watch her wistful look
Following white moths down the brook,
And thrilled to mark her beaming eyes
Brightening in pleasure and surprise
To meet the wild mysterious things
That evening's soothing presence brings;
And stepping on with gentle feet
She strove to shun the lark's retreat;
And as he near the bushes prest,
And scared the linnet from its nest,
Fond chidings from her bosom fell,
Then blest the bird and wished it well.
His heart was into rapture stirred,
His very soul was with the bird;
He felt that blessing by her side
As only to himself applied,
And in his rapture's gushing whim
He told her it was meant for him.
She ne'er denied, but looked the will
To own as though she blessed him still.
Yet he had fearful thoughts in view,
Joy seemed too happy to be true;
He doubted if 'twas Mary by,
Yet could not feel the reason why;
He loitered by her as in pain,
And longed to hear her voice again;
He called her by her witching name,
She answered—'twas the very same,
And looked as if she knew his fears,
Smiling to cheer him through her tears,
And whispering in a tender sigh,
''Tis youth and Mary standing by.'
His heart revived, yet in its mirth
Felt fears that they were not of earth,

428

That both were shadows of the mind,
Picturing the joys it wished to find.
Yet he did feel as like a child,
And sighed in fondness till she smiled,
Vowing that they would part no more,
Nor act so foolish as before.
She nestled closer by his side,
And vowed, 'We never will,' and sighed.
He grasped her hand; it seemed to thrill;
He whispered, 'No, we never will,'
And thought in rapture's mad extreme
To hold her though it proved a dream.
And instant as that thought begun
Her presence seemed his love to shun,
And deaf to all he had to say
Quick turned her tender face away;
When her small waist he strove to clasp,
She shrunk like water from his grasp.

IMPULSES OF SPRING

Day burnishes the distant hills,
    And clouds blush far away;
Life's heart with nature's rapture thrills
    To hail this glorious day.
The morning falls in dizzy light
    On mountain-tops and towers,
But speeds with soft and gentle flight
    Among these valley-flowers.

There's music in the waking woods,
    There's glory in the air;
Birds, in their merry summer moods,
    Now rant and revel there:
Joy wakes, and wantons all around,
    Love laughs in every call,
Music in many hearts is found,
    And poesy breathes in all.

The merry new-come nightingale
   Woos night's dull hours along,
Till daylight at the sound turns pale
   And hastes to share the song.
A waste of sunny flowers is seen,
   And incense fills the air;
No sunless place is found too mean
   Spring's blushing gems to wear.

The horse-blob by the water-mill
   Blooms in the foaming dam,
And pilewort flares around the hill,
   Beside the sleeping lamb.
Spring is the happy breathing time
   For young love's stolen joys;
Spring is the poet's luscious prime—
   He revels in the noise

Of waking insects humming round,
   And birds upon the wing,
And all the gushing soul of sound
   That echoes of the spring;
For in their joys his own are met,
   Though tears stand in his eye;
In their gay mirth he half forgets
   He e'er knew how to sigh.

He feeds on Spring's precarious boon,
   A being of her race,
Where light and shade and shower and sun
   Are ever changing place.
To-day he buds, and glows to meet
   To-morrow's promised shower,
Then crushed by care's intruding feet,
   He fades—a broken flower!

His hopes, they change like summer clouds
   And fairy phantasies;
His pleasures, wrapt in gayer shrouds,
   Are sorrows in disguise;

The sweetest smiles his heart can find
  Possess their tears as well;
His highest pleasures leave behind
  Their heart-ache and farewell.

His are the fading 'joys of grief';
  Care grows his favoured guest;
And sorrow gives his heart relief
  Because it knows him best.
The sweetest flower on pleasure's path
  Will bloom on sorrow's grave,
And earthly joys, and earthly mirth,
  Their share of grief shall have.

True poesy owns a haunted mind,
  A thirst-enduring flame,
Burning the soul to leave behind
  The memory of a name.
Though life be deemed as sweetly sold
  For toil so ill repaid—
The marble epitaph, how cold!
  Although with gold inlaid.

While the rude clown of thoughtless clay,
  In feelings unrefined,
Lives out life's cloudless holiday,
  With nothing on his mind;
Then sound as ever king hath slept,
  On earth's green lap he lies;
While beauty's tears, so sweetly wept,
  And friendship's warmest sighs

Are left upon his lowly grave,
  And live his only fame,
While frowning envy never gave
  One insult to his name;
Yet who would from their cares be free
  For such unconscious bliss?
A living blank in life to be,
  Pain's sympathy to miss?

To meet enthusiastic May
  As but dull winter's hours,
And primrose pale and daisy gay
  As white and yellow flowers
And not as friends in our esteem,
  To cheer dull life's sojourn;
Let me, throughout its cheating dream,
  Much rather feel and mourn

The bliss and grief, though past control,
  That with extremes inflame;
Feelings, blood-rushing through the soul,
  Not uttered in a name;
Where no words live, to free the mind
  From hidden hopes or fears,
Where all the utterance can find
  Are gushing smiles and tears.

Yet woo I not that burning flame,
  Enkindling ecstasy,
Blazing in dreams to win a name
  From fame's eternity.
Fame's yearning breath breeds not my sigh,
  Nor eats my heart away,
Burning life's every channel dry
  To triumph o'er decay.

Yet with the minstrelsy on earth
  I too would love the lyre,
For heaven ne'er gave the meanest birth
  To quench that holy fire:
It owns the muse's sweetest smiles
  And scatters life around;
Grief, sick with hope's heart-broken toils,
  Grows happy at the sound.

The lyre is pleasure's blest abode,
  And round it angels throng;
The lyre is as the voice of God,
  The prophets spake in song.

And as the sun this day brings forth
   Creations every hour,
Care's wreath warms at the muse's mirth,
   And blushes into flower.

THE PROGRESS OF RHYME

O SOUL-ENCHANTING poesy,
Thou'st long been all the world with me;
When poor, thy presence grows my wealth,
When sick, thy visions give me health,
When sad, thy sunny smile is joy
And was from e'en a tiny boy.
When trouble came, and toiling care
Seemed almost more than I could bear,
While threshing in the dusty barn
Or squashing in the ditch to earn
A pittance that would scarce allow
One joy to smooth my sweating brow
Where drop by drop would chase and fall,
Thy presence triumphed over all:
The vulgar they might frown and sneer,
Insult was mean but never near.
'Twas poesy's self that stopt the sigh
And malice met with no reply.
So was it in my earlier day
When sheep to corn had strayed away
Or horses closen gaps had broke,
Ere sunrise peeped or I awoke;
My master's frowns might force the tear,
But poesy came to check and cheer.
It glistened in my shamèd eye
But ere it fell the swoof was by.
I thought of luck in future days
When even he might find a praise.
I looked on poesy like a friend
To cheer me till my life should end.
'Twas like a parent's first regard

And love when beauty's voice was heard,
'Twas joy, 'twas hope, and maybe fear,
But still 'twas rapture everywhere.
My heart were ice unmoved to dwell,
Nor care for one I loved so well
Through rough and smooth, through good and ill,
That led me and attends me still.
Thou wert an early joy to me:
That joy was love and poesy;
And but for thee my idle lay
Had ne'er been urged in early day;
The harp imagination strung
Had ne'er been dreamed of; but among
The flowers in summer's fields of joy
I'd lain an idle rustic boy,
No hope to think of, fear or care,
And even love a stranger there.
But poesy that vision flung
Around me as I hummed and sung;
I glowered on beauty passing by,
Yet hardly turned my sheepish eye;
I worshipped, yet could hardly dare
To show I knew the goddess there,
Lest my presumptuous stare should gain
But frowns, ill humour, and disdain.
My first ambition was its praise,
My struggles aye in early days.
Had I by vulgar boldness torn
That hope when it was newly born,
By rudeness, gibes, and vulgar tongue,
The curse of the unfeeling throng,
Their scorn had frowned upon the lay
And hope and song had died away.
And I with nothing to atone
Had felt myself indeed alone.
But promises of days to come
The very fields would seem to hum,
Those burning days when I should dar
To sing aloud my worship there,

When beauty's self might turn its eye
Of praise: what could I do but try?
'Twas winter then, but summer shone
From heaven when I was all alone;
And summer came, and every weed
Of great or little had its meed;
Without its leaves there wa'n't a bower
Nor one poor weed without its flower.
'Twas love and pleasure all along;
I felt that I'd a right to song
And sung—but in a timid strain—
Of fondness for my native plain;
For everything I felt a love,
The weeds below, the birds above;
And weeds that bloomed in summer's hours,
I thought they should be reckoned flowers;
They made a garden free for all,
And so I loved them great and small,
And sung of some that pleased my eye,
Nor could I pass the thistle by,
But paused and thought it could not be
A weed in nature's poesy.
No matter for protecting wall,
No matter though they chance to fall
Where sheep and cows and oxen lie,
The kindly rain when they're adry
Falls on them with as plenteous showers
As when it waters garden flowers;
They look up with a blushing eye
Upon a tender watching sky,
And still enjoy the kindling smile
Of sunshine though they live with toil,
As garden flowers with all their care,
For nature's love is ever there.
And so it cheered me while I lay
Among their beautiful array,
To think that I in humble dress
Might have a right to happiness
And sing as well as greater men;

And then I strung the lyre agen
And heartened up o'er toil and fear
And lived with rapture everywhere,
Till dayshine to my themes did come.
Just as a blossom bursts to bloom
And finds itself in thorny ways,
So did my musings meet with praise,
And though no garden care had I
My heart had love for poesy,
A simple love, a wild esteem,
As heartfelt as the linnet's dream
That mutters in its sleep at night
Some notes from ecstasy's delight.
Thus did I dream o'er joys and lie
Muttering dream-songs of poesy.
The night dislimned and waking day
Shook from wood leaves the drops away;
Hope came, storms calmed, and hue and cry
With her false pictures herded by,
With tales of help when help was not,
Of friends who urged to write or blot,
Whose taste were such that mine were shame
Had they not helped it into fame.
Poh! let the idle rumour ill,
Their vanity is never still;
My harp, though simple, was my own.
When I was in the fields alone
With none to help and none to hear
To bid me either hope or fear,
The bird or bee its chords would sound,
The air hummed melodies around;
I caught with eager ear the strain
And sung the music o'er again;
Or love or instinct flowing strong,
Fields were the essence of the song.
And fields and woods are still as mine,
Real teachers that are all divine;
So if my song be weak or tame
'Tis I, not they, who bear the blame;

But hope and cheer through good and ill,
They are my aids to worship still,
Still growing on a gentle tide
Nor foes could mar nor friends could guide;
Like pasture brooks through sun and shade,
Crooked as channels chance hath made,
It rambles as it loves to stray
And hope and feeling lead the way.
—Ay, birds, no matter what the tune,
Or 'croak' or 'tweet,' 'twas nature's boon
That brought them joy, and music flung
Its spell o'er every matin sung,
And e'en the sparrow's chirp to me
Was song in its felicity.
When grief hung o'er me like a cloud
Till hope seemed even in her shroud,
I whispered poesy's spell till they
Gleamed round me like a summer's day;
When tempests o'er my labours sung,
My soul to its responses rung,
And joined the chorus till the storm
Fell all unheeded, void of harm;
And each old leaning shielding tree
Were princely palaces to me,
Where I would sit me down and chime
My unheard rhapsodies to rhyme.
All I beheld of grand, with time
Grew up to beautiful's sublime:
The arching grove of ancient limes
That into roofs like churches climbs,
Grain intertwisting into grain,
That stops the sun and stops the rain
And spreads a gloom that never smiles,
Like ancient halls and minster aisles,
While all without a beauteous screen
Of summer's luscious leaves is seen,
While heard that everlasting hum
Of insects haunting where they bloom,
As though 'twas nature's very place

Of worship, where her mighty race
Of insect life and spirits too
In summer-time were wont to go,
Both insects and the breath of flowers,
To sing their maker's mighty powers.
I've thought so as I used to rove
Through Burghley Park, that darksome grove
Of limes where twilight lingered grey
Like evening in the midst of day.
I felt without a single skill
That instinct that would not be still,
To think of song sublime beneath
That heaved my bosom like my breath,
That burned and chilled and went and came
Without or uttering or a name,
Until the vision waked with time
And left me itching after rhyme,
Where little pictures idly tell
Of nature's powers and nature's spell.
I felt and shunned the idle vein,
Laid down the pen and toiled again;
But, spite of all, through good and ill,
It was and is my worship still.
No matter how the world approved,
'Twas nature listened, I that loved;
No matter how the lyre was strung,
From my own heart the music sprung.
The cowboy with his oaten straw,
Although he hardly heard or saw
No more of music than he made,
'Twas sweet; and when I pluckt the blade
Of grass upon the woodland hill
To mock the birds with artless skill,
No music in the world beside
Seemed half so sweet, till mine was tried.
So my boy-worship poesy
Made e'en the muses pleased with me,
Until I even danced for joy,
A happy and a lonely boy,

Each object to my ear and eye
Made paradise of poesy.
I heard the blackbird in the dell
Sing sweet; could I but sing as well,
I thought, until the bird in glee
Seemed pleased and paused to answer me.
And nightingales—Oh, I have stood
Beside the pingle and the wood,
And o'er the old oak railing hung
To listen every note they sung,
And left boys making taws of clay
To muse and listen half the day.
The more I listened and the more
Each note seemed sweeter than before,
And aye so different was the strain
She'd scarce repeat the note again:
'Chew-chew chew-chew,' and higher still:
'Cheer-cheer cheer-cheer,' more loud and shrill:
'Cheer-up cheer-up cheer-up,' and dropt
Low: 'tweet tweet jug jug jug,' and stopt
One moment just to drink the sound
Her music made, and then a round
Of stranger witching notes was heard,
As if it was a stranger bird:
'Wew-wew wew-wew, chur-chur chur-chur,
Woo-it woo-it': could this be her?
'Tee-rew tee-rew tee-rew tee-rew,
Chew-rit chew-rit,' and ever new:
'Will-will will-will, grig-grig grig-grig.'
The boy stopt sudden on the brig
To hear the 'tweet tweet tweet' so shrill,
Then 'jug jug jug,' and all was still
A minute, when a wilder strain
Made boys and woods to pause again;
Words were not left to hum the spell.
Could they be birds that sung so well?
I thought, and maybe more than I,
That music's self had left the sky
To cheer me with its magic strain;

439

And then I hummed the words again,
Till fancy pictured, standing by,
My heart's companion, poesy.
No friends had I to guide or aid
The struggles young ambition made.
In silent shame the harp was tried
And rapture's griefs the tune applied,
Yet o'er the songs my parents sung
My ear in silent musings hung.
Their kindness wishes did regard,
They sung, and joy was my reward.
All else was but a proud decree,
The right of bards and naught to me,
A title that I dared not claim
And hid it like a private shame.
I whispered aye and felt a fear
To speak aloud though none was near;
I dreaded laughter more than blame,
I dared not sing aloud for shame;
So all unheeded, lone and free,
I felt it happiness to be
Unknown, obscure, and like a tree
In woodland peace and privacy.
No, not a friend on earth had I
But my own kin and poesy,
Nor wealth, and yet I felt indeed
As rich as anybody need
To be, for health and hope and joy
Was mine, although a lonely boy,
And what I felt, as now I sing,
Made friends of all and everything
Save man the vulgar and the low;
The polished 'twas not mine to know
Who paid me in my after days
And gave me even more than praise:
'Twas then I found that friends indeed
Were needed when I'd less to need.
The pea, that independent springs,
When in its blossom, trails and clings

To every help that lingers by,
And I, when classed with poesy,
Who stood unbrunt the heaviest shower,
Felt feeble as that very flower
And helpless all; but beauty's smile
Is harvest for the hardest toil,
Whose smiles I little thought to win
With ragged coat and downy chin,
A clownish, silent, aguish boy
Who even felt ashamed of joy,
So dirty, ragged, and so low,
With naught to recommend or show
That I was worthy e'en a smile.
Had I but felt amid my toil
That I in days to come should be
A little light in minstrelsy,
And in the blush of after days
Win beauty's smile and beauty's praise,
My heart with lonely fancy warm
Had even bursted with the charm;
And Mary, thou whose very name
I loved, whose look was even fame,
From those delicious eyes of blue
In smiles and rapture ever new,
Thy timid step, thy fairy form,
Thy face with blushes ever warm,
When praise my schoolboy heart did move,
I saw thy blush and thought it love.
And all ambitious thee to please
My heart was ever ill at ease;
I saw thy beauty grow with days,
And tried song-pictures in thy praise,
And all of fair or beautiful
Were thine akin, nor could I pull
The blossoms that I thought divine
Lest I should injure aught of thine.
So where they grew I let them be,
And though I dare not talk to thee
Of love, to them I talked aloud,

441

And grew ambitious from the crowd
With hopes that I one day should be
Beloved, Mary, e'en by thee.
But I mistook in early day
The world, and so our hopes decay.
Yet that same cheer in after toils
Was poesy, and still she smiles
As sweet as blossoms to the tree,
And hope, love, joy, are poesy.

SHADOWS OF TASTE

TASTE with as many hues doth hearts engage
As leaves and flowers do upon nature's page;
Not mind alone the instinctive mood declares,
But birds and flowers and insects are its heirs.
Taste is their joyous heritage, and they
All choose for joy in a peculiar way.
Birds own it in the various spots they choose:
Some live content in low grass gemmed with dews;
The yellowhammer, like a tasteful guest,
'Neath picturesque green molehills makes a nest,
Where oft the shepherd with unlearned ken
Finds strange eggs scribbled as with ink and pen;
He looks with wonder on the learned marks
And calls them in his memory writing larks;
Birds bolder winged on bushes love to be,
While some choose cradles on the highest tree;
There rocked by winds they feel no moods of fear,
But joy, their birthright, lives for ever near;
And the bold eagle, which man's fear enshrouds,
Would, could he lodge it, house upon the clouds,
While little wrens, mistrusting none that come,
In each low hovel meet a sheltered home.
Flowers in the wisdom of creative choice
Seem blest with feeling and a silent voice;
Some on the barren roads delight to bloom,
And others haunt the melancholy tomb,

Where Death, the blight of all, finds summer's hours
Too kind to miss him with her host of flowers.
Some flourish in the sun and some the shade,
Who almost in his morning smiles would fade;
These in leaf-darkened woods right timid stray
And in its green night smile their lives away;
Others in water live and scarcely seem
To peep their little flowers above the stream,
While water-lilies in their glories come
And spread green isles of beauty round their home.
All share the summer's glory and its good,
And taste of joy in each peculiar mood.
Insects of varied taste in rapture share
The heyday luxuries which she comes to heir;
In wild disorder various routs they run,
In water, earth, still shade, and busy sun;
And in the crowd of green earth's busy claims
They e'en grow nameless mid so many names.
And man, that noble insect, restless man,
Whose thoughts scale heaven in its mighty span,
Pours forth his living soul in many a shade,
And taste runs riot in her every grade.
While the low herd, mere savages subdued,
With naught of feeling or of taste imbued,
Pass over sweetest scenes a careless eye
As blank as midnight in its deepest dye;
From these, and different far in rich degrees,
Minds spring as various as the leaves of trees,
To follow taste and all her sweets explore
And Edens make where deserts spread before.
In poesy's spells some all their raptures find
And revel in the melodies of mind.
There nature o'er the soul her beauty flings
In all the sweets and essences of things.
A face of beauty, in a city crowd
Met, passed, and vanished like a summer cloud,
In poesy's vision lives more lovely fair;
Taste reads o'erjoyed and greets her image there.
Dashes of sunshine and a page of may

Live there a whole life long one summer's day.
A blossom in its witchery of bloom
There gathered dwells in beauty and perfume;
The singing bird, the brook that laughs along,
There ceaseless sing and never thirst for song.
A pleasing image to its page conferred
In living character and breathing word
Becomes a landscape heard and felt and seen,
Sunshine and shade one harmonizing green,
Where meads and brooks and forests basking lie,
Lasting as truth and the eternal sky.
Thus truth to nature, as the true sublime,
Stands a mount Atlas, overpeering time.
Styles may with fashions vary; tawdry, chaste,
Have had their votaries, which each fancies taste:
From Donne's old homely gold, whose broken feet
Jostle the reader's patience from its seat,
To Pope's smooth rhymes that regularly play
In music's stated periods all the way,
That starts and closes, starts again and times
Its tuning gamut true as minster chimes.
From these old fashions stranger metres flow,
Half prose, half verse, that stagger as they go;
One line starts smooth, and then for room perplext
Elbows along and knocks against the next,
And half its neighbour; where a pause marks time,
There the clause ends: what follows is for rhyme.
Yet truth to nature will in all remain
As grass in winter glorifies the plain,
And over fashion's foils rise proud and high
As light's bright fountain in a cloudy sky.
The man of science in discovery's moods
Roams o'er the furze-clad heath, leaf-buried woods,
And by the simple brook in rapture finds
Treasures that wake the laugh of vulgar hinds,
Who see no further in his dark employs
Than village children seeking after toys.
Their clownish hearts and ever-heedless eyes
Find naught in nature they as wealth can prize;

With them self-interest and the thoughts of gain
Are nature's beauties: all beside are vain.
But he, the man of science and of taste,
Sees wealth far richer in the worthless waste,
Where bits of lichen and a sprig of moss
Will all the raptures of his mind engross,
And bright-winged insects on the flowers of May
Shine pearls too wealthy to be cast away.
His joys run riot mid each juicy blade
Of grass where insects revel in the shade,
And minds of different moods will oft condemn
His taste as cruel: such the deeds to them,
While he unconscious gibbets butterflies
And strangles beetles all to make us wise.
Taste's rainbow visions own unnumbered hues,
And every shade its sense of taste pursues.
The heedless mind may laugh, the clown may stare,
They own no soul to look for pleasure there.
Their grosser feelings in a coarser dress
Mock at the wisdom which they can't possess.
Some in recordless rapture love to breathe
Nature's wild Eden, wood and field and heath,
In common blades of grass his thoughts will raise
A word of beauty to admire and praise,
Until his heart o'erflows with swarms of thought
To that great Being who raised life from naught.
The common weed adds graces to his mind
And gleams in beauty few beside may find;
Associations sweet each object breeds
And fine ideas upon fancy feeds.
He loves not flowers because they shed perfumes,
Or butterflies alone for painted plumes,
Or birds for singing, although sweet it be,
But he doth love the wild and meadow lea;
There hath the flower its dwelling-place, and there
The butterfly goes dancing through the air.
He loves each desolate neglected spot
That seems in labour's hurry left forgot,
The warped and punished trunk of stunted oak,

Freed from its bonds but by the thunder stroke,
As crampt by straggling ribs of ivy sere:
There the glad bird makes home for half the year.
But take these several beings from their homes,
Each beauteous thing a withered thought becomes;
Association fades, and, like a dream,
They are but shadows of the things they seem.
Torn from their homes and happiness they stand
The poor dull captives of a foreign land.
Some spruce and delicate ideas feed;
With them disorder is an ugly weed,
And wood and heath a wilderness of thorns
No gardener shears nor fashions nor adorns.
No spots give pleasure so forlorn and bare,
But gravel walks would work rich wonders there.
With such, wild nature's beauty's run to waste
And art's strong impulse mars the truth of taste.
Such are the various moods that taste displays,
Surrounding wisdom in concentring rays,
Where threads of light from one bright focus run
As day's proud halo circles round the sun.

POESY

Oh! I have been thy lover long,
    Soul-soothing Poesy;
If 'twas not thou inspired the song,
    I still owe much to thee:
And still I feel the cheering balm
    Thy heavenly smiles supply,
That keeps my struggling bosom calm
    When life's rude storms are high.

Oh! in that sweet romance of life
    I loved thee, when a boy,
And ever felt thy gentle strife
    Awake each little joy:

To thee was urged each nameless song,
  Soul-soothing Poesy;
And as my hopes waxed warm and strong,
  My love was more for thee.

'Twas thou and Nature bound, and smiled,
  Rude garlands round my brow—
Those dreams that pleased me when a child,
  Those hopes that warm me now.
Each year with brighter blooms returned,
  Gay visions danced along,
And, at the sight, my bosom burned,
  And kindled into song.

Springs came not, as they yearly come
  To low and vulgar eyes,
With here and there a flower in bloom,
  Green trees, and brighter skies:
Thy fancies flushed my boyish sight,
  And gilt its earliest hours;
And Spring came wrapt in beauty's light,
  An angel dropping flowers.

Oh! I have been thy lover long,
  Soul-soothing Poesy,
And sung to thee each simple song,
  With witching ecstasy,
Of flowers, and things that claimed from thee
  Of life an equal share,
And whispered soft their tales to me
  Of pleasure or of care.

With thee, life's errand all perform,
  And feel its joy and pain;
Flowers shrink, like me, from blighting storm,
  And hope for suns again:
The bladed grass, the flower, the leaf,
  Companions seem to be,
That tell their tales of joy and grief,
  And think and feel with me.

A spirit speaks in every wind,
   And gives the storm its wings;
With thee all nature owns a mind,
   And stones are living things;
The simplest weed the Summer gives
   Smiles on her as a mother,
And, through the little day it lives,
   Owns sister, friend, and brother.

O Poesy, thou heavenly flower,
   Though mine a weed may be,
Life feels a sympathizing power,
   And wakes inspired with thee;
Thy glowing soul's enraptured dreams
   To all a beauty give,
While thy impassioned warmth esteems
   The meanest things that live.

Objects of water, earth, or air,
   Are pleasing to thy sight;
All live thy sunny smiles to share,
   Increasing thy delight;
All Nature in thy presence lives
   With new creative claims,
And life to all thy fancy gives
   That were but shades and names.

Though cheering praise and cold disdain
   My humble songs have met,
To visit thee I can't refrain,
   Or cease to know thee yet;
Though simple weeds are all I bring,
   Soul-soothing Poesy,
They share the sunny smiles of Spring,
   Nor are they scorn'd by thee.

TO THE RURAL MUSE

Muse of the fields, oft have I said farewell
To thee, my boon companion, loved so long,
And hung thy sweet harp in the bushy dell,
For abler hands to wake an abler song.
Much did I fear my homage did thee wrong:
Yet, loath to leave, as oft I turned again;
And to its wires mine idle hands would cling,
Torturing it into song.   It may be vain;
Yet still I try, ere fancy droops her wing,
And hopeless silence comes to numb its every string.

Muse of the pasture brooks, on thy calm sea
Of poesy I've sailed; and though the will
To speed were greater than my prowess be,
I've ventured with much fear of usage ill,
Yet more of joy.   Though timid be my skill,
As not to dare the depths of mightier streams,
Yet rocks abide in shallow ways, and I
Have much of fear to mingle with my dreams.
Yet, lovely muse, I still believe thee by,
And think I see thee smile, and so forget I sigh.

Muse of the cottage hearth, oft did I tell
My hopes to thee, nor feared to plead in vain;
But felt around my heart thy witching spell,
That bade me as thy worshipper remain:
I did so, and still worship.   Oh! again
Smile on my offerings, and so keep them green;
Bedeck my fancies like the clouds of even,
Mingling all hues which thou from heaven dost glean.
To me a portion of thy power be given,
If theme so mean as mine may merit aught of heaven.

For thee in youth I culled the simple flower,
That on thy bosom gained a sweeter hue,
And took thy hand along life's sunny hour,
Meeting the sweetest joys that ever grew;

More friends were needless, and my foes were few.
Though freedom then be deemed as rudeness now,
And what once won thy praise now meet disdain,
Yet the last wreath I braided for thy brow
Thy smiles did so commend, it made me vain
To weave another one and hope for praise again.

With thee the spirit of departed years
Wakes that sweet voice which time hath rendered dumb
And freshens—like to spring—loves, hopes and fears
That in my bosom found an early home,
Wooing the heart to ecstasy.   I come
To thee, when sick of care, of joy bereft,
Seeking the pleasures that are found in bloom.
O happy hopes, that time hath only left
Around the haunts where thou didst erst sojourn!
Then smile, sweet cherubim, and welcome my return.

With thee the raptures of life's early day
Appear, and all that pleased me when a boy.
Though pains and cares have torn the best away,
And winters creep between us to destroy,
Do thou commend, the recompense is joy:
The tempest of the heart shall soon be calm.
Though sterner truth against my dreams rebel,
Hope feels success; and all my spirits warm
To strike with happier mood thy simple shell
And seize thy mantle's hem—Oh! say not fare-thee-well.

Still, sweet enchantress, youth's strong feelings move,
That from thy presence their existence took:
The innocent idolatry and love,
Paying thee worship in each secret nook,
That fancied friends in tree, and flower, and brook,
Shaped clouds to angels and beheld them smile,
And heard commending tongues in every wind.
Life's grosser fancies did these dreams defile,
Yet not entirely root them from the mind;
I think I hear them still, and often look behind.

Ay, I have heard thee in the summer wind,
As if commending what I sung to thee;
Ay, I have seen thee on a cloud reclined,
Kindling my fancies into poesy;
I saw thee smile, and took the praise to me.
In beauties, past all beauty, thou wert drest;
I thought the very clouds around thee knelt:
I saw the sun to linger in the west,
Paying thee worship; and as eve did melt
In dews, they seemed thy tears for sorrows I had felt.

Sweeter than flowers on beauty's bosom hung,
Sweeter than dreams of happiness above,
Sweeter than themes by lips of beauty sung,
Are the young fancies of a poet's love,
When round his thoughts thy trancing visions move.
In floating melody no notes may sound,
The world is all forgot and past his care,
While on thy harp thy fingers lightly bound,
As winning him its melody to share;
And heaven itself, with him, where is it then but there?

E'en now my heart leaps out from grief, and all
The gloom thrown round by care's o'ershading wing;
E'en now those sunny visions to recall,
Like to a bird I quit dull earth and sing:
Life's tempests swoon to calms on every string.
Ah! sweet enchantress, if I do but dream,
If earthly visions have been only mine,
My weakness in thy service woos esteem,
And proves my truth as almost worthy thine:
Surely true worship makes the meanest theme divine.

And still, warm courage, calming many a fear,
Heartens my hand once more thy harp to try,
To join the anthem of the minstrel year:
For summer's music in thy praise is high;
The very winds about thy mantle sigh
Love-melodies; thy minstrel bards to be,

Insects and birds, exerting all their skill,
Float in continued song for mastery;
While in thy haunts loud leaps the little rill,
To kiss thy mantle's hem; and how can I be still?

There still I see thee fold thy mantle grey,
To trace the dewy lawn at morn and night;
And there I see thee, in the sunny day,
Withdraw thy veil and shine confest in light;
Burning my fancies with a wild delight,
To win a portion of thy blushing fame.
Though haughty fancy treat thy power as small,
And fashion thy simplicity disclaim,
Should but a corner of thy mantle fall
O'er him who woos thy love, 'tis recompense for all.[1]

Not with the mighty to thy shrine I come,
In anxious sighs or self-applauding mirth,
On Mount Parnassus as thine heir to roam:
I dare not credit that immortal birth;
But mingling with the lesser ones on earth,
Like as the little lark from off its nest
Beside the mossy hill awakes in glee
To seek the morning's throne, a merry guest,
So do I seek thy shrine, if that may be,
To win by new attempts another smile from thee.

If without thee 'neath storms and clouds and wind,
I've roamed the wood and field and meadow lea,
And found no flowers but what the vulgar find,
Nor met one breath of living poesy,
Among such charms where inspirations be,
The fault is mine—and I must bear the lot

---

[1] In another MS. the preceding five lines read:

> That wasteth life away to win a name,
> Of aught else reckless, tho' the chance be small;
> And if so be that death's the price of fame,
> Should but a portion of thy prize befall
> To him who dies to live, 'tis recompense for all.

Of missing praise to merit thy disdain.
To feel each idle plea, though urged, forgot,
I can but sigh—though foolish to complain—
O'er hopes so fair begun, to find them end so vain.

Then will it prove presumption thus to dare
To add fresh failings to each faulty song,
Urging thy blessings on an idle prayer,
To sanction silly themes: it will be wrong
For one so lowly to be heard so long.
Yet, sweet enchantress, yet a little while
Forgo impatience and from frowns refrain;
The strong are ne'er debarred thy cheering smile,
Why should the weak, who need them most, complain
Alone, in solitude, soliciting in vain?

But if my efforts on thy harp prove true,
Which bashful youth 'at first so feared to try;
If aught of nature be in sounds I drew
—From hope's young dreams and doubt's uncertainty,
To these late offerings, not without their sigh—
Then on thine altar shall these themes be laid,
And past the deeds of graven brass remain,
Filling a space in time that shall not fade;
And if it be not so—avert disdain,
Till dust shall feel no sting, nor know it toiled in vain.

The following four stanzas are taken from rough drafts not used in the final version.

Is poesy dwelling in a nice-culled sound,
Or soft smooth words that trifle on the ear
Unmeaning music? Is it to be found
In rhymes run mad, that paint to startled fear
Monsters that are not and that never were?
Is it in declamations frothing high,
Worked like machinery to its mad career?
No, poetry lives in its simplicity,
And speaks from its own heart, to which all hearts reply.

Fame's hopes with me are faint to look upon;
The cloud of doubt with gloom her skies defiles;
Though fluttering pulse and burning thrills urge on,
And hope at intervals the way beguiles,
The flowers she plucks me wear precarious smiles.
Yet do I follow with unwearied eyes
The shadowy recompense for real toils:
Ah, would the heart cease aching and be wise,
And think life vainly spent, staked for a doubtful prize.

Thy smiles are dear to him that needs thy smiles;
He feels their raptures in no less degree
Than bolder votaries, whose ambition toils
Up the steep road of immortality;
And while their souls expand and rise with thee,
On humbler wing, with unpresuming powers,
He shares a portion of thy ecstasy,
Hiding among thy valleys, brooks, and bowers,
Cheered by thy sunny smiles with other lowly flowers.

I've heard of Parnass Hill, Castalia's stream,
And in my dreams have worshipped beauty long;
I've heard, alas, but never could I dream
That aught of birthright did to me belong
In that rich paradise of sacred song.
Yet have I loved and worshipped, and the spring
Of hope—though not an eagle in the sun—
Did like a young bird to thy kindness cling;
Friend of my visions, though my race be run,
I'll feel the triumph still to know thy praises won.

VILLAGE TALES

THE CROSS ROADS *or* THE HAYMAKER'S STORY

Stopt by the storm, that long in sullen black
From the south-west stain'd its encroaching track,
Haymakers, hustling from the rain to hide,
Sought the grey willows by the pasture-side;
And there, while big drops bow the grassy stems,
And bleb the withering hay with pearly gems,
Dimple the brook, and patter in the leaves,
The song or tale the crampt restraint relieves.
And while the old dames gossip at their ease,
And pinch the snuff-box empty by degrees,
The young ones join in love's delightful themes,
Truths told by gipsies, and expounded dreams;
And mutter things kept secrets from the rest,
As sweethearts' names, and whom they love the best;
And dazzling ribbons they delight to show,
The last new favours of some wheedling beau,
Who with such treachery tries their hearts to move,
And, like the highest, bribes the maidens' love.
The old dames, jealous of their whisper'd praise,
Throw in their hints of man's deluding ways;
And one, to give her counsels more effect,
And by example illustrate the fact
Of innocence o'ercome by flattering man,
Thrice tapp'd her box, and pinch'd, and thus began.

'Now, wenches, listen, and let lovers lie,
Ye'll hear a story ye may profit by;
I'm your age treble, with some oddments to't,
And right from wrong can tell, if ye'll but do't:
Ye need not giggle underneath your hat,
Mine's no joke-matter, let me tell you that;
So keep ye quiet till my story's told,
And don't despise your betters 'cause they're old.

'That grave ye've heard of, where the four roads meet,
Where walks the spirit in a winding-sheet,

Oft seen at night, by strangers passing late,
And tarrying neighbours that at market wait,
Stalking along as white as driven snow,
And long as one's shadow when the sun is low;
The girl that's buried there I knew her well,
And her whole history, if ye'll hark, can tell.
Her name was Jane, and neighbours' children we,
And old companions once, as ye may be;
And like to you, on Sundays often stroll'd
To gipsies' camps to have our fortunes told;
And oft, God rest her, in the fortune-book
Which we at hay-time in our pockets took,
Our pins at blindfold on the wheel we stuck,
When hers would always prick the worst of luck;
For try, poor thing, as often as she might,
Her point would always on the blank alight;
Which plainly shows the fortune one's to have,
As such-like go unwedded to the grave:
And so it proved.   The next succeeding May,
We both to service went from sports and play,
Though in the village still, as friends and kin
Thought neighbours' service better to begin.
So out we went.   Jane's place was reckon'd good,
Though she 'bout life but little understood,
And had a master wild as wild can be,
And far unfit for such a child as she;
And soon the whisper went about the town,
That Jane's good looks procured her many a gown
From him, whose promise was to every one,
But whose intention was to wive with none.
'Twas naught to wonder, though begun by guess;
For Jane was lovely in her Sunday dress,
And all expected such a rosy face
Would be her ruin—as was just the case.
The while the change was easily perceived,
Some months went by, ere I the tales believed;
For there are people nowadays, God knows,
Will sooner hatch up lies than mend their clothes;
And when with such-like tattle they begin,

Don't mind whose character they spoil, a pin:
But passing neighbours often mark'd them smile,
And watch'd him take her milkpail o'er a stile;
And many a time, as wandering closer by,
From Jenny's bosom met a heavy sigh;
And often mark'd her, as discoursing deep,
When doubts might rise to give just cause to weep,
Smothering their notice, by a wish'd disguise
To slive her apron corner to her eyes.
Such signs were mournful and alarming things,
And far more weighty than conjecture brings,
Though foes made double what they heard of all,
Swore lies as proofs, and prophesied her fall.
Poor thoughtless wench! it seems but Sunday past
Since we went out together for the last,
And plain enough indeed it was to find
She'd something more than common on her mind;
For she was always fond and full of chat,
In passing harmless jokes 'bout beaus and that,
But nothing then was scarcely talk'd about,
And what there was, I even forced it out.
A gloomy wanness spoil'd her rosy cheek,
And doubts hung there it was not mine to seek;
She ne'er so much as mention'd things to come,
But sigh'd o'er pleasures ere she left her home;
And now and then a mournful smile would raise
At freaks repeated of our younger days,
Which I brought up, while passing spots of ground
Where we, when children, "hurly-burly'd" round,
Or "blind-man-buff'd" some morts of hours away—
Two games, poor thing, Jane dearly loved to play.
She smiled at these, but shook her head and sigh'd
Whene'er she thought my look was turn'd aside;
Nor turn'd she round, as was her former way,
To praise the thorn, white over then with may;
Nor stoopèd once, tho' thousands round her grew,
To pull a cowslip as she used to do:
For Jane in flowers delighted from a child—
I like the garden, but she loved the wild,

And oft on Sundays young men's gifts declined,
Posies from gardens of the sweetest kind,
And eager scrambled the dog-rose to get,
And woodbine-flowers at every bush she met.
The cowslip blossom, with its ruddy streak,
Would tempt her furlongs from the path to seek;
And gay long purple, with its tufty spike,
She'd wade o'er shoes to reach it in the dyke;
And oft, while scratching through the briery woods
For tempting cuckoo-flowers and violet buds,
Poor Jane, I've known her crying sneak to town,
Fearing her mother when she'd torn her gown.
Ah, these were days her conscience view'd with pain,
Which all are loath to lose, as well as Jane.
And what I took more odd than all the rest
Was, that same night she ne'er a wish exprest
To see the gipsies, so beloved before,
That lay a stone's-throw from us on the moor:
I hinted it; she just replied again—
She once believed them, but had doubts since then.
And when we sought our cows, I call'd, "Come mull!"
But she stood silent, for her heart was full.
She loved dumb things; and ere she had begun
To milk, caress'd them more than e'er she'd done;
But though her tears stood watering in her eye,
I little took it as her last good-bye;
For she was tender, and I've often known
Her mourn when beetles have been trampled on:
So I ne'er dream'd from this what soon befell,
Till the next morning rang her passing-bell.
My story's long, but time's in plenty yet,
Since the black clouds betoken naught but wet;
And I'll e'en snatch a minute's breath or two,
And take another pinch, to help me through.

'So, as I said, next morn I heard the bell,
And passing neighbours cross'd the street, to tell
That my poor partner Jenny had been found
In the old flag-pool, on the pasture, drown'd.

God knows my heart! I twitter'd like a leaf,
And found too late the cause of Sunday's grief;
For every tongue was loosed to gabble o'er
The slanderous things that secret pass'd before:
With truth or lies they need not then be strict,
The one they rail'd at could not contradict.
'Twas now no secret of her being beguiled,
For every mouth knew Jenny died with child;
And though more cautious with a living name,
Each more than guess'd her master bore the blame.
That very morning—it affects me still—
Ye know the foot-path sidles down the hill—
Ignorant as babe unborn I pass'd the pond
To milk as usual in our close beyond,
And cows were drinking at the water's edge,
And horses browsed among the flags and sedge,
And gnats and midges danced the water o'er,
Just as I've mark'd them scores of times before,
And birds sat singing as in mornings gone,
While I as unconcern'd went soodling on,
But little dreaming, as the wakening wind
Flapp'd the broad ash-leaves o'er the pond reclined,
And o'er the water crink'd the curdled wave,
That Jane was sleeping in her watery grave.
The neatherd boy that used to tend the cows,
While getting whip-sticks from the dangling boughs
Of osiers drooping by the water-side,
Her bonnet floating on the top espied;
He knew it well, and hasten'd fearful down
To take the terror of his fears to town—
A melancholy story, far too true;
And soon the village to the pasture flew,
Where, from the deepest hole the pond about,
They dragg'd poor Jenny's lifeless body out,
And took her home, where scarce an hour gone by
She had been living like to you and I.
I went with more, and kiss'd her for the last,
And thought with tears on pleasures that were past;
And, the last kindness left me then to do,

I went, at milking, where the blossoms grew,
And handfuls got of rose and lambtoe sweet,
And put them with her in her winding-sheet.
A wilful murder, jury made the crime;
Nor parson 'low'd to pray, nor bell to chime;
On the cross roads, far from her friends and kin,
The usual law for their ungodly sin
Who violent hands upon themselves have laid,
Poor Jane's last bed unchristian-like was made;
And there, like all whose last thoughts turn to heaven,
She sleeps, and doubtless hoped to be forgiven.
But, though I say't, for maids thus wheedled in
I think the wicked men deserve the sin;
And sure enough we all at last shall see
The treachery punish'd as it ought to be.
For ere his wickedness pretended love,
Jane, I'll be bound, was spotless as the dove,
And's good a servant, still old folks allow,
As ever scour'd a pail or milk'd a cow;
And ere he led her into ruin's way,
As gay and buxom as a summer's day;
The birds that ranted in the hedgerow boughs,
As night and morning we have sought our cows,
With yokes and buckets as she bounced along,
Were often deaf'd to silence with her song.
But now she's gone: girls, shun deceitful men,
The worst of stumbles ye can fall agen;
Be deaf to them, and then, as 'twere, ye'll see
Your pleasures safe as under lock and key.
Throw not my words away, as many do;
They're gold in value, though they're cheap to you.
And hussies hearken, and be warn'd from this,
If ye love mothers, never do amiss:
Jane might love hers, but she forsook the plan
To make her happy, when she thought of man.
Poor tottering dame, it was too plainly known
Her daughter's dying hasten'd on her own,
For from the day the tidings reach'd her door
She took to bed and lookèd up no more,

And, ere again another year came round,
She, well as Jane, was laid within the ground;
And all were grieved poor Goody's end to see:
No better neighbour enter'd house than she,
A harmless soul, with no abusive tongue,
Trig as new pins, and tight's the day was long;
And go the week about, nine times in ten
Ye'd find her house as cleanly as hersen.
But, Lord protect us! time such change does bring,
We cannot dream what o'er our heads may hing;
The very house she lived in, stick and stone,
Since Goody died, has tumbled down and gone:
And where the marjoram once, and sage, and rue,
And balm, and mint, with curl'd-leaf parsley grew,
And double marygolds, and silver thyme,
And pumpkins 'neath the window used to climb;
And where I often when a child for hours
Tried through the pales to get the tempting flowers,
As lady's laces, everlasting peas,
True-love-lies-bleeding, with the hearts-at-ease,
And golden rods, and tansy running high
That o'er the pale-tops smiled on passers-by—
Flowers in my time that every one would praise,
Tho' thrown like weeds from gardens nowadays—
Where these all grew, now henbane stinks and spreads,
And docks and thistles shake their seedy heads,
And yearly keep with nettles smothering o'er—
The house, the dame, the garden known no more:
While, neighbouring nigh, one lonely elder-tree
Is all that's left of what had used to be,
Marking the place, and bringing up with tears
The recollections of one's younger years.
And now I've done, ye're each at once as free
To take your trundle as ye used to be;
To take right ways, as Jenny should have ta'en,
Or headlong run, and be a second Jane;
For by one thoughtless girl that's acted ill
A thousand may be guided if they will:
As oft 'mong folks to labour bustling on,

461

We mark the foremost kick against a stone,
Or stumble o'er a stile he meant to climb,
While hind ones see and shun the fall in time.
But ye, I will be bound, like far the best
Love's tickling nick-nacks and the laughing jest,
And ten times sooner than be warn'd by me,
Would each be sitting on some fellow's knee,
Sooner believe the lies wild chaps will tell
Than old dames' cautions who would wish ye well:
So have your wills.'—She pinch'd her box again,
And ceased her tale, and listen'd to the rain,
Which still as usual patter'd fast around,
And bow'd the bent-head loaded to the ground;
While larks, their naked nest by force forsook,
Pruned their wet wings in bushes by the brook.
The maids, impatient now old Goody ceased,
As restless children from the school released,
Right gladly proving, what she'd just foretold,
That young ones' stories were preferr'd to old,
Turn to the whisperings of their former joy,
That oft deceive, but very rarely cloy.

THE SORROWS OF LOVE

'Good shepherd, tell this youth what 'tis to love.'
'It is to be all made of sighs and tears;
        All made of faith and service;
    All made of passion, and all made of wishes;
    All humbleness—all patience and impatience.'
                                SHAKESPEARE.

To sober with sad truths the laughing mirth
Of rosy daughters round the cottage hearth,
And pass the winter's lengthen'd eve away,
A mother told the tale of Sally Grey.
'How time,' she said, 'and pleasure vanish by!'
Then stopp'd to wipe the tear-drops from her eye;
'Time gains upon us distance unawares,
Stealing our joys and changing them to cares:

462

'Tis nine-and-thirty years ago';—the date
To prove, she look'd above her where she sat,
And pull'd the Bible down—that certain guide
When boys and girls were born, and old friends died—
That lay with penny stories rustling near,
And almanacks preserved for many a year;
Stopping her story till she found the place,
Pulling her glasses from their leathern case—
'Twas right: and from her lap, in sadden'd vein,
She took her knitting and went on again.
'Poor thing! she died, heart-broken and distress'd,
Through love.   The doctors, who should know the best,
Said 'twas decline that wasted life away:
But truth is truth; and be it as it may,
She ne'er did aught that malice could reprove;
Her only failing was the fault of love.
'Tis hard enough when Innocence is hurl'd
On the cold bosom of a heartless world;
When Mockery and stony-hearted Pride
Reveal the failings Pity strives to hide,
And with sad cruel taunt and bitter jest
Lay thorns to pillow Trouble's broken rest;
But when a poor young thing like Sally dies
For love, and only love—where are the eyes
Can look in Memory's face without a tear?
Ev'n Scorn no longer turns aside to sneer,
But silent stands; while Pity shakes her head,
And thinks tears just herself declines to shed.
'Twas by another's failings that she fell,
Whose wanton follies were her passing bell:
A clown, as wild as young colts free from plough,
Who saw a prison in a marriage-vow,
Had won her heart, and kept it in his power,
As the rude bindweed clasps the tender flower—
A clown, as shifting as the summer wind,
To whom her heart and love were all resign'd.
Poor girl! I felt in trouble for her end—
A next-door neighbour and an early friend:
Her father kept a cottage next to ours;

463

He was a gardener, and he dealt in flowers,
And Sally's beau would buy his flowers the while
With double prices—money and a smile,
And many a whisper of love's cheating powers,
Calling her fairest of her father's flowers.
Such ways, like spring hopes, youngling blood did move,
And by and by got ripen'd into love.
He then the wishes of his mind express'd,
And was received—a lover, welcome guest!
Go where we would, him we were sure to meet,
Or on the pasture or about the street;
And oft on summer eves or sabbath-days
He'd join our walks and surfeit her with praise;
Nay, she could scarcely to the church repair,
But he held out his arm to lead her there.
Then to her father's house he often went,
Who welcome gave, and deem'd it kindly meant,
And crackt of goods and savings o'er his ale—
Things he had earnèd by his spade and flail;
And often show'd with fatherly regard
The pigs and poultry in his little yard;
How this and that, as matters closer led,
Were marriage-portions when his daughters wed.

   'The children then, her little sisters three,
Began to know him, and would climb his knee
To whisper little stories in his ear;
They call'd him brother, which he smiled to hear,
And, to reward them for each pretty way,
He promised bride-cake on the wedding-day;
And with love's keepsakes brought from fair or wake,
He ne'er forgot the children's toys or cake.
I mark'd these things, for I was often by,
And even thought the wedding-day was nigh:
For, as a neighbour, oft by night and day
I took my work in, to pass time away;
And oft without it on a winter's eve
I've stole away, nor ask'd a mother's leave,
To play at cards, and talk of dress beside—

For wenches' heads are ever after pride.
No holiday e'er came but he was there:
For him the father left his corner-chair;
Her mother bless'd them as she touch'd the glass,
And wish'd him luck, and nodded to the lass;
And all beheld him, when the freak begun,
In kindred prospect as a promised son.

'Thus for a while his fawning love did burn,
But soon doubts rose at every touch and turn:
If she but nodded at a fair or wake
To youths she knew, it made his bosom ache;
Or said "Good morning!" to a passer-by,
She always had a rival in her eye.
Then jealousy would seemingly complain,
And urge to vows ere all was right again:
But when he found her heart indeed his own,
He quickly made his foolish follies known;
And, like a young bird children nurse in play,
He teased and plagued her till she pined away.
He still loved on, but thought it mighty fun
To prove her fondness when the maid was won.
From every night to once a week they met,
And then excuses made it longer yet:
Sometimes he could not stay as heretofore,
But call'd her out to whisper at the door;
And turn'd away and smiled, self-satisfied
To see the tear-drops which she strove to hide.
He danced with other girls, his pride to please,
And seem'd to glory in the chance to tease;
Then look'd around him with a leering eye,
And drank their healths while she was sitting by:
Her face burnt red as any cloak the while,
And tears would startle while she strove to smile.
And oft when nigh a soldier he has sat,
He'd laugh, and put the colours on his hat;
But he too great a coward was to go,
For none but cowards do use women so:
'Twas only to perplex the heart he'd won,

For no one cause but insolence and fun.
Thus did he wound her, though she loved him still,
And patiently put up with every ill,
Nursing the venom of that speckled snake
About her heart, till it was like to break.
Yet, when I caution'd her of love's distress,
And bade her notice the wild fellow less,
Saying she show'd her love too much by half,
"Mary, you jest!" she said, and made a laugh.
Frequent on sabbath-days, in pleasant weather,
We went to walk, and talk of love together;
And often sought a hut beside the wood,
That from the town a gossip's minute stood;
'Twas called the herdsman's hut, for when her spouse
Walked without sticks he kept the village cows,
Ere vile enclosure took away the moor,
And farmers built a workhouse for the poor.[1]
Here an old woman, for some small rewards,
Would tell our fortunes both by cups and cards.
Some call'd her witch, and whisper'd all they dare
Of nightly things that had been noticed there;
Witches of every shape, that used to meet
To count the stars, or mutter'd charms repeat.
Woodmen, in winter, as they pass'd the road,
Have vow'd they've seen some crawling like a toad;
And some like owlets veering overhead,
Shrieking enough to fright the very dead.
Yet she to us appear'd like other folks,
A droll old woman, full of tales and jokes;
And if the old dame's tales were darkly meant,
I ne'er perceived it, though I often went.
Deal as she might with Satan's evil powers,
She read her Bible, and was fond of flowers.
She went to church as other people may,
And knelt and pray'd—though witches cannot pray:
She had her ague-charms, and old receipts
For wounds and bruises labour often meets;
And gather'd wild-flowers in her summer toils,

[1] Preceding four lines added from MS.

To make an ointment that was famed for miles;
And many a one hath own'd her lowly skill,
Who dared not run a doctor's longer bill.
But as to ill-got knowledge of the sky,
She was as innocent as you or I.
She might, no doubt, with pointed finger show
The Shepherd's Lamp, which even children know;
And doubtless loved, when journeying from the town,
To see it rising soon as day was down.
The Tailor's Yard-band, which hangs streaming high,
And Dick's Night-wagon driving through the sky,
And Butcher's Cleaver, or the Seven Stars,
With shooting North-lights, tokening bloody wars;
She might know these, which, if 'tis sin to know,
Then everybody is a witch below.
Well, those are good that never stoop to wrong,
And bless'd are they that 'scape an evil tongue.
Thus to young hopes she would her fortunes tell,
But Sally quickly knew her own too well!
Her tears and sighs did all too fruitless prove,
To keep the shepherd to his vows of love:
He came to vex her oft, and would not stay,
But shut the door again and laugh'd away.
And she was spotless and a maiden still,
Conscience ne'er prickt him that the deed was ill;
And he made promises, to give her pain,
Just for the sake of breaking them again.
On winter's nights for hours I've known her stand,
Listening, with door half open in her hand;
Till, what with colds and an uneasy mind,
Her beauty faded, and her health declined:
The rose, that lovers call so, left her face,
And the pale sickly lily took its place.
Thus she went on, poor melancholy thing!
Just like a bud that's injured in the spring,
That may live on to see the coming day—
A feeble blossom leaning on decay,
As little linnets pine in summer joys
For absent loves a shooting clown destroys.

467

She sorrow'd on, and worse and worse she grew,
And strength declined its labour to pursue:
Yet, wishing still her sorrows to conceal,
She turn'd with feeble hand her spinning-wheel;
Till, weak and weary, when no one was by
She'd lean her backward in her chair to cry.

'At length her parents, though with added fears,
Saw through her heart-throbs and her secret tears;
And when they found the only crime was love,
They joked at times, and would at times reprove,
Saying, if that were all the world possess'd
For causing troubles, few would be distress'd.
But all was vain! she put her best looks on
When they were there, and grieved when they were
    gone;
Till toil and fretting brought her down so low,
That she was forced her labour to forgo.
Her friends, no longer with false hopes beguiled,
Fear'd for the danger of their troubled child:
Her children-sisters oft hung round her chair,
In which she lean'd in silence and despair;
Her troubled looks they could not understand,
But tried to raise her head from off her hand,
And ask'd the reason why she sat so still,
Or if aught wrong'd her that had made her ill?
She kiss'd their prattling lips with struggling sighs,
While anguish rush'd for freedom to her eyes;
Then would she turn away from friends and kin,
To hide the trouble that her heart was in.
They eked her sorrow with her lover's name,
Asking the reason why he never came;
Bringing up childish memories to her cost—
Things they had miss'd, and pleasures she had lost.
Thus they would urge, ending with scornful brow,
"A naughty man! he brings us nothing now."
She stopp'd their mouths with kisses and with sighs,
And turn'd her face again to hide her eyes.
Her mother talk'd of patience all in vain,

And read Job's troubles o'er and o'er again;
Then turn'd to love, and read the book of Ruth,
Making excuses for the faults of youth;
Saying how she in life's young joys was cross'd,
And both a lover and a husband lost,
Yet still hoped on, and overlook'd the past,
And loved her mother, and was bless'd at last.
"And if," said she, "you trust in God and pray,
You may be happy in the end as they."
Then she herself would often try to read
The Bible's comforts in the hour of need;
But soon she fail'd its cheering truths to look,
And grew so weak she scarce could lift the book.
Life to a spider's web was worn and spun,
And e'en her hands, if lifted to the sun,
Were both so wasted that, to fancy's view,
The light would almost seem to glimmer through.
Her lover, by and by, his folly mourn'd;
His conscience prick'd him, or his love return'd:
He begg'd and pray'd, and wish'd again to be
Once more admitted to her company.
The parents thought 'twould save their sinking child,
For trouble's hopes are quickly reconciled,
So let him come.   I sat beside her bed:
He asked her how she was, and hung his head:
The tears burst from her eyes; she could not speak.
Upon her hand her sorrow-wasted cheek
She lean'd; and, when he did his sins recall,
She kiss'd him fondly, and forgave him all,
Then smiled, and bowed her faded face to weep,
And, wearied out, sunk down like one asleep;
Then rose again like one awoke from pain,
And gazed on him, and me—and wept again;
Then on her bosom laid her wasted hand,
Sighing a language brutes might understand!

'Yet hopes were fed, though but the mask of pain,
And she recovered, and got out again.
She seem'd so well, they e'en began to name

The wedding-day. 'Twas set, but ere it came,
The gossips, when they met, would still agree
To shake their heads and say 'twould never be!
Muttering o'er doubts they would not urge aloud,
Saying her bride-dress would turn out a shroud.
God knows, they but too truly prophesied;
For, ere it came, she sickened, sunk, and died.
Upon that very morn that was to see
The wedding sunshine and festivity,
Death did so gently his cold fingers lay
Upon her bosom, that she swoon'd away
Without a groan; and, but for us that wept
About her bed, you might have thought she slept.
For marriage-greetings parents' sorrows fell,
And marriage-peals changed to a passing bell!
Her young sun set 'neath sorrow's gloomy cloud:
Wed to the grave, her bride-sheets were a shroud.
And I, instead of joining in the throng
Of merry faces, and a wedding song,
Instead of seeing her a bride become,
I bore the pall up to her last long home,
And heard the old clerk's melancholy stave,
Who sang the psalm bareheaded by her grave.

'Thus died poor Sally on her wedding-day,
An April bud that could not see the May.
I often stand to gaze upon the stone,
Whene'er I journey to the church alone,
Where gold-winged cherubs hold a flowery wreath
Over a prayer-book open underneath;
Upon whose leaves was writ at her request,
In golden letters,—"Here the weary rest."
Last sabbath-day but one, I loiter'd there
Before the bells had chimed the hour of prayer:
Stopping, as pity seemly did demand,
I wrapp'd my apron corner round my hand,
And pull'd the nettles that had overgrown
The verse, and rambled half-way up the stone;
And then at eve, when ye were at the door,

Whispering with sweethearts your love-secrets o'er,
I took my glasses to amuse myself,
And reach'd the Bible down from off the shelf
To read the text, and look the psalms among,
To find the one that at her grave was sung.
The place had long been doubled down before,
And much I wish that ye would read it o'er;
Your father read it to me many a time
When ye were young, and on our laps would climb.
Nay, keep your work—'tis not worth while to leave,
I'll sit and hear it on to-morrow eve;
For even if the night would time allow,
My heart's too sad—I cannot bear it now.
I've talk'd till I have almost tired my tongue;
Folks say old women's tales are always long;
So here I'll end; and, like it as you may,
I wish you better luck than Sally Grey.'

She ceased her tale, and snuff'd the candle wick,
Lifting it up from burning in the stick,
Then laid her knitting down, and shook her head,
And stoop'd to stir the fire and talk of bed.

THE RIVALS

BENEATH a meadow bridge, whose arch was dry,
Some swains sought shelter till a shower was by.
Upon its smooth half-circling roof of stone
Rude figured scrawls in different colours shone,
Spread hands and birds, and self-imagined flowers,
Pastimes of boys imprison'd there by showers;
Some made with ruddle, which the shepherd swain
Employs, that he may know his sheep again,
Others with fire-sticks, chance would haply find
About the spot, by gipsies left behind;
And many a deeply cut two-letter name,

471

Where knives were spoilt to win an inch of fame,
Which linger on for years about the spot,
Brands of oblivion, living yet forgot.

Here the swains shelter'd till the storm was o'er,
Sitting on stones roll'd in for seats before:
Some spent the hour in leisure's pleasant toil,
Making their apple-scoops of bone the while;
One crimpt a knitting-sheath upon his knees,
To please a maiden whom he wish'd to please;
An older swain did his wet hours employ
In making whistles for an anxious boy,
Who sat in eager watchings by his side,
Waiting their finish with exulting pride;
While two young swains in love's discoursings fell,
Lapping up love-knot plaits and many a spell
With broad green reed-blades, where the shelter'd midge
Danced in their shadows by the mossy bridge.
The swallows, darting through the arch at play,
Heard the rude noise, and popt another way.

RICHARD

My love forgets me never; every spell
Links as I lap it, and betokens well.
When I was young, and went a-weeding wheat,
We used to make them on our dinner seat:
We laid two blades across and lapt them round,
Thinking of those we loved; and if we found
Them linked together when unlapt again,
Our loves were true; if not, the wish was vain:
I've heard old women, who first told it me,
Vow that a truer token could not be.

SIMON

Three times I've lapt mine up, and still 'tis out;
A fatal number, had I cause to doubt;
But Mary Fieldflower still is fond and free,
And shows no token to dishearten me.

I care not what this foolish trifling tells,
For I can bring up better proofs than spells.

Produce them, Simon; for if she be true
To lover's vows, she has no room for two.
Ne'er feast on fancy, 'tis a dangerous food
To take as earnest in a loving mood;
She throws a rosy veil round self-conceit,
Which, like the canker, to the heart will eat,
Till naught is left to cherish her disguise,
Then, like worm-eaten fruit, it drops and dies.
If I judge right, the maid you name is mine;
Nor without proofs will I the maid resign.

These I can give in plenty; though I own
I never knew that she had kindness shown
To other shepherds than myself, till now,
Much less that she chain'd freedom with a vow.
Last April fair, when I got bold with beer—
I loved her long before, but had a fear
To speak—as by a stall she chanced to stand,
With kerchief full of fairings in her hand,
I ventured up, and tapt her on the arm:
She seem'd at first to startle with alarm;
But when I begg'd a fairing at the wake,
She loosed her kerchief and pull'd out a cake;
And in return for her good-natured ways
I offer'd ribbons which I heard her praise:
These she refused, and said she'd plenty got,
But thank'd me kindly, though she took them not.

Whene'er at Sunday feast or noisy fair
I go, and meet with rosy Mary there,
If my dog finds her first he rubs her clothes,
And wags his tail; e'en she to him bestows
A ginger button, and quick turns again,

To wonder why I out of sight remain:
And when she finds me out, in manners free,
She comes unasked to offer things to me;
Never refusing the returns I make,
But meanest trifles condescends to take.
Last Christmas sports, I join'd the skating crew
That yearly race for hats with ribbons blue,
And flew away with young Hope's swiftest pace;
Nor was I cheated, for I won the race:
I took the bunch of ribbons home at night
To Mary, who e'en trembled with delight;
Nor once refused the proffered gift to take,
But said, 'Well done! I'll keep it for your sake.'

SIMON

Once we, with others, at a neighbour's met
To play at cards, when she beside me sat;
Although at first she edged her chair away,
She grew more fond as we began to play,
And soon as ever up my cards I took,
She smiled, and o'er my shoulder stole to look;
To make believe, in true-love's fondling way,
She wish'd to know what cards I had to play.
And when, to try her love, I made pretence
To leave off playing for the want of pence,
She from her lap took out the penny fee,
And put it 'neath the candlestick for me.
Although she would not take, when we retired,
My arm, to guide her home, as I desired,
She often turn'd, as wishing I'd pursue,
And said, 'Good night!' and thank'd me kindly too.

RICHARD

Last Michaelmas, at night, we join'd to play
A hand or two, and keep a holiday:
When we chose partners, not as love regards,
But by the fortunes of the lifted cards,
While Mary look'd at one she took in hand,
She smiled at me to make me understand,

Pointing the colour in her flowery dress;
I took the hint, and well knew which to guess.
'The colour'd card,' said I, 'my wishes seek,
Is something like the rose on Mary's cheek;
A bonny red for me.' She laugh'd outright,
And said, 'Then I'm your partner for the night.'
Blushing, she edged her chair up close to mine,
Paying, with joy, her kiss for every fine.
When time came on us with the hour to part,
Although 'twas late, she seemed as loath to start;
And, though the full moon shone as bright as day,
She even ask'd me if I'd lead the way,
And took my arm without the least to-do:
These are my proofs, and I have morts as true.

SIMON

Once 'neath a huge ash tree she made a stop,
To view a magpie's nest upon the top.
I thought she wish'd the eggs, and up I went,
Nor paused to ask her what her looks had meant;
The grain sway'd like a bulrush in the wind,
But I climb'd on, and left my fears behind.
She praised the spotted eggs, but seem'd in pain,
So up I took them to the nest again.
'Poor birds!' she sighed, to hear them caw and cry,
And more perhaps to think I climb'd so high.
I was embolden'd, from such shown regard,
To beg and take a kiss as my reward;
Although behind her hands she hid her face,
She only blush'd, nor frown'd at my embrace.

RICHARD

Force gives no choice; their own free-will is best;
What we urge earnest, they but take in jest.
One day, while picking sprigs of hillock thyme,
A little pismire in the flowers did climb,
Which to her bosom proved a rebel guest,
And stung her as she placed it in her breast;
Red pimples rose upon her snowy skin,

While sighs bespoke the anguish she was in:
But when she show'd it me with blushing face,
I bent with trembling heart and kiss'd the place,
Urging the charm as cure for all her pain;
She smiled, as wishing to be kiss'd again.

SIMON

Once in the pasture lane, at evening's hour,
She stoopèd down to reach a water flower,
And sure enough, had I not caught her gown,
Headlong the venturing girl had toppled down!
I held her in my arms till danger's fright
Was calm'd, and then she thank'd me in delight;
And smiling, promised as she walked away,
To dance with me on the next holiday.

RICHARD

Once, from her choice black lamb, I stoop'd to pull
A bramble, that got tazzled in the wool,
And prick'd my hand; she seem'd to feel the pain,
While with a pin I pick'd it out again:
Love-sighs the while did her white bosom swell,
And tears e'en started when she wish'd it well,
Owning she wish'd I'd let the lambkin be,
As she had rather it were hurt than me.

SIMON

Ay, some delight to try a gossip's spell,
And flattery's honey suits some lovers well:
I've took her milk full often o'er a stile,
She always thank'd me and would often smile;
And when she miss'd a lamb at morn's young light,
Thinking the fox had stole it off at night,
She'd mourn and sigh, and seek it, and inquire,
Then I too search'd, oft pierced with thorn and brier;
And when she sorrow'd, thought the lamb was free,
I might think too that she was grieved for me.

Thoughts deal in fancies far away from truth,
And folly's shadows shine like suns to youth;
But reason's proofs are never urged in vain,
And what I've witness'd, I'll believe again.
Once 'neath this very bridge, when left alone,
I cut my name in full upon the stone:
'Twas weeding time, and she was toiling nigh,
With others cutting thistles from the rye.
The next day, coming to the place again
Where they had been for shelter from the rain,
I saw her own name in full letters shine,
Scratch'd with a knife or bodkin close to mine,
And link'd together with a true-love's knot:
Mine lingers still upon the much-loved spot;
But some rude fool, with envy at his heart,
Has scratch'd hers out, and torn the links apart.
Well! they may hide love's shadows how they will,
The maid that wrote it is my true-love still:
I told her of the proof with anxious pride,
And though she own'd it not, she ne'er denied.

SIMON

On Plough-witch-Monday, I was in the barn,
Tying up bottles there of foddering corn,
To take afield for sheep, that round the stacks
Lay, with the small snow winnowing on their backs,
When in she ran, with cheeks as pale as death,
And scarce could speak the while for want of breath.
'Keep secrets, Sim,' she said, 'I need them now,
The witch-chaps come'—then skulk'd behind the mow;
And in they rush'd, and laugh'd and stared about,
Threatening rude kisses if they found her out,
While I to screen her, as she wish'd me, swore
That I had seen her bustle by the door:
So off they ran, when she came smiling out,
Saying she hated to be mauled about
With their black faces—but when I began

477

To urge my claims, she never shriek'd nor ran
As from a snake or toad—but said the day
Was short, and Labour had no time for play.

RICHARD

But hark ye, Simon, that's in seasons gone:
On last Plough-Monday I myself was one.
She saw us coming and prepared to flee,
But o'er her shoulder left a laugh on me,
Hiding like one that wishes to be found;
And while the others search'd the house around,
I heard the creaking of the dairy door.
Knowing such secrets by her ways before,
I instant put her hiding-place to rout,
Nor did she hold the latch to keep me out.
She might my blacken'd face a little dread;
'You'll spoil my Sunday cap,' was all she said;
And when I hoped my ways were not unkind,
'Oh, no,' she laughed, 'there's water, never mind.'

SIMON

Some Sundays back, I'd been to fold my sheep,
Just as the red sun down the woods did creep,
And looking back, while wandering home again,
I saw a girl come down the pasture lane;
I slacken'd pace to pull a wild rose down,
That she might catch me ere we met the town;
And turning round again, as near she drew,
'Twas Mary's self, who nodded 'How do ye do?'
She kept my pace, and chatted by my side,
Oft turning round my happy dog to chide,
Who chased the hares, that sat on clover knolls
At feed, and rabbits squatting by their holes.
She praised the blackbird at his evening song,
That in the hedgerow ranted all along
His old song, 'Draw the knave a cup of beer!
Be quick, quick, quick!' in chorus plain and clear.
The path grew narrow as we rambled on,

And through the cornfield made but room for one:
Though she went first, still she would often turn,
The unheard answers of our talk to learn;
Inquiries often urging with a smile,
As if she wish'd to bring up love the while.
I'm sorry since, I tried not ways to woo,
Putting things forward, as a many do.
She let me climb stiles first, then made a stand,
As if she wish'd to offer me her hand;
But I kept backward, wishing still to prove
Yet stronger signals of my Mary's love;
And sure enough, all that have eyes may see,
Through this, the value that she has for me.

RICHARD

They may indeed, and Mary in her mirth
Would say a farthing is of kindred worth.
Last May-day eve she sprained her foot at play;
And when she found she could no longer stay,
She came to me in sorrow, yet in smiles,
And begg'd my aid to help her o'er the stiles;
Some said she feign'd it as excuse to go;
Be as it would, I never sought to know,
But took her arm and went, and on our road
She many a token and a kiss bestow'd.
Once, as she lean'd to rest upon a stile,
The pale moon hanging o'er her looks the while,
'Richard,' she said, and laugh'd, 'the moon is new,
And I will try if that old tale is true,
Which gossips tell, who say that if as soon
As any one beholds the new May-moon,
They o'er their eyes a silken kerchief fling
That has been slided through a wedding-ring,
As many years as they shall single be,
As many moons they through that veil shall see;
And I for once will try the truth, I vow:
For thin, that hangs about my bosom now,
Was drawn through one upon a bridal night,
When we were full of gossip and delight.

Old women, if they heard my talk, would call
Me fond, and think I wish'd the number small;
E'en you may think me foolish, or too free:
Be as it will, I'll take it off and see.'
Then instant from her snowy neck she threw
It first o'er me, and bade me tell her true;
And sure as I stand here, while that was o'er,
I saw two moons as plain as one before;
And when my Mary took it off to try,
Herself saw two, the very same as I,
Although at first she did not like to own,
Saying in blushes she could see but one;
Yet, as her kerchief round her neck she tied,
She smiled, and mutter'd, 'Now I'm satisfied.'
'Mary,' I answered, 'then it rests with you
To suit the tale, and make it false or true.'
'Richard,' she said, 'where I find truth, I find
Nothing to make me of a different mind.'
This was as plain a hint as she could say,
And other proofs were throwing words away;
Yet she made promises that night to me,
That next year's summer may expect to see,
When round our hopes a love-knot shall be twined
As fast as rings and parsons' words can bind.

SIMON

I'll not believe it, though such manners may
Much more of freedom than I wish betray;
Still her good nature I will keep in mind,
And ne'er believe that Mary is unkind:
She always thanks me, very kind and free,
For help in toil, and that's a proof for me.
Last livelong winter through, for such rewards,
I clean'd the paths from snow about the yards,
And litter'd straw in all the pudgy sloughs
About the hovel where she milk'd her cows,
Oft milking when I'd any time in hand;
I've from the heath brought many a load of sand,
Whene'er at plough or dung-cart I have been,

480

Her shining rows of pewter plates to clean;
I've slove up from my dinner many a day,
When master at the market was away,
For her a stolen pear or plum to reach,
Or gait of water from the pump to fetch;
And she has smiled, and thank'd me o'er and o'er—
Love proves itself, I need relate no more;
Yet once, while clambering o'er the orchard wall,
I fell, and from my pocket in the fall
My knife was lost, and Mary, ever free,
Found it, and offered it as mine to me;
But I denied it then, that mine was gone,
On purpose that the maid might keep it on;
So she no more inquiries cared to make,
And I'll be bound she keeps it for my sake.

RICHARD

Well, though I had not time to tend her so,
Or milk her cows, or clean her paths from snow,
Love has no outdoor charms for winter weather—
'Twas spring and summer when we met together;
Yet when a chance fell out, at her desire,
I've waited on her at the kitchen fire,
And often made her evening labour light,
Taking the huge pot off the hooks at night
Brim-full of milk the cading calves to feed;
And soon as chances left no eyes to heed,
In whispering ways she'd o'er my shoulder lean,
While I took kisses for my toil unseen.
Whenever she sat up to bake or brew,
I've strove to help her so that no one knew,
While she would of her own accord agree
To hunt the yard, and seek new eggs for me,
Ne'er dreading striding witch, nor sheeted ghost,
Lapping them up in the hot coals to roast:
Though she'd no cellar-key a horn to fill,
I've fill'd a sweet-wort dish, and sipt at will:
If she drank nothing at those hours of stealth,
She'd sip, and own it was to drink my health.

When summer's morts of blossoms ceased to bloom,
And time to take the honey up was come,
I would for her the brimstone torch alight
To smother in their hives the bees at night;
Though she would call it cruelty, and sigh,
And often take her apron up to cry,
She thought, while troubled o'er each murder'd bee,
To save the whitest honeycomb for me.
Oft would she from her folded apron take
Gifts, venturing clowns had stolen for her sake,
Bidding me choose whate'er I might prefer;
And oft, to prove, I left the choice to her,
When in a moment she'd begin to seek
A favourite apple with the reddest cheek,
Or plum that seem'd the mellowest, the while
Holding them out with many a sweeter smile:
These are not only proofs of love, but speak
Things plain as ever one may wish to seek.
As to the knife, there all your hopes must sink,
For knives cut love, not keep it, as you think.
One that she pick'd up once, you soon may see:
Such *gifts* are dang'rous, so she *sold* it me.
There, own it: if you can, I'll that resign,
But Mary Fieldflower still I claim as mine.
Ay, Simon, lad, why turn ye from the view,
Play with your watch-chain when you've naught to do?
Look up and answer me, or else refrain,
And own you've lost, and we'll be friends again.

'Ay,' said the old man, with a weary smile,
Who sat at rest to listen them awhile,
'Though Love in choosing mates is often blind,
And steers with Folly's whims against the wind,
Poor Simon's baffled hopes have stood too long;
His proofs were seldom right, and often wrong;
His chance is bad, I own, if all be true,
So make it up, and have no more to-do;
Throw down the foolish love ye long have nursed,
And cease, or else the rain will finish first.'

Simon, who from their gaze had turn'd around,
And with his hook progg'd holes about the ground,
Whistled his resting dog, coil'd up asleep,
And in the rain went seeking for his sheep,
Glad from a rival's triumph to retreat,
Yet ne'er acknowledged that himself was beat;
While Richard turn'd his comrades' talk to join,
And proudly laugh'd to see his foe resign.

THE MEMORY OF LOVE

ONCE in the merry toil of clipping time,
When suns are hot and summer in her prime,
An old man, labouring with his fellow men
'Neath two broad walnuts shadowing o'er the pen,
To lighten labour and make short the day,
Tuned ancient songs and chattered time away.
Some boasted of the feats of younger years,
Of quickness some to use the snipping shears,
Others of strength and nimbleness the while,
When they could leap a ditch, or jump a stile;
One told the history of his dog with pride,
That half asleep lay panting by his side;
The younger harp'd o'er coming holidays,
And pretty maids and dances had their praise;
'Twas thought no sin if hearts they only won;
To make them ache, they deem'd it precious fun.
He heard their stories 'tween a sigh and smile,
And bade them listen to his own awhile.
They stopt, and choked the titter as he spoke,
Hearing the story as one hears a joke,
Thinking him childish, as his mind would cling
With joy to every silly-seeming thing:
The vulgar dregs of love were all they knew;
What he had felt was tender, pure, and true.

'My boys,' said he, 'I once was young and wild,
And urged my follies when a maiden smiled;

483

Oft whispering marriage with a lying tongue,
And then excusing me still years too young.
I sought one beauty till the freak was past,
And then found others prettier than the last;
I woo'd and won them, as a sort of pride,
Still seeking new ones till I was denied.
Laugh not, my boys, when slighted maidens mourn,
For fear your follies may be served in turn;
And if in Beauty's net ye once should be,
Ye'll find a puzzle ere your hearts are free.
At last a beauty won my wandering eye,
Binding my fancies with a troubled tie:
I tried to break it, but it would not bend,
So freaks and lies and follies had their end.
Her very image startles on me yet,
She seem'd the loveliest I had ever met;
Her face thrill'd through me, though 'twas only fair
And red and rosy, as the many are;
And though her bosom swell'd and eyes were bright
Like others, yet they overpower'd me quite:
In every feature shone that witching spell
That love adores and language cannot tell.

   'The very day when first her looks I met
Haunts all my musings with its memory yet,
And every trifle then that met my eye
Time cannot pass its recollection by;
Link'd with her name, it holds a pleasing power,
Like spring, whose smile gives even weeds a flower.
Chance doomed us both at the same town to dwell,
When youth's wild visions bade my heart farewell,
And left it love's sick sorrows.   Beauty's fame
Was hot about the village ere she came:
Maids' jealous whisperings did their doubtings raise,
While youths were eager, tho' by guess, to praise;
And I, who meant a season's suit to prove,
Met with a sudden and a lasting love.
I went at Michaelmas, she came at May;
A finer blossom never bloom'd that day.

On that same morn whose memory turns me chill,
I, with a cart, was journeying to the mill;
The time was lovely, and down lane and balk
I went in joy, and mused along the walk,
Gazing on prospects in a happy vein,
O'er fields fresh plough'd and springing crops of grain.
The meadow-closes all about were lined
With cowslip bunches, nodding in the wind;
In every lane, o'erhung with brier and thorn,
Thousands of daisies glitter'd in the morn.
My dog was pleased as I, and often rolled
His curly jacket in the fresh-plough'd mould;
Sheep would our happy walk a moment heed,
Leaving their lairs and stooping down to feed.
The hare oft sturted from the clover lea,
And birds were happy as a song can be;
The redcap often from the hedge would drop,
Perching and twittering on the thistle's top.
The groups of weeders sung their toil away;
And while old women ask'd the time of day,
The young girls halloo'd, merrily and shrill,
If I would take a partner to the mill.
Nor did I think a heart as glad as theirs
Had cause so near to change all joys to cares.

'Beside the mill-brook, whose uneven tide
Grows now and then more than a horse can stride,
Till from its roar released, its windings creep
Narrow and soft, a green grasshopper's leap,
I met the maid whose beauty made me sigh
And turn upon her an admiring eye.
'Twas she, I thought, who wore the village fame,
And as I guess'd it proved the very same.
She asked the way and with a timid smile
Turn'd back to thank me ere she skipt the stile.
Fill'd full of fancies to my journey's end,
I wish'd I'd spoke, then judged I might offend;
And hoped in time a chance might come, to prove
A feeble shadow of my sudden love.

'Within the foldings of her neckerchief
Appear'd a red pink, with its ruddy leaf;
The little trifle gave my bosom pain,
I thought it given by some parting swain;
Yet ever since my memory keeps awake,
To love the blossom for the owner's sake.
Each merry year, as clipping time comes round,
Whene'er I see one in our posies bound,
Though I am old, and love has lost its power,
I pause and sigh, and e'en could kiss the flower.

'I often went on Sundays to the spot
Where she pass'd by, a trifle not forgot;
The very stones she stept to cross the stream,
I've sat for hours to muse upon, and dream:
The stile, too, over which I saw her climb,
Has made my foolish heart ache many a time;
And though I'm old, my palsied memory still,
If I pass'd now, would turn my bosom chill.

'On the next morning, as I cross'd the plain
At milking hour, I saw the maid again;
The cows stood round her in a wondering way,
And kept the stranger with her fears at bay;
They tost their heads and snuff'd the morning gales,
Skewing at her: I gladly took the pails
And milk'd them all; and more her fears to screen,
I took her yokes, and saw her o'er the green.
Then at the pasture gate, with fond delight,
I left a promise I would meet at night,
Urging a kind return, that she'd agree
My May-game partner in the dance to be.
She look'd consent, I even thought she smiled,
For love sees double when by Hope beguiled;
But when the cows grew reconciled and tame,
She always thank'd me and refused the claim.
It made me half my hopeful love resign,
And feel her heart had but small love for mine:
Yet I press'd on, and would my doubts reprove,

486

Thinking her fears might disbelieve my love.
I went to church each leisure Sabbath day,
For every purpose but the right—to pray.
Her seat was opposite to mine: in vain
I tried to read, turning to gaze again,
Till some old matron shook her serious head,
And urged my eye to what I should have read.
My book was open oft when prayers were done,
And I've kept reading till the Psalms begun;
When the clerk's voice, and bassoon booming deep,
Made memory startle as I'd been asleep.
I often tried what signals love would take,
But she seem'd strange to all I had to make;
I often smiled whene'er she turn'd her eye,
But she would pause, as if she wonder'd why:
She seem'd to try to shun me in the street,
And I, scarce conscious, tried the maid to meet.

'At length, some gipsies to our common came,
And, as a change to May-night's evening game,
Maids in the gipsies' nook proposed a dance,
Where I went too, and dream'd upon the chance.
For summer eves to servants then supplied
Sweet leisure hours, when toil was thrown aside;
When we have played, and danced till day was by,
And the moon's horns crept half-way up the sky—
Young miss and master, servant-man and maid;
For none would scold, or question why we stayed.
The maiden came, she whom I wish'd to see,
I ask'd her, trembling, if she'd dance with me;
She smiled, then check'd it, and with half-turn'd eye
Paused for a moment ere she made reply:
Good manners seem'd to urge her to consent,
She blush'd and yielded, and away we went.
Oh! the first time I touch'd her gentle hand,
I felt a joy you'll never understand,
Unless ye thrill 'neath true love's ecstasy,
And then you'll own the pleasant pain with me.
My heart sunk in me like a lump of clay;

My feet e'en trembled as we danced away:
Then fears would leave, and feverish hopes in turn
In fluttering flushes made my bosom burn.
I view'd her face, where beauty ne'er could cloy,
And dream'd o'er raptures till I smiled for joy;
She seem'd to greet my looks with tender eye,
But never smiled, and oft appear'd to sigh.

'Soon as a finish to the sports had come,
I offer'd hints to see her safely home;
She turn'd aside, yet did not answer "No!"
But thank'd my kindness, and prepared to go.
Brooding o'er raptures picturing fancy drew,
I led her homeward on the evening dew,
And ventured gradual hints, mid smiles and sighs,
To clear my passion of its thin disguise.
She seem'd confused at what she had to say,
Nor bade hopes live, nor wish'd my words away:
At length she tried, and having chok'd the sigh,
She gave me hints that made hopes hurry by.
"Nay, you may love," she said, "and I believe
If I had power—but why should I deceive?"
Then paused, as loath the finish to relate,
And would have left me, but I held the gate.
She sigh'd to see me toy mid hopes and fears,
And made excuses to conceal her tears;
While pushing the dark ringlets from her eye,
As shrinking from me, she exclaim'd "Good-bye!"
Bidding me cease to say she had my heart,
And struggling from me as resolved to part;
"Your heart's not mine," she said, "and I must shun
Your urged returns, for mine's already won;
Whatever proofs your vows or words make known,
I cannot give you what is not my own."
I loosed the gate, she hurried to the door,
And I beheld her with hope's eyes no more.

'But often to the town her lover came,
And came at last the marriage day to name.

I went to church, not knowing what I did,
That very Sunday when the banns were bid;
Lord help one's cares, I'd need enough to stay,
And think, when there, of better things, and pray;
But when the parson brought the thing about,
I shut my book and sigh'd and loiter'd out,
Wandering I knew not where, to ease my pain,
Till broken hopes should settle calm again.
The marriage came, it was a woeful day,
And memory gave it an eternal stay:
I heard the bells ring as I cross'd the moor,
And never heard so sad a peal before.
I wish'd to see how she would look a bride,
And started off—and then my courage died;
I would not go; and then I ventured by
The churchyard wall, but nothing met my eye.
I now felt happy that the thing was o'er;
And then was vex'd I did not go before:
Half shamed, I hung my head along the street,
Nor cared to talk with those my path would meet,
Lest they should jeer me or bring up the day,
So, when they spoke, I turn'd, and sneak'd away.

'I thought upon her lovely face for years,
With fondest feelings, almost kin to tears,
Till the heart ached with love.   I cannot tell
What others thought of her I loved so well;
Or how she seem'd to him that call'd her wife—
Her face to me was memory for life.
Her looks, her ways, in winning forms would steal,
Leaving a pain I never ceased to feel;
Her very voice would memory's partner be,
And music linger'd in the sound with me.
Her troubling form was long about my sight,
In day-dreams musing, or in sleep by night:
My dreams wore constantly that pleasing pain,
The face of her I loved and could not gain.

'I sought at first the noise of feast and fair,
To see if tumult yet had joys to spare;

And hope would sometimes join my lonely way,
Through fields and meads, in summer clothing gay:
Half pleased, half sad, I mused o'er days to come,
And idly cropt the meadow flowers in bloom;
Seeking for that which it was vain to find,
To loose the burthen from a troubled mind.
The dance and revel brought its joy no more;
I hated pastimes which I loved before.
The walks on sabbath-days with milking lass,
And every pastime on the summer grass;
Where hunt-the-slipper passed the hours away,
And blind-man's-buff made every bosom gay,
When tittering maidens urged me which to seize:
These lost the relish and the power to please.
I saw no sports to claim an hour from sleep,
And none to care for but my dog and sheep;
I kept no "may-balls" now, of cowslips made;
To toss on May-days to a forward maid:
I ran no "crookhorn" on the pasture grasses,
Nor "duck-'neath-water" played wi' bawling lasses,
Nor danced the "maze" which shepherds fond of play
Cut in the grass to baffle maids at May,
The self-same puzzle which the knowing boy
Oft draws at school and calls "the road to Troy";
Nor "lost love-letter" round the whispering ring
Could one Lent pleasure to my musings bring;
My fancies found none in the merry game
As worth the kisses which the finders claim.[1]
I shunn'd them all, the sports, and loves, and ways,
That used to please me in my younger days.
My Sunday's former pleasures I forsook;
No more I rambled to the pasture brook,
Where in my youth, at Eastwell's fountain side,
Which winter never froze nor summer dried,
Young men and maidens used to talk and play
In the cool shadows of its willows grey,
Drinking love healths in mugs of sugar'd drink
On the soft swellings of its rushy brink,

[1] Preceding twelve lines added from MS.

By the spring head whose water, winter-chill,
Boils up the white sand that is never still,
Now swimming up in silver threads, and then
Slow siling down to bubble up agen:
Where shepherds used to sit, and tell the while
Their tales and jokes to win each maiden's smile.
I shunn'd all these, which I had loved before,
And join'd the children's play-games on the moor,
Nicking the "nine-peg morris" in the grass,
Or tying garlands for some little lass,
Or reaching roses from the hedgerow bowers,
While they fawn'd round me till I got the flowers,
Turning my labours to their changing wills,
Now whistles cutting, and then water-mills:
And thus I tried to loiter time away,
Till they were weary of each idle play.
I was the play-king of the jocund clan,
And often wish'd I could forget the man:
They had but trifles happiness to spoil,
Play all their love, and all their trouble toil.

  'My partners as they passed would point and say,
"There's love-sick Robin with the boys at play!"
While maidens thought me justly served, and smiled
To see crost-love had made me twice a child.
Folks thought me crazed, and you may think the same,
Who know of love no further than the name;
Think as you please, my childish tale is done;
'Tis time it were, for there's the setting sun.
Yet if you e'er should meet with my despair,
To love a girl that has no love to spare,
Then will your weakness to her beauty bow,
And feel the truth that I have told you now.'

SOME childish memories linger while we're men,
Or pains or pleasures, as they touched us then,
Freshing with knowledge as our feelings will,
Till manhood comes—and there they linger still.

Old shepherd Robin, childish ere he died,
I knew him well and every boy beside;
For he has joined our sports with childish glee
And seem'd as happy in our mirth as we.
He twirl'd the top and boasted in his powers
To jilt his pebble farther off than ours,
And smil'd in raptures as we prais'd his skill
While making willow whistles or a mill,
And large keck-trumpets—powers he loved to show,
And much delighted learning us to blow.
And tales he'd tell us while he tended sheep
We wept to hear, and he himself would weep,
For tales of sorrow he would often tell,
And one that touch'd us I remember well.
He often told it, nor left grief to cold;
And still it warms me when it last was told.
'Twas moaning autumn in her oldest hours,
When we'd spent many vainly seeking flowers,
And found him pottering from the rising wind
To the best shelter which the fields could find.
We join'd his steps, and disappointments sigh'd,
And sought a tree and sat us by his side.

'Children,' he said, 'the autumn's withering hours
Have snatch'd away your summer and your flowers.
Far different this to summer's warmer day,
When with my hook I reach'd you boughs of may,
And tied with rushes easy gather'd flowers—
Far different those to these decaying hours.
Yellow are leaves, half naked is the bough,
And ne'er a blossom has the pasture now.
So be content and spend an hour with me,

I'll tell a tale that like the time shall be;
A tale of tender sorrows which I've told
Times out of number both to young and old.

'Poor Mary Lee, she was a child with me,
And one for sorrow she was born to be;
A hard and cruel world in this she found;
She met its vice, and sunk beneath the wound.
She sunk, but kept her hopes, nor fear'd to find
The hard ill usage which she left behind.
Nor lived she long.   Leaves oft have left the tree,
Reminding mortals what their end must be,
And grass and weeds have often spread anew
On other graves, since first on hers they grew.
Tho' wide the world where early hope depends,
Poor Mary met it destitute of friends,
Left a lorn orphan when her years was few—
And parish pity was too early due.
I had a mother, but in shame was born.
She married after, but I kept the scorn.
And she had boys which she as mother prized,
But her first-born was born to be despised.

'With Mary Lee, the parish was my lot,
And its cold bounty all the friends I got;
Dragg'd from our childhood's pleasures and its plays
We pined in workhouse sorrows many days,
Where many wants received their scant supply,
Where pity never came to check the sigh,
Save what laws force from tyrant overseers
Whose bitter gifts was purchased with our tears.
There ragg'd and starved and work'd beyond our powers,
We toil'd those hours you spend in gathering flowers,
Nor mothers' smiles had we our toils to cheer,
But tyrants' frowns and threatenings ever near;
Who beat enfeebled weakness many times
And scoff'd misfortune's agonies as crimes:
While pride's vain children, of a luckier race,
Were taught to shun our presence as disgrace.'

Thus workhouse misery did we both abide
Till our own strength its poverty supplied
And service freed us—freedom did we find
In labour there, to slavery left behind.

'And Mary grew in spite of every harm
To womanhood, and not without its charm;
Tho' pride to me was not of scorn bereft
And yet disdain'd me thro' the fate I left,
It smil'd on her—and she believed the praise
Of men that wrong'd her in her helpless days.
And soon she found she did too soon believe
That worst of foes, befriending to deceive.
A trig young coxcomb, Farmer Folly's son,
Whisper'd in secret how his heart was won;
And Mary sure the person must admire
Of one whose manners aped the country squire,
Who mock'd gentility with dog and gun
And quirk'd the fields as many such have done,
Where humbler gents, their leisure to amuse,
From this pretender oft received abuse,
Branding the honest with a poacher's blame
While he himself deserved a viler name.
He robb'd the game with freedom unreserved
For which his betters paid to be preserved.
And on these walks where Mary sought her cows,
He sought his chances and renew'd his vows:
Where soon his civil flatteries gain'd their end—
While he with pride oft entertain'd a friend
With bragging stories how the fool was won,
And laugh'd it off, and call'd it precious fun.
At length, by time convinced, awakened fears
Their follies learn'd, and she implored in tears;
While the vile wretch, ere she her griefs begun,
Scoff'd her with names for guilt himself had done
And at those tears which shame could not depress
He sneer'd and mutter'd, "Strumpets meet distress."

'So worser fate and added griefs to shun,
Force sought the dungeon where they first begun,

Griefs harmless then, now tortured with disgrace,
Then shameless misery, now a hiding-place.
Worse was her lot, and humbler was her fees,
When justice fail'd her tyrant's power to tease.
Want wins its favour, tho' oft slow to win,
But reason guides it to discourage sin.
Forced, as the father to the child, he paid
But left to want its mother he betray'd.

    'Boys, when ye're men, have better pride to feel
Than wound a heart ye never mean to heal.

    'Now pined and starved, despised by all she knew,
Too weak for toil, yet wishing to pursue
Some means for life now link'd with tender tie,
Which but for that had been a joy to die—
She made her matches, and her burthen bore
To seek compassion at a stranger's door.
But pity deigns not with the proud to live,
And poor that feel it have not power to give.
Small was the sum her last resource supplied
And did but little for her wants provide;
And ragg'd and wretched from sad misery's shed,
While yielding paths betray'd a shoeless tread,
She oft was seen to wander round the fields
And sought the berries which the autumn yields,
Feeding with birds, that twitter'd by her side,
Content to spare her what the proud denied.
Thus oft half famish'd she from town sojourn'd
And went one morning—nor at eve return'd.

    'Search soon was made—tho' one of small respect,
Yet fear'd disgrace forbid them to neglect;
While one heart doubtless in its hopes was high
That fate had freed him and expense was by.
Nor, if that heart could be, were hopes unblest.
Search found the mother, and the child had rest—
But reason's absence did her grief beguile,
And madness gave her sorrow strength to smile.

She kiss'd it oft, and offer'd succour still,
And held it to her bosom cold and chill;
Then moan'd and bow'd as one that tries to weep,
And smiled agen, and hush'd its endless sleep.
Poor perish'd child, what it had linger'd in,
And that night suffer'd for another's sin!
To see such horrors made me quite distrest—
For I was one to seek her with the rest.
As weakness to return that night denied,
She crept for shelter which the fields supplied,
And found an hovel, where she'd seemly ta'en
Grass for her infant's cradle, pull'd in vain.
She seem'd to know me, but she never spoke,
Yet wish'd, it seem'd, to tell her heart was broke.
For to her heart she oft her hand would bear,
And look'd more piteous as she placed it there.

'Again we took her to misfortune's den,
But joys or sorrows knew no difference then.
Pride now felt pity, when she could not live,
And gave its trifle, when too late to give.
No reason e'er return'd to feel the ill,
And death soon came and made her happier still.
There luckless Mary had of pain its share,
There life met grief, and parted with despair.
In the cold grave from every ill she slept,
Nor felt the distance which distinction kept.
North side the church no choice will occupy,
Force finds the workhouse tenants room to lie.
There cold winds frown and sunbeams never come,
There Mary rested in a better home,
A lone cold corner by the charnel pent,
Where nettles spread her only monument.

'Children, ye weep, but few the years ye've met,
And reason's young to think of sorrows yet;
But when ye're men, and infants climb your knee,
Then will ye feel, and think of Mary Lee.'

THE FATE OF GENIUS

FAR from the life of market towns was seen
The humble huts and spire of Topal Green,
Where from the tree-tops that the hamlet shields
The white spire mounts and overlooks the fields,
Meeting the distant view of passing eyes,
Where gentle memory often points and sighs.
For there amidst the ignorance it wears,
Want's chilling views and labour's ceaseless cares,
A rustic genius from the darkness sprung,
And sought the muses mid his toils, and sung;
And warm'd with hopes, while nature round him
    smiled,
He humm'd their raptures and his fate beguiled.

But evil light thro' his oblivion gleam'd;
The world wore smiles his artless hopes esteem'd;
And warm'd with raptures, better days to meet,
They sought applause—and realized the cheat.
Soon envy's wasps around his sweets did swarm,
And peaceful muses fled the rude alarm;
Soon fame's vain follies from their ambush rose,
Friends while they're powerless, but in public, foes.
This praised as fine what that as faults accused;
That urged amendments which the next abused.
Thus 'mid the wild confusion babel raised,
By one advised, by others scoff'd and praised,
The damps of disappointment proved too much,
And warm hopes wither'd at the chilling touch,
Shrinking from life and hope's emblazon'd noon
To witness envy had its own too soon.
And what remains now lingers to be blest
Aside that church where friendship tells the rest,
Who placed a stone to mark his lowly sleep
That kindred hearts might find the spot to weep;
Where the old sexton, death's undaunted slave,
Who knew the bard, and dug his early grave,
To each request inquiry's warmth may raise,

Oft gives the tale of his unnoticed days,
In hope's calm walks, ere flattery smiled his friend,
And black injustice bade their journey end.

'I knew him from a child,' the clerk would say,
'And often noticed his dislike to play;
Oft met him then, lone left by woods and streams,
Muttering about as people do in dreams;
And 'neath lone bushes dropt about the field,
Or peaceful hedges that would shelter yield,
With hand beneath his head in silence bent,
Oft saw him sit and wonder'd what it meant.
Nor did his habits alter with his age,
Still woods and fields his leisure did engage.
Nor friends nor labour would his thoughts beguile,
Still dumb he seem'd in company and toil.
And if one's questions did his dreams surprise
His unconcern oft paused in wrong replies.
We wonder'd many times, as well we might,
And doubted often if his mind was right.
E'en children startled from his oddness ran,
And shunn'd his wanderings as "the crazy man";
Tho' harmless as the things he mix'd among—
His ways were gentle and unknown to wrong.
For I've oft mark'd his pity passing by
Disturb the spider's web to save the fly,
And saw him give to tyrant boys a fee
To buy the captive sparrows liberty.
Each Sunday's leisure brought the woods their guest,
And wildest spot which suited him the best,
As bushy greens and valleys left untill'd
Where weedy brooks went crooking as they will'd,
Where flags and reeds and sedge disorder'd grew,
These would his absence from his home pursue.
And as he rambled in each peaceful round
He'd fancy friends in everything he found,
Muttering to cattle—ay, and even flowers,
As one in visions, claim'd his talk for hours.
And he'd oft wonder where we naught could see,

On blades of grass and leaves upon the tree,
And pointed often in a wild surprise
To trifling hues of gadding butterflies;
While if another made new marvels known,
That seem'd to me more wondrous than his own,
Of ghosts he'd seen that nightly walks deceived,
He heeded not but laugh'd and disbelieved.
Night's dismal tongues that hardest hearts affright,
And all may hear that travel out at night,
Her shadow'd howling tenants fierce and grim—
Tho' trifles struck him—such was naught to him.

'At length 'twas known: his ways by woods and brooks
Were secret walks for making rhymes and books,
Which strangers bought and with amazement read,
And call'd him poet when they sought his shed.
But men, they said, like serpents in the grass
That skulk in ways which learning has to pass,
To slander worth which they would fain possess,
And disappointment urges to suppress,
Snarling at faults too bright for common minds,
And hiding beauties wisdom warmly finds—
Such marr'd his powers, and slander'd in disguise,
And tried to black his merits with their lies.
And tho' his friends the cheating fraud descried,
It hurt too earnest to be wiped aside.
He dwindled down from too severe a blast,
And hopes might wish to live, that died as fast.
Still he did live till real life seem'd as gone,
And his soul linger'd in a shadow'd one.
And yet he mingled in his favour'd ways,
And bared his forehead to the sunny days,
Listening the lark or fountain's moaning wave,
As like a ghost as ever left its grave,
And fled the world at last without a sigh,
And died as gentle as a lamb would die.

'His learned friends said envy's aim was blest,
That malice kill'd him—they might know the best:

Else folks less learn'd to different causes led,
Who read his books and marvell'd as they read,
Where he so free of ghost and fairy talks,
They thought he found them in his lonely walks,
And that some secret which he fail'd to keep
Brought on their anger and his endless sleep.
Be as it might, his life fell in decay,
And that stone tells when it was call'd away,
Where e'en the daisies that around it spread,
The gifts of spring to dress his lowly bed,
Are often stole in garden scenes to grow,
As relics of the dust that sleeps below;
While the stone's verses hid by summer's weed,
Which strangers eager trample down to read,
Are by the curious often written down,
Tho' they tell naught of praises or renown.

   ' "Here sleep the hopes of one whose glowing birth
Was found too warm for this unfeeling earth,
That frown'd and wither'd—yet the fruitful stem
Hides here and buds with others warm as them;
Waiting that sun to warm their bloom to smile,
And welcome heaven as their native soil." '

GOING TO THE FAIR

GAY rose the morn, fulfilling many a prayer
Of anxious maids; the day was Deeping Fair,
The month was May, the meadows they were green
And full of flowers, though paths were far from clean,
Moistened by showers that frequent though not long
Fell and were done ere linnets could their song,
That now by crowds in every thicket sung;
And from the mill-dam up the heron sprung;
In every field larks twittered o'er the grain,
As happy 'twas the fair; so thought the swain
Who hastened o'er his labour to get free

Betimes, the pleasures of the fair to see.
The very air breathed joy, and all the May
To such appeared in joyance with the day,
As if the fair had put their pleasures on:
Thus merry minds shape raptures from their own.
In ivy bowers wood-pigeons sat to coo,
And smooth-voiced cuckoos muttered as they flew;
Free smiled the daisy from dull night's embrace,
Flushed with his dewy kisses on its face.
The sun was peeping o'er the spreading rows
Of dark green elms alive with busy crows,
And round the Lodge that darkened 'neath their shade
Loud was the strife that pigs and poultry made,
A farm-house now, though once a moated hall;
As loud, too, Farmer Thrifty's morning call,
'Come up, boys, up,' re-echoed through the Lodge,
Where last to bed and first to rise was Hodge,
Who heard the unwelcome shout mid yawns and sighs
And spent some minutes to unclose his eyes.
Yet up he must to fetch his horses now:
They needed corn, and waiting lay the plough,
And morning's toil must needs be finished soon
As all had leave to join the fair at noon.
So up Hodge got and soodled down the lane,
Hirpling like one whose joints were stiff with pain,
Though urged by many a call till out of sight
To mend his pace and not be out till night.
And Simon, foremost of the servant clan,
Who next the master ruled as master-man,
Was more than anxious to perform his part,
Who, stript already, stopt his song to start,
As love and hope with mingling fear and glee
Burnt every thought with madness to be free.
Mary, a maid whose fame was in her face,
[Had] lived his partner in his last year's place,
And now, though distant from him many a mile,
Her former fondness cheered his present toil;
For she had vowed, last Martinmas when they
For their new places parted wide away,

That, come what would, on the returning fair
She'd come to see her friends and meet him there.
So Simon's hopes, who painted her as come,
Burnt till they grew all rebels to their home,
Forcing his heart on fancy's wings to wend,
In thought already at its journey's end.
By kindness he had bought in seasons past
The love of Mary, which he hoped would last,
Who young and blushing was and sweet to see,
Yet not like gaudy roses on the tree;
For beauty blazed not in her face, yet there
A twilight splendour owned her more than fair;
The voice of woods and streams was in her looks,
And wise she seemed, though ignorant of books.
Her hair was swarthy brown and soft of hue,
As the sweet gloom that falls with even's dew,
That on her fine white forehead did divide
In the triumphant negligence of pride.
Her eyes were dark, but they wore lights to shine
That love adores and poets call divine,
And her cheeks' summer blooms wore hues the while
Of love's soft innocence without its guile;
And on the pouting of her amorous lip,
Where love delicious nectar longed to sip,
Beauty sat throned, in that bewitching spell
That love adores and language cannot tell;
Where charms triumphant made each gazer pay
Heart-aches for looking, ere he turned away.
And so did Simon's, but the smiles that cured
Paid more than double for the pain endured;
For in love's views to win her kind regard,
He milked, and every Sunday swept the yard,
That she might on her errands safely go
Nor soil the gloss jet of her Sunday shoe;
And from the stack a faggot every night
He threw his Mary's morning fire to light,
Nay, did all toils her Sundays had to do,
When she had on a garment that was new,
And feared with thorns to tear or dirt to soil,

While love was all the payment for his toil.
By all these deeds he strove his love to show,
Nor was she backward what they meant to know;
And though she shrieked to shun a stolen kiss,
A chance to meet his smile she'd never miss;
And oft for syllabubs for cream she crept,
When mistress gossiped and the master slept,
And slove the cellar key from off the nail
Above her master's chair to steal him ale;
While in those favoured hours most like to speed,
Simon had sued and Mary had agreed,
Live where they might, or fair or foul the weather,
They'd meet this morning at the fair together.
Although six lingering months since then had now
Spread in between warm love to cool that vow,
Although six lingering miles with dreary view
Stretched love's frail chain—still he believed her true.

    At length came Hodge, with trouble in his speed;
For when with quicker pace he did proceed,
Bad news was sure the herald of his tale,
To say a portion of his job did fail;
And now he stopt his song ere nigh, to bawl
Of gaps new-broke and horses vanished all,
For he seemed joyed to find them all astray,
Wishing, no doubt, they'd ne'er be found that day;
A truce from plough to rest each weary limb
Was more than fairs or holidays to him.
Simon in silence like a statue stood;
Dire disappointment curdled up his blood;
His hopes of holiday all seemed as done,
While Farmer Thrifty bade them search till noon,
Sending out heralds famed for swifter speed
Than Hodge, grown needless in the time of need;
When soon the horses all were found but one,
And Dobbin, oftenest to transgress, was gone—
Dobbin, a horse well known for miles around
In every village and in every pound;
Although so tame at toil that boys might guide

And children walk uninjured by his side,
When loose from gears, he roved as freedom's mate:
He'd find all gaps and open every gate;
And if aught sweet beyond his pasture grew,
No fence so thick but he would blunder through.
His youth from gipsies did these tricks receive;
With them he toiled and worked his wits to live.
Bare roads he traced all day with naught to bite,
Then stole with them to stacks to feed at night.
Though now a better life was Dobbin's lot,
Well fed and fat, youth's tricks he ne'er forgot;
Still gaps were broke, and Dobbin bore the blame;
Still stacks were pulled, and Dobbin felt no shame.
If fifty partners in his pasture lay,
Dobbin was safe to lead them all astray.
And yet a better horse, all did allow,
Was never yoked to wagon or to plough.
Old Farmer Thrifty now with vengeance ripe
Cursed and laid down half-smoked his morning pipe,
Vowing old Dobbin's tricks would lose his crop
Of corn, if thus whole days they forced to stop
The harrow; and then threw his hands behind him,
'If he's above ground, curse him, we will find him.'
And Simon, as the safest to succeed,
Was posted off, and though to urge his speed
A flagon of the best, ere he did start,
Was drawn, that burnt like brandy round his heart,
Yet nothing cheered it, for his hopes were crost,
And chance of meeting Mary seemed as lost.
Yet he brushed onward on his doubtful route,
With best leg foremost to find Dobbin out,
Muttering his threats in anger's blustering tones,
How he would thrash the wanderer's lazy bones,
Whittling a monstrous cudgel while he spoke,
Proving thereby he did not mean to joke.
Alas for Dobbin! sore will be his back
If Simon finds him; and he marks his track,
For faithless dews his blundering steps betrayed
O'er close and field in crooked marks displayed.

But the kind sun that smiles on all below
Was Dobbin's friend, though Simon was his foe,
Drying the tell-tale dew from off the grass,
Leaving the ploughboy to proceed by guess;
Who asked of almost every one he met,
Searched in each pound, and, ne'er the wiser yet,
Measuring his shadow every now and then
To guess the hour, then hurried on agen;
While Mary's smiles and promise and the fair
Rose o'er all hopes and drove them to despair.
Search where he might, inquire of whom he would,
Dobbin was missing as if lost for good;
For he was reckoned cunning, and at least
Had more of reason than a common beast,
Seeking such secret spots from summer skies
As if he hid from toil as well as flies.
This Simon knew, and searched in every spot
Where he might hide, but yet had hidden not.
So on he searched and cursed and searched again,
Muttering the while his threatening oaths in vain,
Laying to Dobbin's tramp in restless strife
The loss of love and happiness for life;
While short his shadow grew and shifted on
Until it tokened half the day was gone—
And, what was worse, the hour when at the gate
Mary for Simon's coming was to wait,
When he had told her last and vowed as how
That spot should sink ere he would break his vow.
That vow was broke; at least the time expired
When Mary was to wait as love desired:
And wait she did for half the morning there,
Where two paths met the high road to the fair.

She left her father's cot before the time;
To make her lover wait appeared a crime.
'Deceitful man!' doubt burnt hope's taper dim;
She sighed, and muttered, 'I may wait for him.
Here I may stand in doubt the morning long;
Although he knows, he never thinks it wrong.

Last night I came six weary miles in vain,
Cheered with the thoughts of seeing him again.
My mother's love could ill my absence spare,
But without Simon I was restless there.'
So sighed the maid as o'er the stile she bent,
And sighed, and onward to the fair she went,
While every noise that floated in the wind
Would make her pause and turn a look behind;
For Simon's halloo she would list and look,
Loitering and musing to be overtook.
Although still cheated, down each narrow lane
At every turn she'd stop and wait again,
Till tired with hope's excuses for delay
The rosebud in her bosom died away,
Which there was placed new graces to reveal,
Or more for Simon's tempted hands to steal.
But Simon came not; and the withered rose
Was the first omen sorrows to disclose.
So as she journeyed onward to the fair,
Hopes curdled all to malice; and when there,
To lose her thoughts she struggled to be gay,
Passing in freakish whims the merry day,
Mocking gay feelings that had small akin
To the perplexities that lurked within,
Changing her nature, and in freedom's ways
Smiled as if courting amorous eyes to gaze,
Taking with willing hands in merry cue
The glass to kiss from every youth she knew.
Each proffered fairing too was freely ta'en;
She cracked the nuts and threw the shells again,
Resolved to change her old love for a new
And leave off Simon, deemed no longer true.
Yet half-unconscious of the looks she raised,
She blushed and seemed to wonder why they praised;
While Footman Tim in his gilt gaudy suit,
Tapping with pride his cane upon his boot,
Grown bold with ale, nipt up in smirking glee
And rudely made her welcome to his knee.
Soon from his silken purse his cash was flung,

And crown by crown upon the table rung;
For every groat and e'en a penny paid,
This purse and all this silver was displayed.
The while he sat, he'd chink his cash about
To let folk know his pockets wa'n't without.
'Tween thumb and finger oft he swung his cane
In haughty grace, then sipt his glass again,
Still leaving dregs at bottom to throw down
To show how fashion acted from a clown,
And more in Mary's presence to display
A careless waste as heeding not the pay.
Full oft unbidden out his watch was ta'en
To show the hour, but more to show the chain,
And off his gloves were pulled his nails to bite
With vain excuse to show his hands were white;
While open flew his waistcoat at the chin,
Crimpt frills displaying and a golden pin,
To raise his consequence in vulgar eyes
And win the girls to think a blank a prize.
Mary seemed hurt, yet suffered to be held,
Bearing the seat with patience while compelled.

   And Simon, now with weary feet and mind,
Pursuing Dobbin whom he could not find,
Gave up the hunt; his master heard the tale
And swore, yet paid him with a horn of ale,
Saying as morn was by he well could spare
Them all; so all made ready for the fair.
His ash-plant Simon in his hand had got,
Yet paused in doubt, half willing and half not,
Beside the door, with kerchief smoothening down
The ruffled nap upon his beaver's crown;
Then starting off, then still foreboding doubt
With fear's strong impulse made him pause about.
Sweet was the day and sunny gleamed the weather,
While sheep, loud-bleating, called their lambs together.
'Craik' went the landrail in the wind-waved grain,
Whom idle schoolboys hearing chased in vain.
In Simon's mind the noise bespoke his fate:

He thought it muttered he was all too 'late.'
'Chewsit,' the pewit screamed in swopping whews,
'Choose it!' said Simon, 'I know whom to choose.'
Thus ne'er a bird could sing but Simon's cares
Shaped it to something of his own affairs.
The day was swiftly wasting with the wear,
And some few girls were coming from the fair,
Who left gay mirth and all his noisy crew
Not without sighs, their evening jobs to do.
And he, when met, got many a laughing look;
Full loud their fears were urged to cross the brook,
Knocking their pattens when no dirt was near
And finding danger where no dangers were,
Signals to urge the aid of Simon's hand;
But such he could or would not understand.
He hurried by them all and would not stay
To ask a question or salute the day;
Though screams and shouts alternate rung behind,
Raising their wanton echoes on the wind,
He never once turned o'er his arm to see
If they got o'er or in the brook, not he.
His thoughts, already at their journey's end,
Left him no time on trifles to attend.
At length the noisy fair assailed his ear;
Great grew his hope, but greater grew his fear.
And as he crushed among the crowds when there,
His eyes dare scarcely wander o'er the fair
Lest he—for fear was busy to alarm—
Should see his Mary on another's arm;
And as his spirits, worn in feeble guise,
Needed the boldness barley stout supplies,
He sought the ale-house, where by fear repelled
He scarce dare credit what his eyes beheld,
When in a corner, full of outward glee,
He saw his Mary on another's knee.
He turned away nor would his looks repeat;
She turned as white as death, but kept her seat;
For well she thought his carelessness foretold
He for a new love had forsook the old,

While he, with far more cause for dark distrust,
Thought all was over and his actions just;
And though he could not stifle without pain
His love, he thought it useless to explain,
So sat in silence as if none the while
Was worth the notice of a word or smile.
Yet as poor captives oft in hopeless plight
Look through their bars on liberty and light,
So did his eyes beneath his beaver's brim
Steal looks on Mary, half unknown to him,
While lifting up, when not athirst, the quart,
To drown the sigh fast swelling from his heart.
And Mary, smiling, struggled to be gay,
Though disappointment turned her cheek to clay,
And ate like cankers every rose away.
While Footman Tim was busy with his tale
And toasting Mary o'er each draught of ale,
Simon, as able to behold no more,
Emptied his quart and hurried to the door,
To seek amusement in the noise and rout
Within the fair, and keep old memories out.
But all were blanks, and every wish was vain,
And search for peace still added more to pain.
The showman's shout which wonder yearly brings,
The huge hung pictures of outlandish things,
Where grinning tigers wavered in the wind,
Raising more wonders than they hid behind,
The merry fool that would his speeches make
Till at the sport old women's sides would ache—
These without pleasure now he sauntered by,
And only turned a careless ear or eye;
And weary with the frolic and the fun,
He sauntered homeward ere the fair was done;
While as in melancholy mood he went,
In mutterings loud he gave his sorrows vent:
'Is it for this,' he said and turned behind,
As if mistrustful of the listening wind,
'Is it for this I watched, till church was o'er,
Her hens, and scoldings from the parson bore,

Hunting the eggs all church-time through the day,
That none should scold her when they laid away?
Is it for this my credit all at stake,
And even life I ventured for her sake?
When in the orchards, while she milked her cows,
I stole, and clambered to the topmost boughs
To reach the reddest apple, plum, or pear,
For no more payment than a smile could spare.
In this same close which brings up happier hours,
On Sundays when we brushed these self-same flowers,
When glossy slippers did her feet bedeck,
I took my kerchief even from my neck
To wipe off lingering drops of bygone showers,
Or, maybe, tears from crushed and broken flowers,
And dust that would their glossy hues o'ercast,
Powdered from kingcups shaken as we passed.
But what's the use to bring up things gone by?
My best I did, and the worst served am I.'
Here Simon stopt, for loud upon his ear
Stole merry voices fast approaching near,
From many laughing home-returning groups,
Not sad like Simon under broken hopes,
But wild with joy; glad frolicked many a lass,
On ploughman's arms light skipping through the grass;
Old men and women too, with ale inspired,
Felt young again and laughed till they were tired;
While children stooped and shouted by their sides
To see their shadows take such antic strides,
As mocking the old dames who danced and sung,
With aprons spread, as nimble as the young.
Simon, right anxious for the night's disguise,
Hurried along to hide from meddling eyes.
And though at toil next day he bawled and sung,
'Twas but to smother how his heart was wrung;
His mind still laboured over past affairs
And strove in vain to get the start of cares;
While hope proposed a medicine for pain,
Making it up to see her once again,
Resolving, if next Sunday should be fine,

To look o'er all, and ere he would resign
Love's all, he'd go and clear himself from wrong
And tell what kept him from the fair so long.
For he believed, and did his folly scoff,
That Mary fancied he had left her off,
And at the fair in hurt love's jealous whim
To be revenged took up with Footman Tim.
Thus Simon thought and often stopt his song
To curse lost Dobbin that had caused the wrong.

Soon Sunday came, and to make worse the matter
Raindrops from off the eves did quickly patter.
He heard it while abed, for sorrow aches
Around the heart and haunts it while it wakes;
And up he got, and with an anxious eye
From out the window looked upon the sky,
That darkly glowed as if it meant to last,
Raining away so thickly and so fast
That every drop made bubbles as they fell
In the mossed duck-pond and uncovered well;
While brimming ruts did headlong journeys go,
As if like springs they ever meant to flow.
The rain it ceased at noon, the sky looked through
The breaking clouds in many a patch of blue,
As breaks the thick ice in a sudden thaw,
Showing the bottom of the brook below;
When Simon instantly from off the nail
His bran-new beaver reached, and without fail
Brushed o'er the plashy fields and dripping stiles,
Careless of shortening day and lengthening miles;
For Mary's smiles would be to him as light
And make e'en sunshine of the darkest night.
And so they ought, for ere he reached the place
The sun sunk low and bade good night apace;
And while the spire peeped o'er the woodland bough,
He stopt to wipe the moisture from his brow,
Asking a shepherd where the farm might be
About the town where Mary lived; and he
Scarce raised him on his elbow from his lair,

And holding out his sheep-hook halloo'd, 'There';
When on his greedy ear her well-known voice
Echoed amain and made his heart rejoice,
As in a milking nook she called her cows,
While on he sped and hid among the boughs
Of blackthorn growing in disorder near,
The sad revealings of her mind to hear;
For grief in solitude will tell, though vain,
Its sorrows to itself to ease the pain.
So down he dropt amid the thicket's shade,
To list unseen the unsuspecting maid,
Staining his garments with the bruising grass,
For he thought little of his Sunday dress.
Nor was his expectation long deceived;
Her sighs soon told him how her heart was grieved;
And while the brook in mingling mutterings ran,
She milked, and thus her sad complaint began:
'Fie, Simon, fie, to seem to love so true;
Your heedless follies know not what they do.
My heart's nigh broken with his broken vow;
I feel so sad I scarce can milk my cow.
Yet none will free me from my Sunday toil,
So I must milk and Sunday gowns must spoil;
And spoil they may—I feel, in love's despair,
Few are the number I shall live to wear.
Simon's unkindness made all pleasures vain,
And left me wounds that cannot heal again.
Ungrateful man, to do as he hath done,
To take my pails that I the dirt might shun,
And lay fresh stones whene'er the brook was high
That I might cross in safety and be dry;
Then all at once to fling me from his mind
Nor e'en on memory turn a look behind;
Around me, as he did, like ivy cling,
And then to spurn me like a poison thing.
I felt no joy in fussy Footman Tim;
'Twas downright malice made me notice him;
And vain I tried to yield and he to win,
For love and malice claim but small akin.

False Simon first my foolish heart beguiled
And to none else will it be reconciled.
Would I could pluck his memory from my mind,
Just as a dewdrop trembles from the wind.
Oh, dear, I cannot, for my heart must own
The pain it feeleth to be left alone,
To weep unseen and all unheard to sigh;
Left all to silent loneliness am I,
Save that the robin, every time I come,
Peepeth and makes me welcome to his home,
Leaving in neighbouring bush its mossy nest,
To visit and invite me for its guest;
Perk nimble thing, were I but half as free
And half as happy, I might sing with thee;
Thy love proves true, but mine was false and bad,
And that which makes thee happy makes me sad.
Well, foolish griefs are follies, many say,
And long's the night that never looks for day;
Well, if the roads are bad and love unkind,
I've got my pattens still, so never mind;
Thank heaven I'm neither blind nor lame to need
An arm to lean on or a guide to lead;
Yet will my heart be sad,' so said her sighs
As she turned up her apron to her eyes.
Simon heard all, and from his hiding-place
Rushed out and caught her in his heart's embrace.
Cheered was his soul, forgetting former toil,
Glad as the hope that meets a lover's smile.
Then Simon up and told her all, and how
Misfortunes fell and made him break his vow,
And laid it all to Dobbin, who, at large,
Unfound remained, as heedless of the charge.
He told what kept him from the fair so long;
She heard with joy, yet grieved she judged so wrong;
And from that night both pledged eternal love,
Leaving the rest to him who rules above.
And Simon, when they parted in delight,
Could not help singing, though 'twas Sunday night,
And sung so loud, too, on his homeward way

That birds awoke and thought it must be day;
And day it was before he reached the farm,
Where gaping wonder, with inquiry warm,
On tiptoe stood to question his delay,
Where he had been and why he chose to stay;
But Silence, whom no bribe can force to speak,
Kept close her lips and left them still to seek.
Time went on smooth and gaily with him now,
And, glad as larks that sung him to his plough,
He toiled and sung, and labour seemed as naught
While Mary's smiles had share of every thought;
Save now and then, as o'er his memory crossed
The thought of Dobbin whom all reckoned lost.

And many a week went by and grew agen
To two whole months of mystery, and then,
With ribs nigh bare and shoulders galled and sore,
One morn they found him at the stable door,
Waiting as not forgot the accustomed corn
Which he was wont to share of every morn.
Hodge spied him first, and with a joyous shout
Cried, 'Here's old Dobbin!'—when from breakfast out
Came all, and joy in every face did burn,
Pleased as are mothers when their sons return.
One clapped his sides, one did his memory bless,
While Dobbin's looks bespoke his heart's distress.
Low hung his lip, nor in his former way
Did he give signs of frolic or of play;
Yet when his name was called, with freshened will
He pricked his ears as if he knew it still.
The farmer cursed the thieves he hoped to track,
And clapped old Dobbin as right welcome back,
And gave him extra corn and extra rest
Till he grew fat and frolic as the best;
When he his former fame revived again
For breaking gaps and getting in the grain.
And oft in after years, with memory's mirth,
Simon raised laughter round his cottage hearth
With tales of Dobbin's strange eventful life,

When happy Mary had become his wife,
Who often laughed while in his elbow-chair
He told the cause that kept him from the fair,
And all the pains then felt, now banished hence,
Since Mary's love had made him recompense;
Nay, kisses now he claimed back debts to pay,
And thus the winter's evening wore away;
Blessed each with each, like birds in summer weather,
Light was the chain that joined their hearts together.

SONNETS

HOPE SPRINGS ETERNAL

WE well may wonder o'er the change of scene
  Now summer's contrast thro' the land is spread,
  And turn us back where winter's tempest fled
And left naught living but the ivy's green.
  The then bare woods, that trembled overhead
Like spectres mid the storm of what had been
  And wrecks of beauty, ne'er to bloom again,
Are now all glory.   Nature smiles as free
  As the last summer had commenced its reign
And she were blooming in eternity.
  So in this life, when future thoughts beguile
And from past care our spirits get relieved,
  Hope cheers us onward with as sweet a smile
As if before she never had deceived.

TO AN INFANT SISTER

BESSY—I call thee by that earthly name
Which but a little while belonged to thee—
Thou leftst me growing up to sin and shame,
And keptst thy innocence unstained and free,
To seek the refuge of a heaven above
Where life's bud opens in eternity.
Bessy, when memory turns thy lot to see,
A brother's bosom yearns thy bliss to prove,
And sighs o'er wishes that were not to be;
Ah, had we gone together, had I been
Strange with the world as thou thy mother's love,
What years of sorrow I had never seen!
Fullness of joy that leaves no hearts to bleed
Had then with thine been purchased cheap indeed.

EVENING PASTIME

MUSING beside the crackling fire at night,
　While singing kettle merrily prepares
Woman's solacing beverage, I delight
　To read a pleasant volume, where the cares
Of life are sweetened by the muse's voice—
　Thomson, or Cowper, or the bard that bears
Life's humblest name, though nature's favoured choice,
　Her pastoral Bloomfield;—and as evening wears,
Weary with reading, list the little tales
　Of laughing children, who edge up their chairs
To tell the past day's sport, which never fails
　To cheer the spirits.　While my fancy shares
Their artless talk, man's sturdy reason quails,
　And memory's joy grows young again with theirs.

EVENING PRIMROSE

WHEN once the sun sinks in the west,
And dew-drops pearl the evening's breast,
Almost as pale as moonbeams are,
Or its companionable star,
The evening primrose opes anew
Its delicate blossoms to the dew;
And shunning, hermit-like, the light,
Wastes its fair bloom upon the night;
Who, blindfold to its fond caresses,
Knows not the beauty he possesses.
Thus it blooms on till night is by;
When day looks out with open eye,
'Bashed at the gaze it cannot shun,
It faints, and withers, and is done.

SUDDEN SHOWER

BLACK grows the southern sky, betokening rain,
　And humming hive-bees homeward hurry by:

They feel the change; so let us shun the grain,
   And take the broad road while our feet are dry.
Ay, there some dropples moistened on my face,
   And pattered on my hat—'tis coming nigh!
Let's look about, and find a sheltering place.
   The little things around, like you and I,
Are hurrying through the grass to shun the shower.
   Here stoops an ash-tree—hark! the wind gets high,
But never mind; this ivy, for an hour,
   Rain as it may, will keep us dryly here:
That little wren knows well his sheltering bower,
   Nor leaves his dry house though we come so near.

HOME PICTURES IN MAY

THE sunshine bathes in clouds of many hues
And morning's feet are gemmed with early dews;
Warm daffodils about the garden beds
Peep through their pale slim leaves their golden heads,
Sweet earthly suns of spring; the gosling broods,
In coats of sunny green, about the road
Waddle in ecstasy; and in rich moods
The old hen leads her flickering chicks abroad,
Oft scuttling 'neath her wings to see the kite
Hang wavering o'er them in the spring's blue light.
The sparrows round their new nests chirp with glee
And sweet the robin spring's young luxury shares,
Tootling its song in feathery gooseberry tree
While watching worms the gardener's spade unbares.

WOODLAND THOUGHTS

How sweet the wood shades the hot summer hours
   And stretches o'er my head its sheltering green,
As I recline mid grass and cooling flowers
   And seeded stalks of blossoms that have been.

Sure 'tis a pleasure in such secret nooks
    To muse on distant friends in memory's eye,
Or glance on passages in favourite books
    Whose thoughts like echoes to our own reply,
Or shades recall, which substance long forsook,
    From the black nothingness of days gone by,
Blessings of infant hope and love's young bliss.
    Ah, thus to think, the thought of death is sweet
In shaping heaven to a scene like this,
    With loves and friends and feelings all to meet.

SUNRISE

Morning awakes sublime; glad earth and sky
    Smile in the splendour of the day begun.
O'er the broad earth's illumined canopy,
    Shade of its Maker's majesty, the sun
Gleams in its living light from cloud to cloud;
    Streaks of all colours beautifully run
As if before heaven's gate there hung a shroud
    To hide its grand magnificence.   O heaven,
Where entrance e'en to thought is disallowed,
    To view the glory that this scene is giving
What may blind reason not expect to see,
    When in immortal worlds the soul is living
Eternal as its maker, and as free
To taste the unknowns of eternity?

SUNSET

Welcome, sweet eve! thy gently sloping sky,
    And softly whispering wind that breathes of rest;
And clouds unlike what daylight galloped by,
    Now stopt as weary, huddling in the west,
Each, by the farewell of day's closing eye,
    Left with the smiles of heaven on its breast.

Meek nurse of weariness! how sweet to meet
　　Thy soothing tenderness to none denied;
To hear thy whispering voice—ah, heavenly sweet,
　　Musing and listening by thy gentle side;
Lost to life's cares, thy coloured skies to view,
　　Picturing of pleasant worlds unknown to care;
And when our bark the rough sea flounders through,
　　Warming in hopes its end shall harbour there.

THE HAPPINESS OF IGNORANCE

Ere I had known the world and understood
　　How many follies wisdom names its own,
Distinguishing things evil from things good,
　　The dread of sin and death—ere I had known
Knowledge, the root of evil—had I been
　　Left in some lone place where the world is wild,
And trace of troubling man was never seen,
　　Brought up by Nature as her favourite child,
As born for naught but joy where all rejoice,
　　Emparadised in ignorance of sin,
Where Nature tries with never chiding voice,
　　Like tender nurse, our careless smiles to win—
The future, dreamless, beautiful would be;
The present, foretaste of eternity.

TO CHARLES LAMB ON HIS ESSAYS

Elia, thy reveries and visioned themes
　　To care's lorn heart a luscious pleasure proves,
Wild as the mystery of delightful dreams,
　　Soft as the anguish of remembered loves;
Like records of past days their memory dances
　　Mid the cool feelings manhood's reason brings,
As the unearthly visions of romances
　　Peopled with sweet and uncreated things;

520

And yet thy themes thy gentle worth enhances;
  Then wake again thy wild harp's tenderest strings,
Sing on, sweet bard, let fairy loves again
  Smile in thy dreams with angel ecstasies;
Bright o'er our minds will break the witching strain
  Through the dull gloom of earth's realities.

TO DE WINT

DE WINT! I would not flatter; nor would I
  Pretend to critic-skill in this thy art;
Yet in thy landscape I can well descry
  The breathing hues as nature's counterpart.
No painted peaks, no wild romantic sky,
  No rocks, nor mountains, as the rich sublime,
Hath made thee famous; but the sunny truth
  Of nature, that doth mark thee for all time,
Found on our level pastures—spots, forsooth,
  Where common skill sees nothing deemed divine.
Yet here a worshipper was found in thee;
  And thy young pencil worked such rich surprise
That rushy flats, befringed with willow tree,
  Rivalled the beauties of Italian skies.

NOTHINGNESS OF LIFE

I NEVER pass a venerable tree,
  Pining away to nothingness and dust,
Ruin's vain shades of power I never see,
  Once dedicated to time's cheating trust—
But warm reflection wakes her saddest thought
  And views life's vanity in cheerless light,
And sees earth's bubbles, youth so eager sought,
  Burst into emptiness of lost delight,
And all the pictures of life's early day,
  Like evening's striding shadows, haste away.

Yet there's a glimmering of pleasure springs
    From such reflections of earth's vanity;
We pine and sicken o'er life's mortal things,
    And feel a relish for eternity.

THE INSTINCT OF HOPE

Is there another world for this frail dust
    To warm with life and be itself again?
Something about me daily speaks there must,
    And why should instinct nourish hopes in vain?
'Tis nature's prophecy that such will be,
    And everything seems struggling to explain
The close-sealed volume of its mystery.
    Time wandering onward keeps its usual pace
As seeming anxious of eternity,
    To meet that calm and find a resting-place.
E'en the small violet feels a future power
    And waits each year renewing blooms to bring,
And surely man is no inferior flower
    To die unworthy of a second spring.

PROVIDENCE (I)

Folks talk of providence with heedless tongue
    That leads to riches and not happiness,
Which is but a new tune for fortune's song,
    And one contentment cares not to profess.
It knows her seldom and it shuns her long,
    And that kind providence least understood
Hath been my friend that helps me bear with wrong
    And learns me out of evil to find good;
To hearten up against the heartless creeds
    Of selfish interests leading blindly on,
To make one's poor faith wither mid the weeds

Of earth's deceptions; yet when these are gone
A voice within tells peace our one true friend:
And this is providence, right worthy to commend.

PROVIDENCE (II)

It hides the future, and leaves room for hope
  To smile and promise joys that may not come;
And cares from which our fortunes can't elope
  Are robbed of half their terrors, being dumb
And all unable to foretell their speed.
  This blessed ignorance is half the sum
Of providence; thus all are blest indeed,
  The weak and strong, the timid and the bold;
Thus will the hare feel safe in its retreat,
  Where lay the murdering fox an hour before;
And upon boughs warm with the falcon's feet,
  The wren will perch, and dream of harm no more.
Kind providence amid contending strife
Bids weakness feel the liberty of life.

CARELESS RAMBLES

I love to wander at my idle will,
  In summer's luscious prime, about the fields,
To kneel, when thirsty, at the little rill,
  And sip the draught its pebbly bottom yields;
  And where the maple bush its fountain shields,
To lie, and rest a swaly hour away,
  And crop the swelling peascod from the land;
Or mid the upland's woodland-walks to stray,
  Where oaks for aye o'er their old shadows stand,
  'Neath whose dark foliage, with a welcome hand,
I pluck the luscious strawberry, ripe and red
  As beauty's lips;—and in my fancy's dreams,
As mid the velvet moss I musing tread,
  Feel life as lovely as her picture seems.

523

THE OLD WILLOW

THE juicy wheat now spindles into ear,
And trailing pea-blooms ope their velvet eyes;
And weeds and flowers, by crowds, far off and near,
In all their sunny liveries appear,
For summer's lustre boasts unnumbered dyes.
How pleasant, 'neath this willow by the brook—
Its ancient dwelling-place for many a year—
To sit, and o'er these crowded fields to look,
And the soft dropping of the shower to hear,
Ourselves so sheltered, e'en a pleasant book
Might lie uninjured from the fragrant rain,
For not a drop gets through the bowery leaves;
But dry as housed in my old hut again,
I sit, and troublous care but half its claim receives.

THE WRYNECK'S NEST

THAT summer bird its oft-repeated note
    Chirps from the dotterel ash, and in the hole
The green woodpecker made in years remote,
    It makes its nest.   When peeping idlers stroll
In anxious plundering moods, they by and by
    The wryneck's curious eggs, as white as snow,
While squinting in the hollow tree, espy.
The sitting bird looks up with jetty eye,
    And waves her head in terror to and fro,
Speckled and veined with various shades of brown;
And then a hissing noise assails the clown.
    Quickly, with hasty terror in his breast,
From the tree's knotty trunk he sluthers down,
    And thinks the strange bird guards a serpent's nest.

FOREST FLOWERS

YE simple weeds, that make the desert gay,
    Disdained of all, e'en by the youngster's eye,

Who lifts his stick, a weapon in his play,
  And lops your blossoms as he saunters by,
    In mockery of merriment!—Yet I
Hail you as favourites of my early days;
  And every year, as mid your haunts I lie,
Some added pleasure claims my lonely gaze:
  Star-pointed thistle with its ruddy flowers,
Wind-waving rush, left to bewildered ways,
  Shunning the scene which culture's toil devours;
Ye thrive in silence where I glad recline,
  Sharing with finer blooms spring's gentle showers,
That show ye're prized by better taste than mine.

THE ASS

POOR patient creature! how I grieve to see
  Thy wants so ill supplied—to see thee strain
  And stretch thy tether for the grass, in vain,
Which heaven's rain nourishes for all but thee,
  The fair green field, the fullness of the plain
Add to thy hunger; colt and heifer pass,
And roll, as though they mocked thee, on the grass,
  Which would be luxury to the bare brown lane
Where thou'rt imprisoned, humble, patient ass,
  Cropping foul weeds, yet scorning to complain.
Mercy at first 'sent out the wild ass free,'
  A ranger 'of the mountains'; and what crimes
Did thy progenitors, that thou shouldst be
  The slave and mockery of later times?

AUTUMN

AUTUMN comes laden with her ripened load
Of fruitage and so scatters them abroad
That the fern-smothered heath and mole-hill waste
Are black with bramble berries—where in haste
The chubby urchins from the village hie

To feast them there, stained with the purple dye;
While painted woods around my rambles be
In draperies worthy of eternity.
Yet will the leaves soon patter on the ground,
And death's deaf voice awake at every sound:
One drops—then others—and the last that fell
Rings for those left behind their passing-bell.
Thus memory everywhere her tidings brings
How sad death robs us of life's dearest things.

THE WHEAT RIPENING

WHAT time the wheat-field tinges rusty brown
    And barley bleaches in its mellow grey,
'Tis sweet some smooth-mown baulk to wander down
    Or cross the fields on footpath's narrow way
    Just in the mealy light of waking day,
As glittering dewdrops moist the maiden's gown
    And sparkling bounces from her nimble feet,
Journeying to milking from the neighbouring town,
    Making life light with song; and it is sweet
To mark the grazing herds and list the clown
    Urge on his ploughing team with cheering calls,
And merry shepherds whistling toils begun,
    And hoarse-tongued bird-boy whose unceasing brawls
Join the lark's ditty to the rising sun.

TO THE MEMORY OF BLOOMFIELD (I)

SWEET unassuming minstrel! not to thee
    The dazzling fashions of the day belong;
Nature's wild pictures, field, and cloud, and tree,
    And quiet brooks, far distant from the throng,
In murmurs tender as the toiling bee,
    Make the sweet music of thy gentle song.
Well, Nature owns thee: let the crowd pass by;

The tide of fashion is a stream too strong
For pastoral brooks, that gently flow and sing:
  But Nature is their source, and earth and sky
Their annual offering to her current bring.
  Thy gentle muse and memory need no sigh;
For thine shall murmur on to many a spring,
  When prouder streams are summer-burnt and dry.

TO THE MEMORY OF BLOOMFIELD (II)

THE shepherd musing o'er his summer dreams,
The May-day wild flowers in the meadow grass,
The sunshine sparkling in the valley streams,
The singing ploughman and haymaking lass—
These live, the summer of thy rural themes;
Thy green memorials these, and they surpass
The cobweb praise of fashion; every May
Shall find a native Giles beside his plough,
Joining the skylark's song at early day;
And summer, rustling in the ripening corn,
Shall meet thy rustic lover as sweet as now,
Offering to Mary's lips 'the brimming horn';
And seasons round thy humble grave shall be
Fond lingering pilgrims to remember thee.

OLD POESY (I)

SWEET is the poesy of the olden time,
In the unsullied infancy of rhyme,
When nature reigned omnipotent to teach,
And truth and feeling owned the powers of speech.
Rich is the music of each early theme
And sweet as sunshine in a summer dream,
Giving to stocks and stones, in rapture's strife,
A soul of utterance and a tongue of life.
Sweet are these wild flowers in their disarray,

527

Which art and fashion fling as weeds away,
To sport with shadows of inferior kind,
Mere magic-lanthorns of the shifting mind,
Automatons of wonder-working powers,
Shadows of life, and artificial flowers.

OLD POESY (II)

To turn from pages of this modern art
To fame's old pages that real life impart,
We seem as startled from unnatural dreams
To hear the summer voice of woods and streams,
And feel the sunny air, right green and young,
Breathe music round as though a siren sung;
And greet, as art's vain painted scenes are by,
The soul-stirred impulse of a living sky,
As in long droughts of summer's parchèd hours
Falls the refreshment of great rains and showers.
The birds resume their song, the leaves their green,
And brooks, that long dry as the land have been,
Brim-full of the sky's bounty gladly go,
Seeming to sing and wonder why they flow.

IZAAK WALTON

SOME blame thee, honest Izaak! ay, and deem
Thy pastime cruel, by the silent stream
Of the unwooded Lea: but he that warms
In eloquence of grief o'er suffering worms
Throws by his mourning quill, and hunts the hare
Whole hours to death, yet feels no sorrow there.
Yet this mock-sentimental man of moods
On every pastime but his own intrudes:
Not so with thee, thou man of angel-mind!
That, like thy Master, gentle was, and kind;

Fit emblem of the prime apostles' days,
And worthy even of the scripture praise;
For men of God's own heart must surely be
Those honest souls that most resemble thee.

SHADOWS

THE fairest summer hath its sudden showers;
The clearest sky is never without clouds;
And in the painted meadow's host of flowers
Some lurking weed a poisonous death enshrouds.
Sweet days, that upon golden sunshine spring,
A gloomy night in mourning waits to stain;
The honey-bees are girt with sharpest sting,
And sweetest joys oft breed severest pain.
While like to autumn's storms, sudden and brief,
Mirth's parted lips oft close in silent grief,
Amid this chequered life's disastrous state,
Still hope lives green amid the desolate;
As Nature, in her happy livery, waves
O'er ancient ruins, palaces, and graves.

TO MARY (I)

I MET thee like the morning, though more fair,
And hopes 'gan travel for a glorious day;
And though night met them ere they were aware,
Leading the joyous pilgrims all astray,
Yet know I not, though they did miss their way,
That joyed so much to meet thee, if they are
To blame or bless the fate that bade such be.
Thou seem'dst an angel when I met thee first,
Nor has aught made thee otherwise to me:
Possession had not cloyed my love, nor curst

Fancy's wild visions with reality.
Thou art an angel still; and Hope, awoke
From the fond spell that early raptures nurst,
Still feels a joy to think that spell ne'er broke.

TO MARY (II)

THE flower that's gathered beauty soon forsakes;
The bliss grows feeble as we gain the prize;
Love dreams of joy, and in possession wakes,
Scarce time enough to hail it ere it dies:
Life intermingles, with its cares and sighs,
And rapture's dreams are ended.   Heavenly flower,
It is not so with thee! Still fancy's power
Throws rainbow haloes round thee, and thine eyes,
That once did steal their sapphire blue from even,
Are beaming on; thy cheeks' bewitching dye,
Where partial roses all their blooms had given,
Still in fond memory with the rose can vie;
And thy sweet bosom, which to view was heaven,
No lily yet a fairer hue supplies.

ON A SKULL

LIFE'S monitor and fear-inspiring friend,
Picture of our frail origin and end,
Is thine death's quiet sleep? 'Tis horrible
With worms and dust and coffined bones to dwell.
Dost lie in fear of waking wrapt around
In death's dark, sealed, impenetrable cloud?
Dost ever dream and speak without a sound?
'Twould make death's self to shudder in his shroud.
Thy shadow hangeth like a gloomy pall
With more or less of terror over all.

Life, looking in this glass of time, doth freeze
With fear at its own image which it sees.
To think the living head with thoughts so full
Is but the flattered portrait of a skull!

A FAVOURITE NOOK DESTROYED

Poor outcast refugees of mother earth,
    Condemned in vain for rest and peace to roam,
Ye birds and beasts of fate's despited birth,
    Forced from the wilds which nature left your home
By vile invasions of encroaching men,
    By whom wild nature's nearly dispossest—
The rabbit has no waste to make his den,
    And the coy pheasant has not where to rest,
And cawing rook, as spring returns again,
    Scarce finds a tree whereon to build its nest.
Ah, tyrant knaves, while preaching freedom's laws,
    Crying down tyranny in stronger power,
You glut your vile unsatiated maws
    And freedom's birthright in the weak devour.

BEAUTY'S DECAY

Youth speeds its springtide like a princely flower,
And beauty is the jewel of its hour,
That blooms exulting in its triumph there,
'This work is mine and where is aught so fair?'
Nature looks on and doth in raptures move,
Feeling the earnest of delight is love;
Its pains and happiness are sighs and smiles,
And life in bud with opening hope beguiles;
While scarce a pulse beats 'neath the fickle reign
Of present happiness and future pain.

531

For what hath beauty's self to boast and wear,
A lily skin, a cheek of rose, dark hair,
Bright eyes and ruby lips—time's poor display—
When every hour can steal a charm away?

THE LADY-FLY

TENANT of leaves and flowers and glossy stalks,
   The wild profusion that the summer brings,
Hiding in crowding beans and benty baulks,
    Where, on the knapweed while the cricket sings,
    I often watch thee prune thy speckled wings,
On the smooth stem advancing yet more high,
   Till with the help the puffing zephyr brings
Thou'lt stretch thy finer wings of gauze and fly,
In changing scenes more snug and cool to lie.
   Ah, when a cow-boy I at ease reclined
Upon a thymy hill, and thou wert nigh,
   What fond inquiries filled my curious mind!
How have I watched thy pastimes, lady-fly,
   And thought thee happiest creature of thy kind!

SUNDAY EVENING

RELIGION never more calm beauty wears
Than when each cottage joins in Sunday prayers;
The poor man in his ignorance of ill
His Bible reads with unpretending skill.
Unused to argue strange conflicting creeds,
He puts plain comments to the page he reads.
Though venturing not in warm enthusiasts' ways
To offer his own ignorance for praise,
He in his prayer-book's beauteous homilies
His simple reverence to his God reveals,

And while his listening children clasp his knees
A parent's blessing from his bosom steals.
Prayers are the wings on which the soul doth fly
To gather blessings from a bounteous sky.

SUNSET

'TWEEN evening's farewell and the night's approach,
  I love to linger on the garden seat,
While glooms around me sluggishly encroach;
  Or in some neighbouring spot short walks repeat
To watch the west which heaven's best smiles doth bless,
  Where longest clings the memory of the day,
To see it fade and fade, till, colourless,
  The painted record vanishes away,
In time's turned pages to be seen no more.
  Yet gloomy night shall but awhile delay
The past day's offspring that hath smiles in store
  As lovely as the fruit.   Oh, it is sweet
To prove by this, when death's long night is o'er,
  That we shall wake another world to meet.

AN IDLE HOUR

SAUNTERING at ease, I often love to lean
  O'er old bridge walls and mark the flood below,
Whose ripples, through the weeds of oily green,
  Like happy travellers mutter as they go;
And mark the sunshine dancing on the arch,
  Time keeping to the merry waves beneath,
And on the banks see drooping blossoms parch,
  Thirsting for water in the day's hot breath,
Right glad of mud-drops splashed upon their leaves,
  By cattle plunging from the steepy brink;

Each water-flower more than its share receives
    And revels to its very cups in drink:
So in the world, some strive, and fare but ill,
While others riot, and have plenty still.

A SPRING MORNING

THE Spring comes in with all her hues and smells,
In freshness breathing over hills and dells,
O'er woods where May her gorgeous drapery flings,
And meads washed fragrant by their laughing springs.
Fresh are new-opened flowers, untouched and free
From the bold rifling of the amorous bee.
The happy time of singing birds is come,
And love's lone pilgrimage now finds a home;
Among the mossy oaks now coos the dove,
And the hoarse crow finds softer notes for love.
The foxes play around their dens and bark
In joy's excess, mid woodland shadows dark.
The flowers join lips below, the leaves above,
And every sound that meets the ear is love.

CROWLAND ABBEY

IN sooth, it seems right awful and sublime
    To gaze by moonlight on the shattered pile
Of this old abbey, struggling still with time—
    The grey owl hooting from its rents the while,
And tottering stones, as wakened by the sound,
Crumbling from arch and battlement around,
    Urging dread echoes from the gloomy aisle,
To sink more silent still.—The very ground
    In desolation's garment doth appear,
The lapse of age and mystery profound.

We gaze on wrecks of ornamented stones,
  On tombs whose sculptures half erased appear,
On rank weeds, battening over human bones,
  Till even one's very shadow seems to fear.

A PLEASANT PLACE

Now summer comes, and I with staff in hand
  Will hie me to the sabbath of her joys,
To heathy spots and the unbroken land
  Of woodland heritage, unknown to noise
And toil, save many a playful band
  Of dancing insects, that well understand
The sweets of life, and with attunèd voice
  Sing in sweet concert to the pleasant May.
There by a little bush I'll listening rest
  To hear the nightingale a lover's lay
Chaunt to his mate, who builds her careless nest
  Of oaken leaves on thorn-stumps, mossed and grey;
Feeling, with them, I too am truly blest
  By making sabbaths of each common day.

NOVEMBER

Sibyl of months, and worshipper of winds,
  I love thee, rude and boisterous as thou art;
And scraps of joy my wandering ever finds
  Mid thy uproarious madness—when the start
Of sudden tempests stirs the forest leaves
  Into hoarse fury, till the shower set free
Stills the huge swells. Then ebb the mighty heaves,
  That sway the forest like a troubled sea.
I love thy wizard noise, and rave in turn
  Half-vacant thoughts, and rhymes of careless form:

Then hide me from the shower, a short sojourn,
   'Neath ivied oak; and mutter to the storm,
Wishing its melody belonged to me,
That I might breathe a living song to thee.

ROUND-OAK SPRING

SWEET brook, I've met thee many a summer's day
   And ventured fearless in thy shallow flood
And rambled oft thy sweet unwearied way,
   'Neath willows cool that on thy margin stood,
With crowds of partners in my artless play,
   Grasshopper, beetle, bee, and butterfly,
That frisked about, as though in merry mood,
   To see their old companion sporting by.
Sweet brook, life's glories once were thine and mine,
   Shades clothed thy spring that now doth naked lie;
On thy white boiling sand the sweet woodbine
   Darkened, and dipt its flowers: I mark and sigh,
And muse o'er troubles since we met the last,
Like two fond friends whose happiness is past.

MAY (I)

Now comes the bonny May, dancing and skipping
   Across the stepping-stones of meadow streams,
Bearing no kin to April showers a-weeping,
   But constant sunshine as her servant seems.
Her heart is up—her sweetness, all a-maying,
   Streams in her face, like gems on beauty's breast;
The swains are sighing all and well-a-daying,
   Love-sick and gazing on their lovely guest.
The Sunday paths, to pleasant places leading,
   Are graced by couples linking arm in arm;

Sweet smiles enjoying, or some book a-reading,
    Where love and beauty are the constant charm;
For while the bonny May is dancing by,
Beauty delights the ear, and beauty fills the eye.

MAY (II)

BIRDS sing and build, and Nature scorns alone
    On May's young festival to keep a widow;
The children too have pleasures all their own,
    A-plucking lady-smocks along the meadow.
The little brook sings loud among the pebbles,
    So very loud that water-flowers, which lie
Where many a silver curdle boils and dribbles,
    Dance too with joy as it goes singing by.
Among the pasture mole-hills maidens stoop
    To pluck the luscious marjoram for their bosoms;
The greensward's smothered o'er with buttercups,
    And whitethorns, they are breaking down with blossoms!
'Tis Nature's livery for the bonny May,
Who keeps her court, and all have holiday.

MAY (III)

PRINCESS of months!—so Nature's choice ordains,
And lady of the summer still she reigns,
    In spite of April's youth, who charms in tears,
And rosy June, who wins with blushing face,
    July, sweet shepherdess, who wreathes the shears
Of shepherds with her flowers of winning grace,
    And sun-tanned August, with her swarthy charms,
The beautiful and rich, and pastoral gay
    September, with her pomp of fields and farms,
And wild November's sibylline array;—

In spite of beauty's calendar, the year
Garlands with beauty's prize the bonny May.
　　Where'er she goes, fair Nature hath no peer,
And months do lose their queen when she's away.

MAY (IV)

Up like a princess starts the merry morning,
　　In draperies of many-coloured cloud;
And skylarks, minstrels of the early dawning,
　　Pipe forth their hearty anthems long and loud.
The bright enamoured sunshine goes a-maying,
　　And every flower his laughing eye beguiles;
And on the milkmaid's rosy face a-playing,
　　Pays court to beauty in its softest smiles.
For May's divinity of joy begun
　　Adds life and lustre to the golden sun;
And all of life, beneath its glory straying,
　　Is by May's beauty into worship won;
Till golden eve ennobles all the west,
And day goes blushing like a bride to rest.

NUTTING

The sun had stooped, his westward clouds to win,
Like weary traveller seeking for an inn,
When from the hazelly wood we glad descried
The ivied gateway by the pasture side.
Long had we sought for nuts amid the shade,
Where silence fled the rustle that we made;
When torn by briers and brushed by sedges rank,
We left the wood, and on the velvet bank
Of short-sward pasture-ground we sat us down
To shell our nuts before we reached the town.

The near-hand stubble-field, with mellow glower,
Showed the dimmed blaze of poppies still in flower;
And sweet the mole-hills smelt we sat upon—
Again the thyme's in bloom, but where is pleasure gone?

THE WOODMAN

Now evening comes, and from the new-laid hedge
   The woodman rustles in his leathern guise,
Hiding in ditches lined with bristling sedge
   His bill and mittens from theft's meddling eyes,
Within his wallet storing many a pledge
   Of flowers and boughs from early-sprouting trees,
And painted pooties from the ivied hedge,
   About its mossy roots—his boys to please,
Who wait with merry joy his coming home,
   Anticipating presents such as these
Gained far afield, where they, or night or morn,
   Find no school leisure long enough to go,
Where flowers but rarely from their stalks are torn,
   And birds scarce lose a nest the season through.

MORNING PLEASURES

THE dewy virtues of the early morn
   Breathe rich of health, and lead the mind to joy;
While, like a thrilling pleasure newly born,
   Each little hamlet wakes its shouting boy
Right earlily, to wander out afield,
   Brushing the dew-drops from the bending corn,
To see what nests the hedgerow thorns may shield,
   Or gather 'cuckoos' from the neighbouring lawn;
Where, mid the dark dog-mercury that abounds

Round each moss stump, the woodlark hides her nest.
The delicate blue-bell, that her home surrounds,
    Bows its soft fragrance o'er her spotted breast,
Till startled, from the boy's rude step she flies,
Who turns the weeds away, and vainly seeks the prize.

HAYMAKING

'Tis hay-time; and the red-complexioned sun
Was scarcely up, ere blackbirds had begun,
Along the meadow-hedges here and there,
To sing loud songs to the sweet-smelling air,
Whose scent of flowers and grass and grazing cow
Flings o'er one's senses streams of fragrance now;
While in some pleasant nook the swain and maid
Lean o'er their rakes, and loiter in the shade,
Or bend a minute o'er the bridge, and throw
Crumbs in their leisure to the fish below.
Hark at that happy shout, and song between!
'Tis Pleasure's birthday, in her meadow-scene.
What joy seems half so rich, from pleasure won,
As the loud laugh of maidens in the sun!

MORNING

The morning now right earlily in dew
Bathed her sweet naked limbs of fairest hue,
While like a veil all careless thrown aback
On her white shoulders hung her hair so black;
And when the sun a minute earlier rose
The lovely morning sought her cloudy clothes,
But finding none she hasting shrank away;
For night abashed had startled into day.

The sun reigned absolute in cloudless sky
And wooed morn's timid beauty to comply,
And scarlet as the dress she earlier wore
Her white face turned that was so fair before;
While fear in every limb diffused its charms
As soft she sighed and melted in his arms.

THE PARISH: A SATIRE [1]

THE parish hind, oppression's humble slave,
Whose only hope of freedom is the grave,
The cant miscalled religion in the saint,
And justice mocked while listening want's complaint,
The parish laws and parish queens and kings,
Pride's lowest classes of pretending things,
The meanest dregs of tyranny and crime,
I fearless sing: let truth attend my rhyme.
That good old fame the farmers earned of yore,
That made as equals, not as slaves, the poor,
That good old fame did in two sparks expire—
A shooting coxcomb and a hunting squire;
And their old mansions that were dignified
With things far better than the pomp of pride,
At whose oak table, that was plainly spread,
Each guest was welcomed and the poor were fed,
Where master, son, and serving-man and clown
Without distinction daily sat them down,
Where the bright rows of pewter by the wall
Served all the pomp of kitchen or of hall—
These all have vanished like a dream of good;
And the slim things that rise where they once stood
Are built by those whose clownish taste aspires
To hate their farms and ape the country squires.
And where's that lovely maid, in days gone by

---

[1] Clare wrote most of this poem between 1820 and 1824, though he added
several passages at a later date. Both its length and its subject prevented
its inclusion in *The Shepherd's Calendar* or *The Rural Muse*; his plan to
have it published by a local printer fell through, so that he did not prepare
a final draft. Hence the text given here excludes a number of passages
which were not sufficiently worked in. Clare left the following notes on
the poem: 'This poem was begun and finished under the pressure of heavy
distress, with embittered feelings under a state of anxiety and oppression
almost amounting to slavery, when the prosperity of one class was founded
on the adversity and distress of the other. The haughty demand by the
master to his labourer was "Work for the little I choose to allow you and
go to the parish for the rest—or starve." To decline working under such
"advantages" was next to offending a magistrate, and no opportunity was
lost in marking the insult by some unqualified oppression. . . .
'Each character is a true one and as little coloured as possible.'

The farmer's daughter, unreserved though shy,
That milked her cows and old songs used to sing,
As red and rosy as the lovely spring?
Ah, these have dwindled to a formal shade
As pale and bedrid as my lady's maid,
Who cannot dare to venture in the street,
Sometimes thro' cold, at other times for heat,
And vulgar eyes to shun and vulgar winds,
Shrouded in veils green as their window-blinds;
These, taught at school their stations to despise
And view old customs with disdainful eyes,
Deem all as rude their kindred did of yore,
And scorn to toil or foul their fingers more;
They sit before their glasses hour by hour,
Or paint unnatural daubs of fruit or flower;
E'en poetry in these high-polished days
Is oft profaned by their dislike or praise;
Thus housed mid cocks and hens in idle state,
Aping at fashions which their betters hate,
Affecting high life's airs to scorn the past,
Trying to be something makes them naught at last;
These are the shadows that supply the place
Of famous daughters of the vanished race.
And what are these? Rude names will do them harm.
Oh, rather call them 'Ladies of the Farm.'
Miss Peevish Scornful, once the village toast,
Deemed fair by some and prettyish by most;
Brought up a lady, tho' her father's gain
Depended still on cattle and on grain,
She followed shifting fashions and aspired
To the high notions baffled pride desired;
And all the profits pigs and poultry made
Were given to Miss for dressing and parade,
To visit balls and plays, fresh hopes to chase,
And try her fortune with a simpering face;
She now and then in London's crowds was shown,
To know the world and to the world be known;
All leisure hours while Miss at home sojourned
Passed in preparing till new routs returned,

Or tittle-tattling o'er her shrewd remarks
Of ladies' dresses or attentive sparks:
How Mr. So-and-so at such a rout
Fixed his eyes on her all the night about;
And young Squire Dandy, just returned from France,
How he first chose her from the rest to dance;
How this squire bowed polite at her approach,
And lords e'en nodded as she passed their coach.
Thus she went on, and visited and drest,
And deemed things earnest that were spoke in jest,
And dreamed at night o'er pride's unchecked desires
Of nodding gentlemen and smiling squires;
To Gretna Green her visions often fled,
And rattling coaches lumbered in her head;
Till hopes, grown weary with too long delay,
Caught the green sickness and declined away,
And beauty, like a garment worse for wear,
Fled her pale cheek and left it much too fair.
Then she gave up sick-visits, balls, and plays,
Where whispers turned to anything but praise;
All were thrown by like an old-fashioned song
Where she had played show-woman much too long;
She condescended to be kind and plain,
And 'mong her equals hoped to find a swain;
Past follies now were hateful to review,
And they were hated by her equals too;
Notice from equals vain she tried to court,
Or if they noticed 'twas but just in sport;
At last, grown husband-mad, away she ran,
Not with young Squire Dandy, but the servant man.

Young Farmer Bigg, of this same flimsy class,
Wise among fools and with the wise an ass,
A farming sprout with more than farmer's pride,
Struts like a lord and dresses dignified;
They call him squire, at which his weakness aimed;
But others view him as a fool misnamed.
Yet dress and tattle ladies' hearts can charm,
And he's the choice with madams of the farm,

Now with that lady strutting, now with this,
Braced up in stays as slim as sickly miss,
Shining at Christmas rout and vulgar ball,
The favourite spark and rival of them all.
And oft he'll venture to bemean his pride,
—Tho' bribes and mysteries do their best to hide—
Teasing weak maidens with his pert deceit,
Whose lives are humble and whose looks are sweet,
Whose beauty happens to outrival those
With whom the dandy as an equal goes.
Thus maids are ruined oft and mothers made,
As if bewitched, without a father's aid;
Tho' nods and winks and whispers urge a guess,
Weakness is bribed and hides its heart's distress,
To live dishonoured and to die unwed;
For clowns grow jealous when they're once misled.
Thus pointed fingers brand the passing spark,
And whispers often guess his deeds are dark;
But friends deny and urge that doubts mislead,
And prove the youth above so mean a deed.
The town agrees and leaves his ways at will,
A proud, conceited, meddling fellow still.

Nature in various moods pursues her plan,
And moulds by turns the monkey or the man;
With one she deals out wisdom as a curse,
To follow fortune with an empty purse;
The next in opposite extremes is bred—
O'erflowing pockets and an empty head;
Beggars in merit share a squire's estate,
And squires untitled meet a beggar's fate.
Fortune's great lottery owns nor rules nor laws;
Fate holds the wealth, and reason rarely draws;
Blanks are her lot, and merit vainly tries,
While heedless folly blunders on the prize.

Young Headlong Racket's to the last akin,
Who only deals more openly in sin,
And apes forged love with less mysterious guile,

A high-flown dandy in its lowest style;
By fashion hated, with the vulgar gay,
He deems it wit to tempt their steps astray.
No maid can pass him but his leering eye
Attempts to prove her forward or too shy.
He brags o'er wine of loves his wits have won,
And loves betrayed—and deems it precious fun.
Horses and dogs and women o'er his wine
Is all his talk, and he believes it fine;
And fools may join him, but to common sense
His head pleads empty and has no pretence.
He courts his maids and shuns the better sort,
And hunts and courses as a change of sport,
And hates all poachers, game-destroying brutes,
Altho' with both the name as aptly suits,
With this one difference—darkness brings their prey,
And he more brazen murders his by day.
And thus he lives a hated sort of life,
Loves wedded wantons while he scorns a wife,
Prepares by turns to hunt and whore and shoot,
Less than a man and little more than brute.

Next on the parish list in paltry fame
Shines Dandy Flint, Esquire, whose dirty name
Has grown into a proverb for bad deeds;
And he who reads it all that's filthy reads.
Ne'er did a single sentence more express
Of downright evil or of goodness less
Than Dandy Flint, grown old in youthful shame
By loathed diseases which no words can name,
And worn so spare that wit, as passing by,
Swears Nick will thread him through a bodkin's eye;
A sot who spouts short morals o'er his gin,
And when most drunk rails most against the sin;
A dirty hog that on the puddle's brink
Stirs up the mud and quarrels with the stink.

These are the things that o'er inferiors flirt,
That spring from pride like summer flies from dirt,

And tease and buzz their summer season by,
Bantering the poor and struggling to be high.

Some of the old school yet my verse could tell;
And one from boyhood I remember well,
Who ne'er aspired on folly's wings to soar,
A plain, mean man, scarce noticed from the poor,
Who ne'er expected, as he walked the street,
Bows from inferiors whom he chanced to meet;
Inferiors, bred from fashion's idle whim,
Equals and neighbours all appeared to him;
And tho' wealth scorned in such low walks to go,
And pride disdained and called his manners low,
He sought nor paid pride's homage unto man,
But lived unshining in his humble plan;
And when his rights tyrannic power assailed,
His courage triumphed tho' his pocket failed;
For he was doomed to feel that worldly curse,
An upright spirit and an empty purse;
Nor did he try the shameless fault to cure,
Still keeping honest and remaining poor.
But he has left, and one of different race
Spoilt his old mansion and supplied his place.

Proud Farmer Cheetum turned a rogue by stealth,
Whom prosperous times had ripened into health;
Hunting and shooting had its ceaseless charm
When his full purse cared little for a farm;
A trusty hand was left to plough and plan
The double trade of master and of man;
He kept his stud for hunts and races then,
And dogs fed even better than his men,
Bought loves and changed them when the freak was old,
And drank his wine without a wife to scold,
And gained a dashing name and lived in style,
And wore a mask to profit by't the while,
And made large credit while his name was good,
For all would trust him, draw on whom he would;
A man so stylish none could dream to doubt,

Till changing times the secret brought about;
The grain's sunk price o'er knavery's tricks was thrown,
And others' failings well excused his own;
The times, he said, and frowned, disturbed and sad,
Needed no comment to explain them bad.
So ere he broke he honestly confest
His wealth all gone and credit had the rest,
And proved to all a smuggling rogue too late:
Cheat creditors—turn bankrupt—and still great,
Hunts, shoots, and rackets as he did before,
And still finds wealth for horses, dogs, and whore.
And dogs and whore and horses in his train
Are all that have no reason to complain;
These show his kindness in their varied ways
And gild his rotting name with dirty praise;
Like as when brooks are dry, the village sinks
Boast their full dingy tide that flows and stinks.

Old Saveall next, whose dirty deeds and fame
Might put a young bard's silken lines to shame;
But my plain homespun verse lets none escape,
Nor passes folly in its rudest shape;
When satire's muse puts on a russet gown,
Tho' vermin start as game, she runs them down.
So Saveall shall have place—tho' fortune's smiles,
Unmixed with frowns, have made him known for miles;
Who tries to buy a good name and deceive
With fair pretensions that but few believe;
Who seldom swears, and that but now and then
A smuggled oath when vext by better men,
That beard hypocrisy with honest grace
And tear the mask from cant's deceiving face;
Yet in religion he is made elect
And buys with wine the favours of the sect,
Making each spouter welcome when he comes
And turning beggars from their fallen crumbs,
Pleading up charity in whining tones
And driving dogs at dinner from the bones;
The scraps which beggars plead for serve his swine,

So their lorn hopes seek other doors to dine;
The broken bones enrich his land for grain,
So dogs beneath his table wait in vain;
On neighbourly goodwill he often dwells,
And in dry times locks up his very wells,
And if 'twas but of worth we might suppose
He'd even save the droppings of his nose.
Such is this Saveall, first of fortune's fellows,
Famous for wealth, great farms, and small-beer cellars,
With the elect most saintish or most civil,
And with the rest a cunning knave or devil.

Religion now is little more than cant,
A cloak to hide what godliness may want;
Men love mild sermons with few threats perplexed,
And deem it sinful to forget the text;
Then turn to business ere they leave the church,
And linger oft to comment in the porch
Of fresh rates wanted from the needy poor
And list of taxes nailed upon the door;
Little religion in each bosom dwells,
And that sleeps sound till Sunday's chiming bells.
Some with reform religion's shade pursue,
And vote the old church wrong to join the new;
Casting away their former cold neglects—
Paying religion once a week respects,
They turn from regular old forms as bad
To pious maniacs regularly mad,
A chosen race, so their conceit would teach,
Whom cant inspired to rave and not to preach,
A set of upstarts late from darkness sprung
With this new light, like mushrooms out of dung;
Tho' blind as owls i'the sun they lived before,
Conceit inspired and they are blind no more.
The drunken cobbler leaves his wicked life,
Hastes to save others, and neglects his wife;
To mend men's souls he thinks himself designed,
And leaves his shoes to the uncalled and blind;
He then like old songs runs the scriptures o'er

549

And makes discoveries never known before,
Makes darkest points as plain as A B C,
And wonders why his hearers will not see,
Shouts facts on facts to prove that dark is light
And all are blind till he restore their sight,
And swears the old church which he cast away
As full of errors and as blind as they.
Then learning's looked on as an idle jest,
And the old cobbler preaches far the best,
Who soothes with honeyed hopes the deep-dyed sinner,
And earns reward—a lodging and a dinner.
Their former teachers as blind guides they mock,
Nor think them chosen for the crazy flock;
The crazy flock believe and are depraved,
And just in time turn idiots to be saved.

   The Ranter priests, that take the street to teach,
Swear God builds churches wheresoe'er they preach;
While on the other hand Protestant people
Will have no church but such as wears a steeple.
Thus creeds all differ; yet each different sect,
From the free agents to the grand elect,
Who cull a remnant of the promised land,
And wear heaven's mark as sheep their owner's brand,
Each thinks his own as right and others wrong,
And thus keeps up confusion's babel-song;
While half the tribes at bottom are no more
Than saints skin-deep and devils at the core.
Old Ralph, the veriest rake the town possessed,
Felt sins prick deep and all his crimes confessed,
Groaned o'er confessions to his ranting priest,
And prayed and sang and felt his soul released;
The new-birth's struggle made him wondrous wan,
And feebly prayed at first the baby man
'Twixt doubts and fears, yet viewed the cured complaint
And scarce perceived the devil from the saint;
But soon the 'outward man,' grown godly mad,
Felt the good spirit triumph o'er the bad;
He then whined lectures in a happier strain

And coaxed poor sinner to be born again,
Shunned old companions once beloved so well,
As condemned transports on the way to hell,
And prayed and sang from sin and pain released,
And smoothed his hair and strove to act the priest.
And then as priest he exercised his wits,
Forced men to prayers and women into fits,
And heard and cured each difficult complaint,
And midst his flock seemed little less than saint.
But hell, untired with everlasting watch
(The fox grows cunning when prey's hard to catch),
Crept into Ralph's new-planted paradise,
And met success in tempting him to vice.
A simpering Eve did in his garden dwell,
And she was fair, and he grew fond—and fell.
'Twas love at first, but e'en when that began
The sinking saint grew more and more the man,
And with his Eve, so treacherously fair,
Could feel more joy than kneeling down to prayer;
Yet still he prayed nor deemed his case so bad
As stone-blind sinners, tho' his heart was sad;
Tho' sinful love had overpowered his skill,
From other sins he kept unspotted still;
When brethren met he would his joys express,
Groaned when they prayed and said amen by guess;
Till the completion of his serpent sin,
Urged by the devil, sunk him to the chin.
Eve, tho' beguiled forbidden fruit to taste,
Had loved an Adam ere she loved the priest;
And ere disgrace had ripened into light,
Ralph had no power to wed her and be right;
His fate was evident; it came at last;
His sheep were judge and shepherd Ralph was cast;
Then drink and racket joined their former friends,
And new-born saint in the old sinner ends.

In politics and politicians' lies
The modern farmer waxes wondrous wise,
Opinionates with wisdom all compact,

And e'en could tell a nation how to act,
Throws light on darkness with excessive skill,
Knows who acts well and whose designs are ill,
Proves half the members naught but bribery's tools,
And calls the past a dull dark age of fools.
As wise as Solomons they read the news,
Not with their blind forefathers' simple views,
Who read of wars, and wished that wars would cease,
And blessed the king and wished his country peace;
Who marked the weight of each fat sheep or ox,
The price of grain and rise and fall of stocks;
Who thought it learning how to buy and sell,
And him a wise man who could manage well.
No, not with such old-fashioned idle views
Do these newsmongers traffic with the news;
They read of politics and not of grain,
And speechify and comment and explain,
And know so much of parliament and state
You'd think them members when you heard them prate;
And know so little of their farms the while
That can but urge a wiser man to smile.
Young Bragg, a Jack of all trades save his own,
From home is little as the farmer known;
Opinions gratis gives in men's affairs,
Fool in his own but wondrous wise in theirs,
Scrats paragraphs and sends them to the *News*,
Signed 'Constant Reader,' lest they should refuse
The ill-spelt trash on patriotic cavils,
Leaving corrections to the printer's devils:
Skits upon those by whom they're never read
(He might as well write letters to the dead)
Or puffs upon himself in various ways,
Which none but self will either read or praise;
And poems, too, the polished patriot chimes,
Stanzas to Cobbett's truth and comic rhymes,
To which he fits a hackneyed tune that draws
From patriot dinners echoes of applause.
But when election mobs for battle meet,
And dirty flags and ribbons throng the street,

Hunting for votes some dirty borough town,
'Tis then his genius meets the most renown;
When on the hustings bawling spouters throng,
Who fight and war like women with the tongue,
All speakers and no hearers, where the cries
Pile up confusion's babel to the skies,
And croaking at the top in proud renown
Each party sits till t'other pulls them down;
Here shines our orator in all his plumes,
Nor prouder bantam to a dunghill comes
Than he to crow and peck and peck and crow,
And hurl bad English at retorting foe.
He games and drinks and rackets up and down,
A low-lived mocker of high life in town;
And sips his wine in fashionable pride,
And thrusts in scorn the homely ale aside.
His father's riches bought such foolish airs,
But wasting fortunes e'en must need repairs;
As parching summer checks the runnel's haste,
The greatest wealth will lessen, spent in waste;
Tho' credit proves him poor, his stubborn pride
O'eracts his purse and struggles dignified;
Yet, stung with tidings that his conscience vents,
He rails at tithes and hopes for falling rents,
Curses all taxes as tyrannic things,
And hates the pride of government and kings.
Turned radical in spirit and in purse,
He prays reform and deems the laws a curse,
Speaks treasonous things before his friends and cousins
And toasts reforming patriots by dozens,
And aping wit with ignorant delight
A village politician turns outright.
He hails his country's foes his only friends,
Damns peace and prays for war that never ends;
Its ruin's looked on as the way to wealth,
And grace for all meals is reform's good health.
And why is all this hubbub for reforms,
This anxious looking for expected storms,
That turns each fireside into parliaments,

In strong debates of taxes, tithes, and rents?
Is aught of general good or general view
Sketched in the pathway which reform pursues?
Or is the rich man's lands or miser's pelf
But grudged in other to be claimed by self?
With other nations, mid tyrannic strife,
This miscalled mania struggles oft to life;
Fair is the mask that hides its visage first,
But soon the infant to a fiend is nursed,
That like a wolf howls hungrily and high
A cry for blood—and freedom apes that cry;
For freedom, unrestrained, forsakes her cause,
And lawless pleasures are her only laws.

Thus village politics and hopes for pelf
Live in one word and centre all in self;
Thus village politicians urge repairs,
And deem all governments as wrong but theirs,
Versed in low cunning, which, to handle brief,
Is but a genteel title for a thief;
Nay, start not, reader, such harsh words to hear,
Nor think the pen of satire too severe.
What is that shuffling shadow of a man
Where self-deceptions shine in every plan,
Who spouts of wisdom as the thing he craves
And treats the poor o'er whom he rules as slaves,
Who votes equality that all men share
And stints the pauper of his parish fare,
Who damns all taxes both of church and state
And on the parish lays a double rate?
Such is our hero in his tyrant pride,
Then is his honour's title misapplied;
Such with one breath scoff at the poor's distress
And bawl out freedom for their own redress.
These soft politic saints may freedom preach,
And vacant minds believe the lies they teach;
Who think them walking Canaans, flowing o'er
With milk and honey for the starving poor.
And sure enough, their wants may richly fare

If like chameleons they can feed on air;
Their promises, sown thick, degenerate run
And mildew into broken ones when done;
And though a plenteous seed-time dreams of gain,
A blighted harvest falsifies the pain;
Such promises to-day to-morrow straight,
Like an old almanack, are out of date,
And they who break them no more credit break
Than Moore's new year does for the old's mistake;
Thus freedom-preaching is but knavery's game
And old self-interest by another name.

   Churchwardens, constables, and overseers
Make up the round of commons and of peers;
With learning just enough to sign a name,
And skill sufficient parish rates to frame,
And cunning deep enough the poor to cheat,
This learned body for debatings meet;
Their secretary is the parish clerk,
Whom like a shepherd's dog they keep to bark,
And gather rates, and, when the next are due,
To cry them o'er at church-time from his pew.
He as their Jack of all trades steady shines
Thro' thick and thin to sanction their designs,
Who apes the part of king and magistrate
And acts Grand Signior of this Turkish state,
Who votes new laws to those already made
And acts by force when one is disobeyed;
Having no credit which he fears to lose,
He does whatever dirty jobs they choose,
Tasking the pauper labourer to stand,
Or clapping on his goods the parish brand,
Lest he should sell them for the want of bread,
On parish bounty rather pined than fed;
Or carrying the parish book from door to door,
Claiming fresh taxes from the needy poor.
And if one's hunger overcomes his hate
And buys a loaf with what should pay the rate,
He instant sets his tyrant laws to work,

In heart and deed the essence of a Turk,
Brings summons for an eighteen-penny rate
And gains the praises of the parish state,
Or seizes goods and from the burthened clown
Extorts for extra trouble half a crown,
Himself a beggar that may shortly take
A weekly pittance from the rates they make.
But the old proverb suits the subject well:
Mount such on horseback and they'll ride to hell.
Within the church where they on sabbath-days
Mock God with outward blasphemy of praise,
Making His house a Pharisee's at best,
God's for one day and Satan's all the rest,
The parson oft scarce puts his sermon by
Ere, 'neath his pulpit and with mighty cry,
The clerk announces—what? commandments meet?
No—when the parish vestry next shall meet,
To fleece the poor and rob with vile command
Want of its bread, too feeble to withstand,
Although its aching heart too often knows
Knaves call it debtor where it nothing owes;
For in these vestries, cunning, deep as night,
Plans deeds that would be treason to the light;
And tho' so honest in its own disguise,
'Tis but plain robbery in another's eyes;
For the whole set just as they please can plan,
And what one says all sanction to a man;
Their cheating knavery like contagion runs,
And thus the father's card becomes the son's;
Both play one game to cheat us in the lump,
And the son's turn-up shows the father's trump.

Here shines the man of morals, Farmer Finch,
Smooth-tongued and fine, an angel every inch
In outward guise, and never known as yet
To run in taverns, brothels, or in debt;
In public life all punctual, honest, true,
And flattery gives his graces double due;
For pity's gifts are never public made,

But there his name and guinea is displayed.
A Sunday never comes, or foul or fair,
That misses him at church throughout the year.
The priest himself boasts as the man's reward
That he ne'er preached a sermon but he heard.
Such is the man in public; all agree
That saints themselves no better men could be.
But now of private life let's take the view:
In that same church and in that very pew
Where he each Sabbath sings and reads and prays,
He joins the vestry upon common days,
Cheating the poor with levies doubly laid
On their small means, that wealth may be defrayed;
To save his own and others', his compeers,
He robs the poor whom he has robbed for years,
Making the house of prayer the house of sin
And placing Satan as high priest within.
Such is this good, church-going, godly man,
This man of morals on deception's plan;
So knaves by cant steer free from sin's complaints,
And flattery's cunning coins them into saints.
Oppression often mourns the vile abuse
And flies to justice, deemed of little use;
For 'tis well known that justice winks at crimes,
A saying that's in season at all times;
Or why should the poor sinning, starving clown
Meet jail and hanging for a stolen crown,
While wealthy thieves with knavery's bribes endued
Plunder their millions and are not pursued;
Nay, at the foot of Tyburn's noted tree,
They do deserving deeds and still go free;
Where others suffer for some pigmy cause,
They all but murder and escape the laws,
Skulking awhile in bribery's dirty den,
Then start new guilt and pass as honest men.
Gold is a mighty substitute—it buys
The fool sufficient credit to seem wise,
The coward laurels, virtue unto bawds,
A mask for villainy and fame for lords;

Buys knaves an office, traitors trust and power;
Buys lies and oaths, and breaks them every hour;
Buys cant its flattery, hypocrites their paint,
Making a very devil seem a saint;
Buys asses panegyrics and what not,
And makes man worshipped and leaves God forgot;
In fact, buys all and everything, forsooth,
But two poor outcasts—honesty and truth.

Tho' Justice Terror, who the peace preserves,
Meets more of slander than his deed deserves—
A blunt, opinionated, odd, rude man,
Severe and selfish in his every plan—
Tho' pleading want oft meets with harsh replies,
And truth's too often listened to as lies,
Although he reigns with much caprice and whim,
The poor can name worse governors than him.
His gifts at Christmas time are yearly given,
No doubt as toll fees on the road to heaven.
Tho' to complaints his aid is oft denied,
Tho' said too oft to shun the weaker side,
Yet when foul wrongs are uttered in his ear
Farmers themselves meet reprimands severe.
Poor trembling maids, too, learn his looks to dread,
By sad forced errands to his mansion led;
His worship's lectures are so long and keen,
They're dreaded now as penance once has been.
Tho' it is said (what will not rumour say?)
There e'en were seasons when the priest was gay,
That now and then in manhood's lusty morn
His maids turned mothers and were never sworn,
Yet still he reigns, whatever faults they find,
A blunt, odd, rude, good picture of his kind;
Who preaches partial for both church and king
And runs reform down as a dangerous thing.
Ranters and Methodists, his open foes,
In person and in sermons he'll oppose,
And now and then his sermon's length prolongs
To guard his flock against deceitful tongues,

And takes much trouble on a sabbath-day
To lecture drunkards and drive boys from play;
And tho' from year to year unknown to use,
To keep his peace and Sunday from abuse,
Beside the circling cross upon the hill
The dancing-stocks maintain their station still;
And as derision and decaying time
Weaken their triumph o'er abuse and crime,
The priest, still mindful of his ruling cares,
Renews their reign in threatening repairs.
Laws or religion, be what they will,
Self will not yield but stickles to it still;
And still he rules, in every baffling plan
The same headstrong, opinionated man.

But now grown old in reading Sunday's prayers
And keeping village morals in repairs,
Till e'en his very spectacles refuse
To see the largest print that age can choose,
He seeks a curate to supply his place,
A kinsman of his worship's sacred race,
Who wears his priesthood with a trader's skill
And makes religion learn to make her bill;
Who, ere he cures his sheep of their disease,
Like lawyer studies o'er the church's fees,
Who ekes new claims on custom's ancient price,
When reason ruled and priests were not so nice,
And sets on registers his raising mark
That used to fetch their sixpence to the clerk,
And from the aye-inquiring, staring clown
Extorts the monstrous charge of half a crown;
And if a wanderer leaves his wants to roam
And dies on other ills he meets from home,
His churchyard common for a bed is lost,
And forfeits must be paid by double cost;
And marriage pays its earnest for a bride,
Offering the fees before the knot is tied,
And new-made mother that with thanks repairs
Seeks God's kind love and pays the priest for prayers.

Such is the substitute put on to keep
The close-shorn remnant of his worship's sheep;
And by and by hopes at his friend's decay
To be sole shepherd and receive full pay.
And is religion grown so commonplace
To place self-interest foremost in the race
And leave poor souls in Satan's claws confined,
Crawling like crabs a careless pace behind?

Excuse the priest, he's prest with weighty cares;
And tho' the pauper dies without his prayers,
What if such worthless sheep slip into hell
For want of prayers before the passing-bell?
The priest was absent—'twas a daily song—
Yet none except the vulgar thought it wrong.
Perhaps when death-beds might his aid desire,
His horse was sick and might a drink require,
Or friends for just necessities might claim
His shooting skill to track the fields for game;
And when they needed partridges or hares
The parish pauper could not look for prayers;
Or if he did indulge the foolish whim,
What cared the priest?—die and be damned for him!
And he had land to shepherd where the wheat
In a sly way the church's profit beat;
Tho' he kept one to manage of his kin,
Yet self was foreman when the gain dropt in.

And dwells no memory in the days gone by,
No name whose loss is worth a present sigh?
Yes—there was one who priesthood's trade profest,
'One whom the wretched and the poor knew best';
And in yon house that neighbours near the show
Of parish huts, a melancholy row,
That like to them a stubble covering wears,
Decayed the same and needing like repairs
—Superior only was the mansion known
Instead of mud by having walls of stone—
There lived the vicar once in days gone by

When pride and fashion did not rank so high,
Ere poor religion threw her weeds away
To mix in circles of the worldly gay,
Ere hunting parsons in the chase begun,
And added salaries kept their dog and gun,
Ere sheep were driven from the shepherd's door,
And pleasure swallowed what might feed the poor;
In that same time whose loss was keenly felt,
The good old vicar in this mansion dwelt.
Plain as the flock dependent on his cares
For weekday comforts and for Sunday prayers,
He'd no spare wealth to follow fashion's whim,
And if he had she'd little joy for him.
He kept no horse the hunting's sports to share,
He fed no dogs to run the harmless hare;
He'd naught to waste while hunger sought his shed,
And while he had it they ne'er wanted bread.
His chiefest pleasure charity possest
In having means to make another blest;
Little was his and little was required;
Could he do that, 'twas all the wealth desired.
Tho' small the gift, 'twas given with greatest will,
And blessings o'er it made it greater still;
On want's sad tale he never closed his door,
He gave them something and he wished it more;
The beggar's heart, dismantled of its fears,
Leaped up and thanked him for his crust with tears.
The vicar's greensward pathways, once his pride,
His woodbine bowers that used his doors to hide,
The yard and garden roads—his only farms—
And all his stock—the hive bees' yearly swarms—
Are swept away; their produce and their pride
Were doomed to perish when their owner died.
Fresh faces came with little taste or care,
And joyed to ruin what was his to rear;
His garden plants and blossoms all are fled,
And docks and nettles blossom in their stead.
Before the door, where pinks and roses stood,
The hissing goose protects her summer brood,

And noisy hogs are free to wallow o'er
What once was gravelled and kept clean before.
The corner seat where weary hinds had rest,
The snug fireside that welcomed many a guest,
These are decayed as comforts will decay,
As winter's sunshine or as flowers in May;
These all are past as joys are born to pass,
Where life's a shadow and where flesh is grass;
E'en memory's lingering features time shall rot,
And this good man is nearly now forgot,
Save on his tomb and some few hearts beside,
Grey-headed men, left children when he died,
Who from their parents all his goodness knew
And learned to feel it as they older grew.
Yon cot, when in its glory and its pride,
Maintained its priest and half the poor beside;
These are the times that plainness must regret,
These are the times that labour feels as yet,
Ere mock-improvement's plans enclosed the moor,
And farmers built a workhouse for the poor.
The cottage now, with neither lawn nor park,
Instead of vicar keeps the vicar's clerk;
Wolves may devour, oppression's fiends may reign,
None's nigh to listen when the poor complain.
Too high religion looks her flocks to watch,
Or stoop from pride to dwell in cots of thatch.
Too much of pleasure in her mansion dwells
To hear the troubles which the pauper tells,
To turn a look on sorrow's thorny ways
Like good Samaritans of former days,
To heal in mercy when foul wrongs pursue
And weep o'er anguish as she once would do.
Distress may languish and distress may die,
There's none that hears can help them when they cry.
Compassion cannot stoop, nor pride allow
To pass that way with oil or honey now.
Still there are some whose actions merit praise,
The lingering breathings of departed days;
Tho' in this world of vainness thinly sown,

Yet there are some whom fashion leaves alone;
Who, like their Master, plain and humble go,
And strive to follow in his steps below;
Who in the wilderness as beacons stand
To pilgrims journeying to the promised land,
To give instructions to inquiring souls,
To cheer the weak above the world's controls,
To lend their charge and wanderers back restore,
To rest the weary and relieve the poor.

Ah, sure it was a melancholy day
That called the good man from his charge away.
Those poor lorn outcasts, born to many cares,
That shared his table, welcome as his prayers,
To them the bells worse tidings never gave
Than those which called their guardian to the grave;
They'd no more harvests now of hopes to reap;
E'en children wept to see their mothers weep,
And pulled their gowns to ask a question—when
He'd wake and come and give them pence again.
'He'll not sleep there for ever, sure he won't;
'Who'll feed and clothe us if the vicar don't?'
Thus lisped the babes, and while their parents sighed,
Muttering their blessings by the pasture-side,
Warm repetitions of their griefs were given,
And they hoped too to meet their friend in heaven.

Beside the charnel well in humble guise,
A small stone noteth where the vicar lies;
Where age, slow journeying on the sabbath-day,
Oft potters up to wipe the tear away,
And show inquiring youth, with mournful pride,
That good man's name that once its wants supplied,
To hear it read and bring back days to view,
And feel his goodness and his loss anew;
Blessing his name and praying as they weep
To be full soon companion of his sleep,
To share with hin the churchyard's lonely peace,
Where pride forgets its scorn and troubles cease,

Where poverty's sad reign of cares is o'er,
And tells its wants to be denied no more,
The last lorn hope and refuge that appears
Thro' the dull gloom of life's declining years.

Shoved as a nuisance from pride's scornful sight,
In a cold corner stands in woeful plight
The shuttered workhouse of the parish poor,
And towards the north wind opes its creaking door.
A makeshift shed for misery, no thought
Urged plans for comfort when the work was wrought,
No garden spot was left dull want to cheer
And make the calls of hunger less severe
With wholesome herbs that summer might supply;
'Twas not contrived for want to live, but die;
A forced concern to satisfy the law
Built want this covering o'er his bed of straw.
E'en that cheap blessing that's so freely given
To all that live beneath the face of heaven,
The light of day, is not allowed to win
A smiling passage to the glooms within;
No window opens on the southern sky—
A luxury deemed to pride's disdainful eye.
Here dwell the wretched, lost to hopeless strife,
Reduced by want to skeletons in life,
Despised by all; e'en age, grown bald and grey,
Meets scoffs from wanton children in their play,
Who laugh at misery by misfortune bred
And point scorn's finger at the mouldering shed.
The tottering tenant urges no reply,
Turns his white head and chokes the passing sigh,
And seeks his shed and hides his heart's despair,
For pity lives not as a listener there.

Old Farmer Thrifty reigns from year to year
Their tyrant king, yclept an overseer;
A sad proud knave who by a cunning plan
Blindfolds his faults and seems an honest man.
He rarely barters when he buys or sells,

But sets a price, and there his honour dwells;
He rails at cheating knaves for knavery's sake,
And ne'er asks double what he means to take,
Scorns open ways which lesser rogues pursue,
An outside Christian but at heart a Jew.
Old men will tell you when the boy was small
How he blacked shoes and waited at the Hall;
Thro' all the names that wait on wealth and pride,
From shoe-black vile to valet dignified,
He rose successfully without a fall,
And owned the cunning power to please in all.
At length power blessed him with its highest stretch,
Which good men's merits might despair to reach;
No longer doomed in servitude to wait,
Next to the squire he managed his estate,
Yclept a steward; strangers made their bow,
And the squire took him as an equal now,
While to neglect his former steward fell
For no one crime unless 'twas acting well.
And soon the tyrant threw the mask aside,
When wealth thronged in and power was gratified;
He raised the rents of all the tenants round,
And then distressed them as in duty bound,
And then asked leave of the contented squire
To rent the farm, and had his heart's desire.
The storm at first must burst upon the poor,
That urged want's curses as they passed his door;
He viewed their comforts with a jealous heart
And raised their rents and bade their hopes depart;
Yet, loath to leave, their cows were sold for rent,
And the next year left nothing but complaint.
'Twas just as wished; his plans were quickly known;
Each spot was seized and added to his own.
Others resigned and the half-starving poor
Laid down their sufferings at their master's door.
Such whispers urged the easy squire to shift,
And Steward Thrifty then was turned adrift;
But not before his purse was filled with pelf,
For knaves work quick and ne'er lose sight of self;

His nest was feathered ere his fame was old,
And land was bought when farms were cheaply sold.
He now retires at ease and sells his grain
And strives to be an honest rogue in vain;
With big round belly and sleek double chin,
He reads the news and smokes and drinks his gin,
And studies all the week o'er gain's affairs,
And once a week at chapel reads his prayers,
And seems as striving former deeds to mend,
Mild to a foe and coaxing to a friend.
But to the poor his ways are still severe;
Dwindled in office to an overseer,
Still deaf to want that seeks him to be fed,
He gives them curses in the lieu of bread;
Or scoffing at their hopes, tells them they're free
To seek a law as tyrannized as he.
He pleads bad times when justice chides his ways,
Tho' justice' self is ill-deserving praise;
And are bad times the cause of such despair?
Go ask the wretches who inhabit there
If past good times their hopes had ever blest
And left them thus so wretched and distrest;
Ask if their griefs can better times recall;
Their startled tears tell plenty as they fall,
And pity's heart can easy comprehend
That Farmer Thrifty never was their friend.
Art thou a man, thou tyrant o'er distress?
Doubtless thy pride would scorn to think thee less;
Then scorn a deed unworthy of that name,
And live deserving of a better fame;
Hurt not the poor whom fate forbade to shine,
Whose lots were cast in meaner ways than thine;
Infringe not on the comforts they possess,
Nor bid scant hope turn hopeless in distress.
Drive not poor freedom from its niggard soil;
Its independence is their staff for toil;
Take that away which as their right they call,
And thou'rt a rogue that beggars them of all;
They sink in sorrow as a race of slaves,

And their last hope lives green upon their graves.
Still lives unsung a swarm of petty knaves,
Numerous as wasps to sting and torture slaves;
The meanest of the mean, a servile race,
Who, like their betters, study to be base;
Whose dunghill pride grows stiff in dirty state,
And, tho' so little, apes the little-great.
The workhouse keeper, as old Thrifty's man,
Transacts the business on the tyrant's plan,
Supplies its tenants with their scanty food,
And tortures misery for a livelihood,
Despised and hated by the slaves he wrongs,
And e'en too low for satire's scourging songs.

A thing all consequence here takes the lead,
Reigning knight-errant o'er this dirty breed;
A bailiff he, and who so great to brag
Of law and all its terrors as Bumtagg;
Fawning a puppy at his master's side
And frowning like a wolf on all beside;
Who fattens best where sorrow worst appears
And feeds on sad misfortune's bitterest tears?
Such is Bumtagg the bailiff, to a hair,
The worshipper and demon of despair,
Who waits and hopes and wishes for success
At every nod and signal of distress,
Happy at heart, when storms begin to boil,
To seek the shipwreck and to share the spoil.
Brave is this Bumtagg, match him if you can,
For there's none like him living save his man.
As every animal assists his kind,
Just so are these in blood and business joined;
Yet both in different colours hide their art,
And each as suits his ends transacts his part.
One keeps the heart-bred villain full in sight,
The other cants and acts the hypocrite,
Smoothing the deed where law sharks set their gin
Like a coy-dog to draw misfortune in.
But both will chuckle o'er their prisoners' sighs

And are as blest as spiders over flies.
Such is Bumtagg, whose history I resign,
As other knaves wait room to stink and shine;
And, as the meanest knave a dog can brag,
Such is the lurcher that assists Bumtagg.

    Born with the changes time and chance doth bring,
A shadow reigns, yclept a woodland king,
Enthroned mid thorns and briers, a clownish wight,
My Lord's chief woodman in his title's height.
The bugbear devil of the boys is he,
Who once for swine picked acorns 'neath the tree,
And starving terror of the village brood
Who gleaned their scraps of fuel from the wood;
When parish charity was vainly tried
'Twas their last refuge—which is now denied.
Small hurt was done by such intrusions there,
Claiming the rotten as their harmless share,
Which might be thought in reason's candid eye
As sent by providence for such supply;
But Turks imperial of the woodland bough
Forbid their trespass in such trifles now,
Threatening the dithering wretch that hence proceeds
With jail and whipping for his shameless deeds,
Well pleased to bid their feeblest hopes decay,
Driving them empty from the woods away,
Cheating scant comfort of its pilfered blaze,
That doubtless warmed him in his beggar days.
Thus knaves in office love to show their power
And unoffending helplessness devour,
Sure on the weak to give their fury vent
Where there's no strength injustice to resent;
As dogs let loose on harmless flocks at night,
Such feel no mercy where they fear no bite.

    Others of this small fry as mean, as base,
May live unknown, a pigmy reigning race,
And sink to hell from whence their knavery came,
As nameless tribes, unworthy of a name,

Left on the dunghill, where they reigned, to rot,
Hated while living and when dead forgot.
Here ends the song—let jealousy condemn,
And deem reproofs they merit aimed at them;
When pride is touched and evil conscience bit,
Each random throw will seem a lucky hit;
If common sense its ears and eyes may trust,
Each picture's faithful and each censure just.
So let them rail—the proverb's truth is known,
'Where the cap fits, they'll wear it as their own.'
Full many knaves sharp satire's wounds have met,
Who live on aqua fortis dying yet;
In burning ink their scarecrow memories dwell,
Left to the torture of life's earthly hell,
As marked and lasting as the thief's burnt brand,
Who lives and dies with 'Villain' on his hand.

END OF VOL. I

MADE AT THE
TEMPLE PRESS
LETCHWORTH

GREAT BRITAIN